MIKE MEYERS' CERTIFICATION

Passport ★

CISSP®

SHON HARRIS

McGraw Hill OSBORNE

New York • Chicago • San Francisco
Lisbon • London • Madrid • Mexico City
Milan • New Delhi • San Juan
Seoul • Singapore • Sydney • Toronto

The McGraw·Hill Companies

McGraw-Hill/Osborne
2600 Tenth Street
Berkeley, California 94710
U.S.A.

To arrange bulk purchase discounts for sales promotions, premiums, or fund-raisers, please contact McGraw-Hill/Osborne at the above address. For information on translations or book distributors outside the U.S.A., please see the International Contact Information page immediately following the Introduction of this book.

Mike Meyers' CISSP® Certification Passport

234567890 DOC DOC 019876543

ISBN 0-07-222578-5

Publisher
Brandon A. Nordin

Vice President & Associate Publisher
Scott Rogers

Editorial Director
Gareth Hancock

Project Editor
Julie M. Smith

Acquisitions Coordinator
Jessica Wilson

Technical Editor
Eric Ouellet

Copy Editor
Darren Meiss

Proofreader
Susie Elkind

Indexer
Valerie Perry

Computer Designers
Carie Abrew
Tara A. Davis
Lucie Ericksen
Elizabeth Jang
John Patrus

Illustrators
Melinda Moore Lytle
Michael Mueller
Kelly Stanton-Scott
Lyssa Wald

Series Design
Peter F. Hancik

Cover Series Design
Ted Holloday

This book was composed with Corel VENTURA™ Publisher.

About the Author

Shon Harris, CISSP, MCSE, is a security consultant and a member of the Information Warfare unit in the U.S. Air Force. She is a contributing writer to *Information Security Magazine* and *Windows 2000* magazine, a contributing author to the best-selling *Hacker's Challenge*, and the author of *CISSP All-in-One Exam Guide*. Shon is also currently an instructor for the information technology training center Intense School (www.intenseschool.com).

About the Contributing Author

Dusty Hockabout is a technical writer with experience in the telecommunications, information technology, and broadcasting industries. He received his journalism degree from Morningside College in Sioux City, IA. Dusty has worked on key projects involving emerging technologies for Williams Communications and Rhythms NetConnections and is currently a Sr. Technical Writer with Valmont Industries.

Dedication

I would like to dedicate this book to four very important women in my life—Kathleen Conlon, Marge Fairbairn, Diane Marshall, and Kristy Gorenz. I have learned a lot from their strength, I appreciate their love and support, and hope to be more like them.

Acknowledgments

I would like to thank my husband, David Harris, for his continual support, love, and selflessness.

Contents

9   Applications and Systems Development 333

Check-In

May I See Your Passport?

What do you mean, you don't have a passport? Why, it's sitting right in your hands, even as you read! This book is your passport to a very special place. You're about to begin a journey, my friend: a journey toward that magical place called certification! You don't need a ticket, you don't need a suitcase—just snuggle up and read this passport. It's all you need to get there. Are you ready? Well then, let's go!

Your Travel Agent: Mike Meyers

Hello! I'm Mike Meyers, president of Total Seminars and author of a number of popular certification books. On any given day, you'll find me stringing network cable, setting up a web site, or writing code. I love every aspect of this book you hold in your hands. It's part of a powerful new book series called the *Mike Meyers' Certification Passports*. Every book in this series combines easy readability with a condensed format—in other words, the kind of book I always wanted when I went for my own certifications. Putting a large amount of information in an accessible format is certainly a challenge, but I think we've achieved our goal, and I'm confident you'll agree.

I designed this series to do one thing and only one thing: to get you the information you need to achieve your certification. You won't find any fluff in here. Shon and I packed every page with nothing but the real nitty-gritty of the CISSP Certification exam. Every page has 100 percent pure concentrate of certification knowledge! But we didn't forget to make the book readable, so I hope you also enjoy the casual, friendly style.

My personal e-mail address is mikem@totalsem.com, and Shon's e-mail address is shonharris@hotmail.com. Please feel free to contact either of us directly if you have any questions, complaints, or compliments.

Your Destination: CISSP Certification

This book is your passport to CISSP Certification, the leading IT security credential. CISSP certification is a key step in advancing your IT career by definitely identifying yourself as someone who understands the ins and outs of IT security. This book is your passport to success on the CISSP Certification exam.

Your Guides: Mike Meyers and Shon Harris

You get a pair of tour guides for this book, both me and Shon Harris. I've written numerous computer certification books—including the *All-in-One Network+ Certification Exam Guide* and the best-selling *All-in-One A+ Certification Exam Guide*. More to the point, I've been working on PCs and teaching others how to make, fix, and network them for a *very* long time, and I love it!

Shon is the author of the best selling CISSP All-in-One Exam Guide and a recognized expert in the IT security field, as well as author of this book. A CISSP and MCSE, Shon is a security consultant and a member of the Information Warfare unit in the U.S. Air Force. She is a contributing writer to *Information Security Magazine* and *Windows 2000* magazine, and a contributing author to the best-selling *Hacker's Challenge*. Shon is also currently an instructor for Intense School (www.intenseschool.com), an information-technology training center.

Why the Travel Theme?

The steps in gaining a certification parallel closely the steps in planning and taking a trip. All of the elements are the same: preparation, an itinerary, a route, even mishaps along the way. Let me show you how it all works.

This book is divided into 10 chapters with two appendixes. Each chapter begins with an *Itinerary* section that lists the objectives covered in that chapter, and an *ETA* section to give you an idea of the time involved in learning the skills in that chapter. Each chapter is organized by the objectives, which are either drawn from those officially stated by the certifying body, or reflect our expert take on the best way to approach the topics. Also, each chapter contains a number of helpful items to highlight points of interest:

Exam Tip
Points out critical topics you're likely to see on the actual exam.

Travel Assistance
Lists additional sources, such as books and web sites, to give you more information.

Local Lingo
Describes special terms in detail in a way you can easily understand.

Travel Advisory
Warns you of common pitfalls, misconceptions, and downright physical peril!

The end of each chapter gives you two handy tools. The *Checkpoint* reviews each objective covered in the chapter with a handy synopsis—a great way to review quickly—and end-of-chapter *Review Questions* (and answers) test your newly acquired skills.

But the fun doesn't stop there! After you've read the book, take advantage of the free practice exam! Use the full practice exam to hone your skills, and keep the book handy to check your answers. You can learn more about it by reading Appendix A of this book.

If you want even more practice, log onto http://www.osborne.com/passport, and for a nominal fee, you can get additional high-quality practice questions.

When you find yourself acing the practice questions, you're ready to take the exam. Go get certified!

The End of the Trail

The IT industry changes and grows constantly, *and so should you*. Finishing one certification is only one step in an ongoing process of gaining more and more certifications to match your constantly changing and growing skills. Read Appendix B, "Career Flight Path," at the end of the book to find out where this certification fits into your personal certification goals. Remember, in the IT business, if you're not moving forward, you're way behind!

Good luck on your certification! Stay in touch!

Mike Meyers

Series Editor, *Mike Meyers' Certification Passport*

Introduction

CISSP Exam Specifications

When you're serious about security, there's no better way to prove your mettle than by mastering the Certified Information Systems Security Professional (CISSP) exam. Opportunities in the various security fields continue to skyrocket as the need for security is continually rising. Today, the CISSP is the most revered and most sought after security certification. The CISSP certification is continually listed in want ads and job listings, and is specified as a requirement for promotions and pay raises in current positions.

The exam covers an amazing number of concepts pertaining to security, including understanding different access controls, cryptography, physical security, disaster recovery, security models, telecommunication technologies, networking devices, attacks and countermeasures, and operations. It is commonly referred to as a mile wide and an inch deep, because you are not necessarily expected to know the detailed nitty-gritty about each domain of knowledge, but you are expected to be familiar with a wide range of concepts, practices, and technologies.

The CISSP exam is made up of 250 questions, all drawn from the 10 domains that make up the Common Body of Knowledge (CBK) Security Certification Consortium (ISC)^2—a nonprofit corporation with a mouthful of a name, was formed specifically to develop and maintain a security certification program. Several groups came together to develop (ISC)^2, the testing requirements and expectations, and exam objectives. The different domains that the CBK covers are shown here:

- Access control systems and methodology
- Telecommunications and network security
- Security management practices
- Application and system development
- Cryptography
- Security architecture and models

- Operations security
- Business continuity planning and disaster recovery planning
- Laws, investigations, and ethics
- Physical security

Most people who sit for the exam are familiar with 1 to 3 of these domains, not necessarily all 10. To many, studying for the exam can be an overwhelming task because it covers so many different topics, but this book was written to help you zero in on the specific points you need to know.

To pass the exam, you need to score 700 points or higher on the 225 graded questions. The individual questions are weighted, meaning that the harder questions are worth more than the easier ones. The remaining 25 questions are not graded and are there for research purposes, but you will not know which ones are being graded and which are not. You will have up to six hours to complete the exam; most people take four to five hours.

To be able to sit for the exam you must have accumulated three years of experience in any of the 10 domains outlined in the CBK. This does not mean you need three straight years in one of the domains, but throughout your career you must have a total of three years experience in one, two, three, or more domains. Recently, (ISC)² has raised the bar for receiving the CISSP certification. Once a person passes the exam, he may be asked to be sponsored by a person holding a current CISSP credential or by his employer. This is done to help ensure that the exam taker actually has the experience he or she claims. The goal is to ensure that only qualified people sit for the exam and gain the credential and to make sure that the CISSP does not turn into a paper certification that eventually means nothing.

Starting January 1, 2003, the requirements to sit for the CISSP exam will require that a candidate have a minimum of four years of experience or three years of experience with a college degree or equivalent life experience. IT will be up to (ISC)² to determine "equivalent life experience." For more information on these matters, please refer to www.isc2.org.

Recertification Requirements

To keep your CISSP certification current, you will need to obtain at least 120 continuing professional education (CPE) credits over a three-year period. You can also choose to retake the exam instead of accumulating the necessary continuing education credits. Your choice.

Several items count towards CPE credits:

- **Vendor training course**   One CPE credit for each hour of attendance
- **Security conference**   One CPE credit for each hour of attendance
- **University or college security course**   11.5 CPEs per semester hour completed with passing grade at accredited school
- **Publishing a security article or book**   10 CPEs for publishing an article, 40 CPEs for publishing a book—maximum of 40 CPEs over the three-year period
- **Providing security training**   Four CPEs for each hour spent per subject—maximum of 80 CPEs per year
- **Serving on a board of a professional security organization**   10 CPEs per year—maximum of 20 CPEs over the three-year period
- **Self-study**   Maximum of 40 CPEs over the three-year period
- **Reading a security book**   10 CPEs—only one book per year is accepted
- **Volunteer work**   Work for $(ISC)^2$—credits determined by $(ISC)^2$

Now that we have the formal issues of understanding the test, what you need to be able to sit for the exam, and how to keep the certification current, let's dig into the meat that you are looking for—which is, "What do I need to know to pass this test?"

INTERNATIONAL CONTACT INFORMATION

AUSTRALIA
McGraw-Hill Book Company Australia Pty. Ltd.
TEL +61-2-9415-9899
FAX +61-2-9415-5687
http://www.mcgraw-hill.com.au
books-it_sydney@mcgraw-hill.com

CANADA
McGraw-Hill Ryerson Ltd.
TEL +905-430-5000
FAX +905-430-5020
http://www.mcgrawhill.ca

GREECE, MIDDLE EAST,
NORTHERN AFRICA
McGraw-Hill Hellas
TEL +30-1-656-0990-3-4
FAX +30-1-654-5525

MEXICO (Also serving Latin America)
McGraw-Hill Interamericana Editores S.A. de C.V.
TEL +525-117-1583
FAX +525-117-1589
http://www.mcgraw-hill.com.mx
fernando_castellanos@mcgraw-hill.com

SINGAPORE (Serving Asia)
McGraw-Hill Book Company
TEL +65-863-1580
FAX +65-862-3354
http://www.mcgraw-hill.com.sg
mghasia@mcgraw-hill.com

SOUTH AFRICA
McGraw-Hill South Africa
TEL +27-11-622-7512
FAX +27-11-622-9045
robyn_swanepoel@mcgraw-hill.com

UNITED KINGDOM & EUROPE
(Excluding Southern Europe)
McGraw-Hill Education Europe
TEL +44-1-628-502500
FAX +44-1-628-770224
http://www.mcgraw-hill.co.uk
computing_neurope@mcgraw-hill.com

ALL OTHER INQUIRIES Contact:
Osborne/McGraw-Hill
TEL +1-510-549-6600
FAX +1-510-883-7600
http://www.osborne.com
omg_international@mcgraw-hill.com

Security Management Practices

	NEWBIE	SOME EXPERIENCE	EXPERT
ETA	4 hours	2 hours	1 hour

1

There are several types of threats that can affect the security of an organization and the assets it aims to protect. It is up to management to understand these different threats and ensure that the proper countermeasures are implemented. For a company to properly protect itself and its assets, it must implement the correct security management practices. This chapter defines different management practices, provides examples, and shows the possible outcomes if these safeguards are not put into place.

Objective 1.01   Management Responsibilities

Management should dictate the role that security will play within the organization. They should define the scope, objectives, priorities, and strategies of the company's security program. It is their responsibility to get security off the ground, support it, and ensure that it is properly maintained. Without senior management's support, a security program will not usually have the necessary attention, funding, and resources. Also, security recommendations are usually not taken as seriously if employees do not perceive that they are supported and enforced by upper management. Senior management also has an overall understanding of the company's business, vision, goals, and direction, and they should use this insight to direct the role security will play in the organization. Without management taking the lead, there is usually a lack of direction regarding computer, information, physical, and personnel security, and any efforts usually fail before they truly start.

A *top-down approach* is when senior management initiates and fosters the company's security objectives. The other less successful approach is *bottom-up*, where the IT department attempts to develop a security program, which usually does not end up with the necessary support and funding. Security takes a good amount of leadership to be successful because it means things need to change and compliancy needs to be enforced. It is unfair to expect the network administrator to wear this hat on such important issues.

Senior management are the final data owners, meaning they have the ultimate responsibility over the company's assets, including data. If management does not implement the correct security measures, they are not practicing due care. *Due care* is a legal term meaning that a person or company should take reasonable measures to protect itself and to not harm others. If management does not practice this concept, they can be held liable for damages that take place that could have been prevented or mitigated if they *would* have taken the necessary steps. Examples of due care are developing security policies and procedures, performing security awareness training, implementing firewalls and anti-virus software, auditing personnel and computer activities, and the list goes on and on. Practically everything touched upon in this book has some type of due care liabilities associated with it in one way or another. Management is responsible for understanding these issues and what should be put in place for their environment.

Security should be part of business objectives and goals and not treated as an island within itself. The more understanding of how security issues can directly affect business initiatives, production levels, management's liability, and revenue streams, the more security will be incorporated into different business proposals and projects. What is important is to integrate security matters into the psyche of the business decisions makers; security cannot be a continual afterthought or an item that is treated as though it stands alone and does not drastically affect everything around it.

Objective 1.02   Risk Management

Risk management is the process of identifying, assessing, and reducing risk to an acceptable level. The name of the game here is to mitigate all risks, meaning reducing them, to a point that is acceptable to the organization. You cannot totally eliminate risks in life, instead you must learn how to properly identify and deal with them. *Risk analysis* is a tool used to identify the company's assets, calculate their values, identify vulnerabilities, estimate the threats and associated risks, and assess the impact the company would face if these agents took advantage of the current available vulnerabilities. The results of a risk analysis should be used by individuals responsible for risk management to develop and implement the most needed, realistic, and cost-effective procedures and countermeasures. It is all about doing the necessary homework and data gathering activities so that the most informed and logical decisions can be made.

Local Lingo

Threat agents are subjects that take advantage of vulnerabilities as in hackers, viruses, thieves, and malware.

Risk Analysis

The purpose of a risk analysis is to identify what a company actually has and what its potential loss could be for each and every threat identified. It is a tool a company uses to make sure that their security program is cost-effective, relevant, and appropriate for the *real* risks it faces. The four main goals of a risk analysis are

- Identify assets and their values.
- Identify threats.
- Quantify the impact of potential risks.
- Provide an economic balance between the possible impact of the risk and the cost of the countermeasure.

Exam Tip

A risk analysis needs to be initiated, directed, and supported by senior management if it is going to be successful. Senior management needs to define the scope and goals of the analysis, make sure the necessary resources are available during the analysis, and follow up on its results.

The risk analysis team should be appointed by management and made up of individuals from each department to ensure that all risks to all departments are identified and understood.

As stated earlier, each company asset must have a value assigned to it, but this value is not just the amount of money the company spent to purchase the item. The real value is a combination of the purchase amount, the cost of maintenance, the man-hours put into developing the asset, the role it plays within the organization, the cost of replacement, the loss of revenue and productivity if the asset was unavailable, and what competitors would pay for the asset. The combination of these items would give a more clear indication of a true business impact if the actual asset was damaged or unavailable.

Once the team is constructed, assets are identified and values are assigned to them. The next step is to understand the vulnerabilities and possible threats that are current within the environment.

Objective 1.03 Possible Threats

To properly identify a threat, you must know what a threat actually is. The following terms have similar definitions, but distinct roles within security and important interrelationships with each other, as shown in Figure 1-1.

A *vulnerability* is a weakness in a mechanism that threatens the confidentiality, integrity, or availability of an asset. The *threat* is that someone will uncover this weakness and take advantage of it for malicious purposes. The entity that would find and use this weakness is referred to as a *threat agent*. The *risk* is the likelihood of a threat agent finding and using this vulnerability; an *exposure* is an instance of a threat agent exploiting a vulnerability. To reduce a risk, a *countermeasure* is put into place, which is a safeguard used to mitigate the potential losses from an identified threat. Examples of these different concepts and their relationships are shown in Table 1-1.

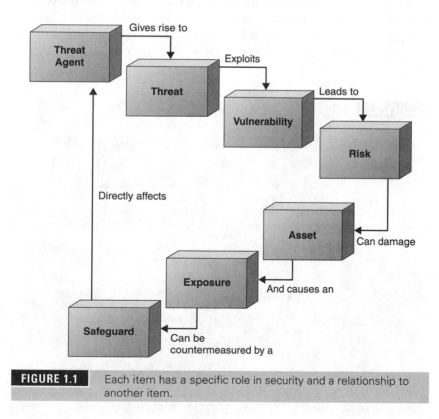

| FIGURE 1.1 | Each item has a specific role in security and a relationship to another item. |

TABLE 1.1   Security definitions and examples

Term	Definition	Example
Vulnerability	Weakness in a mechanism.	Buffer overflow.
Threat	Someone uncovering the vulnerability and exploiting it.	Hacker using an automated tool to exploit the buffer overflow and gain privileged access to system.
Risk	Probability of a threat agent exploiting a vulnerability. (Risk is higher if no countermeasure is in place.)	If code is written poorly, and there is no firewall to restrict access to the system with the buffer overflow, there is a high risk that a threat agent will attempt to overflow the buffer.
Countermeasure	Safeguard put into place to mitigate the risk of a threat.	Rewrite the application or replace it with a more secure application. A firewall and intrusion detection system can also work as countermeasures here.

Applying the right countermeasure can eliminate the vulnerability and reduce the risk. The company cannot eliminate the threat agent, but can protect itself from allowing this threat agent to exploit vulnerabilities within the environment.

Because we now know the definition of a threat, let's look at different threats that can negatively affect an asset's confidentiality, integrity, or availability, as outlined in Table 1-2.

TABLE 1.2   Different threat types and examples

Security Principle	Threat	Explanation
Confidentiality		
	Shoulder surfing	Looking over a person's shoulder to uncover passwords or sensitive data
	Social engineering	Pretending to be someone else with the goal of tricking someone into giving up confidential information
	Message interception	Obtaining data as it is being transmitted
	Browsing	Looking for information without necessarily knowing its format
	Keyboard logger	Software or hardware installed to secretly gather data that a user types in at a keyboard
	Network sniffing	Using a device or software to read data as it travels over the network
Integrity		
	Modifying a message in transmission	Intercepting a message, altering it, and then sending it onto its destination
	Modifying configuration files	Altering critical files on a computer with the goal of changing its functionality

TABLE 1.2	Different threat types and examples *(continued)*	
Integrity		
	Changing audit logs	Modifying audit logs, usually with the goal of covering up misdeeds
	Data diddling	Modifying data before it is inputted into a program or system as soon as it comes out
Availability		
	Man-made or natural disasters	Tornado, fire, vandals, earthquake, terrorist attack, etc.
	Denial of service	Attack that commits so many resources on a victim's system that it can no longer function in one aspect or another
	Failure of a component	Failure of a device or component, which affects other components or devices
	Corruption of data	Modifying data to a point where it is unusable to others

---

Exam Tip

Shoulder surfing can be accomplished by using a video recorder to capture data that is being typed into a system and displayed on a monitor.

Once the vulnerabilities and threats are recognized, the team needs to identify different countermeasures that could help the company protect itself.

Objective 1.04   Security Control Types

A ll security controls are implemented to protect the confidentiality, integrity, and availability of resources. These are the three main principles of security, known as the *CIA triad*. *Confidentiality* prevents unauthorized disclosure of sensitive information; *integrity* prevents unauthorized modification of systems and data; *availability* prevents disruption of service and productivity.

If a security control is providing confidentiality, it is ensuring that the necessary level of secrecy is in place at each junction of data processing and thwarts attempts of unauthorized disclosure. If a control were providing integrity, it is providing the assurance of accuracy and reliability of the data and systems and ensures neither is modified in an unauthorized manner. And if a control were providing availability, it ensures that the system or data is available and in an acceptable form when needed, and that the system and its software executes in a predictable manner with an acceptable level of performance. Every security mechanism that is addressed in this book provides one or more of these security principles in one fashion or another.

There are three main types of controls used to provide these security principles: administrative, technical, and physical. *Administrative controls* are usually management's responsibilities, as in developing security policies, procedures, and standards. Administrative controls also include screening personnel, performing security awareness training, classifying data, developing business continuity and disaster plans, ensuring that rules are enforced, and establishing change control.

Technical controls are logical mechanisms that protect resources and information, as in encryption, firewall, intrusion detection system, and access control software. These technical controls are software and hardware mechanisms used to restrict subjects' access to objects (resources).

Physical controls protect computer systems, departments, people, and the facility. Some examples of physical controls are security guards, perimeter fences, locks, the removal of floppy and CD-ROM drives from computers, and motion detectors.

The secrecy of the control should not be depended upon and should not be the feature that is seen as the actual protection. For example, a company should not depend on the fact that today no one knows that they use an intrusion detection system, thus no one can circumvent it, because someone might find out about this control tomorrow. The dependence upon the secrecy of protection mechanisms is referred to as *security through obscurity* and is not always the best approach toward protection. A company should ensure that the controls put in place provide the necessary level of protection in a uniform fashion and understand that many people know that these types of countermeasures exist and may know how to get around them. This is why *defense in depth* is important, which means to provide layers of protection and not to rely solely on one or two security devices or safeguards.

Local Lingo

The terms *control, safeguard,* and *countermeasure* are used interchangeably throughout this book and refer to a type of protection mechanism.

In most companies, the department that carries out physical security and the department that carries out network security do not usually communicate and do not know or understand what each other is doing. And none of them probably have a good understanding of what management is or is not doing towards security. This is too bad, because they actually have the same goal of protecting the company, they just have different perspectives and focus. If there were more dialog, and these different controls and efforts could work in a synergistic manner, higher levels of protection could be provided, security holes could be more easily identified and understood, and duplicated efforts could be reduced, which saves money and time.

These different controls (administrative, technical, and physical) need to be integrated together to provide a layered approach, as shown in Figure 1-2, and work in concert to provide the necessary level of confidentiality, availability, and integrity for all of the organization's resources.

Exam Tip

Controls should be highly visible to deter misdeeds, but their mechanisms should not be so apparent that individuals can find ways to bypass them.

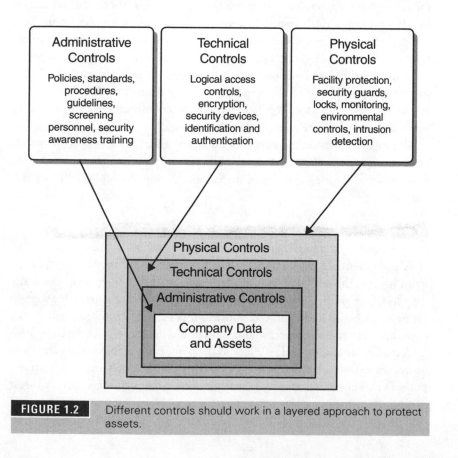

FIGURE 1.2   Different controls should work in a layered approach to protect assets.

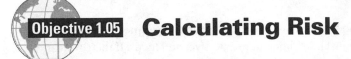

Calculating Risk

Within a risk analysis a *cost/benefit comparison* is performed, where the annualized cost of a countermeasure is compared with the estimated loss potential of each risk. A countermeasure, in most cases, should not be implemented unless the annualized cost of loss exceeds the annualized cost of the countermeasure itself. So if a server is worth $5,000, a countermeasure to protect the server costing $7,000 should not be used.

The team must calculate the risk of the identified threats actually occurring and the accompanying ramifications. The team must estimate the *potential loss* that could be accrued and the delayed loss. *Delayed losses* are ones that do not happen right away but occur down the road, as in loss of customers, failure to meet contractual commitments, tarnished reputation, loss in revenue, and late penalties from not being able to pay expenses. For example, if a company performed e-business by selling widgets on the Internet and its database that held customers' credit card information was compromised, the company could experience potential and delayed loss. If this attack actually caused the company to go offline for several hours, there is a loss in revenue. The cost of calling in experts and consultants to help understand what took place and the cost of getting all systems back online would need to be factored in. These are potential losses. Once this compromise is reported to the customers, and possibly talked about in the media, the company will most likely lose customers, have a damaged reputation, and be financially affected for months or years to come (which are examples of delayed losses).

To properly calculate these types of impact, the likelihood of specific threats needs to be calculated along with their estimated damages. There are two main approaches to figuring out this information: quantitative and qualitative risk analysis.

Quantitative Versus Qualitative Approaches

A *quantitative* risk analysis approach attempts to assign numeric values to all risks and potential losses. This is usually the more useful method to management because the results are in monetary formats that management can easily map to losses, profits, and their bottom line. A *qualitative* approach assigns a rating to each risk and countermeasure and is derived from "gut feelings" or opinions of internal employees who are considered the "experts" in the company.

A qualitative analysis uses scenarios laying out the possible threats and their outcomes so that the different people can conceptually walk through each hypothesis and give their opinions. Once the scenario explaining a specific threat is examined, the individuals are asked to indicate if they feel that the particular issue is an actual threat to the company and to what degree. The rating can be on a scale of 1–5 or a "low, medium, high" scale. Then, the different countermeasures are explained and the same group of people rate the individual countermeasures. The end result is obtaining the opinions of the people who are closest to the possible threats and are seen to have the most expertise in these different areas.

The steps to a qualitative analysis:

1. Develop risk scenarios.
2. Gather company "experts."
3. Work through the scenarios to understand an identified threat.
4. Rank seriousness of the threats and estimate their probability of taking place.
5. Rank effectiveness of different countermeasures.

Exam Tip

A Delphi method can be used, which allows individuals to give their opinions anonymously. This provides an atmosphere where people feel more at ease to give their honest opinions and will not be as influenced or intimidated by others.

Quantitative Risk Analysis Because quantitative assessments deal with numbers and monetary values, formulas must be involved. The two main formulas are the *single loss expectancy* (SLE), which is then plugged into the *annualized loss expectancy* (ALE) formula. The goal of the SLE is to figure out the possible business impact if an asset was damaged by a specific threat. The goal of the ALE is to understand how much the company could logically spend to protect the asset from this identified threat. The actually formulas are as follows:

Exposure factor (EF) × asset value = Single loss expectancy

SLE × annualized rate of occurrence (ARO) = Annualized loss expectancy

The *exposure factor* (EF) is the estimated percentage of damage that could take place. The *annualized rate of occurrence* (ARO) is the estimated frequency of that threat occurring. Because the ARO is an annualized value, its maximum value is 1.0. If the threat were estimated to happen once in ten years, the ARO value would be 0.1, and once in 100 years would have an ARO value of 0.01.

If the analysis team identified a tornado as a threat to the company, they may walk through the following calculations: A tornado is estimated to damage 50 percent (EF) of a facility, and the value of the facility is $200,000; thus, the SLE would be $100,000. If the probability of it occurring is one in ten years, the ALE is $10,000.

$$\$200,000 \times .5 = \$100,000$$

$$\$100,000 \times .1 = \$10,000$$

What the resulting value tells the team, and management, is that up to $10,000 could be budgeted per year to protect the facility from tornado damage. Spending over $10,000 would be excessive and not make good business sense.

This information is gathered and calculated for every asset and every identified threat and given to management so that they can make informed and logical decisions when it comes to security. The results of the analysis help management prioritize different risks, allows them to understand the full extent of risks that the company faces, and helps them properly construct a security budget.

Travel Advisory

When an actual risk analysis is performed, it requires many other formulas and calculations; SLE and ALE are just two of them. But for test purposes, these are the formulas that you need to understand.

A purely quantitative risk analysis is impossible because many of the items that are being evaluated and estimated are qualitative in nature. Estimating that a tornado would cause damage of only 50 percent to the facility is a qualitative measurement in that no one really knows if 10 percent or 100 percent of the damage will actually take place. Risk analysis is about making educated estimates with all of the available information.

An overview of the steps of a risk analysis are as follows:

1. Understand the goal and scope of the analysis.
2. Estimate and assign values to assets that are to be protected.
3. Identify each vulnerability and its threat agents.
4. Estimate the full loss potential of each risk.
5. Estimate the probability and frequency of a risk becoming a reality.

6. Suggest cost-effective safeguards and remedial measures that can be implemented to mitigate risks.

7. After the risk analysis is completed, all information is documented and presented to management.

Dealing with Risk

The point of risk analysis and risk management is to find ways to mitigate risk. There is no such thing as a 100 percent secure system or facility, and there is no way to get rid of all risk, so risk must be identified, understood, and properly dealt with. In most cases, this means there is always a level of risk that will need to be accepted. *Total risk* is what exists before a countermeasure is put into place; *residual risk* is the remaining risk after a countermeasure is implemented. The following are conceptual formulas that can be used to understand these different risk types:

$$\text{Threats} \times \text{vulnerability} \times \text{asset value} = \text{Total risk}$$

$$\text{Total risk} \times \text{countermeasure} = \text{Residual risk}$$

Management has several ways of dealing with risk:

- **Transfer the risk** Purchase insurance.
- **Reduce the risk** Implement a countermeasure.
- **Accept the risk** Accept total risk without any action.
- **Reject the risk** Ignore the risk.

If a countermeasure costs more than the estimated potential loss value, management may decide to accept the risk and take no further action. If they do not want to take all the risk on themselves, they may purchase insurance and transfer the risk. If a countermeasure is implemented, risk is reduced to residual risk. And if management is in denial or afraid of the risk, they may reject it, which is irresponsible and could make them liable if the threat actually occurred.

Countermeasure Selection

If a company decides to reduce their risk by implementing countermeasures, there are a few requirements of the countermeasures that must be met, as outlined here:

- It must provide a security solution to an identified problem and be cost-effective.

- Its security should not depend upon the secrecy of its mechanisms.
- It must be testable to ensure that it provides the claimed level of protection.
- It must provide uniform protection for all assets and users.
- It should be isolated from other safeguards and have a low dependency on them.
- It should require minimal human intervention and be tamper-proof.
- It should have override and fail-safe defaults.
- During reset or recovery, it should still protect the intended asset.
- There should be different access rights; administrative for configuration and user, which may not configure or disable the safeguard.

Local Lingo

A fail-safe default means that if the partition mechanism fails for any purpose, it does not put the asset at risk. For example, if a firewall fails, it should disallow any traffic through it instead of failing to open, which means any type of traffic is allowed access to the environment.

Objective 1.06

Security Policies and their Supporting Counterparts

Up to this point, the risk analysis team has identified the company's assets, assigned values to them, and identified threats and corresponding countermeasures. Management has been made aware of all of these issues, and they have determined how they will deal with the risks and have agreed upon the necessary countermeasures that should be put into place. All of these steps should take place *before* a security program is developed because it allows for educated decisions to be made and provides a solid foundation and direction for the program to follow.

A security program is all of the policies, procedures, documents, standards, compliancy enforcement measures, devices, software, awareness training, and personnel that work together to protect the company and its assets. The rest of the chapter takes a deeper look at some of these items that make up the security program.

Security Policy

The next step is for management to develop a *security policy*, which is a document that contains generalized terms of management's directives pertaining to what type of role security is to play in the organization. It establishes how a security program will be set up, dictates the program's goals, assigns responsibilities, shows the strategic and tactical value of security, and outlines how enforcement should be carried out. This policy must address relative laws, regulations, and liability issues the company is faced with and how they are to be satisfied. The organizational security policy provides scope and direction for all future security activities within the organization.

After the security policy is created, standards, guidelines, baselines, and procedures can be developed. Each of these supports and enforces the directives outlined in the security policy and give the policy structure and substance.

Standards

Standards are rules indicating what employees should and should not be doing at their place of business, what different devices are to be used for, and acceptable software configurations of different products. They are compulsory in nature, meaning that there is not much flexibility in choosing whether to follow them or not. The goal of standards is to ensure a consistency in the use of company assets, users' actions, and approaches to security. Standards may be drawn up indicating that users cannot download pornographic material, that inappropriate materials cannot be sent via e-mail, servers must be installed in a specific way, that an identification badge must be worn by employees at all times, and that user activities must be audited and monitored. These standards are derived directly from the security policy.

Exam Tip

If a person is continually not abiding by the company's policy and standards, this information should be presented to a supervisor and not addressed one-on-one.

Baselines

A *baseline* establishes a minimum level of security that is required throughout the organization. Baselines can be applied directly to computers where they are required; for example, all systems within the accounting department must meet at least a C2 security rating. This is just a minimum, and more security can be added on top of it, but all systems must at least meet this requirement. A baseline is sometimes referred to as an abstraction of a standard, meaning that the baseline is the intended goal and the standard is how to get there. We follow rules (standards) to accomplish a level of security (baseline).

Procedures

Procedures are detailed, documented step-by-step actions to be taken to achieve a specific task. For example, there can be a procedure outlining the necessary steps to set up a user account, assign rights, and configure a new mailbox. There can be a procedure indicating how people should install a new server, what configurations should be set, and what service packs should be installed. This ensures that no matter who makes changes to the environment, they are done in a standardized manner across the board (thus, they are meant to be repeatable).

Guidelines

Many times companies do not know where to start and stop when developing a security program, what items should be addressed, what pieces should make up their security program, and how specific issues should be handled. *Guidelines* are recommendations and operational guides for companies and are often referred to as "Best Practices."

There are standardized guidelines that provide guidance for companies, security professionals, and data custodians, as in the ISO I7799. And a company may also have their own internal guidelines that indicate how certain issues should be handled. For example, in an IPSec implementation, a company may have a guideline indicating that a stronger algorithm should be used for encryption whenever possible, as in using 3DES instead of DES.

Local Lingo

ISO I7799 is an international set of guidelines that address how a company should develop a security policy, classify assets, implement system access controls, enforce compliance, and much more.

Standards, guidelines, and baselines are all derived from, support, and implement the security policy. Where the policy is very general and vague, these other components are very specific and granular.

Roles and Responsibilities

Everyone has their role in life and corresponding responsibilities. This is also true for security programs within companies. Providing clarity of roles and responsibilities helps ensure that everyone knows what is expected of them, curbs the "It's not my job" attitude, and above all else, provides us with someone to blame because we seem to need that.

Data Owner

Each individual within a company has a different level of responsibility as it relates to security. The ultimate *data owner* is a member of senior management who is responsible for the protection of company assets, including data. It is this person who is bound to due care responsibilities and is responsible if and when an asset is compromised. It is the data owner's responsibility to dictate the classification level of the data, indicate how assets should be protected and who should have access to them, and delegate day-to-day tasks to others to carry out and enforce these instructions.

Data Custodian

The *data custodian* is delegated the responsibility of the maintenance and protection of the company's assets and data. This person, or department, installs and configures hardware and software, performs backups, validates the confidentiality, availability, and integrity of resources, and performs the day-to-day procedures of keeping systems functional and their data protected. This role is usually given to the IT department.

User

The *user* is any individual who routinely uses company assets and data to fulfill her role and responsibilities within the company. The user must have the necessary level of access to the assets to perform her duties and is responsible for following operational security procedures and standards to ensure resources' confidentiality, integrity, and availability. Users should have a limited amount of access rights and permissions when it comes to configuration of resources and manipulation of data.

Security Auditor

A *security auditor* is an individual or group that does periodic reviews of the company's security procedures and in-place mechanisms to make sure they meet a predefined level of protection. This is usually required in industry-specific organizations, such as financial institutions, government agencies, and medical facilities. Approval needs to be given by the data owner, or a delegate, before an audit is carried out. This approval should be documented and traceable through the management chain of the company.

Exam Tip
If an auditor needs access to data protected by logical controls, approval should be given in written form before the auditor attempts to access any information.

Decisions about security goals should not be placed in the hands of the data custodians, but should sit squarely in senior management's lap. They have a larger understanding and vision of the company and are ultimately responsible if something goes wrong. The next layer under senior management is functional management, which has more intimate understanding of how individual departments work and how security affects those departments directly. Under functional managers are operational managers and staff who are closer to the actual operations of the organization and understand the technical details of the security mechanisms in place. Each layer has its own insight to security as a whole; it is important that they are all on the same road with the same objectives.

Objective 1.08 **Information Classification**

It was stated earlier that all assets should be identified and a value assigned to them; this also includes information. Information is very important—and sometimes critical—to companies. Assigning a value to an asset helps determine how important it is to a company, how much protection should be put in place to protect it, and how much money should be earmarked in the security budget to continue to protect it. This is the same reason data is classified. The classification level indicates its importance to the company, the sensitivity of the data, who should be able to access it, and what security mechanisms should be put into place to protect it.

Classifying data ensures that the information receives the appropriate level of protection by indicating the level of confidentiality, integrity, and availability that is required. Each classification level should have separate handling requirements, access procedures, standards of how the data is to be used, and procedures for properly destroying it when its lifetime is over. A criteria should be developed and used when classifying new data, instead of arbitrarily assigning classification levels here and there.

Travel Advisory

One problem with data classification is declassification. Many times, companies do not take the necessary steps to declassify data, so it wastes resources and degrades the overall effort of protecting only critical and relevant information. Declassification issues should be addressed in a policy, and steps for declassification should be outlined in a procedure.

Classification also helps ensure that the protection put in place is cost-effective by not spending the money and overhead of protecting sensitive *and* nonsensitive data. If you try to protect everything, usually in the end you protect nothing.

Exam Tip

Data owners are responsible for classifying data.

Military Versus Commercial Classifications

The military and government agencies, when compared to the private commercial sector, are usually much more concerned about keeping their information secret. Because of these differences in objectives, these organizations implement different classification sets for different purposes. The classification structure is usually dissimilar, and the controls that are implemented to enforce these classifications can range.

The commercial sector usually uses the following levels (highest to lowest):

- Confidential
- Private

- Sensitive
- Public

The military and government usually use the following levels (highest to lowest):

- Top Secret
- Secret
- Confidential
- Sensitive but Unclassified
- Unclassified

Once the classification scheme is agreed upon, a criteria needs to be developed to help decide how information is assigned one classification over another one. The following items are examples of some of the characteristics that need to be examined to determine the necessary classification level:

- Usefulness of data.
- Value of data.
- Age of data.
- The level of damage that could be caused if the data was disclosed.
- The level of damage that could be caused if the data was modified or corrupted.
- Laws, regulations, or liability responsibilities pertaining to protecting data.
- Effects the data has on national security.
- Who should be accessing this data?
- Who should be maintaining this data?
- Where should this data be stored?
- Who should be able to reproduce this data?
- What data would require labels and special marking?

From here, the necessary controls and countermeasures identified in the risk analysis that were approved by management need to be put into place to protect each data classification properly. Data custodians must be identified and assigned the responsibility of implementing these controls and performing the necessary procedures to keep this level of security at all times.

Here are the procedures for properly classifying data:

1. Outline classification levels that will be used and what they mean.
2. Indicate security controls that are required for each classification level.
3. Develop criteria that will be used to determine how data is classified.
4. Data owner dictates the classification of the data he is responsible for.
5. Identify the data custodian responsible for maintaining the determined security levels.
6. Document any exceptions to previous classification issues.
7. Develop termination procedures for declassifying data.
8. Integrate all issues into security awareness program.

Objective 1.09 # Employee Management

People are almost always the weakest link in security, and most of the security breaches that take place within companies are done by employees, not outside hackers. Employee management is a crucial piece to a security program and can minimize a long list of risks. The following subjects are considered to be administrative controls pertaining to employee management.

Prospective employees should be required to sign a nondisclosure agreement, and the following items may need to be fully investigated:

- Background check, including education and references
- Drug screening
- Security clearance
- Credit check

When an employee is being terminated for one reason or another, the following steps should be taken:

- The individual must leave facility immediately under supervision.
- The individual must surrender ID badges, keys, and company belongings.
- An exit interview must be completed.
- The user's accounts must be disabled.
- Passwords must be changed immediately.

Although these things should take place for each and every employee termination, if the employee that is leaving is disgruntled in any way, it is imperative to disable his accounts and change all of his passwords on different resources right away.

Operational Administrative Controls

Separation of duties needs to be enforced, which means that one person or department cannot complete a critical task by itself. With separation of duties in place, someone who wanted to commit fraud would need to participate in *collusion*, meaning that more than one person would need to work together to cause some type of destruction or fraud, thus drastically reducing the probability of fraud being committed.

Travel Advisory
A security officer should be a separate entity from management and the IT department to ensure that all decisions are made for security purposes only. The security officer's findings and recommendations should be presented to a group that has anonymity from others.

Another administrative control is *job rotation*, which means that individuals are trained and rotated throughout different positions within the company. This ensures that knowledge is shared, that a company is not too dependent upon one person, and that others may be able to identify fraudulent activities if they are taking place.

Exam Tip
Rotation of duties can also be a countermeasure to reduce collusion possibilities.

The last control we will look at is *security awareness*. For security to be effective and successful, senior management on down needs to be fully aware of its importance and what is expected of them. The training should explain the *what, when, how,* and *whys* of computer information, personnel, and physical security so that the attitudes of the individuals will be modified to try and help the cause instead of trying to get around it or disrupt it.

If employees are not told what is expected of them and what management considers unacceptable behavior, the company will have a much harder time enforcing rules and may be held liable for negative activities because security awareness and communication falls under due care directives.

CHECKPOINT

✔**Objective 1.01:   Management Responsibilities**   Senior management is ultimately responsible for all that takes place within a company and must follow due care stipulations for developing, maintaining, and supporting a security program and all of the elements within it. Security within a company should follow a top-down approach, instead of bottom-up.

✔**Objective 1.02:   Risk Management**   Risk management is identifying and dealing with vulnerabilities and threats in the best way to protect the company. The company should establish the level of risk they are willing to accept; risk management ensures that this threshold is never exceeded. A risk analysis is a tool used in risk management and is the process of identifying all assets, assigning values to them, identifying all possible threats, calculating the possible risks of those threats, and coming up with countermeasures.

✔**Objective 1.03:   Possible Threats**   There are several different types of threats a company actually faces. It is important to recognize all of them and identify the corresponding countermeasures that should be put in place to protect against them. A vulnerability is a weakness; a threat is something that takes advantage of that weakness; a risk is the probability of a threat agent exploiting a vulnerability; and a countermeasure reduces this risk and provides protection.

✔**Objective 1.04:   Security Control Types**   There are several types of controls that can be used to protect a company and its assets. They fall into one of these three categories: administrative, technical, and physical. These controls are implemented to protect the confidentiality, integrity, and availability of assets.

✔**Objective 1.05:   Calculating Risk**   A risk analysis can take a quantitative or qualitative approach. A quantitative method assigns numbers and monetary values to the items being assessed. Qualitative uses ratings, "gut feelings" of a set of experts, and scenarios. Companies can choose to accept, transfer, reduce, or ignore the risks the analysis uncovers.

✔**Objective 1.06:   Security Policies and their Supporting Counterparts**   A security policy contains management's views and directives towards security. Standards are rules that must be followed; procedures are step-by-step instructions; baselines are required minimum levels of security; and guidelines are recommendations. These items are derived from the security policy and work to support it.

✔**Objective 1.07:   Roles and Responsibilities**   Each person within a company has a role and individual responsibilities when it comes to security. Management must outline these roles, dictate their associated responsibilities, and assign people to these roles. The main roles we need to understand are data owners, data custodians, auditors, and users.

✔**Objective 1.08:   Information Classification**   As with other assets, information must be protected. This happens through identifying it, assigning values to it, indicating what needs to be put into place to protect it, and outlining how it will be accessed, maintained, and destroyed. It is the data owner's responsibility to assign a classification level to the data he is responsible for. The different classifications levels are set to describe the level of sensitivity of the data. Each classification level has different handling procedures and security requirements.

✔**Objective 1.09:   Employee Management**   Employees are a large part of every company and are usually security's worst enemy. Employees need to go through proper hiring and termination processes, and they should be made aware of what is expected of them. The awareness comes from training, which should happen at least once a year. Separation of duties and job rotation should be enforced to help fight against fraudulent activities.

REVIEW QUESTIONS

1. Which of the following make up the CIA triad?
   - **A.** Confidentiality, Integrity, Assurance
   - **B.** Confidentiality, Integrity, Availability
   - **C.** Confidentiality, Integration, Assurance
   - **D.** Confidentiality, Integration, Availability

2. How is the annualized loss expectancy (ALE) calculated?
   - **A.** $SLE \times ARO$
   - **B.** $ARO \times EF$
   - **C.** $SLE \times EF \times ARO$
   - **D.** $ARO \times SLE - EF$

3. Of the following, who has the responsibility of determining the classification levels for information?

    A. User

    B. Data owner

    C. Auditor

    D. Security manager

4. Which of the following best describes organizational security policies?

    A. General guidelines defining access control requirements

    B. Suggestions on how to achieve compliance with standards

    C. High-level statements that indicate management's intentions

    D. High-level statements indicating specific technical controls to be used

5. For a company to properly protect its intellectual property and other assets, which of the following would be the best approach when terminating an employee?

    A. Perform an exit interview, have employee review nondisclosure agreement, disable accounts, and change passwords.

    B. Perform an exit interview, disable accounts, and change passwords.

    C. Have employee agree to a transborder agreement.

    D. Outline all employee duties relating to due care before being dismissed.

6. Which of the following best describes the difference between quantitative and qualitative approaches to risk analysis?

    A. A qualitative approach assigns monetary values to assets and percentages to risk probabilities.

    B. A quantitative approach gets experts' advice.

    C. A quantitative approach supplies a rating to each risk and countermeasure.

    D. A qualitative approach uses risk scenarios.

7. Which of the following is a compulsory rule pertaining to computer or information security?

    A. Standard

    B. Security policy

    C. Guideline

    D. Procedure

8. Which best describes the purpose of a risk analysis?

    A. Identify liability issues and regulations in place to protect assets.

    B. Identify assets and what technical controls should be put into place to protect them.

    C. Identify assets, vulnerabilities, and calculate potential risks.

    D. Identify threats that have a direct relationship to liability.

9. Which of the following most clearly indicates whether specific countermeasures should be put into place?

    A. ALE results

    B. Countermeasure cost/benefit analysis

    C. Threat and risk analysis

    D. Risk evaluation

10. When is it acceptable for a manager overseeing the execution of a risk analysis to not take action on an identified risk?

    A. When the cost of the necessary countermeasure outweighs the potential cost of the realized risk.

    B. When the risk reduction measures improve the productivity of the business.

    C. When the conditions that cause the risk to arise is outside the control of the department.

    D. It is never acceptable.

11. A browsing attack is referred to when which of the following takes places?

    A. Attacker is shoulder surfing to identify confidential information.

    B. Attacker is looking for sensitive data without knowing its format.

    C. Attacker is collecting electrical radiation and recompiling to uncover sensitive information.

    D. Attacker is performing dumpster diving.

REVIEW ANSWERS

1. **B**   The CIA triad includes the main principles of security, which are confidentiality, integrity, and availability. Every security control provides one or more of these principles.

2. **A**   The annualized loss expectancy (ALE) is calculated by multiplying the single loss expectancy (SLE) and the annualized rate of occurrence

(ARO). The resulting value gives management an idea of what can be spent to protect the asset from the identified threat.

3. **B**   The ultimate data owner is senior management because they are the ones that are liable. They need to understand what data is important and how it should be protected, which is the reason for classification. Senior management can also delegate the responsibility of data ownership.

4. **C**   Policies are general statements that outline the senior management's intentions and directives pertaining to computer, information, personnel, and physical security within the company.

5. **A**   A company should carry out an exit interview for each individual terminated, have each person review the nondisclosure contract that was signed previously, disable accounts, change passwords, and escort the individual out of the building.

6. **D**   A qualitative approach uses risk scenarios to get experts' advice to then rate risks and countermeasure. A quantitative approach applies monetary values to assets and risks and estimates the possibility of the risk.

7. **A**   A standard is a rule that outlines how the management expects an employee to react or behave. Standards can also indicate how equipment is to be used and what configurations are required for specific computers.

8. **C**   The reason to perform this type of analysis is to see what the company has (assets) and how much they are worth and to identify potential risks. It deals with more than just technical controls, as stated in answer B, and is a tool to calculate risk.

9. **B**   The countermeasure itself needs to be judged on its own merits and on the cost and benefit it can provide the company. The ALE calculates the potential loss, but does not calculate the cost of a countermeasure, thus it looks at part of the story.

10. **A**   If the countermeasures cost more than the estimated potential and delayed losses, it is a good business decision not to implement the countermeasure.

11. **B**   A browsing attack is when an intruder is looking through a person's files, hard drive, or personal belongings. She is looking for information but does not know if it is held in a database, spreadsheet, or document; thus, she does not know the format it is in.

Access Control

	NEWBIE	SOME EXPERIENCE	EXPERT
ETA	5 hours	3 hours	2 hours

Companies have many types of resources they need to ensure that only the intended people can access and need to make sure that these intended users have only the level of access required to accomplish their tasks. These resources can be physical (a facility, sensitive room, or expensive equipment), informational (intellectual property, confidential data), or personnel (employees, contractors, and Bob).

Access control is more than simply requiring usernames and passwords when users want to access resources. It can be much more. There are multiple methods, techniques, technologies, and models that can be implemented, there are different ways to administer controls, and there are a variety of attacks that are launched against many of these access control mechanisms. We cover it all. So get comfortable—this is an important chapter.

Objective 2.01   Identification and Authentication

Access controls exist to keep the bad guys out and to keep the good guys honest. Companies need to ensure that unauthorized access is not allowed and that authorized users' cannot make improper modifications. The controls exist in a variety of forms, from passwords and ID badges to remote access authentication protocols and security guards. The tricky part is that they must be incorporated in a layered approach and that each layer needs to be understood, along with its relationship to the other layers, to ensure that vulnerabilities are not overlooked or introduced and that different controls do not step on each other's toes.

Definitions

Before we get too far ahead of ourselves, let's go over some basic definitions of terms you will see often throughout this chapter:

- **Subject**   Active entity that requests access to an object or the data within an object. The subject is the actor.
- **Object**   Passive entity being accessed, or the item being acted upon.
- **Access**   Ability of a subject to do something, such as read, create, delete, or modify. Access is also considered the flow of information between a subject and object.
- **Access control**   Security features that control how subjects and objects communicate and interact with each other and the flow of information.

An entity can be a subject or an object, depending upon its activity. For example, a program can be an object when a user requests information from it or requests it to process data. The program can also be a subject if it initiates communication with another program.

Three Steps to Access Control

There are three important components of access control: identification, authentication, and authorization. *Identification* is the activity of the subject supplying information to identify itself to an authentication service. Some examples of identification mechanisms are username, account number, and memory card. *Authentication* is the second part of a credential set to verify the identity of the subject. These mechanisms could be passphrases, passwords, cryptographic keys, PIN numbers, or tokens. You may tell me your name, but I have no proof that you are who you say you are until you demonstrate the secret handshake. Only then will I be convinced of your identity. *Authorization* is the process of determining what this identified subject can actually access and what operations it can carry out. Authorization is based on some type of predefined criteria, which is enforced through access control lists, security labels, capabilities tables, or user profiles.

These three components of access control usually work together in a synergetic relationship and can be found in applications, operating systems, firewalls, routers, databases, domain controllers, and more.

Authentication

Identification is usually providing a public piece of information (username, account number) and authentication is providing a private piece of information (PIN number, passphrase, digital signature). Three important characteristics of the mechanisms that can be used for authentication are as follows:

- Subject must prove something he knows   Example = password
- Subject must prove something he has   Example = smart card
- Subject must prove something he is   Example = fingerprint

If one mechanism providing one of these characteristics is used, it is referred to as *one-factor*; if two mechanisms are being used, it is *two-factor*; and you guessed it, an authentication process that requires all three is referred to as *three-factor*. For the authentication process to be considered *strong authentication*, it must be at least two-factor.

User identification values should be unique to ensure accountability of individual activity. They should be nondescriptive of job functions to make them not as easily guessed and so that attackers will not know what type of account the credentials are tied to. There should also be secure and documented processes for issuing identification and authentication values and mechanisms to ensure standardization.

There are several mechanisms that can be used for authentication, each one with its own strengths and weaknesses. We take a look at the following items:

- Biometrics
- Passwords
- Token devices
- Memory cards
- Smart cards
- Cryptographic keys

Biometrics

Biometrics is a type of access control mechanism that can be used to verify an individual's identity with a unique personal attribute. Examples are fingerprints, palm scans, retina scans, and voice prints. These kinds of authentication systems gather a lot of information that can be hard to imitate, thus they provide a higher level of protection when compared to other authentication technologies.

Biometric systems are usually more expensive, relative to other approaches, and do not usually have a high acceptance rate by society because they are perceived to be intrusive and they obtain personal information. Biometrics are sometimes seen as too "Big Brother-ish" and an encroachment into our personal privacy through automated means. For these reasons, they have usually been seen only in environments that require a very high level of security. But after what happened on September 11, 2001, they are being implemented into more locations because of society's increased awareness of security.

Each subject must go through an enrollment period where personal attributes are captured and then stored in a reference file. The reference file can be held in a local or remote database or even within a biometric template of a smart card. So, when Truman presses his finger on the reader in order to enter his highly secure work facility, the reader references the image Truman presents against his stored reference file. If the two match, and he supplies the correct PIN or password, he is successfully authenticated and allowed access.

The accuracy of different biometric systems can be evaluated by two separate measurements: Type I error and Type II error. A *Type I error*, false reject rate, is rejecting a subject that should be authenticated and allowed access. If Truman is rejected when he presents his fingerprint, and he really should have been authenticated, this is referred to as a Type I error. If an imposter is successfully authenticated by the system, this is called a *Type II error*—false accept rate. Each of these error rates should remain low for the system to provide the necessary level of protection and efficiency. A metric has been developed to measure different biometric systems' overall protection and accuracy level, which is a combination of these two error types, called the *crossover error rate* (CER). CER is the point at which Type I errors (false rejection) equal Type II errors (false acceptance), as shown in Figure 2-1.

The CER can be accomplished by calibrating the system to ensure that it does not provide more Type I errors than Type II errors and vice versa. For example, if a system was calibrated so that it resulted in only 2 Type I errors out of 100 authentication attempts and 2 Type II errors out of 100 attempts, it would have the CER value of 2. This system would provide a higher accuracy level than a system that provided a CER value of 3. This metric can be used when evaluating different biometric systems for purchase.

Types of Biometrics Different biometric systems gather different types of biometric information. The following explains the different physical attributes that various systems can use for authentication purposes:

- **Fingerprint** Ridge endings and bifurcations on the finger.
- **Finger scan** Selective points on the fingerprint are collected and stored. This uses a smaller amount of data compared to fingerprint systems.
- **Palm scan** Creases and ridges on the palm and all fingerprints are used to identify individuals.
- **Hand geometry** The shape of a person's hand (length and width of hand and fingers).
- **Retina scan** The patterns of the blood vessels on the backside of the eyeball.

- **Iris scan** The unique patterns, rings, and corona in the iris, which is the colored portion of the eye.
- **Signature dynamics** Electrical signals, pressure used, slant of the pen, the amount of time and patterns used in creating a signature are captured. There is much more information and variables to look at when compared to a static signature, thus harder to counterfeit.
- **Keyboard dynamics** Mechanism that analyzes electrical signals when a person types a certain phrase on a keyboard, such as speed and movement.
- **Voice print** This mechanism recognizes subtle differences in people's speech sounds and patterns.
- **Facial scan** Attributes of a person's face, bone structure, nose ridges, and eye widths.
- **Hand topology** Looks at a side view of a person's hand and reviews the height and length from that perspective.

Travel Advisory

Although retina scanners provide a very high level of protection, they are usually one of the least accepted systems by society because the eyeball must be placed close to the system and a puff of air may need to be blown into the eye. And we all just love that.

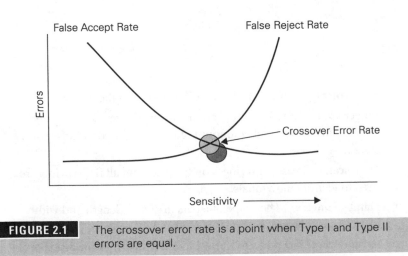

FIGURE 2.1 The crossover error rate is a point when Type I and Type II errors are equal.

Passwords

A *password* is a string of characters that should be different for each user and highly protected. It is something that a subject knows and is the most widely used authentication method in place today. The problem is that it is the most insecure mechanism when compared to other authentication technologies, because users and administrators do not usually practice the necessary disciplines required to provide a higher level of protection. Also, specialized utilities have been developed to uncover passwords and compromise this type of authentication method.

The following is a list of best practices that should be implemented and enforced as part of a company-wide password policy:

- Passwords should have at least eight characters (alphanumeric and symbols) and a combination of upper- and lowercase.
- Users should not be able to reuse the same passwords (password history).
- Systems should have a threshold (clipping level) configured that limits the number of unsuccessful logon attempts.
- An accurate audit log should be maintained that includes information about each logon attempt, which includes date, time, user ID, and workstation.
- The password lifetime should be short but practical.
- Passwords should not be shared.
- Passwords should not be easily guessable nor should they be dictionary words.

Passwords should never be stored in clear text; some type of encryption scheme, as in a one-way hashing method, should be used to ensure that passwords are not easily read. Servers that store passwords should have limited physical and logical access and should be highly protected.

Some companies choose to use password generators, which are software applications that create complex passwords for users instead of allowing them to come up with their own. Although this sounds like a great approach, many times the passwords that are created are too complex for the users to remember and they are quickly written down on yellow sticky notes that are then stuck to the monitor or secretly hidden underneath the keyboard. Writing down passwords and making them publicly available defeats the whole purpose of passwords and access control.

Attacks on Passwords   There are two types of attacks that are commonly used against passwords: dictionary and brute force attacks. *Dictionary attacks* are performed by software tools that contain hundreds or thousands of words that are commonly chosen as passwords. The attacker usually captures a hashed value of a password, or password file, and the tool then compares each of the words preloaded into the tool to the captured password until a match is uncovered.

Another type of attack on passwords is a *brute force* attack. In this attack type, a tool is used that tries every possible character and sequence of characters until the correct password is uncovered. So whereas a dictionary attack will attempt to match the password using a long list of words, a brute force attack will try and crack a password one character at a time.

Dictionary and brute force programs are not just used by evildoers. Oftentimes, systems administrators will use them to test the strength of users' passwords to enforce a set password policy. Because many useful tools reside on the Internet, or are accessible to the general public, attackers and security professionals are typically equipped with the same firepower. Security professionals simply need to be smarter and take more precautions to protect against these never-ending threats. The following are some countermeasures for password attacks:

- Do not allow passwords to be sent in clear text.
- Encrypt the passwords with encryption algorithms or hashing functions.
- Employ one-time password tokens.
- Rotate passwords on a frequent basis.
- Employ intrusion detection systems (IDS) to detect dictionary or brute force attacks.
- Use dictionary tools to find weak passwords chosen by users.
- Protect password files properly.

Cognitive Password

A *cognitive password* is based on fact or opinion used as the secret code, which is usually easier for a user to remember and is more difficult for an attacker to uncover. The user goes through an enrollment process by answering questions that typically deal with personal experiences and the answers to these questions are documented and used as cognitive passwords when the user needs to authenticate herself at a later time. For example, when Chrissy calls a help desk for the first time, she is enrolled for proper authentication by being asked the following questions:

- What is your mother's maiden name?
- What is your dog's name?

- What city were you born in?
- What is your favorite color?

When Chrissy calls back to get assistance from the help desk at a later time, she is presented with one or more of these questions to prove her identity. Once the help desk person is convinced of her identification, he can move on to assisting Chrissy.

One-Time Password

A *one-time password* is a set of characters that can be used to prove a subject's identity one time and one time only. After the password is used, it is destroyed and no longer acceptable for authentication. If the password were obtained by an attacker as it was being transmitted, she would have a small window of time to try and use it and most likely it was already used once, thus it is useless to the attacker. This greatly reduces the vulnerability of someone sniffing network traffic, obtaining a password, and being able to successfully authenticate as an actual legitimate user.

One-time passwords are usually generated and supplied to the user via a handheld device with an LCD display, referred to as *token device*. The user reads the password provided by the token device and enters it, along with a username, into a system for authentication purposes. The password is good for only that session and when the user needs to authenticate again, another password is dynamically created. Token devices, also referred to as one-time password generators, are either synchronous or asynchronous.

Synchronous token devices are synchronized with an authentication service via clocking mechanism or by events. When a clocking mechanism is used, the token device and authenticating service agree upon a timing scheme. The token device presents encrypted time values to users, and they enter these values along with their usernames into their workstations, as shown in Figure 2-2. This credential set is sent to the authentication service. Because the token device and authentication service are synchronized, the authentication service is expecting a specific value to be submitted as the password. If the correct value is submitted, and it correlates with the given username, the user is successfully authenticated.

When *events* are used to establish authentication, the user is usually required to initiate the logon process, which tells the token device and authentication system to increment the one-time values. The token device and authentication system share the same list of values to be used for one-time passwords; the token device encrypts and presents the next value in the list to the user, which she enters as her password.

Asynchronous token devices use a challenge-response method to create one-time passwords. The authentication service sends the user a value, which he

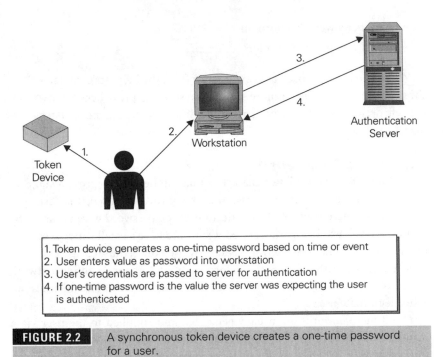

1. Token device generates a one-time password based on time or event
2. User enters value as password into workstation
3. User's credentials are passed to server for authentication
4. If one-time password is the value the server was expecting the user
   is authenticated

| FIGURE 2.2 | A synchronous token device creates a one-time password for a user. |

enters into his token device. The token device modifies this value, through encryption or a hashing process, and presents the new value to the user. The user then enters this new value as his password to authenticate to the authentication service. If this set of characters is the same that the authentication service originally sent to the user, the user is properly authenticated.

Token devices protect against password guessing, replay attacks, and electronic eavesdropping, but can be exposed to masquerading attacks, where an attacker gains control of the token device and uses it to impersonate the valid user. This is why many token devices require the user to enter a proper PIN value before it can be used. If a user has to provide a PIN and uses the token device for authentication, this is a two-factor authentication process.

Exam Tip

A replay attack is capturing a message, packet, or credential set and resubmitting it with the goal of impersonating a legitimate user.

Cryptographic Keys

Another authentication method is the use of cryptographic keys and digital signatures to prove one's identity. This can be an alternative to using passwords and biometric systems or can be used in combination with these technologies.

A private key is a cryptographic key that should be available to only one person, and this is how it offers authentication purposes. It should be highly protected and not shared in any way. The private key can be used to create a digital signature, which also provides authentication of a user. These items are covered further in Chapter 6, but for now understand that they are mechanisms that can be used for authentication purposes.

Passphrase

A *passphrase* is a long string of characters that are easier for the user to remember in most cases than a password because it is an actual phrase of some type. Once the passphrase is entered into the computer, a software program converts it into a *virtual password*, which is the actual information used for authentication purposes. For example, Chip, a sales executive, could use the passphrase "AlwaysBeClosing." The application will put this phrase through a process, either encryption or hashing, and work with the resulting value. Passphrases usually provide a higher level of protection than passwords because they are longer and harder for attackers to guess or break.

Memory Cards

A *memory card* is an authentication mechanism that holds user information within a magnetic strip and relies on a reader of some sort to process the information. The user inserts the card into the reader and then enters a set of credentials to be properly authenticated. An example of a memory card is an automated teller machine (ATM) card. The user inserts the ATM card into the ATM machine and then enters his or her PIN number. The card supplies the account number (user information) and then the user provides the secret code (PIN), together providing a credential set.

Within companies, employees will often carry ID badges with magnetic strips. In many of these implementations, a PIN is hashed and stored on the magnetic strip. In order to enter a building, the employee must enter a PIN number and swipe the badge through a reader. The reader hashes the inputted PIN number and compares it to the value on the card itself. If they match, access is granted.

Smart Cards

A *smart card* is a step above a memory card, in that it can actually process information because it has a microprocessor and integrated circuits. The user inserts the smart card into a reader, which has electrical contacts that interface and power the smart card processor. The user then enters a PIN value, which "unlocks" the information and processing power contained on the smart card. The card can hold a user's private key, generate a one-time password, or respond to a challenge-response request.

Smart cards are much more tamperproof when compared to memory cards and after a certain number of incorrect PIN values have been inputted, the card can actually "lock" itself, which would require the user to contact the vendor to receive an overriding PIN value to "unlock" the card again. Some cards zeroize themselves after too many invalid login attempts, which means they render themselves totally useless and must be reprogrammed.

Both memory and smart cards have the extra expenses of creating new cards and purchasing the required readers, which must be calculated in their implementation and lifetime costs. If the cards require a second credential set to be provided (password or PIN), it is referred to as two-factor authentication (something that you have and something that you know).

Smart cards can be *contact cards*, meaning they need to be inserted into a reader, or *contactless*, meaning they do not need to be inserted into a card reader but need to be within a certain proximity of the reader. Contactless cards need only to be passed within range of a radio frequency acceptor to read information from the chip. Some smart cards have both contact and contactless functionality. A *hybrid card* has two chips on it, one for contact readers and one for contactless readers. And a *combi card* has a single chip with both the contact and contactless interfaces.

Authorization

Authorization is a process of assigning authenticated subjects access and the right to carry out specific operations, depending upon their preconfigured access rights and permissions outlined in an access criteria. An access criteria is developed by the administrator, or security officer, to support and carry out the organization's security policy. A criteria can be based on one or both of the following items:

- **Clearance**   The security level the subject holds, which directly dictates the objects that are accessible to it.
- **Need-to-know**   The formal access level approved that correlates to what information should and should not be available to a subject.

Mandatory access control (MAC) environments use clearances, classifications, and need-to-know to determine if a subject can access an object and what operations can be carried out. Discretionary access control (DAC) environments use access control lists (ACLs), which are developed based strictly on the subject's need-to-know. MAC and DAC environments are described in the "Access Control Models and Techniques" section of this chapter.

It is important to only give the subject access to the objects (resources, devices, and information) that are required for it to complete its tasks. This concept is referred to as *least privilege*. This reduces the possibility of fraud and damaging accidents by limiting access to objects based purely on business needs.

It is best for mechanisms that are making access decisions to default to "no access." This means that if a subject is not explicitly allowed, it is implicitly denied. In other words, if I don't tell you specifically you can do something, you can do nothing.

If a task must be completed by two or more individuals coming together to carry out their piece of the task, it is referred to as *dual control*. For example, in a cryptographic key recovery technology, the master key needed to decrypt a lost key is usually split up into two or more pieces and each piece is given to an individual. If this master key needs to be reconstructed to recover a lost key, each individual with a piece of the key must submit their portion, which the system combines to create the original master key. This is dual control, because it requires more than one person to complete an important task.

| Objective 2.02 | # Single Sign-On Technologies |

B ecause users are usually accessing multiple systems and networks many times within a given workday, different *single sign-on technologies* were created. This enables a user to enter his or her credentials only once and remain authorized throughout the day within the entire network. He can access different resources within the environment without having to supply another set of credentials. This makes life easier on users, because they will not need to remember (or write down) several different passwords; it can make administration easier by controlling and maintaining one system that is responsible for all access requests.

There are four types of single sign-on technologies that are covered in this section:

- Directory services
- SESAME

- Kerberos
- Thin clients

Exam Tip

Scripts can work as a single sign-on technology by logging in users automatically. These scripts need to be secured because they contain user credentials.

A security concern relating to single sign-on technologies is that if an attacker figures out a valid credential set, he can now access all resources within that environment. Once he is in, he is really in.

Travel Advisory

If a user's access needs to be revoked, it is easier to carry out in a single sign-on instead of having to revoke rights in many different systems throughout a network.

Directory Services

A network service is a mechanism that identifies resources (printers, file servers, domain controllers, peripheral devices) on a network and provides a way to make them available to users and programs. A network directory service contains information about these different resources, providing a naming scheme, and a hierarchical database that outlines characteristics such as name, logical and physical location, subjects that can access them, and the operations that can be carried out on the resources.

Network directory services provide users access to network resources transparently without needing to know their exact location and access steps required to access them. These issues are taken care of for the user in the background. Some examples of directory services are Novell's Netware Directory Service (NDS) and Microsoft's Active Directory.

Kerberos

Kerberos is a ticket-based authentication protocol based on symmetric cryptography. The following components are used in Kerberos:

- **Key distribution center (KDC)**   Holds user and service cryptographic keys (secret keys), provides authentication services, and creates and distributes session keys.

- **Authentication service (AS)**   Functional component of the KDC that actually performs the authentication.

- **Principals**   All entities that use the Kerberos protocol for authentication are referred to as principals, which could be users, applications, resources, or services.

- **Realm**   A set of principals, which are grouped together logically by an administrator. A KDC is responsible for one or more realms of principals.

- **Ticket granting service (TGS)**   The part of the KDC that creates and distributes tickets to the principles containing session keys.

- **Ticket**   An authentication token.

- **Secret and session keys**   Symmetric keys used for authentication purposes and data encryption.

When a user logs in to the network first thing in the morning, his or her authentication information is sent to the AS, which is part of the KDC. The AS returns an encrypted ticket to the user's computer, which is decrypted with the user's password (secret key). If the user enters the correct password, he is then properly authenticated to the network and his computer. When the user needs to access a resource on the network, let's say a file server, the user's computer sends the initial ticket to the TGS. The TGS creates another ticket, containing the user's authentication information and two instances of the same session key, and sends it to the user's system, as shown in Figure 2-3. One instance of the session key is encrypted with the user's secret key and the other instance of the session key is encrypted with the file server's secret key. The user's Kerberos software decrypts and extracts one instance of the session key, inserts his or her authentication information into the ticket, and sends it onto the file server. The file server decrypts the second instance of the session key with its secret key and reviews the user's authentication information.

> ### Local Lingo
> The initial ticket sent from the AS to the principle is also referred to as the Ticket Granting Ticket (TGT).

These steps are taken because the principals do not directly trust each other, but they do trust the KDC. Only the KDC is supposed to have a copy of each principal's secret key. So, when the file server received a ticket that contained a session key encrypted with its secret key, it was convinced that the ticket came from the KDC. The file server also compared the user authentication information the TGS put into the ticket and what the user inserted into the ticket to ensure the user's true identity.

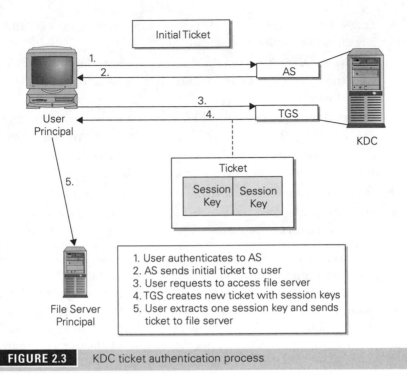

1. User authenticates to AS
2. AS sends initial ticket to user
3. User requests to access file server
4. TGS creates new ticket with session keys
5. User extracts one session key and sends
   ticket to file server

FIGURE 2.3   KDC ticket authentication process

The following are characteristics and weaknesses pertaining to Kerberos you need to be aware of:

- Provides authentication, confidentiality, and integrity, but not availability or nonrepudiation.
- The KDC can be a single-point-of-failure.
- Secret keys are stored on users' workstations.
- Session keys are stored on users' workstations in a cache or key tables.
- Kerberos is vulnerable to dictionary attacks.
- Network traffic is not protected if encryption is not enabled.
- KDC must be readily available and support the number of requests it receives from principals.
- All principals must have Kerberos software installed.
- Requires trusted, synchronized clocks within the network.
- The KDC should not allow any non-Kerberos network activity to take place.

Kerberos is an authentication technology where users must prove their identities to each application and service before they can actually be used.

> **Local Lingo**
>
> Kerberos, which is the name of a three-headed dog in Greek mythology, was designed in the mid-1980s as part of MIT's Project Athena.

SESAME

The *Secure European System for Applications in a Multi-vendor Environment* (SESAME) project is a single sign-on technology that was developed to extend Kerberos functionality and improves upon its weaknesses. SESAME uses symmetric and asymmetric cryptographic techniques to protect the exchange of data and to authenticate subjects to network resources (objects). (Kerberos is a strictly symmetric key-based technology.)

> **Local Lingo**
>
> Asymmetric cryptography is also referred to as public key cryptography.

Kerberos uses tickets for authenticating subjects to objects; SESAME uses *privileged attribute certificates* (PAC), which contain the subject's identity, access capabilities for the object, access time period, and lifetime of the PAC. The PAC is digitally signed so that the object can validate that it came from the trusted authentication server, which is referred to as the privilege attribute server (PAS). The PAS holds a similar role as the KDC within Kerberos. After a user successfully authenticates to the authentication service (AS), she is presented with a token to give to the PAS. The PAS then creates a PAC for the user to present to the resource she is trying to access, as shown in Figure 2-4.

Thin Clients

Computers without operating systems or limited instruction sets are referred to as *thin clients*. They provide an alternate method of distributed computing when compared to traditional desktop personal computers. They are networked systems that totally depend upon a centralized server for all functionality. The centralized server has all of the applications the clients would need and centrally controls access to all network resources. The thin client must properly authenticate to the server before it can participate on the network. Once the thin client and user are

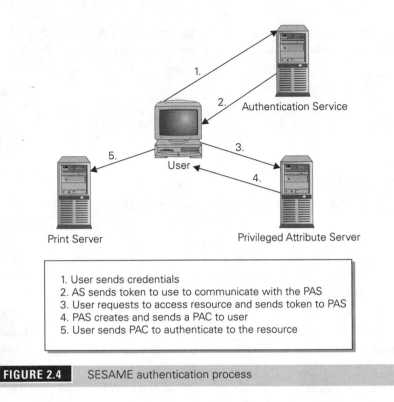

1. User sends credentials
2. AS sends token to use to communicate with the PAS
3. User requests to access resource and sends token to PAS
4. PAS creates and sends a PAC to user
5. User sends PAC to authenticate to the resource

FIGURE 2.4   SESAME authentication process

properly authenticated, there is no reason for the user to have to enter a second set of credentials to perform tasks, thus it is a single sign-on technology.

Objective 2.03   Access Control Models and Techniques

Access control models are created to enforce the rules and objectives of an established security policy and to dictate how subjects can access objects. There are three models that will be covered in this section: discretionary access control (DAC), mandatory access control (MAC), and role-based access control (RBAC).

DAC

A *discretionary access control* (DAC) model allows the owners of objects (resources) to control who accesses them and what operations can be performed on the objects. For example, if Dan creates a share on his system containing documents and WAV files, he can control and dictate who can access this share and the items within it. This is typically done through access control lists (ACLs), where permission is granted on a need-to-know basis.

DAC systems are used in environments that do not require the structure and higher level of protection that mandatory access control (MAC) models provide and enforce. Operating systems must be built differently depending upon whether they are going to provide DAC or MAC functionality. For example, Windows-based platforms provide a DAC access structure instead of MAC. Specially developed operating systems, usually created for government agencies and the military, provide a MAC access structure and the controls and mechanisms necessary to enforce this level of control.

Some characteristics of DAC systems are the following:

- Access is based entirely on the identity of the user or role that user plays within the company.
- Data owners determine who can access their resources.
- No security labels are used.
- Usually implemented through access control lists (ACLs).

Travel Advisory

Malicious code, such as a Trojan horse, can inherit the DAC access rights of a user and operate within that user's security context.

MAC

Mandatory access control (MAC) models do not leave access decisions up to the data owner, instead systems compare the subjects' clearances and need-to-know to the objects' classification to either grant or disallow access. Every object has a *security label* assigned to it, which includes classification information (top secret, secret, etc.). In order to access an object, the subject's clearance level must be equal to or greater than the object's classification. For example, if Dave has a "top secret" clearance, and an object has a "secret" classification, Dave's clearance dominates the objects classification. But Dave cannot access all top-secret information within his military branch, his access is also based on his need-to-know. The second piece of a security label is referred to as categories, as shown in Figure 2-5. Categories outline the groups that a subject must have a need-to-know of before access to the object can be granted. If Dave has a need-to-know for one of these categories, and his clearance is equal to or dominates the object's classification, he can access it.

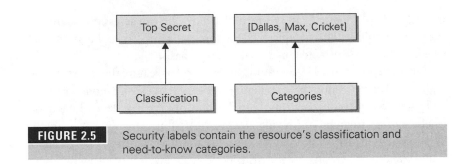

FIGURE 2.5   Security labels contain the resource's classification and need-to-know categories.

Security labels are the core decision-making component in MAC environments; they are assigned by system administrators or security officers and should be changed only in a well-defined manner so the security policy is supported and enforced. Systems that implement MAC models are used in highly secured environments, such as military or government organizations.

Local Lingo
Rule-based access controls use global rules imposed upon all subjects. MAC is sometimes referred to as a rule-based access control.

RBAC

Role-based access control (RBAC) models, also called nondiscretionary models, make access decisions based on the rights and permissions assigned to a role or group, not an individual user. Administrators create roles, or groups, which act as containers for users. The administrators assign access rights and permissions to the role instead of directly to the user. The user that is placed into a role or group inherits the permissions and access rights from the role, thus is *implicitly* assigned access rights. This kind of model is effective in large companies that have high turnover rates because it allows the administrator to simply place new employees into roles instead of creating new permissions for each and every person who joins the company.

Local Lingo
Implicit access rights are inherited from roles or groups; explicit rights are assigned directly to the individual users.

Roles usually map to specific roles outlined in the company's organization chart. For example, if a company has an accounting department, the administrator can create an accounting group with access rights to the resources anyone within the department would need. Users can be assigned to one or more roles and each role can have limited or many access rights and permissions assigned to it. The upper and lower bounds of access are referred to as a *lattice* of access rights, which is illustrated in Figure 2-6.

Travel Advisory

DAC, MAC, and RBAC controls can be used together in combination within different environments to support and implement the organization's security policy.

Access Control Techniques

Once an organization decides upon the access control model it will implement (DAC, MAC, or RBAC), then it needs to look at the different possible access control techniques that are available to work within these models and supplement

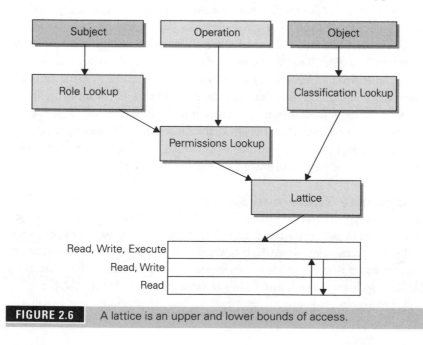

FIGURE 2.6   A lattice is an upper and lower bounds of access.

their mechanisms. The following sections explain some of the available access control techniques.

Restricted Interfaces

Users' environments can be constructed and controlled, which is another approach to controlling the objects they have access to. An administrator can create a user profile that will provide a user's working environment. This profile allows the administrator to dictate what icons, menus, applications, commands, and functionality is available within that environment. It is considered a restricted interface because the user utilizes the provided environment, desktop, and profile to interface with the operating system, installed applications, and resources.

Another example of a restricted interface is a database view. A database administrator can implement *database views*, which will show only the information within the database that the user has the necessary access rights to view. So the payroll department may be able to view employee salary and commission information, but not individual's employment records and human resource information. Different department managers may be able to view their employees' employment records, but not their salary and commission information. Database views are controls that allow the database administrator to logically partition the database and present these specific pieces to different authenticated users.

The last restricted interface access control technique we look at is a *physically constrained interface*. The best example of this type of access control is an automated teller machine (ATM). These systems have operating systems that have many more capabilities than transferring, depositing, and withdrawing funds, but users of these machines are presented only with buttons for these specific functions and no more. Thus, the physically constrained interface provides limited options and only a few buttons so any other functions that the operating system can actually perform are not accessible by regular users.

Capability Table and ACLs

An *access control matrix* is a mechanism used to associate access permissions of a subject to an object. The actual permissions assigned to a subject, which is a row within the access control matrix, is referred to as a *capability table*. And the different subjects that can access an object are referred to as an access control list (ACL), which are the columns of the matrix, as shown in Figure 2-7.

When a subject requests to access a specific object, the operating system will refer to this access control matrix to see if the access and requested operation is allowed.

Access Control Matrix				
Subject	**File 1**	**File 2**	**File 3**	**File 4**
Larry	Read	Read, Write	Read	Read, Write
Curly	Full Control	No Access	Full Control	Read
Mo	Read, Write	No Access	Read	Full Control
Bob	Full Control	Full Control	No Access	No Access

Capability →

ACL

FIGURE 2.7   Capability tables are bound to subjects; ACLs are bound to objects.

Exam Tip

A capability can also refer to a ticket within a ticket-based infrastructure. Capability-based systems protect access to objects by forcing a subject to possess the necessary capability (ticket) before access is allowed.

Content-Dependent Access Control

Content-dependent control is another technique used, which is based on the object's content that the subject is trying to access. It is usually implemented in databases. For example, a database may contain sensitive medical information; the more sensitive this data is, the fewer the number of people that will be able to access it. Let's say the database holds the results of different tests that have been performed on a particular patient. If a lab technician requests to see these results, she may be shown only that the tests were completed successfully, on what date, and by whom. If a nurse requests to see this information, she may be given access to a little bit more of the information than the lab technician, but not sensitive information, as in the patient has positive signs of malaria. And when a physician requests to see the same set of information, she may have access to all test data and results.

Content-dependent access controls require a lot of resources and overhead because the database will need to scan the object to determine if a particular subject can actually access it. The more granularity that is configured and expected from these types of controls will equate to more resources needed to evaluate requests.

Other Access Techniques

The following access control types are more granular in nature and can be used in combination with any of the previously discussed controls and models. The operating system or application would need to provide these types of controls for them to be available to be configured by the administrator or security officer.

- **Physical location**   A user may be allowed access to a resource only if she has interactively logged in to a computer, meaning that she is physically at a computer and not logged in remotely.
- **Logical location**   An administrator can restrict access to resources by IP addresses, which is a logical location on a network.
- **Time of day**   A control mechanism can be configured to only allow access to resources between certain hours of the day and certain days of the week.
- **Transaction type**   Restrictions based on operations that are requested to be carried out. A bank teller may be able to deposit checks but not cash checks. This would be a type of transaction access restriction.

Objective 2.04   Access Control Administration

So, you've picked your model and identified the techniques you want to use, now it's time to actually manage the thing. How do you do that? You have three choices of administration methods: centralized, decentralized, or hybrid. This section explains each type.

Centralized Access Control Administration

In a *centralized access control administration*, one group is controlling how subjects access objects. This obligation usually falls upon the IT group and security officers. They are responsible for configuring the systems that will enforce this type of access control. The systems need to have at least a database of known users, their credential sets, and allowed operations dictated by the access criteria.

The systems are used to identify, authenticate, and authorize users before access to network resources is granted. The three types of centralized access control technologies discussed are RADIUS, TACACS+, and Diameter. Each of these are usually used when remote users need to access a corporate network either from a remote site, a home office, or for road warriors that access the network through Internet Service Providers (ISPs).

These three centralized access control technologies are referred to as AAA protocols, which stand for authentication, authorization, and auditing. They provide the same overall functionality, but each has differences that would be best used in different environments.

RADIUS

Remote Authentication Dial-in User Service (RADIUS) is an authentication protocol that allows users to dial into an environment and authenticate over a PPP or SLIP connection. The components that are typically involved are a modem pool, an access server, and a RADIUS server. Users dial into the modem pool, which is connected to an access server. The access server prompts the user for credentials and then passes this information on to the RADIUS server. The RADIUS server compares the credentials to its user database and then authenticates authorized users. This process is shown in Figure 2-8.

The user is a client to the access server and the access server is a client to the RADIUS server. The access server just works as a middleman between the user and RADIUS server. When a user is authenticated, the RADIUS server may send connection requirements to the access server, as in a requirement to set up a virtual private network (VPN) or an allotted amount of bandwidth users can use during connections.

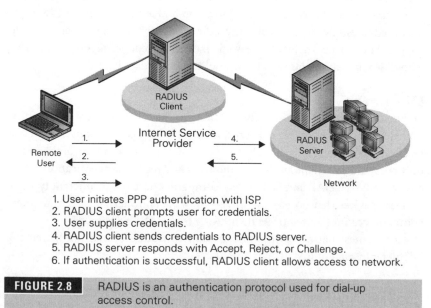

1. User initiates PPP authentication with ISP.
2. RADIUS client prompts user for credentials.
3. User supplies credentials.
4. RADIUS client sends credentials to RADIUS server.
5. RADIUS server responds with Accept, Reject, or Challenge.
6. If authentication is successful, RADIUS client allows access to network.

FIGURE 2.8   RADIUS is an authentication protocol used for dial-up access control.

This technology allows users to use a local ISP to connect to a corporate network instead of enduring long-distance phone calls. It also allows for centralized control, in that the administrator configures the RADIUS server to dictate who is granted access and to what extent.

Travel Advisory
When using RADIUS, only the user's password is encrypted when being passed from the access server to the RADIUS server.

TACACS

Terminal Access Controller Access Control System (TACACS)+ provides basically the same functionality as RADIUS and uses the same type of components: modem pool, access server, and TACACS+ server. TACACS+ is a Cisco proprietary protocol and has a few extras that are not included in RADIUS. As stated earlier, RADIUS encrypts only the user's password when an access request is passed between the RADIUS client and server. TACACS+ encrypts all the negotiation data being passed back and forth, which provides a higher level of security. TACACS+ also splits up the authentication, authorization, and auditing functionality, which RADIUS does not. This gives the administrator more flexibility in being able to decide which functionality she actually wants to use. It also allows another mechanism to provide the authentication, as in a Kerberos KDC, and the TACACS+ would still provide the authorization piece. Because the authentication and authorization pieces are split up, the administrator can also configure individual user profiles. So when Kandi dials into the company's network, she would have a different profile, or environment, with different access rights than Keith would when he dials in.

Diameter

Diameter is an authentication protocol that has the capability of authenticating many different types of devices over different types of connections. RADIUS is restricted to working only over PPP and SLIP connections and can authenticate only computers and laptops that use modems and regular authentication protocols, as in PAP, CHAP, and EAP. Today, companies have many different types of wireless devices that do not use these protocols and mechanisms, thus these companies cannot authenticate them using the RADIUS protocol.

Companies that need this extra flexibility would look at implementing Diameter instead of RADIUS or TACACS+.

> **Travel Advisory**
>
> Diameter was developed to be able to work with IPSec if network layer security and encryption is required.

Decentralized Access Control Administration

The alternative administration approach is *decentralized access control*. In this structure, users do not authenticate to one specific system, and one group is not enforcing specific access rules. The environment may work in more of a peer-to-peer relationship. In this type of environment, users access network resources without being centrally authorized. The different resources may be owned and maintained by different departments or users and they will make the decisions on who can access and use these resources.

In many environments, centralized and decentralized methods of access control are combined, which ends up in a hybrid administration. The network administrator may control who can access network resources (file servers, printers, remote sites), and individual users can control who accesses their resources (shares, local printers, directories). This provides more flexibility for the users, but ensures that the critical assets are closely monitored and at less risk of being misused.

Objective 2.05 Intrusion Detection System

Intrusion detection systems (IDS) are dedicated appliances or software-based components that monitor network traffic or individual computer activity with the goals of identifying malicious actions, resource misuse, attempts to gain unauthorized access, and attacks. There are different types of IDS systems—host and network-based, and signature and behavior-based—which we will be covering in the following sections.

Network-Based and Host-Based

Network-based IDS can be hardware appliances dedicated to their tasks or software applications installed on a computer system. In either case, the network interface card works in promiscuous mode and collects and monitors network traffic looking for malicious activity. There are sensors placed in the network segments that are to be monitored, and they are all connected to a central management console. The IDS software analyzes protocols and relevant packet information to uncover misdeeds.

Host-based IDS, on the other hand, are applications installed on individual computers with the goal of monitoring activities taking place on specific systems instead of monitoring network traffic. Host-based IDS have a more myopic view and can be used to ensure that critical system files are not modified in an unauthorized manner, scrutinize event logs, monitor use of system resources, and possibly detect ping sweeps and port scans that are taking place on those individual systems.

Local Lingo

A ping sweep is a method of determining if a system is up and running; a port scan is a way to determine what services are running on a computer. These are usually the steps that take place before an actual attack.

Host-based IDS can take a lot of maintenance if they are installed on each and every system within a network. In most environments, only the critical servers have host-based IDS installed because the whole network could be negatively affected if one or more were compromised.

The goal of both the network and host-based IDS is to detect ongoing attacks or potentially dangerous activities and alert the network staff so that they can properly react and mitigate damages. Depending on the product and its configuration, the IDS can page or e-mail the network administrator or engineer to alert her of a specific type of activity. The IDS may also attempt to reset the connection of an ongoing attack and even reconfigure a router or firewall to cut off traffic from the identified source of the attack.

Travel Advisory

Many attacks use spoofed addresses, so cutting off traffic from the apparent source of an attack can actually cut off access for legitimate users.

Network and host-based systems will be either a signature or behavior-based product, which are described in the following section.

Signature-Based and Behavior-Based

When different attacks are identified, IDS vendors write signatures that fit the patterns of these attacks. These signatures are installed into the IDS software by the customer so that the product can detect and identify all attacks that are currently known. This is similar to how anti-virus software products are continually updated so that they can identify the latest and greatest viruses and malware.

A *signature-based IDS,* also referred to as rule-based IDS, keeps these signatures in a database and compares network traffic or host-based activities to the contents of the database. If a signature is matched to an ongoing activity, the IDS takes whatever action it is configured to carry out (e-mail or page an individual, reset connection, or reconfigure perimeter device). So if a network-based IDS sensor picks up a packet that is fragmented and malformed in a way that matches a signature in its database, it will conclude that this is an identified attack and will take the steps it is configured to follow.

> **Travel Advisory**
>
> Signature-based IDS cannot detect new attacks that do not have signatures written for them.

There are two types of rule engines that can be used in rule-based IDS systems, ones that implement a state-based model and another type that implement a model-based approach. The *model-based* approach works on the assumption that attackers use specific known procedures to breach an environment's security, as in performing scans and exploiting certain vulnerabilities. The IDS system looks for these specific activities to identify an intrusion.

A *state-based IDS* looks at the full exchange of data between source and destination systems to fully understand the dialog that is going on between the two systems. This provides a more in-depth look at the possible attack underway instead of comparing individual packets to a database of individual signatures. This type of IDS combines the packets and reviews the full conversation to look for malicious activity.

A *behavior-based IDS,* on the other hand, compares current traffic to a reference model of normal behavior. When it sees something out-of-the-ordinary that does not match its definition of "normal," it signals an alarm. When a behavior-based IDS is first installed into an environment, it goes through a process of learning about the environment, its traffic patterns, user activities, traffic types, bandwidth use, and much more. This data is collected and a profile for the current environment is built. After this learning period, all future traffic and activities are compared to this reference profile. Anything that does not match is seen as an attack. This approach usually produces a lot of false positives.

Local Lingo

Behavior-based IDS is also referred to as statistical-based and anomaly-based IDS systems.

The behavior-based IDS can detect new attacks, unlike the signature-based systems, because they are not depending upon matching specific attack signatures to traffic patterns.

Exam Tip

Statistical anomaly detection may be carried out by expert systems.

Downfalls of IDS

Intrusion detection systems have characteristics and downfalls that security professionals should be aware of:

- Cannot always process all packets in busy networks
- Cannot analyze encrypted data
- Not as effective in switched-based networks
- Many false alarms
- Not an answer to all prayers—still need firewalls, anti-virus software, security policies, and other types of controls

It is important to realize the IDS is just one piece of a security program and should be used as one of the layers that protects the company and its assets.

Objective 2.06   Unauthorized Access Control and Attacks

This section covers the many tricks and ploys that attackers use to gain unauthorized access into a company's assets and information. These items need to be understood, along with the necessary countermeasures, to ensure that all threats are properly identified and eliminated or mitigated.

Unauthorized Disclosure of Information

Sensitive information can be disclosed intentionally or accidentally, but the results are the same, individuals have access to information that was not intended for their eyes. A big part of access control is preventing this type of activity from taking place. Many times, different types of media are used by different people within an organization. Floppy disks are shared, hard drives are checked out from a media library for different employees to use, and shares on servers are used by many to store information. These different media types can hold sensitive information that can be accessed by more individuals than should be allowed. Also, new employees often inherit old computers, which could contain sensitive information, from former employees. These are some examples of *object reuse*, which means that some type of media (object) that could contain sensitive data is being used by a different subject. The following issues should be considered when dealing with unauthorized disclosure of information:

- Media containing sensitive information may need to be degaussed to properly erase all data.
- Deleting files on a disk removes only the pointers to those files, not the files themselves, thus they are still available for unauthorized disclosure.
- Formatting a drive rewrites only the allocation table, but does not actually remove the information held within the drive's sectors.
- If media containing sensitive information cannot be properly erased, it should be physically destroyed.
- Processes within an operating system should erase their memory segments before other processes are allowed to use the same memory portions.
- Social engineering can be used to trick someone into providing confidential information to unauthorized individuals, thus is a possible threat to sensitive data.
- Zeroization is the process of writing null values over media several times to ensure that data is not available to others.

Keystroke monitoring tools are hardware- or software-based utilities that are used to capture each and every keystroke an individual inputs into a computer. They can be used to monitor employees for suspicious activities or can be used by attackers to gain access to confidential information. A common trick is to load a Trojan horse onto a user's system, which then installs a keystroke-monitoring program to capture usernames and passwords and send them back to the attacker. The attacker then uses these credentials to fraudulently authenticate as that user and access resources and information not intended for him.

Emanation Security

Another method that attackers use to steal information is to intercept electrical signals that radiate out of computers and devices. Every electrical device emits some amount of electrical signals or radiation, which attackers can intercept using specialized equipment. These signals can carry sensitive information. With the right hardware and software, the attackers can reconstruct this data without the individuals using the devices ever knowing about it.

We see these types of activities in spy movies where there is a white van in the parking lot of a building, trying to pass itself off as a utility vehicle. But the van is actually filled with specialized equipment and highly skilled individuals with the goal of gaining access to information that they are not supposed to be able to access. This may seem as though it only exists in spy novels and movies, but there are actually countermeasures that are often used to protect against these types of attacks. The three main countermeasures to emanation attacks are TEMPEST, white noise, and control zones.

TEMPEST was a study of monitoring these signals and preventing others from being able to monitor specific devices. TEMPEST then graduated into being a standard that vendors must meet if they want their products to be considered TEMPEST protection mechanisms. The devices have a special shielding, referred to as a *faraday cage* that allows only an acceptable amount of radiation to escape. Typically, only highly secure organizations implement TEMPEST products because it is expensive, and the buying and selling of TEMPEST devices is highly controlled by the government.

White noise is another countermeasure that can be used to fight emanation attacks. In this case, a uniform spectrum of random electrical signals is purposely emitted to jam the signals that are released from an environment. White noise makes it difficult for an attacker to decipher real electrical signals that could be deemed beneficial.

Finally, *control zones* can be used within buildings to block the electrical signals as they leave a facility or room, as shown in Figure 2-9. Walls, ceilings, and floors can be constructed with materials that greatly reduce the amount of signals that are released from that area.

Attack Types

Attackers have been very busy and creative over the years and have come up with many different types of attacks that can be used to threaten an organization's access controls that are put into place to protect assets. The following list describes many of these types of attacks:

- **Man-in-the-middle attack**   An intruder injects himself into an ongoing dialog between two computers so that he can intercept and read messages being passed back and forth. These attacks can be countermeasured with digital signatures and sequence numbers.

- **Sniffing**   A passive attack where an intruder monitors the network in order to gain information about the victim, usually for a later attack. A countermeasure is encryption of data as it is being transmitted.

- **War dialing**   A brute-force attack in which an attacker has a program that systematically dials a large bank of phone numbers with the goal of finding ones that belong to modems instead of telephones. These modems can provide easy access into an environment and the counter-measures are not to publicize these telephone numbers and implement tight access control for modems and modem pools.

- **Ping of Death**   A type of DoS attack where oversized ICMP packets are sent to the victim. Systems that are vulnerable to this type of attack do not know how to handle ICMP packets over a specific size and may freeze or reboot. Countermeasures are patching the systems and implement ingress filtering to detect these types of packets.

- **WinNuk**   A type of DoS attack that sends out-of-band packets to port 139. Windows 9x and NT can be vulnerable to this kind of attack. The countermeasures to this attack are to patch the system or upgrade to a later operating system version.

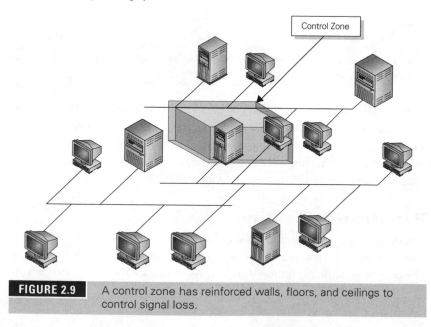

FIGURE 2.9   A control zone has reinforced walls, floors, and ceilings to control signal loss.

- **Fake login screens**   A fake login screen is created and installed onto the victim's system. The user then attempts to log in to the system by entering his or her credentials into it. The screen captures the credentials and exits showing the user the actual login screen for his or her system. Usually, the user just thinks he mistyped the password and attempts to authenticate again without knowing anything malicious just took place. A host-based IDS can be used to detect this type of activity.

- **Teardrop**   An attack that sends malformed fragmented packets to a victim. The victim's system usually cannot reassemble the packets correctly and freezes as a result. Countermeasures to this attack are patching the system and ingress filtering to detect these packet types.

- **Traffic analysis**   A method of uncovering information by watching traffic patterns on a network. For example, heavy traffic between HR and headquarters could indicate an upcoming layoff. Traffic padding can be used to counter this kind of attack, in which decoy traffic is sent out over the network to disguise patterns and make it more difficult to uncover patterns.

Local Lingo
Ingress filtering is filtering traffic as it enters an environment; egress filtering is filtering traffic as it leaves an environment.

Exam Tip
A danger to sniffers is that their presence and activity cannot be detected and audited, in most cases.

Script kiddies are individuals that do not necessarily have a high-level of computer skills, but perform attacks using already-made programs that perform attacks for them. In most cases, they do not fully understand what these programs do, and do not understand the full extent of the damage that they can cause and the extended ramifications of these types of attacks.

Penetration Testing

Penetration testing is the process of simulating attacks on a network and the systems that make it up at the request of the owner, usually senior management. The goal of penetration testing is to identify vulnerabilities, estimate the true protection the security mechanisms within the environment are providing, and how suspicious activity is reported.

The penetration team must have signed consent from the owner of the environment outlining what is to be accomplished in the test and to what degree the vulnerabilities should be tested. The team then goes through a process made up of five steps, outlined here:

- **Discovery**   Footprinting and gathering information about the target.
- **Enumeration**   Performing port scans and resource identification methods.
- **Vulnerability mapping**   Identifying vulnerabilities in identified systems and resources.
- **Exploitation**   Attempts to gain unauthorized access by exploiting vulnerabilities.
- **Report to management**   Documentation of findings of test goes to management along with suggested countermeasures.

The team can have varying degrees of understanding of the target before the tests are actually carried out:

- **Zero-knowledge**   Team does not have much knowledge of target and must start from ground zero.
- **Partial-knowledge**   Team has some information about target.
- **Full-knowledge**   The team has intimate knowledge of target.

It is important that the team start off with only basic user-level access to properly simulate different attacks. They need to utilize a variety of different tools and attack methods and look at all possible vulnerabilities because this is how actual attackers will function.

CHECKPOINT

✔**Objective 2.01:   Identification and Authentication**   Access is the flow of information between a subject and an object. A subject is an active entity; an object is passive entity. Access controls require identification, authentication, and authorization of subjects requesting to access objects. Authentication is verifying the identity of a subject. Possible authentication mechanisms are biometrics (verifies the identity by a unique personal attribute), passwords (the weakest form of authentication), token devices (create one-time passwords), passphrases, cognitive passwords, memory, and smart cards. Each authentication mechanism has one of the following characteristics: something that you know, something that you have, or something that you are.

✔**Objective 2.02: Single Sign-On Technologies** Kerberos, SESAME, directory services, and thin clients are examples of single sign-on technologies. Users enter only one set of credentials, which allows them to access all the network resources they require. Kerberos is a ticket-based authentication protocol that uses symmetric cryptography. SESAME is similar to Kerberos, was developed to overcome some of Kerberos shortcomings, and uses public key cryptography. Kerberos and SESAME are both vulnerable to dictionary attacks.

✔**Objective 2.03: Access Control Models and Techniques** Access control can be implemented by operating systems that are developed with one of the three types of access control models: discretionary, mandatory, and role-based. The discretionary access model allows data owners to decide what subjects can access resources; mandatory access models do not allow data owners or users such flexibility. Discretionary uses ACLs and mandatory models use security labels to enforce access control policies. The role-based model allows roles and groups to be developed, and users are assigned to these logical containers.

✔**Objective 2.04: Access Control Administration** There are three types of access control administration: centralized, decentralized, and hybrid. Centralized administration means that one group is responsible for ensuring that the subjects are identified, authenticated, and authorized. Some examples of centralized administration technologies are RADIUS, TACACS+, and Diameter authentication protocols. Decentralized administration does not have one group responsible for enforcing access rules and a hybrid administration is a combination of centralized and decentralized.

✔**Objective 2.05: Intrusion Detection System** Intrusion detection systems (IDS) can be used to monitor network segments (network-based) or individual systems (host-based). There are two types of IDS: signature-based and behavior-based. Signature-based IDS cannot recognize new types of attacks, but instead looks for patterns of previously identified attacks. Behavior-based IDS builds a profile of a network's usual activities and compares all future activities to this profile to detect unusual behaviors.

✔**Objective 2.06:   Unauthorized Access Controls and Attacks**   The unauthorized disclosure of information can happen by object reuse, social engineering, keystroke monitoring, and radiation of signals. Emanation security involves protecting against attackers intercepting electrical signals that radiate from computers. There are three countermeasures for emanation attacks: white noise, control zones, and TEMPEST. There are many attacks on access controls, however, dictionary and brute force attacks are the most common.

REVIEW QUESTIONS

1. Which of the following is not used in biometric systems to authenticate individuals?

   A. Fingerprinting
   B. Keyboard dynamics
   C. Iris scan
   D. Cognitive password

2. Which of the following is the most important when evaluating different biometric systems?

   A. Type I error
   B. CER
   C. Type II error
   D. The total amount of errors between Type I and Type II

3. Which of the following attacks is most commonly used to uncover passwords?

   A. Spoofing
   B. Dictionary attack
   C. DoS
   D. WinNuk

4. Which of the following is not a weakness of Kerberos?

   A. The KDC is a single point of failure.
   B. Kerberos is vulnerable to password guessing.
   C. All devices must have Kerberos software to participate.
   D. Kerberos is the de facto standard for distributed networks.

5. Which of the following access control models uses security labels?

   A. Discretionary
   B. Non-discretionary

    C. Mandatory

    D. Role-based

6. A capability table is bound to which of the following?

    A. Subject

    B. Object

    C. ACLs

    D. Permissions

7. Which of the following is not an example of centralized access control administration technology?

    A. RADIUS

    B. TEMPEST

    C. TACACS

    D. Diameter

8. Which of the following best describes the difference between memory and smart cards?

    A. A memory card has a microprocessor and integrated circuits used to process data, whereas a smart card has a magnetic strip that is used to hold information.

    B. A smart card has a microprocessor and integrated circuits used to process data, whereas a memory card has a magnetic strip that is used to hold information.

    C. Memory cards are more tamperproof than smart cards.

    D. Memory cards are cheaper to develop, create, and maintain.

9. Which of the following is a true statement pertaining to intrusion detection systems?

    A. Signature-based systems can detect new attack types.

    B. Signature-based systems cause more false positives than behavior-based systems.

    C. Behavior-based systems maintain a database of patterns to match packets and attacks against.

    D. Behavior-based systems have higher false positives than signature-based systems.

10. Which of the following is a countermeasure to traffic analysis attacks?

    A. Control zones

    B. Keystroke monitoring

    C. White noise

    D. Traffic padding

11. If several subjects access the same media or memory segments, sensitive data may be at risk of being uncovered. This is referred to as…

    A. Degaussing

    B. Zeroization

    C. Object reuse

    D. Mandatory access

12. Which of the following is not a critical piece in developing a penetration test?

    A. Obtain management approval

    B. Conduct war dialing

    C. Establish and outline goals before testing begins

    D. Establish timeline for testing

REVIEW ANSWERS

1. **D**   Biometrics authenticates an individual by a unique personal trait. A cognitive password is a fact or opinion-based password extracted from that person's life experience.

2. **B**   Crossover error rate (CER) is the point in which Type I and Type II errors are equal and represents the most important evaluation rating for a biometric system.

3. **B**   Dictionary attacks use programs that have thousands of the most commonly used passwords. The program goes through these different words until one is matched as a valid password for a given user.

4. **D**   Kerberos is incorporated in many products and environments today. It started out in UNIX systems, but is now the default authentication mechanism in Windows 2000 systems. The previous three items listed are considered weaknesses of Kerberos.

5. **C**   Mandatory access control models use security labels. These labels hold the classification of the object and the categories that the subject must have a need-to-know of before being allowed access. When a subject attempts to access the object, its security clearance and need-to-know is compared to the information held in the security label.

6. **A** Capability tables are bound to subjects and specify the operations it can perform on different objects. The capability table is the row of an access control matrix and the access control list is the column of the matrix.

7. **B** TACACS+, Diameter, and RADIUS are all AAA protocols that provide centralized access control. TEMPEST is the study and standard for products that are used to protect against unauthorized disclosure of information through radiation.

8. **B** Smart cards have microprocessors and integrated circuits that allow for data to be processed, which provides much more functionality than memory cards. Smart cards are more tamperproof but more expensive than memory cards.

9. **D** A behavior-based IDS learns about an environment and builds a profile. All future network activity is compared to the profile to try and uncover malicious events. A signature-based IDS maintains patterns of identified attacks.

10. **D** Traffic padding is the process of generating traffic on the network in order to make it more difficult for individuals to identify patterns.

11. **C** If sensitive data is held on some type of media (floppy disk, hard drive, memory segments) it should be properly erased before allowing another subject to use the media. This can happen through degaussing or zeroization.

12. **B** Testers need to obtain management support, understand and establish the goals of the test, and decide how long the testing should be conducted. War dialing may or may not be part of a penetration test. It is just one tool and not critical to the planning and development of the testing procedures.

Security Models and Architecture

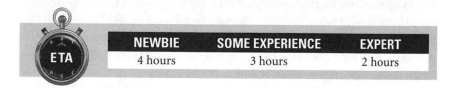

	NEWBIE	SOME EXPERIENCE	EXPERT
ETA	4 hours	3 hours	2 hours

In this chapter, we look at how some of the components of a computer work, how an operating system interacts with these components, identify different security mechanisms, explain the many different access control models, and learn how security products are evaluated and rated. It is a lot to cover, but this chapter, in particular, includes the concepts that are the foundation of creating and implementing security in a computer-driven environment.

Objective 3.01 System Components

The operating system is the core of every computer because it provides the environment for applications and users to work within, interacts with and controls hardware components, provides access control and security mechanisms, supplies and maintains the file system, and has the necessary services that allows a computer to participate in a networked environment. First, we look at some of the hardware components within a computer system that the operating system has to understand and work with.

Central Processing Unit

The *central processing unit* (CPU) processes the operating system and applications' instructions and the data that is used or called upon during these procedures. The CPU contains a control unit, an arithmetic logic unit (ALU), and registers. When instructions and data need to be processed by the CPU, they are cued to a memory location, which are the CPU's registers. The *control unit* dictates the timing of when these instructions and data are passed to the CPU for processing. The ALU performs mathematical and logical functions, such as number crunching and data manipulation, on the data that is passed to the CPU. The results are passed back to the application's memory so that they can be used and presented to the user. These steps are illustrated in Figure 3-1.

When a process, or application, sends data to be processed by the CPU, it can be working in one of two states: supervisor and problem state. When the CPU is processing instructions working in *supervisory mode*, the process has access to most or all of the resources within the operating system and computer. Only the most trusted software can work in this mode because of the damage that it could cause if it were to act unruly. When the CPU processes data for an application that works in *user mode*, or nonprivileged mode, the CPU is working in a *problem state*. The application is not trusted enough to work in the higher-privileged supervisory state, thus has less access to resources, and its operations within the system are limited. In most cases, the operating system program code is

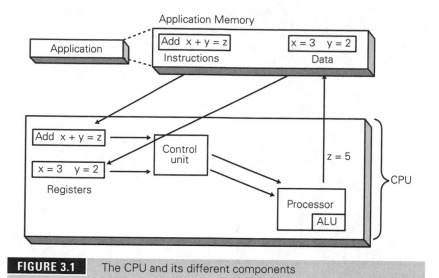

Application Memory

FIGURE 3.1   The CPU and its different components

executed by the CPU in a supervisory state, and applications are executed in a problem state.

Local Lingo

Problem state is sometimes referred to as user state or user mode.

Computers can have multiple applications running at one time, which means many processes are running at once. The operating system must know how to handle all of these activities and provide the processors with timely access to the CPU without causing bottlenecks or collisions. Before we get into the different techniques a computer uses, let's cover two terms that will be used often in this section: process and thread.

An application runs as a *process*. A process is basically the application's instructions in memory and is identified by a process ID. A process can perform several different functions: send data to a printer, accept user input values, and communicate with the operating system, but each of these different activities takes a different string of code, referred to as a *thread*. A process is made up of one or more threads, and the threads carry out the different functions for that process, as illustrated in Figure 3-2. Threads can be dynamically created and destroyed when needed.

The processes themselves can also run in different states, shown in Figure 3-3, which are outlined here:

- **Stopped**   The process is not running.
- **Waiting**   The process is waiting for an interrupt to be able to be processed by the CPU.

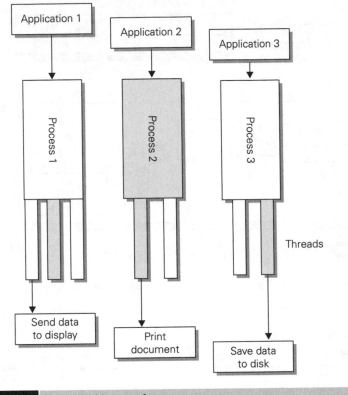

FIGURE 3.2   A thread is part of a process.

- **Running**   The process's instructions are being executed by the CPU.
- **Ready**   Available to be used and waiting for an instruction or input.

Local Lingo

Interrupts are mechanisms used to split up the CPU's time between different applications and requests.

So now that those terms are understood, let's discuss how the operating system handles them. If a computer system is *multithreading*, it is capable of processing more than one request, or thread, at a time. A *multitasking* system can process more than one process, or task, at a time. A *multiprocessor* system has more than one CPU, and *multiprocessing* is parallel processing by two or more processors in a multiprocessor computer. A system can also be referred to as *multiprogramming*, meaning that it can interleave the execution of two or more programs. If these terms are new to you, they can all sound a lot alike and confusing.

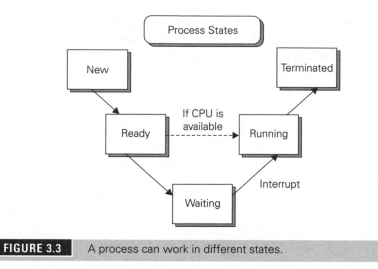

Process States

New

Terminated

If CPU is available

Ready ----------> Running

Interrupt

Waiting

| FIGURE 3.3 | A process can work in different states. |

An older system may be multiprogramming, because it allows you to have two applications running at the same time, but it does not mean that the CPU and operating system are multitasking. If it is not multitasking, the system must dedicate the CPU and resources to one application and then to the other, instead of accepting instructions in a time-sliced manner.

In multiprogramming systems, when a process is using the CPU, that process cannot be interrupted; with multitasking, a process can be interrupted, which allows for time-sharing of the CPU.

Travel Advisory

The CPU and the operating system must be able to provide these different functionalities (multitasking, multiprogramming, etc.) The operating system "feeds" the instructions and data to the CPU in these different fashions.

Storage and Memory Types

The CPU can access data held in memory directly, which is referred to as *primary storage*, or main memory. The CPU can access these memory segments directly because it is highly trusted by the system, and the system has confidence that the CPU will not negatively affect data held in memory.

The CPU is the only component in the computer with direct access to memory, which means there are physical buses that connect the CPU microprocessor to the various memory chips. The applications installed on the system, on the other hand, have to access memory through a memory mapper. The *memory mapper* ensures that applications do not directly access physical memory, makes sure they work within their own memory segments, and do not access memory that is "off-limits" to them. This mapper works as an index to the different memory areas and enforces access control, which protects the operating system and the different applications that are installed.

To be able to store and retrieve data from memory segments, they must have addresses assigned. The memory mapper assigns logical addresses to the memory that can be used by applications. These logical addresses are translated into physical addresses by the CPU when the instructions and data held in those memory portions need to be processed. The physical address is the *absolute address* or actual location of the memory segment.

A *base address* is a reference point for other addresses. For example, in Figure 3-4, we see that an application has been allocated a memory segment with the base address of D. Now the segment is actually chopped up into sections itself, which are offsets of the beginning address (base address), which holds instructions and data. When the application needs to access a specific information set, it needs to know where it is. The application will call upon a relative address, which indicates the distance from the base address.

The operating system uses distinct address spaces so that multiple processes can run concurrently and not interfere with each other; it allows the system to

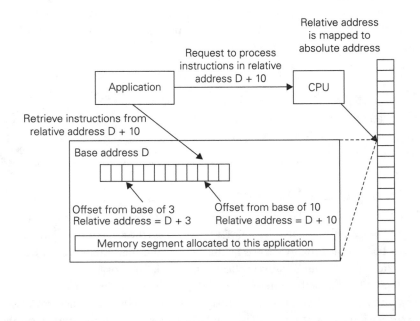

FIGURE 3.4 Applications are given portions of memory that are then mapped to physical memory segments.

know where to retrieve these different data sets when there is a request for them to be processed by the CPU.

There are other types of memory and storage units used in computers:

- **Volatile storage** Temporary storage, which loses its data if the system is shut down or power is lost.
- **Nonvolatile storage** Memory as in read-only memory (ROM) and erasable and programmable read-only memory (EPROM) that holds data even if power is lost.
- **Secondary storage** Nonvolatile storage components such as CD-ROMs, tapes, hard drives, or floppy disks.
- **Cache storage** Parts of memory used by the system to store data that it anticipates will be called upon within a short period of time. This improves the system performance.

Figure 3-5 illustrates how many of these components are used.

Virtual Memory

Virtual memory is a combination of the computer's main memory and secondary storage to make it seem as though the computer has a much larger memory bank than it actually does. When the storage area within the main memory fills up, it will begin saving the data to the computer's hard drive in units of *pages*,

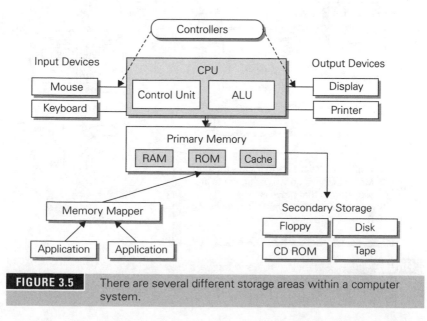

FIGURE 3.5 There are several different storage areas within a computer system.

which are 4 or 8KB in size. The space on the hard drive that is used for this function is referred to as *swap space*, and the act of transferring pages between memory and the swap space is called "swapping." When an application makes a call for data that is actually now stored on the hard drive, the operating system moves this information back into memory, which is called a *page fault*.

The operating system's memory manager must keep track of all of these activities and more. The memory manager first splits the memory into equal-sized slots, called *page frames*. It allots certain page frames to each process, meaning it assigns each application a memory segment to work with. The memory manager must also maintain a page table that keeps track of available frames, which can be allocated to new processes, and which pages have been moved to the hard drive's swap space. These activities are illustrated in Figure 3-6.

The memory manager is responsible for physical and logical organization of memory and the data it holds, relocation of data between different types of memory, protecting data that is held in memory frames, and overseeing the sharing of certain memory segments.

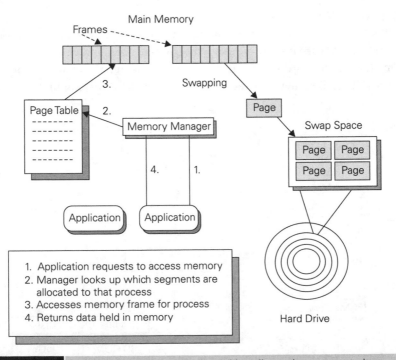

1. Application requests to access memory
2. Manager looks up which segments are allocated to that process
3. Accesses memory frame for process
4. Returns data held in memory

FIGURE 3.6 Swapping pages to the hard drive allows the system to have more memory space.

Data Access Storage

Sometimes data needs to be accessed in different ways, which requires unique storage methods. *Sequential storage* facilities are media types that hold data that must be searched from beginning to end, or sequentially. An example of a sequential storage media is a magnetic tape. A different approach is a *direct access storage* area, which is how memory and disk drives are accessed. The information on this type of media does not need to be accessed sequentially, so a program can go directly to the end of the memory segment, then to the front, and then to the middle, wherever the needed information is located.

It is important to realize that if someone needs to access information held on a sequential storage media type, all data held on that storage media may be available to her, not just one segment. For example, if you want me to review information you have saved to the middle portion of a magnetic tape, all the information I must skim through until I get to this portion is available to me. Sensitive and non-sensitive data should not be stored on a sequential storage media if the data needs to be accessible to a subset of people with different access levels.

Processing Instructions

The CPU understands only data presented in binary, called *machine language*, through electrical signals that represent 1s and 0s. Although this works great for the CPU, it doesn't work so great for programmers and developers who need to write the software. The first language that was developed to make programming easier for people was an *assembly language*, which did not represent data in 1s and 0s but a type of hexadecimal format. This code is passed through an assembler to translate it into machine language when it needs to be processed by the CPU.

Then, higher-level languages were developed to make it even easier to write programming code and to provide languages that contained more power and functionality. These languages are either *compiled*, meaning all of the source code is translated into machine code, or they are *interpreted*, meaning only one line at a time is converted into machine language that the CPU can understand.

Local Lingo

Source code is the program code that the developer creates.

Operating States

If users with different security clearances need to use the same operating system, and the system has to keep track of these clearances and the different classifications of data, then a *multilevel security* operating system is implemented. This means that Keith, with the clearance of "top secret," can log into a computer and access the data that is available to him. And David, with the clearance of "secret," can log in later to the same system and access the different data that is available to him. Some centralized servers or mainframes allow different users with different clearances to be logged in and interact with different data sets at the same time.

Not all operating systems can handle and keep track of these different security levels. If multilevel security is a requirement for an environment, specialized operating systems must be built and implemented.

Multilevel systems can operate in one of the following modes:

- **Dedicated security mode**   All users have the clearance or authorization and need-to-know to access *all* data processed within the system. The system handles a single classification level of information.
- **Compartmented security mode**   All users have the clearance to access all the information processed by the system, but might not have the need-to-know and formal access approval. In this mode, users can access a segment, or compartment, of data only.

Objective 3.02

Operation System Security Mechanisms

We have looked at how the computer processes instructions, how data is stored, and how the key components function together, but there is a particular area of computer technology that should draw considerable interest from a security professional: self-protection. Computers are designed with many protection mechanisms to ensure constant stability. Some of these mechanisms are

- Process isolation
- Security domains
- Protection rings
- Virtual machines
- Trusted computing base (TCB)

The following sections cover these protection mechanisms.

Process Isolation

An operating system is a very busy and complex beast. It has several services and processes of its own to worry about and keep track of, and then add in several different applications and all of their drama—it might just make you want to get into another profession. But operating systems, for the most part, seem to deal with all of this complexity and perform amazing feats at a high level of performance.

With this many processes that need to interact and use the same resources, the operating system has to be able to control each process's activities in an isolated way. Each process has a trust level assigned to it, which determines the level of access to system resources it has. The level of trust assigned to a process dictates its security domain. A *security domain*, also referred to as an execution domain, is all the resources a process has to work with. Processes that work in supervisory mode have a high level of trust, thus a large security domain to work within. The operating system has protection mechanisms that ensure that processes work only within their own security domain (allocated resources), and if two processes actually share resources, that it takes place in a controlled manner.

The following is a list of some of these protection mechanisms used to properly isolate processes:

- Encapsulation of objects
- Time multiplexing of shared resources
- Naming distinctions
- Virtual memory mapping

Protection Rings

When we talk about an operating system assigning different trust levels to processes, we are really discussing protection rings. *Protection rings* are conceptual boundaries that a system uses to make distinctions between what it deems as trustworthy and untrustworthy. The center rings with the lower ring numbers contain the more trusted elements; as the numbers of the rings increase, the level of trust reduces. As stated in the last section, the lower the trust level, the smaller the amount of resources available to a process and the more restrictions that are placed on what that process can do with its available resources.

As you can see in Figure 3-7, the operating system kernel is the most trusted component and can access all of the resources in a privileged mode within the system. Ring 1 contains the rest of the operating system instructions, Ring 2 contains utilities that need a certain level of access to the system components, and all applications reside in Ring 3. This is done because the operating system does not know how these applications were written or what they are programmed

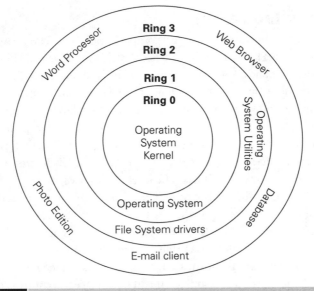

FIGURE 3.7 Protection rings separate processes based on levels of trust.

to do, thus they need to be as restricted from critical system components and resources as possible.

When processes that reside in different protection rings need to communicate, this communication takes place through interfaces, usually application programming interfaces (APIs), that must be carefully constructed and restrictive in nature. The interfaces need to be restrictive because processes at different levels of trust are exchanging data, and a less trusted process may attempt to corrupt or compromise processes at a higher level.

Processes can access data and resources within the same ring level or a less privileged ring. If the process needs to communicate to an object or process in a higher protection ring, it must call upon an operating system service to perform this type of communication. This prevents the chance of the less trusted component from compromising the more highly trusted component because it cannot directly communicate with it.

Local Lingo

A service is a process running in the security context of the operating system, thus at a privileged mode.

All operating systems implement protection rings. The different systems may not implement the four ring architecture, as shown in Figure 3-7, it depends upon the model and architecture the operating system was developed on.

Virtual Machine

Virtual machines are simulated environments for applications to run in. The virtual machine works as a container and will have a specified security domain assigned to it, including allocated memory segments for the application to use, and every operation is mediated by a virtual machine layer. A virtual machine may be necessary for a 16-bit application to be able to run within an environment that it does not understand, as in a 32-bit operating system. The virtual machine provides the 16-bit application with an environment that simulates a 16-bit operating system.

Virtual machines are also used for allowing untrusted programming code to run, as in Java applets. The virtual machine (called a sandbox) acts as a container by allowing the code to interact only with a certain amount of system resources in a very controlled manner.

A popular product, VMWare, allows different operating systems to run simultaneously on one computer. Each operating system has its own virtual machine, which provides an environment that allows it to "think" it is the only one running on that system.

Multilevel security systems can be developed to allow different virtual machines to be able to run at different security levels and contexts on the same computer.

Virtual machines, as well as the other protection mechanisms we are covering, are used to protect the operating system from rogue applications and to protect the applications from each other.

> ### Local Lingo
> The actual operating system is called a real machine; the simulated environments are called virtual machines.

Trusted Computing Base

The *trusted computing base* (TCB) is the combination of all security mechanisms within a computer, including software, hardware, and firmware. These items are highly trusted to support and implement the security policy of a particular system. The TCB components maintain the confidentiality, integrity, and availability of processes and their domains and controls the following functions:

- Input/output operations
- Process activation
- Execution of domain switching
- Memory protection
- Hardware management
- Interprocess communication

The components the make up the TCB are the ones that are stringently scrutinized if the system is submitted to be evaluated and given a security rating, because they are providing the protection for the system. Not all of the components within a system are trusted protection mechanisms, thus not part of the TCB. An imaginary boundary, referred to as a *security perimeter*, delineates between the components that are part of the TCB and which ones are not, as shown in Figure 3-8.

Reference Monitor and Security Kernel

The reference monitor and security kernel work hand in hand. The *reference monitor* is an abstract machine that ensures that only authorized subjects (programs, users, or processes) can access objects (file, program, or resource). It must mediate all access attempts between subjects and objects and is basically the access policy that must be enforced for that system.

The *security kernel* is what actually enforces the rules of the reference monitor. The security kernel is a combination of hardware, software, and firmware that lies within the TCB. It is the core of the TCB and is crucial for building trusted computing systems. The reference monitor and security kernel must have the following characteristics:

- Must be protected from modification and be tamperproof.
- Must be invoked for every access attempt.
- It must be small enough to be able to be tested and verified in a complete and comprehensive manner.

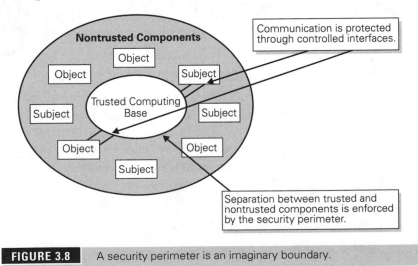

FIGURE 3.8   A security perimeter is an imaginary boundary.

So the reference monitor contains the rules, and the security kernel is the enforcer of those rules. An analogy is a list of rules you might have had as a child—don't run with scissors, don't talk to strangers, always wear clean underwear, etc. The enforcer of these rules would be your mom.

> **Local Lingo**
>
> A trusted computing system is one that performs to its documented specifications, prevents unauthorized entry, and acts in a predictable manner.

Objective 3.03 Security Models

This section goes over the different security models that have been created to provide much of the foundation for the security built into many systems today. Different sectors of the computing world have specific needs when it comes to security. For them to know how to actually implement the security needs, they need to have a model to follow.

It is easy to climb to a high mountain and dramatically state, "We shall build a system, and they will call it secure!" But how do you actually go about implementing the necessary components within an operating system to match the protection level your customer base will require? Thankfully, a lot of smart people did the legwork for us and developed different models that can be followed and integrated into new operating systems and applications.

> **Local Lingo**
>
> The terms security models and access control models are used interchangeably here.

The Different Models

Access control models provide rules and structures that specify how access decisions will be made. The main components included in the models are subjects, objects, operations, and their relationships. The reason for an access control model is to outline how objects are accessed, to ensure that the operations that are allowed are safe, and to ensure that the overall security of the system is never compromised. The access control models that we cover are

- State machine
- Bell-LaPadula
- Biba
- Clark-Wilson
- Non-interference
- Information flow
- Brewer and Nash (Chinese Wall)
- Graham-Denning
- Harrison-Ruzzo-Ullman models

Remember, these models are used to bring formation to a security policy that a vendor wants to be implemented and enforced in its new product. Instead of having a hundred programmers run to their cubicles and start pounding away at their keyboards developing code, a model ensures that they are on the same track and working towards the same goal.

I could have a pile of sticks that I am suppose to put together to build a small model airplane, but without the actual model and directions for me to follow I will most likely end up with just a pile of sticks glued together. In the same sense, a security model offers directions for implementing security principles into a software product.

State Machine Models

The *state machine model* is a conceptual model for all computers which ensures that no matter what activities take place within the system, it is protecting itself and will not slip into an insecure state. It dictates that subjects can only access objects in accordance with the security policy and that each activity, referred to as a *state transition*, is secure and safe. The developers of a system that implements this model must review all possible state transitions and make sure the necessary components and countermeasures are in place to protect the system.

The goal of a computer system following the state machine model is to make sure that it is in a secure state for each and every instance of its existence. This model has actually been integrated into many of the following models we look at.

Bell-LaPadula Model

In the 1970s, the U.S. military used time-sharing mainframe systems and was concerned about the security of these systems and leakage of classified information.

The *Bell-LaPadula model* was developed to address these concerns. Its development was funded by the government to provide a framework for computer systems that would be used to store and process sensitive information. The model's main goal is to prevent sensitive information from being accessed in an unauthorized manner, thus keeping secrets secret.

A system that employs the Bell-LaPadula model is called a multilevel security system because users with different clearances use the system, and the system processes data with different classifications. The classification level of information determines the handling procedures that should be used for the different data sets, and the operating system must understand and enforce these procedures.

The Bell-LaPadula model is a state machine model enforcing the confidentiality aspects of access control. The subject's clearance is compared to the object's classification; if the clearance is higher or equal to the object's classification, the subject can access the object without violating the security policy.

The model uses subjects, objects, access operations (read, write, and read/write), and security levels. Subjects and objects can reside at different security levels and the operating system creates the relationships and rules that dictate the acceptable activities between them. If properly implemented and enforced, this model has been mathematically proven to prevent data from a higher security level from flowing to a lower security level. It is an *information flow security model* also, which means that information does not flow to an object of lesser or noncomparable classification.

This model uses two main rules, which dictate how subjects and objects at different levels should interact:

- **Simple security rule**   A subject cannot read data at a higher security level—"no read up."
- ***-security rule**   A subject cannot write information to a lower security level—"no write down."

So a subject that has a lower security clearance will not be able to read data that has a higher security classification, otherwise sensitive secrets may be revealed. And a subject cannot write to an object at a lower security level, meaning users cannot declassify documents themselves and cannot create documents that will be available to others that hold a lower clearance.

Local Lingo

The rules within this model may also be referred to as properties; for example, simple security property and star security property.

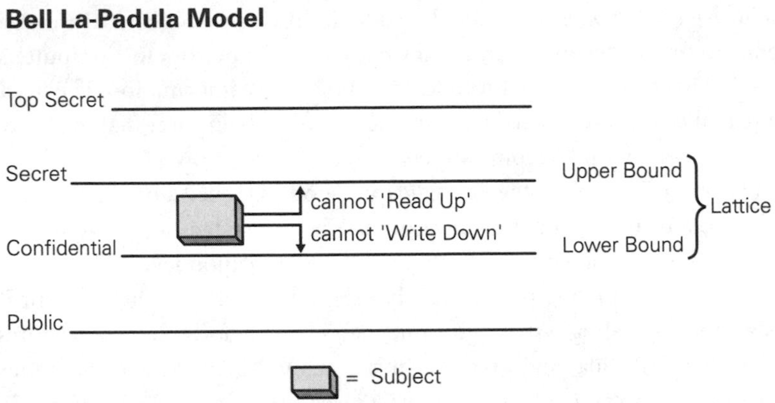

Bell La-Padula Model

FIGURE 3.9 The Bell-LaPadula model is used for multilevel secure systems.

The rules of the Bell-LaPadula model are illustrated in Figure 3-9.

Although this model is effective at achieving confidentiality for military-based operating systems, it is not the most practical of models for other types of environments because it does not deal with protecting the integrity of data.

Exam Tip

The Bell-LaPadula model was the first mathematical access control state machine model that is used to protect the confidentiality of data.

Biba

Because not everyone is in the military and not everyone is worried about protecting national secrets, other models were developed for other purposes. The *Biba model* was developed after the Bell-LaPadula model. It is a state machine model that addresses the integrity of data, and if implemented and enforced properly, prevents data from the different *integrity* levels from interacting in a way that could threaten the integrity of the information and the system.

The Biba model also has two fundamental rules:

- **Integrity star property** A subject cannot write data to an object at a higher integrity level—"no write up."
- **Simple integrity property** A subject cannot read data at a lower integrity level—"no read down."

This second rule might sound a little odd, but it is protecting the data at a higher integrity level from being corrupted by data in a lower integrity level.

When first learning about the Bell-LaPadula and Biba models, they seem very similar, and the reasons for their differences may bring about some confusion. The Bell-LaPadula model was written for the government, which is very paranoid about the leakage of their secret information. So, in their model, a user cannot write to a lower level because that user might let out some secrets. Similarly, a user at a lower level cannot read anything at a higher level because that user might learn some secrets. However, not everyone is so worried about confidentiality and has such big, important secrets to protect. The commercial industry is usually more concerned about the integrity of its data. An accounting firm is more worried about keeping their numbers straight and making sure decimal points are not dropped in a process carried out by an application or that extra zeros are not accidentally added. The accounting firm is more concerned about the integrity of this data and is usually under little threat of someone trying to steal these numbers, so they would employ the Biba model. Of course, the accounting firm does not look for the name Biba on the back of a product nor does it have to ensure that it is in the design of their software. It is something that was decided upon and implemented when the system or application was being developed. So even if the accountants are using a system that was built upon the Biba model, they would not necessarily know it and we're not going to tell them.

Clark-Wilson Model

The *Clark-Wilson model* is another integrity model, which takes a different approach than the Biba model. The Biba model uses a lattice of integrity levels and plugs the subjects and objects into one of those levels. The Clark-Wilson model dictates that subjects must access data through an application, separations of duties must be enforced, and auditing is required.

> ### Exam Tip
>
> A lattice is a logical structure that provides upper and lower bounds of access. Each subject and object are associated with one or more classes within a matrix, which dictates the access levels the subject has on that particular object.

Transactions that take place within a system using this model must be "well-formed," meaning that they must take place in a structured, predictable, and secure way. Subjects can only access and manipulate data held within an object through the use of a program. The program will ensure that the activity is acceptable and that it will not corrupt the internal consistency of the data or system. This is referred to as *access triple* (subject – program – object).

Critical operations are divided into subparts and require more than one subject (or user) to execute each part. This is the separation of duties portion of the model and is implemented to prevent authorized users from making improper modifications.

The Clark-Wilson model addresses all three integrity goals:

- Prevent unauthorized users from making modifications.
- Maintain internal and external consistency.
- Prevent authorized users from making improper modifications.

The Clark-Wilson model is used in the commercial industry where data integrity is deemed critical.

> ### Exam Tip
>
> The Biba model enforces the first integrity goal; the Clark-Wilson enforces all three integrity goals.

Non-Interference Model

In multilevel systems, users that work at different security levels (top secret, secret, confidential) work in different domains or environments. This means that the environment the computer provides for the different users is developed with a security context dictated by their clearance, which also dictates the resources available to the user and permission levels.

Most multilevel systems implement the *non-interference model*, which ensures that whatever a user does at one security level does not directly or indirectly affect the security domain (or environment) of another user. For example, nothing that Keith does, who works at a "top secret" level, while logged into the computer should affect David's experience, who works at a "secret" level, on the same computer. If changes from Keith's domain "leaked" to David's domain or David's domain changed because of Keith's activities, David may be able to figure something out that he is not suppose to know. This is similar to the inference issues discussed in Chapter 9.

> ### Local Lingo
> The non-interference model was developed by Goguen and Meseguer and is sometimes referred to as the Goguen and Meseguer model.

Access Control Matrix Model

The *access control matrix model* uses a two-dimensional matrix where subjects' access rights are presented in rows and objects are presented in columns, as shown in Figure 3-10. The matrix dictates the specific operations and access rights that each subject can implement when interacting with each object.

Access control lists (ACLs) are bound to the objects themselves, whereas capabilities are bound to the subjects (or users). These items are explored more in Chapter 2.

Information Flow Model

The *information flow model* is what the Bell-LaPadula and Biba models are based on. It focuses entirely on how data flows in accordance with the set security policy and restricts the flow that goes against this policy.

Access Control Matrix

Subject	File 1	File 2	File 3	File 4
Larry	Read	Read, Write	Read	Read, Write
Curly	Full Control	No Access	Full Control	Read
Mo	Read, Write	No Access	Read	Full Control
Bob	Full Control	Full Control	No Access	No Access

Capability →

ACL

FIGURE 3.10 Access control matrix

Biba prevents data from flowing from one *integrity* level to another; Bell-LaPadula restricts data from flowing from one *security* level to another.

The goal of the information flow model is that information is not shared with other subjects and objects in a manner that threatens the integrity or confidentiality of the data and the system.

> **Travel Advisory**
>
> Remember that some models integrated other models. For example, the Bell-LaPadula and Biba models integrated portions of the state machine and information flow models.

Brewer and Nash Model

The *Brewer and Nash model*, also called the Chinese Wall model, was created to provide access controls that can change dynamically depending upon a user's previous actions. The main goal of the model is to protect against users accessing data that could be seen as conflicts of interest. For example, if a large marketing company provided marketing promotions and materials for several banks, one individual that is working on a project for Bank A should not be looking at information the marketing company has for Bank B. So this marketing company could implement a product that tracks the different marketing representatives' access activities and disallow certain access requests that would present a conflict of interest. In Figure 3-11, you can see that when a representative accesses Bank A's information, the system automatically makes Bank B's information off-limits. If the representative accessed Bank B's data, Bank A's information would be off-limits. These access controls change dynamically depending upon the user's activities and previous access requests.

Graham-Denning and Harrison-Ruzzo-Ullman Models

Remember that these are all models, thus they are not very specific in nature. Each individual vendor must decide how it is going to actually meet the rules outlined in the chosen model. Neither the Bell-LaPadula nor the Biba specifies how the security and integrity ratings are defined and modified nor do they provide a way to delegate or transfer access rights. The *Graham-Denning model* addresses these issues and defines a set of basic rights in terms of commands that a specific subject can execute on an object. The *Harrison-Ruzzo-Ullman model* outlines how access rights can be changed and how subjects and objects should be created and deleted.

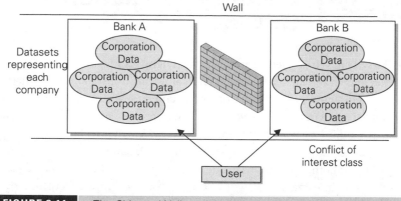

FIGURE 3.11 The Chinese Wall model provides dynamic access controls.

So these newer models provide more granularity and direction for vendors on how to actually meet the goals outlined in the earlier models.

Table 3-1 summarizes the access control models covered in this section.

TABLE 3.1 Summary of Access Control Models

Model	Type and Function
Bell-LaPadula	Multilevel security mathematical state machine model that addresses confidentiality.
Biba	Integrity model that uses integrity levels and addresses the first goal of integrity.
Clark-Wilson	Integrity model that addresses all three goals of integrity by using an access triple approach and separation of duties.
State Machine	System is secure through all transactions and state transitions.
Information Flow	Ensures that information flows in a way that does not negate the security policy.
Non-interference	Ensures that one domain does not affect another domain.
Brewer and Nash	Allows for dynamically changing access controls that protect against conflicts of interest.
Graham-Denning	Creates rights for subjects which correlate to the operations that can be executed on objects.
Harrison-Ruzzo-Ullman	Allows for access rights to be changed and specifies how subjects and objects should be created and deleted.

Security Evaluation Criteria

No system is completely secure, not ever. There is always the potential for the unknown to rear its ugly head and compromise a system. And, the unknown cannot be tested, planned for, or prevented. So where does that leave us? Well, if we do all of our homework and make sure our vendor does its homework and a third party evaluates and tests the system, it leaves us with a pretty darn secure computing system. How's that for a guarantee?

Doing our homework means making sure a system has been evaluated properly. Vendors implement different levels of protection to meet customer demands. The vendor usually targets a specific market, evaluates that market's security needs, builds a system to those specifics, and submits the product to a third party for evaluation, where an assurance rating can be obtained.

The third party evaluation entity that tests these products must have a predetermined evaluation criteria to follow. This criteria allows the vendor to know what needs to be implemented into the product to achieve a certain rating, and the evaluation team knows exactly what to test and how to test it; the resulting rating values are used as a metric. This metric gives everyone a common language so that if one company states that their product provides an Orange Book B2 rating, everyone will know exactly what level of protection that product provides. The other choice is the vendor telling you that their product is "really secure" and it is up to you if you take their word for it.

When security is rated, the level of trust is gauged, which provides assurance that a system will perform in a secure and predictable manner. Let's look at trust and assurance a little bit deeper; they are important concepts when discussing the evaluation of computing systems:

- A *trusted system* has undergone sufficient benchmark testing, verification, and validation to ensure that the product meets the user's requirements pertaining to security, reliability, and functionality.

- *Assurance* is a degree of confidence that the system will act in a correct and predictable manner in each and every computing situation.

The point really is that the evaluation team will not state that a product is secure, instead it will state that the system provides a certain level of assurance, which is determined by the amount of testing and scrutiny of the development practices and design that went into the verification process. The higher the assurance rating the product is trying to achieve, the more intense testing and analysis will go into the process, and the higher the potential for the degree of trust that will be put into the product.

Security Evaluations

There are three evaluation criterion we look at: Trusted Computer System Evaluation Criteria (TCSEC), Information Technology Security Evaluation Criteria (ITSEC), and Common Criteria.

The security evaluation criteria provides a structured way to test and assess many of the items covered earlier in this chapter and book; TCB, access control mechanisms, reference monitor, kernel, design, development practices, and security policy. Each of the security evaluation types has different approaches to rating these internal components and overall systems.

Trusted Computer System Evaluation Criteria

The *Trusted Computer System Evaluation Criteria* (TCSEC) evaluates operating systems and products. It was developed by the National Computer Security Center (NCSC). It is based on the Bell-LaPadula model, so it focuses on confidentiality instead of integrity or availability.

The alias for TCSEC is the *Orange Book*, because that was the color of the cover of the book and probably because it is easier to say than TCSEC.

The rating system is broken down into different classifications:

- A   Verified protection
- B   Mandatory protection (systems that uses security labels)
- C   Discretionary protection
- D   Minimal security

The A classification provides the highest level of assurance, and D provides the lowest. If a product receives a D rating, that means that it did not meet any of the specifications of the other ratings.

Each higher rating takes on the responsibility of meeting the specifications of the lower ratings. For example, a B3 rating must meet all the requirements of all the lower ratings (D through B2) plus some extra elements that must be implemented and verified. The following provides a short list of some of the different requirements at each level.

- **C1 Discretionary Security Protection**
  - Identification and authentication
  - Discretionary protection of resources
- **C2 Controlled Access Protection**
  - Object reuse
  - Protect audit trail

- **B1 Labeled Security**
  - Labels and mandatory access control
  - Process isolation in system architecture
  - Design specifications and verification
  - Device labels

- **B2 Structured Protection**
  - Device labels and subject sensitivity labels
  - Trusted path
  - Separation of operator and administrator functions
  - Covert channel analysis

- **B3 Security Domains**
  - Security administrator role defined
  - Trusted recovery
  - Monitor events and notify security personnel

- **A1 Verified Design**
  - Formal methods

Rainbow Series

The Orange Book addresses only stand-alone systems and does not address networking components, databases, and many other important features of today's computing environment. So, more books had to be developed to address all of these different issues, which ended up being over 20 books. And to keep with the theme of the Orange Book, they each have a different color cover and are referred to collectively as the *Rainbow Series*.

Exam Tip
The Red Book focuses on security issues pertaining to networking components.

The Orange Book also has received a number of criticisms:

- Deals primarily with operating systems and not other issues such as networking and other computing technologies
- Does not address integrity and availability
- Works with government security classifications and not protection classifications used in the commercial industry
- Provides a small number of ratings that does not allow for a lot of flexibility

Information Technology Security Evaluation Criteria

The *Information Technology Security Evaluation Criteria* (ITSEC) is a European standard for rating operating systems and applications. ITSEC evaluates functionality and assurance separately, where the TCSEC evaluates these two items together and represented them with one rating value.

The assurance ratings in ITSEC are E0 through E6, where E6 provides a greater level of assurance; functionality ratings are F1 through F10, with F10 providing the highest rating value. The ratings were developed this way because a system can provide low functionality and high assurance or vice versa. If these ratings are clumped into one value, as in the TCSEC, it is hard to determine the actual performance and protection levels involved. Table 3-2 maps the ITSEC rating to TCSEC rating.

Common Criteria

The TCSEC fit like a shoe that is too tight and ITSEC like a shoe that is too loose, so in 1993, the International Organization for Standardization (ISO) developed a new evaluation criteria that took the best of these two, and other criterion that were in use in different parts of the world, and developed the Common Criteria. Hopefully, this fits like a more comfortable shoe and fits everyone's needs.

The TCSEC has been seen as too restrictive in nature and not flexible enough, and ITSEC tried to provide a better approach, but provided too much

TABLE 3.2	Comparison of ITSEC and TCSEC ratings
ITSEC Rating	**TCSEC Rating**
E0	D
F1 + E1	C1
F2 + E2	C2
F3 + E3	B1
F4 + E4	B2
F5 + E5	B3
F5 + E6	A1
F6 = high integrity	
F7 = high availability	
F8 = data integrity during communications	
F9 = high confidentiality (encryption)	
F10 = networks with high demands on confidentiality and integrity	

flexibility, which brought about a lot of confusion. Both are being phased out and the Common Criteria is being used for today's evaluations of products. The Common Criteria has been developed to be used globally, which will help out the vendors that sell their products around the world. Under the other method, the vendors have to meet the specifications of several different evaluations criterion, which provided a lot of complexity, confusion, extra expense, and required a good amount of time and effort to be evaluated by several different groups.

The Common Criteria provides a universal structure and language for expressing product and system requirements. It uses *protection profiles* (PP), which are specific sets of functional and assurance requirements for a category of products that fulfill a specific customer's needs. A PP can actually be written by several different groups (customers, accrediting agencies, vendors) and will express a need for a security solution that is currently not available in other products.

The *security target* (ST) is written by the product vendor, or developer, that explains the specifications of a product, including functionality and assurance requirements that will be used to evaluate the product against. Basically the vendor states, "This is what our product does," and the evaluators take this statement and reply, "Well, we'll see about that." The *target of evaluation* (TOE) is the product or system that will be evaluated and rated. The ST explains the components, mechanisms, and design of the TOE.

The Common Criteria defines two sets of security requirements: functional requirements and assurance requirements. The functional requirements define the security behavior of the product (What protection level does this product provide?), and the assurance requirements establish the confidence in the product based on how it satisfies the requirements and objectives and the correctness of the product's implementation. Table 3-3 shows a breakdown of the classes contained within each security requirement set.

The different classes contain families that have the same objectives, but that differ in terms of rigor of testing and evaluation.

TABLE 3.3   The Two Sets of Requirements for Evaluation Purposes for the Common Criteria

Security Functional Requirements	Security Assurance Requirements
Identification and authentication	Guidance documents and manuals
Audit	Configuration management
Resource utilization	Vulnerability assessment
Trusted paths/channels	Delivery and operation
User data protection	Life cycle support
Security management	Assurance maintenance

TABLE 3.3	The Two Sets of Requirements for Evaluation Purposes for the Common Criteria *(continued)*	
Security Functional Requirements	**Security Assurance Requirements**	
TOE access	Development	
Communications	Testing	
Privacy		
Protection of the TOE security functions		
Cryptographic support		

The functional and assurance requirements are combined into a package, which is intended to be reusable for evaluating other products. These packages have seven *evaluation assurance levels* (EALs) assigned to them, as outlined here:

- EAL 1 Functionally tested
- EAL 2 Structurally tested
- EAL 3 Methodically tested and checked
- EAL 4 Methodically designed, tested, and reviewed
- EAL 5 Semiformally designed and tested
- EAL 6 Semiformally verified, designed, and tested
- EAL 7 Formally verified, designed, and tested

As with other criterion, as the assurance level increases so does the scrutiny of the design of the product and the vigor of the testing. The statement of TOE in the ST defines the functional requirements drawn from the security functionality classes and assurance requirements outlined in the list of classes. The relationships of these different items are shown in Figure 3-12.

> **Exam Tip**
>
> The following evaluation criterion went into the development of the Common Criteria: TCSEC, ITSEC, Canadian Trusted Computer Product Evaluation Criteria (CTCPEC), and the Federal Criteria.

Certification Versus Accreditation

So, your newly rated system is resting on a rack, and you're smiling at your desk while you look over the product's glowing evaluation report. Nothing to worry about now, right? Unfortunately, there are a few more steps.

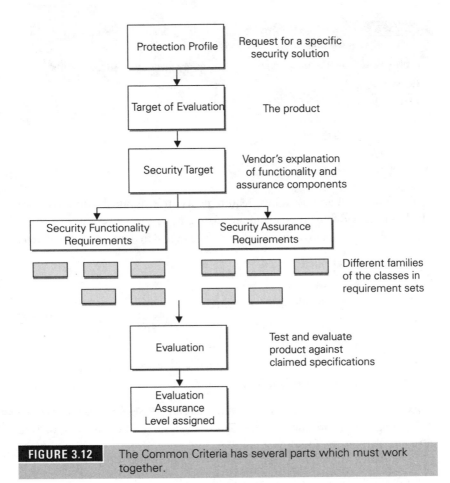

The Common Criteria has several parts which must work together.

The evaluation simply assured us that the product has the possibility of providing the assurance and functionality rating assigned to it. The product will still need to be installed, implemented, and configured properly. And you need to ensure that it provides the necessary assurance level and functionality for *your* environment and that it is the right component to be processing *your* data. This is when the certification and accreditation processes come in.

Certification is a technical evaluation of security components within a system, the overall system, and its interactions with its surrounding environment. Companies specialize in this type of service by performing tests, diagnostics, risk analysis, and auditing to ensure that security levels are being met. This is a formal process that is usually done by an independent agency that had nothing to do with the product evaluation process. A company can instead decide to have their own staff perform this certification procedure. A certification evaluates the following:

- Security modes of operation
- Data sensitivity handling procedures
- System and facility configuration
- Intercommunication with other systems

When the certification is complete, the results need to be taken to management for approval. This formal approval process is referred to as *accreditation*. Basically, management reviews the results and outcome of the certification process and decides if the system provides the necessary level of protection for their specific environment. If management elects to accept the system, it is officially accredited. At this point, management is accepting any risk the new system may bring to the company.

> **Travel Advisory**
>
> If there are changes to the system or environment, the certification and accreditation process may need to be repeated.

CHECKPOINT

✔**Objective 3.01:   System Components**   A CPU contains a control unit, which controls when instructions and data are processed by the CPU. The ALU is the brain of the CPU, and the CPU is the brain of the computer. Applications run as processes, and a thread is an individual function that the process can carry out. A process can be made up of one or more threads. Processes, the operating system, and the CPU can work in different states. And there are several types of storage areas within a computer (primary, secondary, volatile and nonvolatile), each with its own characteristics and uses.

✔**Objective 3.02:   Operating System Security Components**   Systems protect themselves by separating and isolating processes so that they do not interfere with each other's resources. Processes should be configured with least privileges, which means they have only the necessary permissions and access rights to complete their tasks. The security kernel enforces the rules of the reference monitor, and the TCB contains all the protection mechanisms within the system. The TCB components will be carefully analyzed if the product is evaluated for the purpose of achieving an assurance rating. Computers implement protection rings, which segment processes of different trust levels.

✔**Objective 3.03:   Security Models**   A security model gives a description of how a security policy will be enforced by controlling the interactions between subjects and objects. The Bell-LaPadula model was designed for U.S. military systems and focuses on ensuring the confidentiality of data. The Biba and Clark-Wilson models address data integrity. A state machine model dictates that the system is in a secure state if each state transition happens safely and does not negate the security policy. The non-interference model ensures that one environment does not affect another; the Chinese Wall model allows for dynamic access controls that prevent conflicts of interest.

✔**Objective 3.04:   Security Evaluation Criteria**   Security evaluations deal with the functionality and assurance of products and systems. TCSEC is based on the Bell-LaPadula, emphasizes confidentiality, and is referred to as the Orange Book. A set of books called the Rainbow Series was developed to cover the items that the Orange Book does not. ITSEC is an evaluation criteria developed and used in Europe that evaluates a product's functionality and assurance separately. Common Criteria is the new evaluation method that the world is shifting towards using because of its flexibility and that it does a better job of addressing today's security concerns. Common Criteria uses a rating scheme referred to as the Evaluation Assurance Levels (EAL). Certification is the testing and verification of a system and its components, and accreditation is the formal approval of the certification by management.

REVIEW QUESTIONS

1. Which of the following computer components controls when instructions are processed by the CPU?
   A. Registers
   B. Control unit
   C. Primary storage
   D. ALU

2. Which of the following terms describes a CPU that can process more than one process or task at time?
   A. Multiprocessing
   B. Multithreading
   C. Multitasking
   D. Multileveling

3. Which of the following best describes the security kernel and reference monitor relationship?

   A. The security kernel holds the access rules, and the reference monitor enforces them.

   B. The reference monitor holds the access rules, and the security kernel enforces them.

   C. The reference monitor is a core piece of the operating system, and the security kernel is an abstract machine.

   D. The security kernel is trusted and within the TCB, and the reference monitor is untrusted.

4. Which of the following is not a characteristic of the Clark-Wilson model?

   A. Access triple

   B. Integrity model

   C. Addresses all three goals of integrity

   D. Uses a lattice of integrity levels

5. Which of the following best describes the difference between compartmented and dedicated security mode systems?

   A. In dedicated security mode systems, all users have access to all data.

   B. In compartmental security mode systems, all users have access to all data.

   C. In dedicated security mode, not all users can access all data.

   D. In compartmental security mode, all users can access only directories and not files.

6. Which of the following is the total combination of protection mechanisms within a computer system?

   A. TCB

   B. Security perimeter

   C. Security kernel

   D. Security policy

7. Which of the following does not describe the Biba model?

   A. Integrity model that addresses the first goal of integrity

   B. Has a "no write up" rule

   C. Uses a lattice of integrity levels

   D. Has a "no read up" rule

8. Which of the following accurately characterizes the Bell-LaPadula model?

    A. Uses "no write up" and "no read down" rules

    B. Uses "no read up" and "no write down"

    C. Integrity model enforcing the separation of duties

    D. Mathematical theory used to address dynamically changing access permissions

9. In the Orange Book, which of the following ratings is the first to require security labels?

    A. B3

    B. B2

    C. C2

    D. D

10. In the Common Criteria, which of the following outlines requested security solutions in future products?

    A. TOE

    B. EPL

    C. Protection profile

    D. Accreditation

11. Which of the following best describes a lattice model?

    A. Subjects and objects are associated to classes within a matrix.

    B. Confidentiality levels outlined in the Bell-LaPadula model.

    C. An imaginary boundary that dictates what is trusted and within the TCB.

    D. A component that works with the security kernel to ensure there are no untrusted paths.

REVIEW ANSWERS

1. **B** The control unit controls when data and instructions from different applications are sent to the ALU for processing.

2. **C** Multitasking is the act of executing more than one process at a time. The CPU must be developed for this type of functionality, as well as the operating system.

3. **B**   The reference monitor is an abstract machine that holds the access permissions and ensures that the security policy of that system is supported and enforced. The security kernel enforces the reference monitor's rules and must be invoked for each access request.

4. **D**   The Clark-Wilson model is an integrity model that enforces access triple and separations of duties. It addresses all three goals of integrity and does not use a lattice of integrity levels. The Biba model uses integrity levels for access decisions.

5. **A**   If a system works in a dedicated security mode, all users have the necessary clearance and a need-to-know to access all data. If a system is working in a compartmented security mode, all users may have the required clearance, but not necessarily the need to know. Thus, all data is not necessarily available to all users in compartmented mode.

6. **A**   The trusted computing base (TCB) encompasses every component that enforces the stated security policy, including software, hardware, and firmware.

7. **D**   The Biba model is an integrity model that addresses the first goal of integrity (Do not allow unauthorized users to make modifications.) It has a "no write up" rule and a "no read down" rule and makes access decisions based on the integrity levels of the subjects and objects.

8. **B**   The Bell-LaPadula model deals with confidentiality and was originally built for U.S. military systems. The model dictates that subjects cannot write data down to objects of lower security levels and cannot read data that has a higher classification.

9. **B**   In TCSEC ratings, the B classifications deal with mandatory access control models, thus they require security labels. The C classification deals with discretionary access control models and does not require security labels. Notice the question asked for the first rating. B3 would also require labels but comes after B2 in succession.

10. **C**   Protection profiles can be written by a number of different groups and outlines a specific security need that is not currently available in other products.

11. **A**   A lattice model is a structure that represents subject and object access relationships outlined in a matrix. The subjects and objects are associated with one or more classes within the matrix, and this association dictates the upper and lower bounds of access.

Physical Security

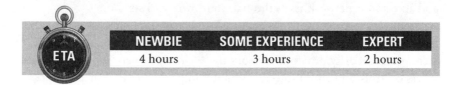

	NEWBIE	SOME EXPERIENCE	EXPERT
ETA	4 hours	3 hours	2 hours

Employees all over the world have to deal with the effects of physical security every day, such as wearing ID badges, putting parking stickers on their cars, punching in access codes to get through certain secure doors, and being aware of suspicious individuals and their behaviors. What a pain, right? Well, maybe, but these physical security controls, while bothersome and at times annoying, are critical to maintaining protection of a company's employees, data, equipment, systems, and the facility itself. This chapter explains the different issues pertaining to physical security and identifies potential threats.

Objective 4.01   Controls Pertaining to Physical Security

Physical assets can be just as vulnerable as computer and information assets, but these vulnerabilities have more to do with physical destruction, intruders, environmental issues, and employees misusing their privileges and causing unexpected damage to data or systems. When security professionals are looking at *computer* security, they are thinking about how bad guys can enter an environment in an unauthorized manner through a port or modem. When they are looking at *physical* security, they are concerned with how bad guys can physically enter an environment, how employees and customers should be protected, or what type of intrusion detection system is best for a particular facility or department. What good is it if you ensure that no one can access your assets through a firewall, but someone can physically stroll in, sit down at a computer, and access your network assets through your own workstation?

Physical security controls are not usually what comes to mind first when we think of security because a different group of folks take care of these issues while a computer security professional looks more closely at network technologies, access controls, and virus protection. But it is important to look at all the possible threats in an environment if we truly want to protect it. The following are some examples of the security controls we look at in this chapter, along with some of their associated threats.

Physical construction of the facility

- Building structure
- Surroundings

Technical controls

- Proximity devices
- Intrusion detection systems

Supporting facility controls

- Electrical power
- Heating, ventilation, and air-conditioning
- Fire detection and suppression

Threats

- Physical damage
- Theft
- Interruption of services
- Unauthorized disclosure of information
- Natural disasters
- Fires
- Vandalism
- Terrorism
- Environmental issues

To determine the degree of risk of each area within the company, a vulnerability assessment should be completed. Inspections, facility and construction, training issues, history of losses, and evaluating current controls are all aspects of a vulnerability assessment. As with the items we addressed in Chapter 1, we need to know what to be afraid of to know how to properly protect ourselves.

Travel Advisory
One of the biggest problems in physical security is that people do not notice that an incident has even occurred.

Facility Location

New companies or companies about to erect a new building have to think about physical security issues from day one. Before the first batch of cement is poured, there are several issues that should be considered. Of course, land prices, customer population, and local competition are reviewed, but security professionals are also interested in the confidence and protection a specific location can provide. Some organizations that deal with sensitive information make their facilities unnoticeable so they do not attract the attention of would-be attackers. The building may be hard to see from the surrounding roads, the company signs and logos are small and not easily noticed, and the markings on the buildings do not give away any information that pertains to what is going on inside that facility. It is a type of city or urban camouflage that makes it harder for the enemy to seek them out.

Some buildings are put into areas that are surrounded by hills to help prevent eavesdropping of electrical signals emitting from the facility's equipment. Other facilities are built underground or right into the side of a mountain, as in Cheyenne Air Force Base, for concealment and disguise in the natural environment, and protection from radar tools and spying activities.

Location selection also means identifying other types of risks related to specific areas. These issues deal with natural disaster possibilities, crime rates, surrounding neighbors, and proximity to airports and railways. If a company is considering the possibility of building a facility in Kansas, tornado insurance will certainly have to be built into cost and maintenance equations. If the company is also looking at erecting a building in a low-income area, although the land prices will most likely be cheap, there will be a need for higher physical and perimeter security levels, which bring along costs and overhead. The following is a list of issues to consider when building a new facility:

Visibility

- Surrounding terrain
- Building markings and signs
- High or low population in the area

Surrounding area and external entities

- Crime rate
- Adjacent neighbors and companies
- Proximity to police, medical, and fire stations
- Possible hazards from surrounding area

Accessibility

- Road access
- Proximity to airports, train stations, and highways

Natural disasters

- Likelihood of floods, tornados, earthquakes, or hurricanes
- Hazardous terrain (mudslide, falling rocks from mountains, or excessive snow or rainfall)

An inspection of the area should be done to reveal the vulnerabilities and the extent of each. If the company is going to be manufacturing rocket fuel, it might be important to be close to the fire station and medical facilities; if a company is going to be manufacturing and selling stuffed animals it might be more important to be accessible to customers, and it might be important for the stuffed animal company to not erect a building next to a company that manufactures rocket fuel. It's all relative.

The value of the facility and property within the facility should be determined as well to help in deciding how much money can be budgeted towards the physical security. Risk management, analysis, and cost/benefit analysis were discussed in Chapter 1, but the same approaches and disciplines should be practiced in physical security. Make informed and responsible decisions *before* filling out that purchase order.

Exam Tip

Physical security controls are the first line of defense; people are the last.

Facility Construction

The needs of a business should be thought about when constructing a new facility. For instance, a facility used for the National Security Agency (NSA) should have a more fortified and secure environment than what would be required for a company that creates food products.

The physical materials being used in construction are very important. This addresses issues such as fire protection, environmental issues, and structural decisions. Another question to ask is, "What is this building going to be used for?" If a facility is going to be used to store documents and old equipment, it has far different regulations and legal requirements than if it is going to be used for employees to work in every day of the week.

When looking at the actual structural components of a facility, the *load* (how much weight that can be held) of a building's walls, floors, and ceilings needs to be estimated and projected to ensure that the building will not collapse in different situations. The walls, ceilings, and floors must meet fire codes and, sometimes just as importantly, provide protection against water damage. The windows (interior and exterior) may need to provide ultraviolet (UV) protection, be shatterproof or bulletproof, or be translucent or opaque depending on the placement of the window and the contents of the building. The doors (exterior and interior) may need to have a specific directional opening, have equal fire rating as the surrounding walls, protect against forcible entries, contain emergency egress markings, and depending on placement, may require monitoring and attached alarms. In most buildings, raised floors are used to hide and protect wires and pipes, but in turn these floors need to be electrically grounded because they are raised.

There are a ton of things to consider when constructing a new facility and fortunately, building codes will regulate most of these issues. However, there are still many options within each category that help to accomplish the company's security and functionality needs while still being cost-effective. Some of these issues are listed here:

Walls

- Combustibility material (wood, steel, concrete)
- Fire rating
- Reinforcements for secured areas

Ceilings

- Combustibility material (wood, steel, concrete)
- Fire rating
- Load and weight bearing rating
- Drop ceiling considerations

Doors

- Combustibility material (wood, pressed board, aluminum)
- Fire rating
- Resistance to forcible entry
- Emergency marking
- Placement
- Alarms
- Directional opening
- Electric door locks may need to revert to a disabled state if a power outage occurs for safe evacuation

- Type of glass (if necessary, this may need to be shatterproof or bulletproof)
- Strike-plates, reinforced doors
- Tamper-resistant hinges

Windows

- Translucent or opaque requirement
- Shatterproof
- Alarms
- Placement
- Accessibility (unavailable to intruders)

Flooring

- Load and weight bearing rating
- Combustibility material (wood, steel, concrete)
- Fire rating
- Raised flooring (electrical grounding)
- Nonconducting surface and material

Heating and air conditioning

- Positive air pressure (air flows out, not in)
- Protective intake vents
- Dedicated power lines
- Emergency switch-off valves
- Placement of equipment

Power supplies

- Backup and alternate power supplies
- Clean power source
- Dedicated feeders to required areas
- Placement and access to distribution panels and circuit breakers

Water and gas lines

- Shutoff valves
- Positive flow (material should flow out of building, not in)
- Placement of lines

Fire Detection and suppression

- Placement of sensors and detectors
- Placement of sprinklers
- Type of detectors and sprinklers

Exam Tip

If an electric door defaults to fail-safe, it will unlock if the power supply fails. If the door defaults to fail-secure, the door will lock if the power supply fails for one reason or another.

Computing Area

Computers are expensive and usually hold critical information; therefore, their protection should be well thought out. Data centers should not be located on the top floor of a building in case of a fire or in the basement in case of a flood. Instead, it is a good idea to locate them at the core of a building to provide protection from natural disasters or bombs. Another location to avoid is right next to a cafeteria, stairs, bathrooms, or the watering hole where people mill around drinking coffee talking about rumors of the next layoff. Although the employees who work in the data centers would be pleased to have such close access to necessities, it is not smart to place these high-risk facilities in areas with heavy traffic or where people tend to gather.

Computing areas should have the following characteristics:

- No more than two doors
- Full-height walls (partitions are not used)
- Walls, doors, and ceiling must have the proper fire rating

Internal partitions can be used to segment separate work areas, but should not be used to provide protection for critical areas. Many buildings have dropped or suspended ceilings, meaning the interior partitions may not extend above the ceiling; therefore, an intruder can lift a ceiling panel and climb over the partition. An example of intrusion is shown in Figure 4-1.

The bad guys should have to work harder than this to get to your highly valued assets!

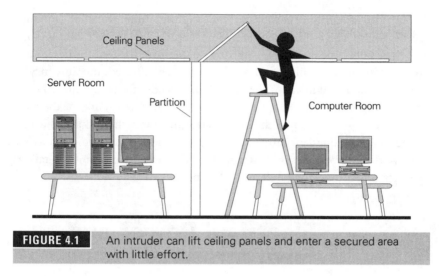

| **FIGURE 4.1** | An intruder can lift ceiling panels and enter a secured area with little effort. |

Hardware Backups

Providing redundant hardware is important for the smaller emergencies that can take place. If a particular file server provides critically needed services to the company 24 hours a day, 7 days a week, it is usually mirrored or RAID capabilities are put into place to protect the data. But what about the hardware itself? If there is physical damage to a system, having the necessary files is useless without a healthy system to install them on. Service level agreements (SLAs) with hardware vendors need to be kept up-to-date to ensure that they can provide the necessary level of protection and availability. If the vendor promises to repair a product within three days, but the business could lose massive profits if the system is down for three hours, this is not a realistic protection mechanism.

Each device has a *mean time between failure* (MTBF) and a *mean time to repair* (MTTR) values. The MTBF estimate is used to determine the expected lifetime of a device or when a component within that device is expected to go kaput. The MTTR value is used to estimate the amount of time needed to repair the device and get production back at the same level.

These estimates can also be used to calculate the risk of utility failure and evaluate other devices that may have better MTBF or MTTR values. If a company depends greatly on a specific cooling device for their server room that contains over 200 servers, they may have one or two backup devices in place; or they may send George, the network engineer, to classes so that someone on staff knows how to deal with this type of critical equipment failure. Or, the company may pay more to have the necessary SLA put into place.

The crux of hardware backups is how long the company can be without a specific device. This estimation is compared to the MTBF and MTTR values and SLA agreement timelines. If the company can perform without the device, and productivity or profitability will not be negatively affected, the SLA may be more than enough. If this item blowing up will directly affect the company's revenue flow, a more expensive approach (redundant hardware) may be the more logical choice. A cost analysis should be performed for each product, which includes costs for redundant hardware, SLAs, MTBF, and MTTR. Doing your own homework on these issues is a better approach than believing a smooth-talking salesman that brings you donuts and a free pen.

Objective 4.02 Electrical Power and Environmental Issues

Without electrical power, most companies cannot operate. Having redundant power capabilities is an absolute must.

Companies operate on a day-to-day basis by using a *primary power source*, usually a power feed that comes directly from a utility substation. But, just as your electricity at home can go out during a lightning storm, so can the electricity of a company that is only operating off of one primary power source. This is why most organizations have an *alternate power source*, which can be an UPS (uninterruptible power supply) or a generator.

UPS

UPS uses batteries that range in size and capacity and can be online or standby systems. *Standby UPS* devices stay inactive until a power line fails. The system has sensors that detect a power failure, and the load is then switched to the battery bank. *Online UPS* systems are in continual use because the main power source voltage goes through the online system to the computers and devices. If there is a power failure, the online system uses its charged battery power supply and works to provide the same level of voltage as the primary source. These systems can usually switch the load to the battery supply more quickly than standby UPS systems, which can help ensure that components will not be damaged and data will not be lost or corrupted.

Some UPSs provide just enough power to allow systems to be shut down cleanly, whereas some will allow the systems to run for a longer period of time.

The following should be considered when purchasing and implementing an UPS system as an alternate power source:

- What size load can the UPS support?
- How long can it support the load (battery duration)?
- How quickly can the UPS take on the load once the primary source fails?
- How much physical space does it require?

Travel Advisory

UPS systems provide relief for short power outages; generators provide relief for longer power outages.

Power Interference

When clean power is being used, it means that the power supply contains no interference or voltage fluctuation. The types of interference, or line noise, that are possible are either from *electromagnetic interference* (EMI) or *radio frequency interference* (RFI) and transient noise, and all cause a disturbance to the flow of electric power as it travels across a power line, as shown in Figure 4-2.

EMI is created by the difference between three wires: hot, neutral, and ground. Lightning and electrical motors can also induce EMI; RFI is usually created by electrical cables and fluorescent lighting.

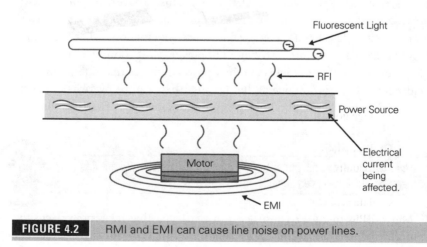

FIGURE 4.2 RMI and EMI can cause line noise on power lines.

A fluctuation is an unexpected change in voltage level. The following are the different types of fluctuations that are possible with electrical power:

Power increase

- **Spike** Momentary high voltage
- **Surge** Prolonged high voltage

Power loss

- **Fault** Momentary power outage
- **Blackout** Prolonged loss of power

Power degradation

- **Sag** Momentary low voltage
- **Brownout** Prolonged power supply that is below normal voltage

Exam Tip

Utility companies sometimes plan rolling brownouts for areas that have high power demands to try and ensure that blackouts do not occur.

Lightning storms, intense cold or hot temperatures, and generators turning on and off are all normal occurrences that can cause voltage fluctuations. In fact, these scenarios happen often enough that mechanisms have been put in place to provide constant protection. *Voltage regulators* and *line conditioners* are commonly used to detect and protect against power fluctuations. They are used to ensure a clean and smooth distribution of power. Most computers and devices have a built-in line conditioners in their power supplies that filter the voltage before it reaches its components, but because these can be overwhelmed with surges, it is best to have every device plugged into some type of surge protector.

Local Lingo

An inrush current is the initial surge of current required when an increase in power is demanded.

Many data centers are constructed in a manner that takes power-sensitive equipment into consideration. Because surges, sags, brownouts, blackouts, and voltage spikes frequently cause data corruption and component damage, the centers are built to provide a high level of protection from these threats. Other environments, such as basic office space, do not provide this level of protection, and plugging vacuum cleaners or microwaves into the same outlets can negatively affect the systems dependent upon a steady and reliable power supply. In these environments, it is typical to have multiple devices plugged into one outlet using power strips and extension cords. This can cause more line noise, reduction of voltage to each device, and fire hazards; thus this should not be in place for any data processing environment.

When dealing with electrical power issues, the following safeguards can be taken to protect devices and the environment:

- Voltage regulators and line conditioners should be used to maintain a clean power supply.
- Shutting down devices in an orderly fashion helps avoid data loss or damaging devices due to voltage changes.
- Every device should be connected to a surge protector.
- Power line monitors should be employed to detect frequency and voltage amplitude changes.
- Connections need to be grounded from the device to the Earth.
- Protection from magnetic induction should be provided through shielded lines.
- UPS or generators should be available for backup power supply.
- Long cable runs should be shielded.
- Three-prong connections and adapters should be used instead of two-prong.
- Outlet strips and extension cords should not be plugged into each other.

Nothing is worse then feeling safe and secure because you have a backup power supply and then having that knot quickly arrive in the pit of your stomach during a disaster because you just realized you never actually tested its functionality. A UPS or generator should be tested periodically to make sure it can keep the company up and running when called upon, and that you will not need to be looking through the want ads for a new job once the disaster has passed.

Travel Advisory

The electrical system needs to have an emergency power off (EPO) switch to allow the power to be quickly shut off if required.

Environmental Considerations

Just about every engineer has been stuck doing testing in a cold equipment room at one time or another. Although these cool temperatures can be frustrating after a few hours, it is this kind of environmental control that prolongs the life of electronic equipment and keeps a network running smoothly.

Maintaining appropriate temperature and humidity levels is an important part of an electronic environment. High humidity can cause corrosion, and low humidity can cause excessive static electricity. This static electricity can short out devices, cause the loss in information, or provide amusing entertainment for unsuspecting employees. Relative humidity between 45 and 60 percent is acceptable for areas that are processing data. A *hygrometer* can be used to monitor humidity manually or automatically.

Lower temperatures can cause mechanisms to slow down or stop altogether. Higher temperatures can cause devices to use too much fan power and eventually shut down. An acceptable temperature for an area containing computing devices is between 70 and 74 degrees Fahrenheit.

Static electricity is a common problem in dryer climates, or during the winter when the air contains less moisture. The following steps can be taken against static electricity:

- Use antistatic flooring in data processing areas.
- Ensure proper humidity.
- Have proper grounding of building and outlets.
- Do not have carpeting in data centers, or if necessary, have static-free carpet.
- Wear antistatic bands when working inside of computer systems.

Ventilation

Heating, ventilation, and air conditioning (HVAC) are used to control humidity, temperature, and contaminations. *Positive pressurization* and ventilation should be implemented to control contamination, which can be dirt, dust, smoke, gas, or manufacturing particles. Positive pressurization means that when an employee opens a door, the air goes out and outside air does not come in. If a facility were on fire, you would want the smoke to go out the doors instead of being pushed back in.

Electronic devices also rely on proper ventilation. Dust can impact a device's functionality by clogging up the fan that is supposed to be cooling it, and excessive concentrations of certain gases can accelerate corrosion and cause performance issues or device failure. Although most disk drives are hermetically sealed, other storage devices can be affected by airborne contaminants.

> **Travel Advisory**
>
> During a fire, HVAC should be turned off so smoke is not spread and the fire is not given a supply of oxygen.

Water, Steam, and Gas

Water, steam and gas are all environmental factors that need to be monitored regularly. During facility construction, it must be made certain that these facilities have proper shutoff valves, and *positive drains*, which means that their contents flow out instead of in. If there is ever a break in a main water pipe, the water flow must be able to be turned off. In case of a surrounding flood, a company wants to ensure that material cannot travel up through the water pipes and into their water supply or facility.

If there is presence of fire within a building, gas lines need to be able to be terminated. Having these emergency shutoff valves is a wonderful thing, unless people don't know where they are or what to do with them. Facility, operating, and security personnel should know where these valves are and there should be strict procedures to follow for these types of emergencies.

Objective 4.03 # Fire Detection and Suppression

The subject of physical security would not be complete without a discussion about fire safety. The most basic approach to fire safety is asking the question, "How do I get out of here?" But someone should probably stay behind to ask, "How can I put this fire out?" and "How did it start?"

A fire begins because something ignited it. That could be the failure of an electronic device, combustible materials stored improperly, carelessly discarded cigarettes, a malfunctioning heating device, or arson. Fire needs fuel and oxygen to continue to burn and grow; the more fuel per square meter, the more intense the fire will become. Fuel could be items like wood, paper, liquids, chemicals, or wiring.

To put out a fire, one or more of its four legs (heat, fuel, oxygen, chemical reaction) must be affected. The heat (temperature) must be reduced, the fuel and oxygen must be removed, or the chemical reaction must be disrupted. Different fire suppressants provide these services, as covered in the "Fire Suppression" section.

Fire Prevention

There are national and local standards that must be met pertaining to fire prevention, detection, and suppression methods. *Fire prevention* comes from proper construction of buildings, proper wiring, training employees how to react properly when faced with a fire, supplying the right extinguishing equipment and ensuring that it is in working order, making sure there is an easily reachable fire suppressant, and storing combustible elements in the proper manner.

A fire prevention program should be developed to protect people first and equipment next. This means that a proper reaction to a fire is not to shove the irritating guy from accounting into the fire and save the file server instead. A fire prevention plan should incorporate scenarios with the highest probability, such as an electrical fire in a computing center, and how to properly react to each of these different scenarios.

Fire Detection

If you cannot properly prevent a fire, you want to make sure it can be properly detected. *Fire detection response systems* come in many different forms. This can be an automatic sprinkler system or discharge system that dispenses carbon dioxide, Halon, or another fire suppressing substance. Automatic water sprinkler systems are widely used and highly effective in protecting buildings and their contents, although water does not usually have a good relationship with computers and electrical devices. We will look at other possible fire suppressants soon that may be better suited for data processing environments.

There are four types of detectors available today:

- **Smoke-activated (ionization detector)**   Reacts to the charged particles of smoke and can sound an early warning alarm before actually releasing a supression agent.
- **Optical (photoelectric device)**   This has a light source and a receiver and it sounds an alarm if its light beam is interrupted before reaching the receiver (assumes the light is interrupted by smoke). Another type of photoelectric device samples the surrounding air by drawing air into a pipe. If the light source is obscured, the alarm will sound.
- **Heat-activated**   Sounds an alarm when a predefined temperature is reached, which is a *fixed-temperature sensor*. If the sensor looks for a drastic rise in temperature in a short period of time, it is a *rate-of-rise temperature sensor*. Rate-of-rise temperature sensors usually provide a quicker warning than fixed-temperature sensors because they are more sensitive, but they can also cause more false alarms.

- **Flame-activated (infrared detector)** Depending on the actual device, it will either sense the pulsations of a flame or sense the infrared energy that is associated with flames and combustion.

Newer fire detection products combine the different functionalities from the preceding list for the best effectiveness in detecting a fire.

Fire detector systems can be programmed to automatically call the fire station, as well as shut down the HVAC system, which is a good thing. At these times in our lives, we need all the help we can get.

It is not enough to have these fire and smoke detectors installed in a facility; they must be installed in the right places. Detectors should be on and above suspended ceilings and below raised floors because these are the places that wires are often strung and they can start electrical fires. Detectors should also be placed in enclosures and air ducts because smoke can gather in these areas and not be seen until it is too late. Figure 4-3 illustrates the proper placement of smoke detectors.

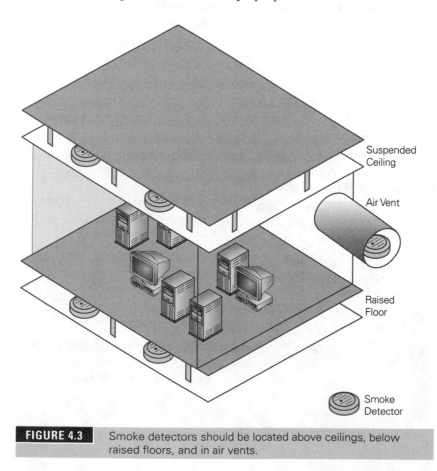

Suspended Ceiling

Air Vent

Raised Floor

Smoke Detector

FIGURE 4.3 Smoke detectors should be located above ceilings, below raised floors, and in air vents.

It is important that people are alerted about a fire as quickly as possible so the damage may be reduced, fire suppression activities may start quicker, and lives may be saved. This means you should not quietly slip out the side door once you notice a fire, but alert others so that they too may be saved. They'd do it for you.

Fire Types

It is important to know the types of fires that can take place and what should be done to properly suppress them. Each fire type has a class that indicates what materials are actually on fire. Table 4-1 shows the four fire types and their corresponding suppression methods.

Different environments will have more of a likelihood of one type of fire than another, which means the proper suppression agent should be readily available in those areas. For example, a warehouse containing documents and paper files will be more likely to experience a Class A fire, whereas a data processing facility will more likely experience a Class C fire, a rocket fuel plant a Class B fire, and a chemical company or airplane brakes manufacturer would be more susceptible to a Class D fire. This is important to understand so that you don't put dry powder on a Class B fire or water on a Class C fire.

Fire Suppression

There are several ways of suppressing a fire, and certain precautions that should be taken. In many buildings, there are suppression agents located in different areas that are designed to initiate after a specific trigger has been set off. Each agent has a zone of coverage, meaning an area that the agent is responsible for, thus full coverage must be planned for.

There are different types of suppression agents: water, Halon, or CO_2. Table 4-2 shows how different suppression substances interfere with elements of fire.

TABLE 4.1	Four Types of Fire and Their Suppression Methods		
Fire Class	**Type of Fire**	**Elements of Fire**	**Suppression Method**
A	Common combustibles	Wood products and paper	Water or soda acid
B	Liquid	Petroleum products and coolants	Gas (Halon), CO_2, or soda acid
C	Electrical	Electrical equipment and wires	Gas (Halon) or CO_2
D	Combustible metals	Magnesium, sodium	Dry powder

TABLE 4.2	How Different Substances Interfere with Elements of Fire	
Combustion Elements	**Suppression Methods**	**How Suppression Works**
Fuel	Soda acid	Removes fuel
Oxygen	CO_2	Removes oxygen
Temperature	Water	Reduces temperature
Chemical combustion	Gas – Halon or Halon substitute	Interferes with the chemical reactions between elements

One document used for research for this book states that CO_2 is not compatible with life. That is an important tidbit of information to be aware of when selecting a fire suppression agent. CO_2 actually displaces oxygen from the surrounding air. This is good for fighting fires, because oxygen is a major fuel of fires, but it is pretty important for people also, so any suppression system using it should have a delayed reaction to allow people to evacuate. It should be used only in facilities that do not have people working in them.

> **Travel Advisory**
>
> CO_2 is colorless and odorless and may result in unconsciousness.

Halon

Halon is a gas that is used in many fire extinguishers but is quickly being phased out. It is used because of its capability to interfere with the chemical combustion in fires, and it does not harm electronic equipment. However, it has been found to be harmful to people in certain amounts and that it actually eats away at our precious ozone layer. It was determined that the ozone layer is pretty important, so Halon is federally restricted and you will not find new extinguishers filled with this stuff. Anyone with extinguishers filled with Halon does not need to throw them out the window with disgust, but when it comes time to have them refilled, they need to be filled with a different and less harmful substance. There are several Environmental Protection Agency (EPA)–approved chemicals that can be used instead of Halon, FM-200 being one of them.

Fire Extinguishing Issues

Fire extinguishers have markings indicating what type of fire they should be used on, which is a pretty nifty idea. The markings indicate what types of chemicals are within the canisters and what types of fires they have been approved to be used on. Portable extinguishers should be located within 50 feet of any electrical equipment and near exits. The extinguishers should be marked clearly, with an unobstructed view. They should be easily reachable by employees, and should be inspected quarterly.

This means that they should not be stored in closets, behind doors, and should actually be checked to ensure they really work.

Water Sprinklers

Water sprinklers can be less expensive than Halon and FM-200 systems, but can initiate unnecessarily, which in turn causes water damage. Sensors should be put in place to shut down electrical power before water sprinklers activate. Each sprinkler head should activate individually to avoid wide-area damage and there should be shutoff valves so the water supply can be stopped if necessary. There are four main types of water sprinklers:

- **Wet pipe** Wet pipe systems hold water in the pipes and are usually discharged by temperature control sensors. This is the most common sprinkler systems used today. Its biggest disadvantage, however, is the tendency for pipes to freeze and break in colder climates.

- **Dry pipe** Dry pipe systems do not hold water in the pipes, but instead water is held back by a valve until a specific temperature is reached. This delay can be good because it allows time to shut down the system if needed, but in the event of an actual fire, the response time is slower than a wet pipe system. The biggest benefit of this type of water system is that pipes will not freeze and break in colder environments.

- **Pre-action** Pre-action systems combine the functionality of wet and dry pipe systems. Water is held back from the pipes by a valve, but when a predefined temperature is met, the pipes fill with water. However, the water is not released immediately; a delay mechanism holds the water in the pipes, which allows adequate time to shut down the system in case of false alarms.

- **Deluge** Deluge systems are the same as dry pipe systems, except the sprinkler heads are open to allow for a larger volume of water to be released in a shorter period of time.

A continual mantra of people who are in the fire-fighting business is, "Fires cause water damage, water sprinklers and water do not cause water damage," which means do not choose to be passive and not put a fire fighting system in place because you are afraid of water damage. Water damage will usually occur because of the presence of a fire, which can be exponentially more dangerous and damaging.

Exam Tip
The best water suppression systems to be used in data processing environments are pre-action, because they allow someone to put the fire out through other means or shut down the system in case of a false alarm.

Emergency Response

Good management must have the foresight to look into the future and understand that some things may not go as planned, situations may arise that need special handling, and employees might be faced with emergency situations. It is management's responsibility to think through many types of scenarios and ensure that procedures and responses are developed that should take place when these situations arise. This is an example of practicing due care, and if these items are not addressed, a company can be held negligent and liable. So if a disaster takes place, and everyone just runs out of the building screaming instead of treating the situation with more calmness and responsibility, we can just blame management.

Although much of this planning will most likely be rolled into a disaster recovery and business continuity plan, it is a good idea to understand basic emergency procedures as they relate to physical security. How can management better prepare their people for these stressful and possibly dangerous types of situations? The following items should be put into place to aid in such times of trouble:

- Emergency response planning
- Periodic inspections and reports
- Awareness efforts and training
- Drills and exercises
- Documentation of necessary procedures

Objective 4.04 Perimeter Security

This is the part that most people think of when the subject of physical security is discussed. Security guards, door locks, and burglar alarms are what first come to mind. But, there are other controls that are used and that are necessary to ensure proper perimeter security.

External boundary protection consists of the following physical controls: locks, fencing and physical barriers, security force, outside lighting, access control mechanisms, intrusion detection, and monitoring devices. We address each in the following sections.

Lock Types

Locks are the most inexpensive access control mechanisms, but should be viewed as only a delaying device to dedicated intruders. Because locks can be picked or broken, and keys can be lost or duplicated, this access control type should be only one part of the overall protection scheme that a company employs.

Locks come in all types and sizes. It is important to have the right type of lock so that it provides the correct level of protection. The following is a list of lock types:

- **Conventional locks**   Traditional lock and key mechanism. Locks can be easily picked or broken, and keys can be lost or duplicated.
- **Pick-resistant locks**   More expensive than conventional locks. Locks are harder to pick, and keys are not as easily duplicated.
- **Electronic combination systems**   An access code is needed to access a building or room. Uses a keypad for individuals to enter pre-assigned codes. This is also called *cipher* or keyless locks.
- **Deadbolt locks**   A bolt, which is not operated by the door handle, is connected to the frame of the door.
- **Smart locks**   Allow only authorized individuals in through specific doors at certain times. It may require a time-sensitive magnetic stripe card.

There are some different options to use with cipher locks to improve performance and increase security levels:

- **Door delay**   If a door is open for a long period of time, an alarm will trigger to alert personnel of possible suspicious activity.
- **Key-override**   A specific combination can be programmed to be used in emergency situations to override usual procedures or for supervisory overrides.
- **Master-keying**   This option enables supervisory personnel to change access codes and other features of the cipher lock.
- **Hostage alarm**   If an individual is in duress and/or held hostage, there can be a combination she can enter to alert the proper authorities.

> ### Exam Tip
>
> The best protection from theft of corporate information from a laptop is not a device lock, but encryption.

Facility Access

A common problem with controlling authorized access into a facility or area is called *piggybacking*. This occurs when an intruder uses someone else's access card or access code or simply follows them into the building without being noticed. The best prevention of piggybacking is increased security at each building entrance, security guards, and employee education. So, while you think you are being nice by holding the door open for someone, you could be freely allowing an intruder into your building.

> ### Exam Tip
>
> Piggybacking is a general term that means to use someone else's credentials, thus it can take place in other places, not just physical security. Piggybacking in the physical security context is also referred to as tailgating.

If a company is employing a card badge reader, there are several different types of systems to choose from. The magnetic card can contain a magnetic strip, containing authorization information, a magnetic dot, or an embedded wire (resists tampering). A proximity card may be used, which means it does not need to be swiped through a reader. A proximity system has a reader that senses someone approaching and can communicate with the access card when an individual gets within a certain distance of the reader.

There are two types of wireless proximity readers: user activated and system sensing. A *user-activated* system requires the user to enter an access code that is transmitted over the airwaves to a centralized device for approval. When the correct sequence is delivered, access is granted. A *system-sensing* proximity card, on the other hand, will recognize the presence of the coded card within a specific area and send interrogating signals to the card to retrieve the encoded access code. A system-sensing access control system is a device that does not require the individual to enter any sequence or numbers or perform any action.

> **Exam Tip**
>
> Electronic access control (EAC) tokens are used in physical security to authenticate individuals. They can be proximity readers, programmable locks, or biometric systems that identify and authenticate users before allowing them entrance.

Entrance Protection

Stationary and revolving doors can be used as physical access control mechanisms. They are used in mantraps and turnstiles so that unauthorized individuals entering or leaving a facility cannot get in or out if it is activated. *Mantraps* protect physical access by routing personnel through a small area with two doors. The second door is not actually unlocked until the individual is authorized to enter. The authorization can include showing a badge to a security guard, swiping a card through a reader, or authenticating to a biometric system. Some mantraps actually weigh individuals to ensure that only one person is trying to enter the facility at a time.

Turnstiles are the entertaining doors that go around and around. If there is a suspect trying to flee the area these can be locked so that they are not allowed to use the door or they can be locked inside the turnstile like a goldfish in a bowl.

Another protective action is keeping accurate access logs of who enters and exits the facility. Usually, this can be done by a security guard or front desk personnel. The log should include the exact time an individual entered the building, who was responsible for this individual, and when the person actually left. This is a detective control, in that one would consult the log *after* something bad has taken place with the effort of trying to piece together who was in the facility at the time of the disturbance.

> **Exam Tip**
>
> Different security mechanisms can provide a main service and secondary services. An access or audit log is actually a *detective* control, because it will be used after an event takes place. It can be preventive because if someone knows their actions are being logged, they may not carry out some actions, but that is a secondary service. When exam time comes around, these logs are considered detective controls, not preventive.

Fencing

Fencing is not always the most attractive way to enclose and protect an area, and is actually quite costly, but in some cases it is definitely necessary. Plus, bushes and flowers can be planted to hide embarrassingly ugly fences and still keep the bad guys out.

Fencing is quite an effective physical barrier because it works as a preventive and deterrent mechanism. Fencing can provide crowd control and helps control access to facilities and their surrounding areas.

Fences come in varying heights; each height provides a different level of security:

- Fences three to four feet high only deter casual trespassers.
- Fences six to seven feet high are considered too high to climb easily.
- Fences eight feet high with strands of barbed wire at the top mean you are serious about protecting your property. This will deter even the more serious intruders.

> ### Exam Tip
>
> If using barbed wire on top of a fence, it should be slanted at a 45° angle. If a company is trying to keep individuals in (as in a prison), the slant will be toward the building. If the company wants to keep individuals out, the slant is away from the building.

Sometimes it is good to show your fences, as the military and prisons proudly do. This is strictly for deterring people who may consider accessing the environment in an unauthorized manner. These determined intruders may take such bold actions as trying to climb or cut the fence. In these situations, a *perimeter intrusion and detection assessment system* (PIDAS) can be implemented. PIDAS is a fencing system that can detect if an intruder is approaching or damaging the fence and sounds an alarm. It consists of mesh wire and passive cable vibration sensors that can set off an alarm. Although this provides a high level of security, it is vulnerable to many false alarms, such as passing deer and bunnies.

Some companies will even go so far as to construct a perimeter wall that surrounds their facility. These are reinforced concrete or brick walls that should stand at least ten feet high and sometimes have barbed wire or sharp spikes on their tops. These companies usually really have something to hide and protect.

Bollards are usually small, round concrete pillars that are constructed and placed around facilities at risk of being damaged by someone running a vehicle into the side of the building. They should be placed on the sides of a facility that are in close proximity to parking lots or roads.

As with all security mechanisms and procedures addressed in this book, fences should provide the necessary level of protection and be a cost-effective solution.

Lighting

Lighting should be used to discourage intruders and provide safety for personnel in entrances, parking areas, and other critical sections. Lighting is a physical control that provides preventive and deterrent protection. A company practices due care when it supplies the correct type of lighting for areas that could be considered dangerous. For example, if an employee was attacked in the company's parking lot, that employee could sue the company for not providing the proper security measures, one of them being proper lighting.

The National Institute of Standards and Technology (NIST) standard pertaining to perimeter protection states that critical areas should be illuminated eight feet in height with two-foot candle power.

There are several types of lights a company can choose to implement: searchlights, streetlights, floodlights, and Fresnel units, which contain small lenses that can be focused.

Surveillance Devices

One of the best security mechanisms is a security guard and/or a patrol force to monitor facility grounds. This type of security control is more flexible than other security mechanisms, can provide good response to suspicious activities, and works as a great deterrent. However, it can be the most costly because it requires additional headcount to the company's payroll, meaning a salary, benefits, paid vacations, and an invitation to the company picnic. The best security program has a combination of security mechanisms and does not depend on just one component for security. A security guard should be accompanied by other surveillance and detection mechanisms.

Exam Tip
A security guard is chosen as a security mechanism when discriminating judgment is required.

Another option is using dogs to protect a facility. Dogs have proven to be highly useful in detecting intruders and other unwanted conditions. Their hearing and sight capabilities outperform humans, and their intelligence and loyalty can be used as protection measures. Dogs can be trained to hold an intruder at bay until security personnel arrive, or they can chase an intruder and attack.

Some dogs are even trained to recognize smoke so that they could alert others of an ongoing fire.

Because surveillance is based on sensory perception, surveillance devices usually work in conjunction with guards to extend their capabilities and range of perception. Cameras can be used to take still pictures, which are stored for later viewing, or a company can choose to use *closed-circuit TVs* (CCTVs). A CCTV enables a guard to monitor many different areas at once from a centralized location.

When looking to purchase and implement a CCTV, the size of the area to be monitored should be understood to ensure that the device can cover the complete area (height and width) and the lighting requirements of the area (which will determine the lens type). CCTVs should not be the only control in place, and like others, work the best when used with other types of prevention mechanisms.

Intrusion Detection Systems

Surveillance techniques are used to watch for unusual behaviors, whereas detecting devices are used to sense changes that take place in an environment. Both are monitoring methods, but they use different technologies and approaches. The different detection technologies are listed here:

- **Proximity detection system**   A proximity detector, or capacitance detector, emits a measurable magnetic field while in use. The detectors monitor this electrical field, and an alarm sounds if the field is disrupted. These devices are usually used to protect specific objects (artwork, cabinets, or a safe) versus protecting a whole room or area.

- **Photoelectric or photometric system**   This type of system detects the change in the level of light within an area, and thus must be used in windowless rooms. This system emits a beam of light towards a receiver. If the beam is disrupted, an alarm sounds. The light beams can be visible or invisible.

- **Wave pattern**   These detectors generate a wave pattern that is sent over a sensitive area and is then reflected back to a receiver. If the patterns are returned undisturbed, the device does nothing. If the patterns return altered, then an alarm sounds. These devices can detect microwave, ultrasonic, and low frequency ranges.

- **Passive infrared system**   This type of system identifies the changes of heat waves within an area. If the particles within the air rise in temperature, it could be an indication of the presence of an intruder and an alarm will sound.

- **Acoustical-seismic detection system** This type of system detects the changes in the noise level of an area. These devices do not emit any waves; they use microphones to listen for sounds within an area, and are considered passive devices.

Travel Advisory

Acoustical-seismic systems can cause many false alarms because of their sensitivity. Storms, airplanes, and local noises can set them off.

Other types of sensors may be used in intrusion detection systems, as shown here:

- **Contact** Electrical circuit is broken (usually a door or window is opened).
- **Pressure mat** If an intruder steps on a mat, an alarm sounds.
- **Video motion** Movement is sensed on a video camera.
- **Closed circuit** Electrical circuit is broken (cutting a wire or breaking a window).
- **Vibration** Uses fine embedded wires to detect movement of walls, screens, ceilings, and floors.
- **Duress** Used for someone to activate during an emergency (usually a switch). Bank tellers use this to sound silent alarms during robberies.

Unfortunately, intrusion detection systems are not silver bullets and have issues of their own to understand before implementation:

- They are expensive.
- They require human intervention.
- They require redundant power supply and emergency backup power.
- They should be linked to a central security system and local police station.
- They should default to fail-safe.
- They should be resistant to and detect tampering.
- They can cause a large amount of false alarms.
- They can be penetrated.

CHECKPOINT

✔**Objective 4.01:   Controls Pertaining to Physical Security**   Physical security is the first line of defense against environmental risks and unpredictable human behavior. The use of automated environmental controls can help minimize the resulting damage and speed of the recovery process. Manual controls can be time-consuming, error-prone, and require constant attention. Environmental issues such as local crime rate, natural disaster potential, and distance to hospitals, police and fire stations, airports, and railroads are all considerations when deciding on a new facility location. The materials used in the construction of a facility can greatly reduce many types of threats to the building and contents of the building.

✔**Objective 4.02:   Electrical Power and Environmental Issues**   Companies should have a backup power source in place, such as UPS or a generator. Power noise is a disturbance of voltage to a device and can be caused by electromagnetic interference (EMI) or radio frequency interference (RFI). Regulators can condition a line to keep voltage steady and clean. Positive pressurization and ventilation should be implemented within companies to keep air and contaminants flowing out of the building and not in.

✔**Objective 4.03:   Fire Detection and Suppression**   A fire needs high temperatures, oxygen, fuel, and chemical reactions, so to suppress it, one or more of the those items needs to be reduced or eliminated. Fire detectors should be located on and above suspended ceilings, below raised floors, and in air ducts. Portable fire extinguishers should be placed within 50 feet of electrical equipment and should be inspected quarterly.

✔**Objective 4.04:   Perimeter Security**   Physical access controls restrict the entry and exit of personnel. There are many types of access control mechanisms, from cipher locks to proximity readers. Piggybacking is when unauthorized access is achieved to a facility via another individual's legitimate access credentials. Proximity detection systems (motion detectors, vibration sensors, and light beams) require human response, can cause false alarms, should be tamperproof, and depend on a constant power supply. Fencing is a common way to provide external boundary security.

REVIEW QUESTIONS

1. What is the first step that should be taken when a fire has been detected?

    A. Turn off the HVAC system and activate fire door releases.

    B. Determine which type of fire it is.

    C. Advise individuals within the building to leave.

    D. Activate fire suppression system.

2. When should a Class C fire extinguisher be used instead of a Class A?

    A. When electrical equipment is on fire

    B. When wood and paper is on fire

    C. When a combustible liquid is on fire

    D. When the fire is in an open area

3. Which is not a preventive physical security control?

    A. Fences

    B. Locks

    C. Security guard

    D. Access and audit log

4. How does Halon fight fires?

    A. It reduces the fire's fuel intake.

    B. It reduces the temperature of the area and cools the fire.

    C. It disrupts the chemical reactions of the fire.

    D. It reduces the oxygen in the area.

5. What is a mantrap?

    A. A trusted security domain

    B. A logical access control mechanism

    C. A double-door facility used for physical access control

    D. A fire suppression device

6. When is a security guard the best choice for a physical access control mechanism?

    A. When discriminating judgment is required

    B. When intrusion detection is required

    C. When the security budget is low

    D. When access controls are in place

7. Critical areas should have illumination of _____.

    A. Three-foot candles and eight feet in height

    B. Two-foot candles and eight feet in height

    C. Three-foot candles and six feet in height

    D. Two-foot candles and six feet in height

8. What is a common problem with vibration-detection devices used for perimeter security?

    A. They can be defeated by emitting the right electrical signals in the protected area.

    B. The power source is easily disabled.

    C. They cause false alarms by things that do not involve a threat to the environment.

    D. They interfere with computing devices.

9. What are the problems with humidity in an area with electrical devices?

    A. High humidity causes excessive electricity, and low humidity causes corrosion.

    B. High humidity causes corrosion, and low humidity causes static electricity.

    C. High humidity causes power fluctuations, and low humidity causes static electricity.

    D. High humidity causes corrosion, and low humidity causes power fluctuations.

10. When deciding on a location to build a facility, which item is not as important as the rest?

    A. Possibility of natural disasters

    B. Crime rate

    C. Proximity to downtown facilities

    D. Proximity to fire station

11. What is a cipher lock?

    A. A lock that uses cryptographic keys

    B. A lock that uses a type of key that cannot be reproduced

    C. A lock that uses a token and perimeter reader

    D. A lock that uses a keypad

12. Water and gas lines should have shutoff valves and positive drains. What is a positive drain?

   A. Water does not go into the drain until a fire has been detected.
   B. This characteristic ensures that the pipe is unbreakable.
   C. Water, or gas, flows out instead of in.
   D. Water, or gas, flows in instead of out.

13. Which of the following is true pertaining to CCTV systems?

   A. Best if used in a synergistic manner with other security controls
   B. Best used in small, populated areas
   C. Best used in areas with little or no light
   D. Lighting has no affect on lens type that should be used

REVIEW ANSWERS

1. **C** Protecting human life is the first and most important step in fire safety. Individuals should be told and then steps should be taken to suppress the fire.

2. **A** Class C is an electrical fire that should be suppressed with some type of gas (Halon or FM-200) or carbon dioxide, but not water.

3. **D** Access and audit logs are detective controls, while fences, locks, and security guards are all examples of preventive controls.

4. **C** Halon interferes with the chemical combustion of the elements within the fire.

5. **C** Mantraps route personnel through a double-door area where the individuals are subject to further identification and authentication processes.

6. **A** Security guards are the one control mechanism that offers discriminating judgment.

7. **B** The NIST standard states the critical areas should be illuminated with two-foot candles that reach eight feet in height.

8. **C** Vibration-detection devices are susceptible to false alarms and are better suited to be used inside a facility rather than outside.

9. **B** Moisture in the air can cause corrosion in electrical devices and the lack of moisture can cause static electricity.

10. **C**   Natural disasters, crime rates, and the proximity to a fire station are all legitimate issues that concern physical security. The proximity to downtown facilities is not usually considered as important as the other items.

11. **D**   Cipher locks are also known as programmable locks. They use keypads to control access into an area or facility.

12. **C**   Water and gas should flow out of a facility for safety reasons and should be able to be terminated from within the building.

13. **A**   CCTV systems should not be used by themselves or solely depended upon, thus they should be used with other controls. Lighting is important to ensure that the proper depth of the items being monitored is provided. The type of lens that should be used correlates to the lighting of the environment and the size of the coverage required.

Telecommunications and Networking Security

ETA	NEWBIE	SOME EXPERIENCE	EXPERT
	6 hours	4 hours	3 hours

This is the largest chapter in the book and for good reason. Telecommunications and networking are enormous beasts considering the multiple technologies, protocols, devices, and services that they encompass. Throw in the added task of securing these beasts, and you should have your hands full for a while. Let's start with a simple definition. Telecommunications is defined as the electrical transmission of data between systems, whether it is through analog, digital, or wireless communication medium. The data can flow across copper wires, fiber, or airwaves and can take place within a company's network, on a cable company's infrastructure, go through the telephone company's public-switched telephone network, or through a service provider's fiber cables, switches, and routers. There are definitive lines drawn within the media used for transmissions, technologies, protocols, and whose equipment is being used. But, these definitive lines get a little blurry when you look at how data from a workstation flows through a complex path of Ethernet cables, through to a router that divides the company's network and the rest of the world, into and out of an ATM switch, through a mysterious cloud in the sky (actually it's underground), onto another company's network, through their router, and finally arriving at another user's workstation within seconds. I also didn't mention that the data would be converted, encrypted, and multiplexed several times taking on the many different names from datagram, to packet, to cell and so on. I know, "blurry" was an understatement. This is why the chapter is so long. Have no fear though; it won't be blurry much longer! Put on your glasses, pull up a comfortable chair, and get ready to see things more clearly.

Objective 5.01 TCP/IP Suite

Before any of the copper wires, multiport switches, or complex routers can work, something has to tell the data how to move across the network. Let's face it, you can have all the expensive hardware and infrastructure you want, but without flowing data, you have nothing but idle equipment and an unused network. Thankfully, some really smart people invented something called a *protocol*, which is a set of instructions or rules for systems and data to follow in order to communicate with one another. In this section, we discuss the set of rules designed specifically for moving data with a specific protocol suite: TCP/IP.

Transmission Control Protocol/Internet Protocol (TCP/IP) is a suite of protocols that governs the way data travels from one device to another. It has two main components, TCP and IP, although there are other protocols that make up this suite. The protocols within the TCP/IP suite work together to break the data passed down from the application layer into pieces that can be moved along a network. Then, they work with other protocols to transmit the data to the destination computer and then reassemble the data back into a form that the application layer can understand and process.

Let's start with TCP. TCP is referred to as a *connection-oriented* protocol because handshaking takes place between the two systems that want to communicate. Just as people shake hands to introduce themselves, protocols perform handshakes as an introduction and as a negotiation to begin a connection. The negotiation includes agreeing upon how much data will be transmitted at a time, as well as sequence numbers, error detection, and correction techniques. Once the handshaking completes successfully, a virtual connection is set up between the two systems.

TCP uses ports to communicate with the upper OSI layers and to keep track of different conversations that take place at the same time. These ports have numbers, which are inserted into the header of the packet so the data message can be properly passed off to the correct protocol, which will eventually get to the user's application. Packets use address and port information to find their destination. The following are some of the "well-known" ports and the services that are usually bound to them:

- Ports 20 and 21   Used for FTP
- Port 25   Used for SMTP
- Port 161   Used for SNMP
- Port 80   Used for HTTP
- Port 23   Used for Telnet

A protocol that works along side TCP at the transport layer is User Datagram Protocol (UDP). While TCP ensures that packets are delivered to their destinations by handshaking, setting up a virtual connection, and using sequence numbers, UDP simply sends the data to the destination without ensuring that it actually got there. Because of this, UDP is referred to as a *best-effort* and *connectionless-oriented* protocol. TCP has many more advantages than UDP, but does require much more overhead to operate, so there are occasions when it makes sense to use UDP. For example, UDP would be a good choice for a server that sends out status messages to computers on a network segment at regular intervals. It is not critical that each system receives the message because another message will be sent out at the next interval. There is no reason to waste the overhead to run TCP in this case. On the other hand, SMTP is used to transmit e-mail messages and uses TCP because it needs to verify that the data is delivered, and if the destination does not acknowledge that the message was received, then the source computer will resend it.

Table 5-1 lists the major differences between TCP and UDP.

Travel Advisory

All connectionless-oriented protocols are referred to as "best-effort" protocols, not just UDP.

Travel Advisory

UDP is easier to spoof because it has no session identifiers such as sequence numbers or acknowledgments.

TABLE 5.1	Major Differences Between TCP and UDP	
Service	**TCP**	**UDP**
Reliability	Ensures that packets reach their destinations, returns ACKs when a packet is received, and is a reliable protocol.	Does not return ACKs and does not guarantee that a packet will reach its destination, and is an unreliable protocol.
Connection	Connection-oriented, thus it performs handshaking and creates virtual connections with destination computers.	Connectionless, thus it does no handshaking and does not set up a virtual connection.
Packet sequencing	Uses sequence numbers within packets to make sure that each packet within a message is received.	Does not use sequence numbers.
Congestion controls	The destination computer can tell the source if it is overwhelmed and to slow the transmission rate.	The destination computer does not communicate back to the source computer about the flow control.
Usage	Used when reliable delivery is required, as in e-mail and domain name service (DNS) zone transfers.	Used when reliable delivery is not required, as in streaming video and status broadcasts.
Speed and overhead	Uses a considerable amount of resources and is slower than UDP.	Uses fewer resources and is faster than TCP.

Internet Protocol (IP)

The term IP is thrown around a lot, but do many people really know what it is and what it does? This section should help explain its functionality.

Internet Protocol (IP) is the network layer protocol that provides routing services. The main task of IP is to support internetwork addressing and packet routing, meaning it figures out what path a packet should take to arrive at its destination. It is a connectionless protocol that envelopes data passed to it from the transport layer and addresses the packet with the source and destination IP addresses. IP is like the envelope that you put a letter in before you mail it with the necessary addressing information. The data is the letter and the network it travels over is analogous to the postal system.

We are currently using IP version 4, although IP version 6 has been developed and is waiting in the wings, but it hasn't been fully implemented yet. It provides more possible addresses, because addresses are 128 bits in length, whereas IP v4 uses addresses made up of 32 bits. It adds quality of service functionality and includes IPSec capabilities. The IP version 4 address scheme is broken down into the following address classes:

- Class A 1.0.0.0   126.255.255.255
- Class B 128.0.0.0   191.255.255.255
- Class C 192.0.0.0   223.255.255.255
- Class D 224.0.0.0   239.255.255.255—multicasting
- Class E 240.0.0.0   254.255.255.255—future use

Networks

A *local area network* (LAN) is a network that allows for shared communication and resources in a relatively small area. Usually, a LAN is the internal network within a company or within a building. A LAN is defined by its physical medium, networking protocols, and media access technology. For example, a LAN could use 10Base-T cabling, TCP/IP protocols, and Ethernet media access technology to allow users in the same building to communicate with each other.

A *metropolitan area network* (MAN) is usually a backbone that connects businesses to WANs, the Internet, and other businesses within a city. What differentiates a LAN from a MAN is distance and the protocols used to transport data. For example, a LAN may be one internal corporate network using IPX/SPX, and a MAN could be a network connecting that LAN to another LAN using Switched Multimegabit Data Service (SMDS). A majority of today's

MANs use Synchronous Optical Network (SONET) or FDDI rings provided by the telephone companies and service providers.

The only thing left is the outside world, which is where the *wide area network* (WAN) comes into play. A WAN is a technology used when data needs to travel over a larger geographic area. When a computer on one network needs to communicate with a network on the other side of the country or in a different country altogether, it uses a wide area network. A WAN will use different protocols and technologies to get the data across these distances, as in frame relay, X.25, and ATM.

Intranets and Extranets

Most companies today have developed intranets and extranets for their employees, customers, or partners to access. Intranets use the same type of technologies used on the Internet. Web-based technologies use the TCP/IP protocol suite. Web pages are written in Hypertext Markup Language (HTML) or Extensible Markup Language (XML) and are accessed via HTTP. Web technologies and their uses have exploded in functionality, capabilities, and popularity.

An *intranet* allows companies to provide the same information to all employees in a standardized format, provides the users with working environments, and allows the use of Web servers and Web browsers to access company data and perform tasks.

An *extranet* extends outside the bounds of the company to allow two or more companies to share common information and resources. Business partners commonly set up extranets to allow for business-to-business communication to take place. Many times trading partners use *Electronic Data Interchange* (EDI), which provides structure and organization to electronic documents, orders, invoices, purchase orders, and data flow. EDI provides robust communication and confirmation that messages have been sent and read, and it supplies receipts indicating that the message has been properly delivered. Companies that want EDI provided and maintained for them would purchase a value add network (VAN), which just means a third-party company ensures that all necessary parts of the EDI are customized for the customer's needs and mailboxes can be provided for companies to use to communicate with other companies. Usually, suppliers use these mailboxes so that their customers can submit purchase orders.

When two networks are connected, as in extranets, there is usually a difference in security policies, technologies, security levels, and discipline on each side. It is important that the extranet does not introduce any vulnerabilities or possible security compromises. Each company has a responsibility in providing a certain level of protection so that connecting companies are not negatively affected. This is referred to as *downstream liability*. Just like other things seem to fall down hill, so do liabilities, so companies need to be sure to practice due care in these situations.

Objective 5.02 Cabling and Data Transmission Types

An important part of data travel is understanding the types of cabling and media that are being used. Just as people use umbrellas and raincoats to protect themselves in a rainstorm, we can use cabling to protect data from motor noise, magnetic forces, fluorescent lighting, and electrical devices. Electrical signals travel as voltage through cables and can be negatively affected by these kinds of disturbances. This is the very reason that there are cable standards that indicate what cable type should be used in specific environments, shielding, transmission rates, and distances.

Cabling has bandwidth and data rate values associated with it. Although these two terms are related, they are also very different. The bandwidth of a cable indicates the highest frequency range that it uses. For instance, 10Base-T uses 10 MHz and 100Base-TX uses 80 MHz. This is different than the actual amount of data that can be pushed through a cable. The data rate is the actual data throughput of a cable after compression and encoding has been used. For example, 10Base-T has a data rate of 10 Mbps and 100Base-TX has a data rate of 100 Mbps. So, the bandwidth can be thought of as the size of the pipe, and the data rate is the actual amount of data going through that pipe.

Coaxial Cable

Just about everyone has seen a coaxial cable at one time or another. If you're not sure, go look behind your TV and you'll probably find one. *Coaxial* cabling has a copper core, which is surrounded by a shielding layer and grounding wire, as shown in Figure 5-1. This is all encased within a protective outer jacket. Coaxial cable is more resistant to electromagnetic interference (EMI), provides a higher bandwidth, and has longer cable lengths than twisted-pair cabling. So why is twisted-pair more popular? Twisted-pair is cheaper, easier to work with, and the move to switched environments that allows for hierarchical wiring schemes has overcome the cable length issue of twisted-pair cables.

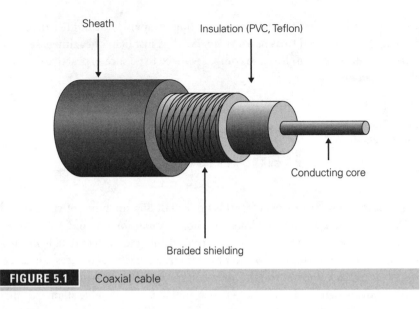

Sheath

Insulation (PVC, Teflon)

Conducting core

Braided shielding

FIGURE 5.1   Coaxial cable

The two main types of coaxial cables used within LAN environments are the 50-ohm cable (used for digital signaling) and 75-ohm cable (used for high-speed digital signaling and analog signaling). The coaxial cables types are

- 10Base-2 (thinnet) or RG58; segment limited at 185 meters
- 10Base-5 (thicknet), RG8, or RG11; segment limited at 500 meters

Twisted-Pair Cable

Twisted-pair cabling has insulated copper wires that are surrounded by an outer protective jacket. If the cable has an outer foil shielding, it is referred to as *shielded twisted-pair* (STP). The shielding provides added protection from radio frequency and electromagnetic interference. Another type of twisted-pair cabling which does not have this extra outer shielding is called *unshielded twisted-pair* (UTP) wiring. STP is less vulnerable to interference, cross talk, and eavesdropping.

The cable contains copper wires that twist around each other, as shown in Figure 5-2. This twisting of the wires protects the signals they carry and prolongs the signal's strength, allowing it to reach further distances. Each wire forms a balanced circuit because the voltage in each pair uses the same amplitude, just with opposite phases.

The tighter the twisting of the wires, the more resistant the cable is to interference and attenuation. UTP has different categories of cabling that have different

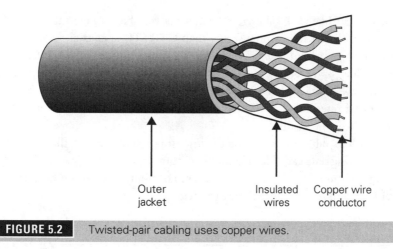

Outer jacket | Insulated wires | Copper wire conductor

FIGURE 5.2   Twisted-pair cabling uses copper wires.

characteristics. One of the characteristics that differentiate the categories from each other is how tightly the wires are twisted.

Copper cabling has been around for many years; it is inexpensive and well understood. A majority of the telephone systems today use copper cabling with the rating of voice-grade. Twisted-pair is the preferred network cabling, but it also has its drawbacks. Copper actually resists the flow of electrons, which causes a signal to degrade after it has traveled a certain distance. This is why there is a need for recommended cable lengths. Copper also radiates energy, which means that information can be monitored and captured by intruders.

Coaxial cabling and twisted-pair cabling are used in different areas and offer different advantages. Coaxial is typically used in *broadband*, where the cable carries several channels, as in cable TV. However, it can also transmit data using a *baseband* method, where the cable carries only one channel. Coaxial offers much higher performance than twisted-pair, but it is also much more expensive. Along with being used for residential phone systems, twisted-pair cabling is used extensively in LAN environments due to its low cost and ease of use.

Fiber

Twisted-pair and coaxial cabling use copper wires as their data transmission media, but *fiber-optic* cables use a type of glass. The glass carries light waves, which represent the data that is being transmitted. The glass core is surrounded by a protective cladding and is completely encased within an outer jacket.

Because of the use of glass, fiber-optic cabling has higher transmission speeds that can travel over longer distances and is not as affected by attenuation and EMI interference when compared to cabling that uses copper. It does not radiate signals like UTP cabling, either, and is very hard to tap into. Thus, fiber-optic cabling is much more secure than UTP, STP, or coaxial.

So fiber optic sounds like the way to go; why even bother with UTP, STP, and coaxial? Fiber-optic cabling is extremely expensive and very hard to work with. It is usually used in backbone networks and environments that require the high data transfer rates that it can deliver. Most networks use UTP and connect to a backbone, which uses fiber.

Fiber-optic cables can experience *dispersion*, which means that the light pulses carrying data can "bleed" into each other or some light rays arrive at the destination at different times. This is more common when using fiber with a larger core, and it can reduce cable distance.

> ### Exam Tip
> Fiber is the most secure of the different cables because it is hard to tap into and does not radiate signals.

Cable Issues

Noise on a line is usually caused by surrounding devices or by the characteristics of the environment. This noise can be caused by motors, computers, copy machines, florescent lighting, or even microwave ovens. It is referred to as background noise and can combine with the data being transmitted over the cable and distort the signal, as shown in Figure 5-3. The more noise that interacts with the cable, the more likely the receiving end will not receive the data in the form that was originally transmitted

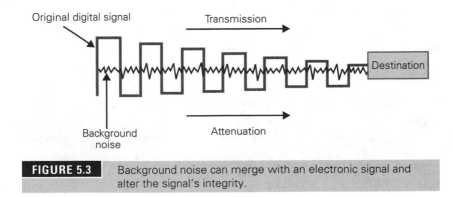

FIGURE 5.3 Background noise can merge with an electronic signal and alter the signal's integrity.

Attenuation is the loss of signal strength as it travels. The longer a cable is, the more attenuation will be introduced, and thus, the signal that is carrying data will deteriorate. Attenuation effects increase with higher frequencies. So, 100Base-TX at 80 MHz has a higher attenuation rate than 10Base-T at 10 MHz. This means that cables used to transmit data at higher frequencies should have shorter cable runs to ensure that attenuation does not become an issue. Attenuation can also be caused by cable breaks and cable malfunctions. This is why cables should be tested. If a cable is suspected of attenuation problems, testers can inject signals at the front end and read the results at the back end.

Cross talk is when electrical signals of one wire spill over to another wire. When the different electrical signals mix, their integrity lessens and there is a higher chance of data corruption. UTP is much more vulnerable to cross talk than STP or coaxial because it does not have the extra layers of shielding for protection.

Fire Ratings

Just like buildings must meet certain fire codes, so must certain wiring schemes. A lot of companies string their network wires in drop ceilings, (the space between the ceiling and the next floor). Network cabling in these hidden places, or plenum spaces, become a much greater fire hazard and must meet specific fire rating criteria to ensure that they will not produce and release harmful chemicals in the event of a fire.

Nonplenum cables usually have a polyvinyl chloride (PVC) jacket covering; *plenum-rated cables*, which should be used in drop ceilings, have jacket covers made of fluoropolymers. When setting up a network or extending an existing network, it is important to know which wire types are required in which situation.

There are several things to consider when choosing cabling for a network. The cabling needs to fit the needs of the company and associated network: cost, ease of handling, possible signal interference, distance of cable runs, necessary speed of transmission, security, and fire rating.

Broadband and Baseband

Broadband transmissions divide a cable into channels so that different types of data can be sent at the same time. As mentioned earlier, coaxial cable is used extensively in the broadband cable television industry. Several television channels are sent over one cable using this technology. The types of broadband communication systems available today are leased lines (T1, T3), ISDN, ATM, digital subscriber line (DSL), broadband wireless, and CATV.

Baseband uses the full cable for its transmission permitting only one signal to be sent at a time. The signals, or currents, hold binary information. High voltage usually represents the binary value of 1, while the low voltage usually represents the binary value of 0. The actual voltage interpretation depends upon the media access technology being used and its signaling structure.

Signals

In order for the data to get from one place to another, it can go through many conversions and transformations. One form that it can take on is called a signal, and there are two types that we cover: analog and digital.

Analog transmission signals are continuously varying electromagnetic waves that can be carried over air, water, twisted-pair, and coaxial or fiber-optic cable. Through a process of modulation, the analog signal is combined with a carrier signal on a specific frequency. The modulation of a signal differs in amplitude (height of the signal) and frequency (number of analog waves in a defined period of time). This means that data is "put on the back" of a carrier signal and it is the different carrying signals that provide radio stations, frequency ranges, and communication channels. (You can think of the signal as the horse and the data as the cowboy.) Each radio station is given a certain carrier signal to use for its transmission. This is how there can be three different country music stations on three different radio channels.

Computers use *digital signals* when moving data internally from one component to another component over a network. When this computer is connected to a telephone line, a modem (modulate/demodulate) must translate this digital data into an analog signal, because this is what is expected and used on the telephone lines. The modem actually modulates the digital data onto an analog signal (places the cowboy on the horse). Once the data reaches the destination computer, it must be transformed back into a digital state by the destination modem.

Digital signals represent binary digits as electrical pulses. Each individual pulse is a signal element and represents either a 1 (on) or a 0 (off). Bandwidth refers to the number electrical pulses that can be transmitted over a link within a second, and it is these electrical pulses that carry individual bits.

So why has digital become so prevalent today? Simple. Digital signals are more reliable, and because of their simple format (1s and 0s), it is much easier to extract noise from them, which produces a clean transmission. This allows for higher speeds and less data loss, which increases network performance.

Asynchronous and Synchronous

When two devices are not synchronized in any way and they need to talk, it is referred to as *asynchronous communications*. The sender can initiate a data transmission at any time, and the receiver must always be ready. In contrast, *synchronous communications* takes place between two devices that are synchronized, usually via a clocking mechanism.

Modems use asynchronous data transmissions. Because the data can travel at any time and be any length, there must be stop and start deliminators to tell the receiving end when to start processing a request and when to stop. Each character, which is really just a string of 1s and 0s, has a "start-of-character" bit and a "stop" bit before and after each character. This produces a lot of overhead and extra bits, but is necessary in asynchronous communications.

Synchronous communications, on the other hand, transfers data as a stream of bits. The synchronization can happen with both systems using the same clocking mechanism signal, which can be encoded into the data stream to let the receiver synchronize with the sender of the message. This synchronization needs to take place before the first message is sent, so the sending system will transmit a clock pulse to the receiving system, which translates into, "We will start here and work in this type of synchronization scheme."

> **Exam Tip**
>
> Asynchronous communication uses start and stop bits; synchronous does not.

Transmission Methods

Sometimes a packet needs to go to only one workstation, a set of workstations, or to all workstations on a particular subnet. If a packet needs to go from the source computer to one particular system, a *unicast* transmission method is used. Unicast is simply a one-to-one transmission.

If the packet needs to go to a specific group of systems, the sending system will use the *multicast* method. Multicast can best be described as a one-to-many transmission. A good example is receiving music from a radio station on a computer. Some computers have software that allows users to determine if they want to listen to different radio stations. Once they select their choice, the software must tell the NIC driver to not only pick up packets addressed to its specific IP address, but also pick up packets that contain a specific multicast address.

And if a system wants all computers on its subnet to receive a message, it will use the *broadcast* method. Broadcast is a one-to-all transmission.

The difference between broadcast and multicast is that in a broadcast everyone gets the data, and in a multicast only a few who have chosen to receive the data actually receive it. So an analogy is if you tell your friend something, that is a unicast; if you tell a group of friends, that is a multicast. If you scream your message to a whole neighborhood, that is broadcasting (and quite annoying).

Objective 5.03   LAN Technologies

To this point, we've figured out how data is moved along by protocols to be able to reach its destination, and we learned that certain types of cables make for a smoother ride and a happier datagram, but we haven't figured out how all of these multiple systems will communicate with one another. Because of the complexities in LAN environments, systems need a multitude of technologies, protocols, and interfaces to assure successful communications and interoperability. We will dig into how this takes place through media access technologies, but first let's look at how we should physically connect computers and network devices.

Network Topologies

The actual physical arrangement of computers and devices is called a *network topology*. Topology refers to the manner in which a network is physically connected, and it shows the layout of resources and systems. There is a difference between the physical network topology and the logical network. A logical network "sits on top of" the physical topology. For example, a network can be configured as a physical star, but work logically as a ring. The systems are all plugged into a central device (the star), but communicate as though they are connected in a ring configuration. This is because the physical star is at the physical layer and the logical ring resides at the data link layer and is not restricted by physical cabling.

There's a lot to think about when trying to decide what type of topology to use in a network. Some things to consider are how nodes are supposed to interact, the protocols being used, the types of applications available, reliability, expandability, physical layout of the facility, fault tolerance, existing wiring, and the technologies that have been implemented. Whew! That's a lot to consider, but it's important to know that choosing the wrong topology or combination of topologies can negatively affect the network's performance, productivity, and growth possibilities.

In a simple *bus topology*, a single cable runs the entire length of the network with nodes attached to it at drop points. Data communications transmit the length of the medium, and each packet transmitted is looked at by all nodes. Each node will decide to accept, process, or ignore the frame.

There are two main types of bus topologies: linear and tree topologies. The *linear bus topology* has the single cable with nodes attached to it. A *tree topology* has branches from the single cable, and each branch can contain many nodes. In simple implementations of a bus topology, if one workstation fails, other systems can be negatively affected because of the interdependencies between the nodes. And because all nodes are connected to one main cable, the cable itself becomes a potential single point of failure.

A *ring topology* has a series of devices connected by unidirectional transmission links. These links form a closed loop and do not connect to a central system as in a star topology. In a physical ring formation, each node is dependent upon the preceding nodes. In very simple networks, if one system failed, all other systems can be negatively affected because of this interdependence. Today, most networks have redundancy in place or other mechanisms that will protect the network as a whole from being affected by one workstation that is on the fritz. However, this possibility does still exist. A ring formation is usually used in LAN and WAN networks. A ring backbone is a high-speed network that connects many slower speed networks.

In a *star topology*, all nodes connect to a central hub or switch with their own dedicated link. This central hub needs to provide enough throughput to support the nodes and eliminate any bottlenecking in the network. Because a central device is required, it is a potential single point of failure, thus redundancy may need to be put into place. Hubs and switches can be configured in flat or hierarchical implementations, which allows larger organizations to use them.

When one workstation fails on a star topology, it does not affect other systems as in a ring or bus topology. Each system is not as dependent upon each other as they are dependent upon the central-connection device.

It could be said that a *mesh topology* is a mess, although people in charge of these types of networks would wholeheartedly disagree. So to avoid any squabbles, the proper definition of a mesh topology is when all systems and re-sources are connected to each other in a way that does not follow the uniformity of the previous topologies. It is a network of interconnected routers and switches that provide multiple paths to all the nodes on the network. This provides a greater degree of complexity and redundancy than the other types of topologies. A *full mesh topology* has every node connected to every other node, which provides a great degree of redundancy. If one link fails, the communications can use any of the alternate paths available to it.

A *partial mesh topology* does not have every node connected to each other and may be used to connect full-mesh networks. The Internet is an example of a partial mesh topology.

Media Access Technologies

Media access technologies deal with how computers and devices will format their data to be sent over a specific type of media, how errors will be detected and corrected, the maximum transmission unit (MTU) size of frames, and how proper sharing of the LAN cabling will take place. Access methods define how computers will gain access to the shared network in a way that does not interfere with other computers' transmissions. Each participating entity needs to know how to properly communicate so that all other systems will understand the transmissions, instructions, and requests. This is taken care of by the different LAN media access technologies that work at the data link layer.

Ethernet

Ethernet is a LAN technology, which allows several devices to communicate on the same network by sharing the media. Ethernet usually uses a bus or star topology. It became the IEEE 802.3 standard after being developed in the 1970s and commercially available in 1980. Ethernet has seen quite an evolution in its short history starting at purely coaxial cable installations (which worked at 10 Mbps) and then going to mostly twisted-pair cable (which works at 10Mbps, 100 Mbps, 1,000 Mbps, and 10 Gbps).

So how does Ethernet work anyway? It uses a media sharing process called *carrier sense multiple access with collision detection* (CSMA/CD). The devices on the network monitor the transmission activity, or carrier activity, on the wire so that they can determine when would be the best time to transmit data. Each node monitors the wire continuously and waits until the wire is free to transmit its data. When using the CSMA/CD access method, computers listen for the absence of a carrier tone on the cable, which indicates that no one else is transmitting data. If two computers sense this absence and transmit data at the same time, this is called a *collision*. If a computer puts frames on the wire and its frames collide with another computer's frames, it will abort its transmission and will alert all other stations that a collision just took place. Then, all stations will start a random collision timer that forces a delay before they attempt to transmit data again. This random collision timer is called the back-off algorithm.

When a system receives a message, it will send an acknowledgment indicating that the message was delivered successfully. If the sending system does not receive this acknowldgement, it will assume that the frame did not arrive and will retransmit the data.

Carrier sense multiple access with collision avoidance (CSMA/CA) is another access method where each computer signals its intent to transmit data before it actually does so. This tells other computers on the network not to transmit data right now or there is a possibility for collision.

> **Exam Tip**
>
> Any technology that requires devices to share one medium is referred to as a contention technology because all devices have to compete for the same resource.

Token Passing

Like Ethernet, *token passing* is a technology that allows for communication and sharing of networking resources. A token is a 24-bit control frame used to control which computers communicate at what intervals. The token is passed from computer to computer and only the computer that has the token can actually put data onto the wire. When a system is ready to transmit data, it has to wait to receive an empty token. The computer then fills the empty token with the source and destination addresses and its data and puts it onto the wire.

This type of network access method is used by Token Ring, FDDI, and ARCnet LAN technologies. Token passing methods do not cause collisions because only one computer can communicate at a time. Token Ring technology uses a token-passing technology with a star-configured topology. The ring part of the name pertains to how the signals travel, which is in a logical ring within a hub or centralized device. Each computer is connected to the centralized device, called a *multistation access unit* (MAU). So physically, the topology is a star, but the signals and transmissions move in a ring.

> **Exam Tip**
>
> The IEEE standard for Token Ring is 802.5.

Polling

Polling is a method of monitoring multiple devices or controlling network access transmission. In a polling environment, some systems are configured to be primary stations and others are secondary stations. At predefined intervals, the primary station will ask the secondary station if it has anything to transmit. This is the only time a secondary station can communicate. So basically, the secondary stations cannot speak unless spoken to.

Protocols

We've already discussed the TCP/IP protocol suite that handles the movement of data. However, there are many more protocols that have a wide array of functionality that deal with how systems communicate over networks. Several of the most widely used protocols are discussed in this section.

Address Resolution Protocol (ARP)

On a TCP/IP network, each computer and network device requires a unique IP address and also a unique hardware address. Each network interface card (NIC) has a unique physical address that is programmed into the read-only memory chips on the card by the manufacturer. The physical address is also referred to as the *media access control* (MAC) address. The network layer works with and understands IP addresses, and the data link layer works with and understands physical or MAC addresses.

So how do these two types of addresses work together? When data comes from the application layer, it goes to the transport layer for sequence numbers, session establishment, segmenting, and whatever needs to take place. The data is then passed to the network layer, where routing information may be added to the packet, and the source and destination IP addresses are inserted into a header. Then, it goes to the data link layer, which must find the MAC address and add it to the header portion of the frame. When a frame hits the wire, it knows only what MAC address it is heading towards. At this lowest layer of the OSI model, the mechanisms do not even understand IP addresses. So, if a computer cannot resolve the IP address passed down from the network layer to the corresponding MAC address, it cannot communicate with the destination computer.

Travel Advisory

MAC addressing is used only to forward frames on the same network segment. IP addresses are used for routing across network segments.

MAC and IP addresses must be properly mapped so that they can be correctly resolved. This happens through the *Address Resolution Protocol* (ARP). When the data link layer receives a data packet, the network layer has already attached the destination IP address to it. But, the data link layer cannot understand the IP address and invokes the ARP for help. ARP broadcasts a frame that requests the MAC address corresponding with the destination IP address. Each computer on the subnet receives this broadcasted frame but only the computer with the destination IP address will respond with its MAC address. ARP then adds the hardware address onto the frame and passes it onto the physical layer, which allows the frame to hit the wire and go to the destination computer. ARP keeps track of these addresses in a table for a predefined amount of time.

Beware, however, ARP tables are not immune to attacks. Sometimes attackers alter a system's ARP table so that it contains incorrect information. This is called *ARP table poisoning*. ARP does not have authentication capabilities, so an attacker can send ARP replies, which can put her own destination address into ARP tables in order to receive messages that were intended for others, as shown in Figure 5-4.

Reverse Address Resolution Protocol (RARP)

There are a few different ways for a computer to receive its IP addresses when it first boots up. If it has a statically assigned address, nothing needs to happen. If a computer depends upon a Dynamic Host Control Protocol (DHCP) server to assign it the right IP address, it will boot up and make a request to the DHCP server. The DHCP server will then assign the IP address, and everyone is happy and healthy. But what if the environment has diskless workstations, meaning they have no operating system?

Diskless workstations have just enough code to know how to boot up, broadcast for an IP address, and may have a pointer to the server that holds its operating system. The diskless workstation does know its hardware address, however, so it broadcasts this information so that a server can assign it the correct IP address. As with ARP, *Reverse Address Resolution Protocol* (RARP) frames go out to all systems on the subnet. But, only the RARP server will respond. Once the RARP

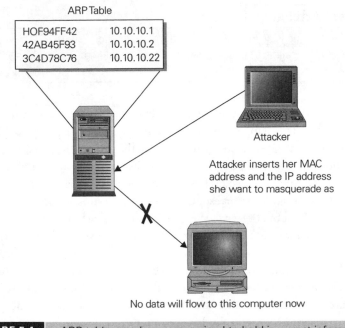

ARP Table

HOF94FF42	10.10.10.1
42AB45F93	10.10.10.2
3C4D78C76	10.10.10.22

Attacker

Attacker inserts her MAC
address and the IP address
she want to masquerade as

No data will flow to this computer now

FIGURE 5.4 ARP tables can be compromised to hold incorrect information.

server receives this request, it finds the IP/hardware address match in its table and then sends a message containing the IP address back to the requestor.

Boot Protocol

BOOTP was created after RARP to enhance the functionality that RARP provided for diskless workstations. The BOOTP protocols can retrieve the computer's IP address from the BOOTP server, the name server address for future name resolutions, and the default gateway address. BOOTP usually provides more functionality to diskless workstations than RARP.

Switches and routers may also use BOOTP as an external service to retrieve their configuration information. The BOOTP server is seen as a trusted source for a system's boot up information, and if this data comes from this trusted entity, the device can be assured that the configurations have not been modified.

> **Exam Tip**
>
> ARP knows the IP address and finds the MAC address. When using RARP or BOOTP, the station knows its MAC address and needs to find its IP address.

Internet Control Message Protocol (ICMP)

The *Internet Control Message Protocol* (ICMP) is basically IP's message boy. ICMP, a protocol within the TCP/IP suite, delivers status messages, reports errors, replies to certain requests, reports routing information, tests connectivity, and can be used to troubleshoot problems on IP networks.

The most commonly understood use of ICMP is the Ping and Traceroute utilities. When a person wants to test the connectivity to another system, he may ping it, which sends out ICMP ECHO packets. When the user sees replies on his screen from the Ping utility, this is really ICMP REPLY packets that are responding to the ECHO packets. If a reply is not returned within a predefined time period, the Ping utility sends more ECHO packets. If there is still no reply, Ping indicates that the host is unreachable.

ICMP can indicate when there are problems with a specific route and recommends better routes to devices based on the overall health and congestion of the network. Routers also use ICMP to send messages to indicate that specific packets could not be delivered.

Other TCP/IP Protocols

Here is a list of other protocols within the TCP/IP protocol suite:

- **Simple Network Management Protocol (SNMP)**   Allows for remote network monitoring and status checks on network devices. The manager component periodically polls the agent on the actual device and presents the administrator with an overview of the network. If something goes wrong, the agent can send a trap message to the manager. Community strings are used as passwords. The public community string allows SNMP data to be viewed and the private community string allows for the SNMP data to be viewed and modified.

- **Simple Mail Transfer Protocol (SMTP)**   It is used to send and receive electronic mail. Mail agents send the mail to mail servers, and the server makes sure the mail reaches its destination. SMTP specifies how two mail servers interact and the type of controls they use to transfer mail.

- **Line Printer Daemon (LPD)**   LPD is used with a line printer program (LPR) to allow users to send print jobs to a printer that is not directly connected to their computers. LPD maintains the print jobs in the print queue and sends them to the actual printer device.

- **Network File System (NFS)**   NFS provides file sharing functionality between two different file systems that would not otherwise be able to communicate.
- **Trivial File Transfer Protocol (TFTP)**   TFTP is a file transferring protocol with much less functionality when compared to FTP. It cannot implement any authentication or encrypt data, thus it is an insecure protocol.
- **File Transfer Protocol (FTP)**   FTP allows file transfers to take place between two systems, but cannot execute files as programs. Data and passwords are sent in clear text.
- **Telnet**   Terminal emulation software that allows a remote user to access files and resources on a remote computer.

> **Travel Advisory**
>
> SNMP version 1 passes community strings in clear text, which can be easily sniffed and used.

Objective 5.04   Networking Devices and Services

There are several types of devices used in LANs, MANs, and WANs. Understanding how these devices communicate with one another is an important part of securing a network, not to mention a part of the CISSP exam. The differences in these devices lie in their functionality, capabilities, intelligence, and network placement.

Repeater

A *repeater* provides the simplest type of connectivity because it only repeats and amplifies electrical signals between cable segments. A repeater extends a network because it receives data from one cable segment and transmits it onto another segment. Signals lose strength with distance (attenuation) and need to be amplified. A repeater, which is located in the physical layer, amplifies the signal and serves as an add-on device to extend the network over a greater distance.

Repeaters are also known as line conditioners because some of them can actually clean up the signals that they are repeating. But if a repeater is amplifying an analog signal, it will also amplify any noise or distortion that is present in the signal, so the distortion is also amplified.

The repeater has no true intelligence. Their functions are simple: signal repeating, strengthening, and conditioning.

Local Lingo

A device used to connect multiple LAN devices, also referred to as a multiport repeater or concentrator, works at the physical layer.

Bridge

A *bridge* is also a LAN device used to connect different LAN segments. But unlike the repeater, a bridge works at the data link layer and makes decisions on what port a frame should be sent out of based on MAC addresses. When a frame comes to a bridge, the bridge will determine if the MAC address is on the local network segment or not. If the MAC address is not on the local segment, the bridge will forward it onto the correct network segment.

A bridge is also used to divide overburdened networks into smaller segments to ensure better use of the bandwidth and traffic control. It extends the LAN and amplifies the signal like the repeater, but the bridge is an intelligent device also. The functions of the bridge are outlined here:

- Segments a large network into smaller, more controllable pieces.
- Performs forwarding and filtering based on MAC addresses.
- Joins different types of network links while retaining the same broadcast domain.
- Isolates collision domains within the same broadcast domain.
- Bridging can take place locally within a LAN or remotely with two distant LAN's.
- Some bridges translate between protocol types.

Switches

Switches actually combine the functionality of a hub and the functionality of a bridge. It amplifies the electrical signal, like a hub, and has the built in circuitry and intelligence of a bridge. A switch is a multiport device that provides connections for individual computers, network devices, hubs, or other switches. Any device connected to one port can communicate directly to a device connected to another port with its own virtual private link.

How is this different than how devices communicate using a bridge or a hub? Well, when a frame comes to a hub, the hub will send it out through all of its ports. When a frame comes to a bridge, the bridge will send it to the port that the destination network segment is connected to. When a frame comes to a switch, it will send the frame directly to the destination computer, thus there is a reduction of traffic.

On Ethernet networks, computers have to compete for the same shared network medium. Each computer must listen for activity on the network and transmit its data when it thinks the coast is clear. This contention and resulting collisions cause traffic delays and use up precious bandwidth. When switches are used, however, contention and collisions are no longer issues. Each switch port has dedicated bandwidth to the device attached to it and each port is connected to another port giving the two devices their own private link, which result in more efficient use of the network bandwidth and decreased latency.

Basic switches work at the data link layer and forward traffic based on MAC addresses. But today there are layer 3 and layer 4 switches, referred to *multilayer switches*, which have more enhanced functionality than the traditional layer 2 switches. These higher-level switches have routing functionality, packet inspection, traffic prioritization, and quality-of-service (QoS).

> **Travel Advisory**
>
> Switches make it harder to sniff traffic because broadcast and collision information is not available. This also makes it harder for network-based intrusion detection systems to detect attacks.

VLAN

Virtual LANs (VLANs) allow administrators to logically separate and group users based on resource requirements, security, or business needs instead of the standard physical location of the devices. When using hubs, bridges, and routers, users are grouped in a manner that is dictated by their physical location. VLANs allow users to be grouped logically instead of physically.

VLANs, which are located on the top of the physical layer, also allow an administrator to apply different security policies to different logical groups. This way, if tighter security is required for the payroll department, the administrator can develop a policy, add all payroll users to a specific VLAN, and apply the security policy only to the payroll VLAN, as shown in Figure 5-5.

Router

Repeaters work at the physical layer, bridges and switches work at the data link layer, and routers work at the network layer. As we go up one layer at a time, each

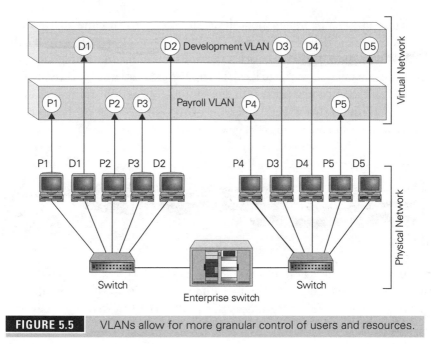

FIGURE 5.5   VLANs allow for more granular control of users and resources.

device has more and more intelligence and functionality. This is because each device can look deeper into the frame. A repeater just looks at the electrical signal. The bridge can look only at the MAC address within the header. But the router can peel back the first headers and look into the frame for IP addressing and other routing information. The deeper a device can look into a frame, the more complex decisions it can make. We will see later that gateways can look all the way to the core of the frame, which is the data that the user sent in the first place, not just addresses and routing information.

Routers are layer 3, or network layer, devices that are used to connect similar or different networks. (This means that a router can connect two Ethernet LANs or an Ethernet LAN to a Token Ring LAN.) A router is a device that has two or more interfaces and a routing table. The routing table provides paths for packets to take and gives traffic filtering capabilities and the capability to fragment packets if necessary. Because routers have more network-level knowledge, they can perform higher-level functions such as calculating the shortest and most economical path between the sending and receiving hosts.

Why are routers so intelligent? Because they have intelligent protocols (RIP, BGP, OSPF) to discover information about routes and changes that take place in a network. These protocols tell routers if a link has gone down, if a route is congested, and if another route is more economical. Protocols also update routing tables and indicate if a router is having problems or has gone down.

The router may be a stand-alone device or a computer running a networking operating system that is dual homed. One of the great features of a router is the *access control list* (ACL). When packets arrive at one of the router interfaces, the router compares that packet to its ACL. This list indicates what packets are permitted and what packets are denied. For example, an administrator may block all packets coming from the 10.10.12.0 network, any FTP requests or any packets headed towards a specific port on a specific host.

> **Exam Tip**
>
> Routers versus bridges: Routers work at the network layer and filter packets based on IP addresses. Bridges work at the data link layer and filter frames based on MAC addresses. Routers will not, usually, pass on broadcast information. Bridges will pass on broadcast information.

Routers use routing protocols, which specify how to get packets to their destination and how routers should share information. The most commonly used routing protocols are routing information protocol (RIP), exterior gateway protocol (EGP), border gateway protocol (BGP), and open shortest path first protocol (OSPF).

> **Travel Advisory**
>
> Many routing protocols do not use authentication, thus their routing tables can be compromised. This can be done to maliciously reroute traffic or reduce availability.

Brouters

A *brouter* is a hybrid device that combines the functionality of a bridge and a router. A brouter can understand and route certain protocols and will forward the rest. When a packet is received, it will first try to route the packet, but if this is unsuccessful and the packet cannot be properly routed, the device will step back and punt by forwarding the data based on its MAC address.

Gateway

A *gateway* is a general term for software running on a device that connects two different environments and acts as a translator for them and possibly restricts and controls their interactions. Usually, a gateway is needed when one environment speaks one language (protocol) that the other environment does not understand. The gateway can translate the IPX protocol packets to IP packets, convert mail from one mail format to another, and connect and translate different data link technologies like FDDI to Ethernet.

A gateway almost always works at the application layer because it needs to see a majority of the information within a packet and not just the address and routing information that a router or bridge requires. Gateways perform much more complex tasks than these types of connection devices. However, routers are often referred to as gateways when they connect two unlike networks (Token Ring and Ethernet) because the router has to translate between the data link technologies.

Summary of Devices

Table 5-2 shows the different devices covered in this section and points out their important characteristics.

TABLE 5.2	Summary of Devices	
Device	**OSI Layer**	**Functionality**
Repeater	Physical layer	Amplifies signal and extends networks.
Bridge	Data link layer	Forwards frames and filters them based on MAC addresses; forwards broadcasts traffic, but not collision traffic.
Router	Network layer	Separates and connects LANs creating internetworks; routers filter based on IP addresses, port numbers, and protocol type.
Brouter	Data link and network layers	A hybrid device that combines the functionality of a bridge and a router. A brouter can route packets and forward the frames it cannot successfully route.
Switch	Data link layer; more intelligent switches work at the network layer	Provides a private virtual link between communicating devices, allows for VLANs, reduces traffic, and impedes network sniffing.
Gateway	Applications layer (although different types of gateways can work at other layers)	Connects different types of networks, performs protocol and format translations.

Local Lingo

A message at the application layer is called "data" or "message." At the network layer, it is referred to as a "packet," and at the data link layer, it is a "frame." These names indicate at what stage the data encapsulation is at and what types of headers and trailers have been attached to the data. Also, a router routes packets and a bridge forwards frames because that is the layers they work at and functions they perform.

Firewalls

Firewall is probably the most common term used when information and network security is brought up. It's a well-known word, but not necessarily well understood.

Most companies have firewalls to restrict access into their network from Internet users. They may also have firewalls to restrict one internal network from accessing another internal network. An organizational security policy will give high-level instructions on acceptable and unacceptable actions as they pertain to security. The firewall should support that policy and have its own policy that is more granular in nature. Its policy dictates what services are accessible, what IP addresses and ranges are restricted, and what ports can be accessed.

The firewall is described as a choke point in the network where all traffic flows to, is inspected, and is potentially restricted. A firewall is actually a type of gateway that can be a router, computer, authentication server, or specialized hardware device. The firewall monitors packets coming in and out of the network and based upon its predefined rules, will discard these packets, repackage them, or redirect them.

Packet Filtering

Packet filtering is a security method of controlling what data can flow to and from a network. Packet filtering takes place by using access control lists (ACLs), which are created and applied to a router. The ACL is just lines of text, called rules, that the device will apply to each packet that it receives. These rules indicate what packets can be accepted and what packets should be denied.

This filtering is based on network layer information, which means the device cannot look too far into the packet itself. It can only make decisions based on header information, which is limited. Access decisions are based on source and destination addresses, source and destination port numbers, protocol type, and possibly flags within the headers themselves. The router cannot look at the actual data payload because it works only at the network layer.

The following are the pros and cons of packet filtering:

Pros

- Scaleable
- Provides high performance
- Application-independent

Cons

- Does not look into the packet past the header information
- Low security relative to other firewall types
- Does not keep track of the state of connections

Travel Advisory

Packet filtering cannot protect against mail bombs or similar attacks because it cannot read the content or data payload of the packet.

Proxy Firewalls

A proxy is a middleman that stands between two entities and decides whether these entities should really communicate to each other and how that dialog should take place. The *proxy firewall* is the middleman between a trusted and untrusted network. It will impersonate the destination computer while it looks for suspicious information. If the proxy decides that the packet is safe, it sends it onto the destination computer. When the destination computer replies, the message goes back to the proxy firewall, which repackages the packet with its own source address instead of the host system address on the internal network.

The proxy firewall is the only machine that directly talks to the outside world. This ensures that no outside computer has direct access to an internal computer and hides information about the company's addressing scheme and topology information. This also means that the proxy firewall is the only computer that needs a valid public IP address. The rest of the computers on the internal network can use private (nonroutable IP addresses on the Internet) addresses, because no computers on the outside will see their addresses anyway.

The real claim to fame for proxy firewalls is that they "break the connection" by not allowing untrusted systems to have direct connection to trusted internal systems. The firewall will accept a packet, make a copy of it, change the source address, and put it on the wire to the destination system. These steps help ensure that malformed packets or skillfully crafted packets cannot get through to the vulnerable internal computers. Because of this, they provide a higher level of protection than packet filters.

Just like the packet filtering firewalls, proxy firewalls also have a list of rules that are applied to packets. When the proxy firewall receives a packet, it compares it to this list of rules to see if the packet should be allowed or rejected.

There are two main types of proxy firewalls, application-level and circuit-level, explained next.

Application-Level Proxy Firewalls *Application-level proxies* inspect the entire packet and make access decisions based on the header information and the actual content of the packet. They understand different services and protocols and the commands that are used within them. For example, an application-level proxy can distinguish between an FTP GET command and an FTP PUT command and can make access decisions based on this type of information, which is more granular in nature when compared to what other firewall types use. Packet filtering firewalls can only allow or deny FTP requests as a whole, not the commands used within the FTP protocol.

However, one proxy is required per protocol or service because such a detailed understanding of the protocol and its command structure is required. A computer can have many different types of services and protocols (FTP, NTP, SMTP, Telnet, etc.), thus there must be one application-level proxy per service.

Application-level proxy firewalls provide the highest level of security because they allow for the greatest level of control, but can also drastically affect network performance because of the extra processing that is required.

Circuit-Level Proxy Providing application-level proxy services can be much trickier than it appears. The proxy must totally understand how specific protocols work, what commands are legitimate, and be aware of what applications use these protocols and services. This is a lot to know and requires many components of the protocol to be examined during the transmission of data. If the application-level proxy firewall does not understand a certain protocol or service, a *circuit-level proxy* can be used instead. The circuit-level proxy understands a wider variety of protocols because it makes access decisions based on header information; IP addresses, ports, protocol type, and protocol flags. Circuit-level proxy firewalls provide more flexibility, but less security.

The characteristics of each type are shown here:

Application-level proxy firewall

- One proxy is required for each protocol used.
- Makes access decisions based on header information and data payload contents.
- Provides more intricate control than circuit-level proxy firewalls.
- Reduces network performance.

Circuit-level proxy firewall

- Access decisions based on same type of information packet filters use.
- Does not require a proxy for each and every protocol.
- Does not provide the granular control that an application-level proxy firewall provides.
- Provides security for a wider range of protocols, thus is seen as more flexible.

If a circuit-level firewall makes access decisions based on the same type of information a packet filter uses, what is the difference between the two? A big difference between circuit-level proxy firewalls and packet filters is that the proxy actually breaks the connection (definition of a proxy) and the packet filtering device does not.

SOCKS   SOCKS is an example of a circuit-level proxy firewall that controls the data flow between internal and external systems. SOCKS requires clients to have proprietary software (SOCKS-ified) installed, and it offers additional services that many proxies do not, such as accounting, management, auditing, and security functionality.

Stateful Firewalls

Stateful firewalls keep track of actual dialogs between systems by using a state table to record each step of the communication process. The state table is like a scorecard keeping track of who said what when. This firewall type also makes decisions on what packets to allow or disallow, but their functionality goes a step farther. For example, a packet-filtering device may deny any UDP packets requesting service on port 25 on an internal server. A stateful firewall may have the rule to allow only UDP packets passage to the server if they are responses to packets the server previously sent out. This equates to, "You cannot send any UDP packets to this server unless it sent ones to you first and you are just replying to its request." Other types of firewalls do not have the intelligence and understanding of how dialogs take place between computers and could not make distinctions like this.

The following are characteristics of a stateful firewall:

- The firewall maintains a state table that tracks each and every communication channel.
- It provides a high degree of security and does not introduce the performance hit that proxy firewalls do.
- It is scaleable and transparent to users.
- It provides functionality for tracking connectionless protocols as in UDP.
- The state and context of the data in the packets are stored in the state table and updated continuously.

> **Exam Tip**
>
> Packet filtering is the first generation firewall, proxy is second generation, and stateful is the third generation of firewalls.

Firewall Architecture

A *dual-homed firewall* has at least two interfaces: one connected to an untrusted network and the other connected to an internal, trusted network. Firewalls can have multiple interfaces if they are connecting and controlling access to several networks or subnets.

Routing and forwarding needs to be disabled on the device acting as a dual-homed firewall because these services could send a packet on its way to its destination without passing it up to the firewall software for inspection. This means that a firewall administrator can configure ACLs, proxies, settings, or stateful configurations, but the packets would never be affected by these rules and instead just be put on the wire to their destinations.

When a packet from an untrusted network comes to the external NIC on a dual-homed firewall, the computer does not know what to do with it, so it passes it up to the firewall software. The software inspects it for legitimacy and makes decisions pertaining to if it should be allowed passage, dropped, or if an error should be sent back to the sender.

Learning about all the types of firewalls is one thing, but actually placing them in the proper position within the network is another thing. It can get a little tricky, but here is some general information that can help in putting together a secure firewall architecture.

Firewalls can be placed in different areas of a network for different reasons. They can be used as a choke point between internal and external networks, can be used to segment network sections and enforce access controls, and can be used to construct a *demilitarized zone* (DMZ) or a buffer zone between two networks.

> **Local Lingo**
>
> A DMZ is a network segment between a trusted and untrusted network that is created by firewall devices. These devices can be actual firewalls or screening routers.

The *bastion host* is a locked down system, meaning it has no unnecessary services or subsystems running, it has no third-party applications or utilities installed, it is patched, and has no unnecessary user accounts configured. All systems that are placed within the DMZ should be bastion hosts because they will be the first to be hammered on by curious attackers.

The bastion host(s) is the system that will be accessed by many entities trying to access or leave the network, thus it is a highly exposed device because it acts as the front line in a company's network and its existence is known to the Internet. In short, there can be no holes for an intruder to find within these systems, thus they must be tightly locked down and controlled.

A *screened host* is a firewall that is being protected by a screening packet filtering router. It receives data that has already passed through one level of security, which is the packet filtering on the router. This means a smaller amount of traffic will need to be processed by the firewall, which allows for it to do more detailed inspections on the packets themselves. This architecture provides two layers of protection and reduces the load of the firewall but does not provide a protective DMZ.

Traffic that comes in from the untrusted network is first filtered via packet filtering on the outer router. The traffic that makes it past this phase is then sent to the screened host firewall (bastion host system), which applies more rules to the traffic and drops the denied packets. After this phase, the traffic finally moves to the internal destination hosts. The screened host, the firewall, is the only device that receives traffic directly from the router. No traffic goes from the untrusted network, through the router, and into the internal network.

The *screened-subnet* approach provides more protection than a stand-alone firewall or a screened-host architecture because there are three devices that must be compromised before an attacker can get access to the internal network. In this configuration, there is an outer screening router, a firewall, and an interior screening router as shown in Figure 5-6.

This architecture sets up a DMZ between the two routers. The DMZ network functions as a small buffer zone isolated between the trusted internal and untrusted external networks. The outer and internal routers should have different configurations because each has a different focus on the protection it is providing. The outer router needs to allow traffic that is heading towards the systems within the DMZ and the internal network and the internal router applies much more strict rules only allowing traffic into and out of the internal network.

Once you've got the firewalls up and running, you're in the clear, right? Not necessarily. Unfortunately, once companies erect firewalls, they have a false sense of security. Firewalls are only one part of an overall security program, and many times

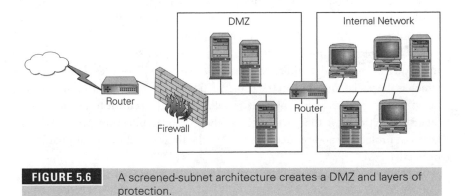

FIGURE 5.6   A screened-subnet architecture creates a DMZ and layers of protection.

they do not provide the necessary level of protection due to misconfiguration. The following list addresses some of the limitations of firewalls:

- Security is concentrated in one spot, versus a distributed approach that secures many different places within a network.
- Firewalls present a potential bottleneck to traffic flow.
- Most firewalls do not protect from viruses being downloaded or passed through e-mail.
- Firewalls provide little protection against the inside attacker.
- Firewalls do not automatically protect the modems that are used for remote connectivity.

Travel Advisory

If you are familiar with the items in this chapter already, you can tell we are giving an overview of the basics of these devices and technologies. Today, we have technologies that provide much more functionality than being described here, but we are providing you with what you will most likely see on the CISSP exam.

Firewall Administration

Administering firewalls can be a complex task. Most vulnerabilities are related to misconfigurations and improper monitoring of firewall devices and their findings and not reacting properly to activities that can take place. It is better to think ahead and plan for situations that could occur so that reactions will be beneficial and not carried out in a confusing and chaotic manner.

For example, if an incident occurs to the firewall device, it may need to be brought down temporarily. A smart approach in this situation is to disable Internet services until the firewall can be reconfigured and brought back online or to implement a backup firewall during the primary firewall's downtime. When reinstating the primary firewall, return it to its original state before the incident occurred to ensure that no insecure doorways have accidentally (or intentionally) been created during the incident, which may allow attackers into the environment.

The following is a list of best practices for firewall administration:

- There should be two firewall administrators (primary and secondary). The primary makes all of the changes to the firewall(s), and the secondary serves as a backup to the primary administrator.
- Contact information for both administrators should be available to the staff.

- Remote access for administrators should not take place over untrusted networks without strong authentication and a secure channel.
- The only accounts on a firewall with privileges to make changes should be the administrators.
- Configurations should be backed up at least monthly and stored on read-only media.
- A backup firewall may be required, ready to go online.
- Anomalies need to be recorded, reported, and investigated.

Remote Connectivity

We are slowly moving from our interior LAN devices, protocols, and technologies out into the big scary world. We will start off by looking at how remote sites and road warriors can connect to the LANs through dial-up connections, and the authentication mechanisms involved there. Then, we look at more secure connections, as in virtual private networks.

PPP

Point-to-Point protocol (PPP) is used to encapsulate messages and transmit them over a serial line, which is usually used for telecommunications. PPP can encapsulate many different types of protocols (IP, IPX, NetBUI), which allow two different networks to be connected by a serial line and still communicate with their native protocols.

PPP is used for dial-up connections and dedicated transmission links. So a PPP connection is established between the user's system and an Internet service provider (ISP), and the ISP connects the user to another network that could be his company's network or the Internet.

SLIP

PPP has, for the most part, replaced *Serial Line Internet Protocol* (SLIP). SLIP is an older protocol that was used for encapsulating data to be sent over serial lines, which is what PPP does. However, PPP has several capabilities that SLIP does not have:

- PPP implements header and data compression for efficiency and better use of bandwidth.
- PPP has error detection and correction.
- PPP supports different authentication methods.
- PPP can encapsulate protocols other than IP.

PPP supports different authentication methods that are used during the initial link establishment, which are PAP, CHAP, and EAP.

PAP

Password authentication protocol (PAP) is an authentication protocol used by remote users to provide identification and authentication information when attempting to access a network from a remote system. This protocol requires a user to enter a username and password before being authenticated. Unfortunately, PAP is one of the least secure ways of authenticating because the credentials are sent in clear text. This allows them to be easily captured by network sniffers. Although it is not recommended, some systems revert to PAP if they cannot agree on any other authentication protocol. PAP is also vulnerable to *replay attacks* because it uses a static username and password scheme. This means the attacker can resend the captured credentials and be authenticated to the network very easily.

CHAP

Challenge Handshake Authentication Protocol (CHAP) uses a challenge/response mechanism to authenticate users instead of sending a password over the wire. When a user requests to access a network, the authentication server responds with a challenge to the user, which is a random value. This challenge is encrypted with the use of a predefined password as an encryption key. The encrypted challenge value is then returned to the server for authentication. The server uses the user's password it has in its database and decrypts the response it received from the user. If the decryption takes place properly and the resulting value is the same value the server sent over in the first place, the server is assured that the user entered the correct password and authenticates.

Travel Advisory
Many times the password is actually hashed instead of encrypted, but the CHAP concept and steps are just the same.

The steps that take place in CHAP are depicted in Figure 5-7.

CHAP is not vulnerable to man-in-the-middle or replay attacks because it continues this challenge/response activity throughout the connection to ensure that the authentication server is still communicating with the authorized user.

EAP

Extensible Authentication Protocol (EAP) is different than PAP and CHAP in that it merely provides a framework for authentication to take place instead of the actual protocol itself. As the names states, it extends authentication possibilities from the norm and allows such things as one-time passwords, token cards, digital signatures, and biometrics to be used. Enabling EAP allows for more possibilities and flexibility with requesting different types of identification and authorization information from users.

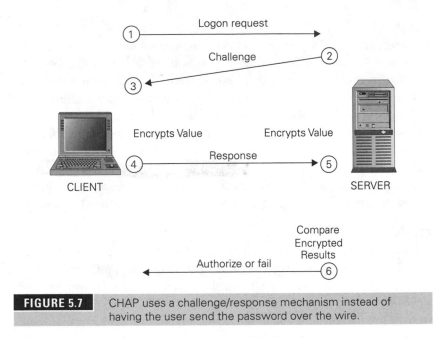

Logon request

Challenge

Encrypts Value   Encrypts Value

Response

CLIENT   SERVER

Compare
Encrypted
Results

Authorize or fail

FIGURE 5.7   CHAP uses a challenge/response mechanism instead of having the user send the password over the wire.

VPN

Virtual private network (VPN) is a popular technology that companies use to provide secure communication tunnels through untrusted networks. The connection is made private and secure by encryption and tunneling protocols, which we discuss in this section. Typically, VPN functionality is provided by firewall software, which then filters the traffic after it has been decrypted and before it is allowed into the internal network.

We look at the three protocols that can be used to provide VPN functionality: Point-to-Point Tunneling Protocol (PPTP), IPSec, and L2TP.

When a protocol provides tunneling functionality, it encapsulates a packet inside of another protocol. The tunneling protocol is usually needed to move data through a network that the original protocol does not understand. For example, if we needed to connect two sites that used IPX/SPX across the Internet, we would need to use a tunneling protocol that understood and could be routed on the Internet. Tunneling does not mean that data is encrypted by default. Encryption can be added, but some tunneling protocols do not encrypt data, but instead just move it through (or tunnel it) to the destination network.

PPTP

Point-to-Point Tunneling Protocol (PPTP) is a connection-oriented encapsulation tunneling protocol based on PPP. It works at the data link layer, and it allows a single point-to-point connection, usually between a client and a server. PPTP actually encrypts and encapsulates PPP packets, which creates the virtual private connection. PPTP does provide a level of security because it authenticates and encrypts data, but there are a few weaknesses. When the negotiation takes place, PPTP cannot encrypt all of the negotiation information because encryption is in the process of being invoked. So data that actually goes through the tunnel is protected, but some of the negotiation information is done in clear text and can be easily sniffed.

L2TP

Cisco had developed a tunneling protocol called Layer 2 Forwarding (L2F), which was later combined with the PPTP protocol. The result was *Layer 2 Tunneling Protocol* (L2TP). It is similar to PPTP in that it provides tunneling functionality over serial lines, but it does not provide encryption for the data it is tunneling. The differences between L2TP and PPTP are shown in Table 5-3.

IPSec

Internet Protocol security (IPSec) is a tunneling protocol with strong encryption and authentication methods used to create and maintain VPNs. IPSec is

TABLE 5.3	Difference Between Tunneling Protocols PPTP and L2TP
PPTP	**L2TP**
Can only run on top of IP networks because it is dependent upon that protocol.	L2TP, on the other hand, can run on top and tunnel through networks that use other protocols such as frame relay, the Internet, and ATM connections.
PPTP is an encryption protocol.	L2TP is not an encryption protocol, thus L2TP lacks the security to be called a true VPN solution. L2TP needs to be used in conjunction with IPSec to provide encryption services.

described in more detail in Chapter 6, but a list of its primary characteristics is shown here:

- Allows for multiple connections at the same time
- Provides secure authentication and encryption
- Can protect just the payload (transport mode) or the payload and the headers (tunnel mode)
- Supports only IP networks
- Focuses on a LAN-to-LAN communication rather than a dial-up protocol
- Works at the network layer
- Usually implemented by firewall software as VPN solutions

Network Services

A network service is a mechanism that is aware of network devices, resources, protocols, and services and knows how to communicate with them. Network services are the components that allow computers and devices to participate in a networked environment by tracking down the necessary objects that offer critical networking functionality. There is a long list of network services in use today, but we look at just two: DNS and NAT.

DNS

The *Domain Name Service* (DNS) is a method of resolving host names to IP addresses. Host names are used purely for people, not for the computers themselves. It is easier for us to remember www.msn.com than the actual IP address of this site. Because we understand and use host names, and the computer uses and understands IP addresses, there must be a mechanism that does the necessary mapping of the two, which is DNS.

The Internet, and most networking, is dependent upon DNS services. A DNS server is a collection of resource records that contain the necessary information to map host names to addresses, and these resource records are split into zones. One zone may contain all resource records for the marketing and accounting departments, and another zone may contain resource records for the administration, research, and legal departments. The DNS server that holds the files for one of these zones is said to be the *authoritative* name server for that particular zone.

For a message to actually get routed, the IP address is needed. When a user's computer needs to resolve a host name to an IP address, it looks to its TCP/IP settings to find out what DNS server it is configured to use. A request is sent and the DNS server checks its resource records and resolves the name to the corresponding address. This address is sent back to the requesting computer, which puts the correct address in the packet's header for routing purposes.

It is a good idea to have a *primary* and *secondary* DNS server for each zone for redundancy purposes.

Travel Advisory

DNS servers can be poisoned, where a resource record is modified to provide the client with an incorrect IP address. This will point the user to an incorrect system or Web site.

NAT

Unfortunately, IP addresses have become scarce (until the full adoption of IPv6) and expensive. One way of working around this problem is using *network address translation* (NAT), which allows a network that does not follow the Internet's addressing scheme to still have the ability to communicate over the Internet.

NAT hides internal addresses by forwarding only the source address of the NAT device within the frames that leave the network. So when a message comes from an internal computer with the address of 10.10.10.2, the message is stopped by the device running NAT. This device changes this private address (or non-Internet routable address) to a public address that will be recognized and properly routed on the Internet. This provides a level of protection because anyone on the external network (Internet) does not see any of the internal computers' addresses. This helps ensure that attackers will not be able to make direct connections to internal systems and makes it harder for the attacker to learn about a company's network.

Private address ranges are as follows:

- 10.0.0.0–10.255.255.255
- 172.16.0.0–172.31.255.255
- 192.168.0.0–192.168.255.255

Most NAT implementations are stateful, meaning they keep track of the communications between the internal and external hosts until the session is ended. The NAT device keeps state on these dialogs because it needs to remember the internal private IP address and port number so that it knows where to send the reply messages, as shown in Figure 5-8. This stateful characteristic is similar to stateful firewalls, but NAT does not perform scanning or filtering on the packets themselves to make access decisions.

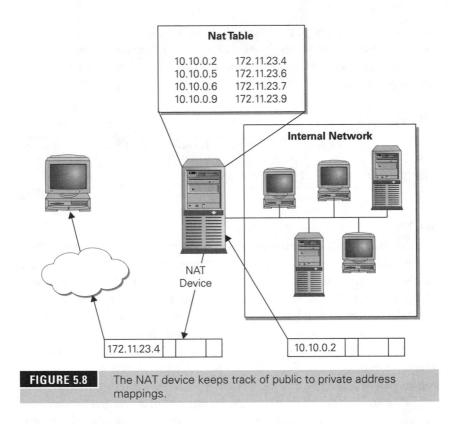

Nat Table

10.10.0.2   172.11.23.4
10.10.0.5   172.11.23.6
10.10.0.6   172.11.23.7
10.10.0.9   172.11.23.9

Internal Network

NAT
Device

| 172.11.23.4 | | | |

| 10.10.0.2 | | | |

FIGURE 5.8   The NAT device keeps track of public to private address mappings.

Travel Advisory

The public IP address used in this graphic was randomly chosen. It is being used only to explain the NAT concept.

Objective 5.05 **Telecommunications Protocols and Devices**

Now, we're getting somewhere. In this section, we dive into the telecommunications protocols and technologies that are being used today, and the different devices that interface with MAN and WAN media. We've already discussed the differences in functionality between LANs, MANs, and WANs. But we have yet to uncover how WAN networks really work and how they interact with other technologies.

FDDI

Fiber Distributed Data Interface (FDDI) is a high-speed, token-passing media access LAN and WAN technology with a data transmission speed of 100 Mbps. It is usually used as a fiber-optic backbone network because it has a unique fault-tolerance architecture and high data throughput capabilities. FDDI is made up of two rings. The primary ring has data traveling clockwise and is used for regular data transmission. The second ring transmits data in a counterclockwise fashion and is usually invoked only if the primary ring goes down.

> **Travel Advisory**
>
> Both rings can be used for data transmission if configured that way.

FDDI can be used as a LAN backbone network, as shown in Figure 5-9, or it can be used as a MAN technology that connects different LANs over a larger geographical area. In either scenario, the systems need to be connected to both rings, or devices need to be connected to both rings that allow for proper fail-over to take place if the primary ring goes down, as shown in Figure 5-9.

There is also a version of this technology that can work over UTP cabling called *Copper Distributed Data Interface* (CDDI).

> **Travel Advisory**
>
> FDDI-2 extends the functionality of FDDI and allows for voice, video, and data to be transmitted.

SONET

Synchronous Optical Network (SONET) is actually a standard for telecommunication transmissions over fiber-optic cables. SONET rings cover large areas that businesses can connect to via T1, fractional T1s, and T3 lines. SONET's main claim to fame is its ability to be self-healing; meaning that if there is a break in one of its lines due to an earthquake or a fiber-seeking backhoe, it can use a backup redundant ring to ensure that transmission continues.

SONET networks transmit voice and data over optical networks. Many times, slower-speed SONET networks feed into larger, faster SONET networks

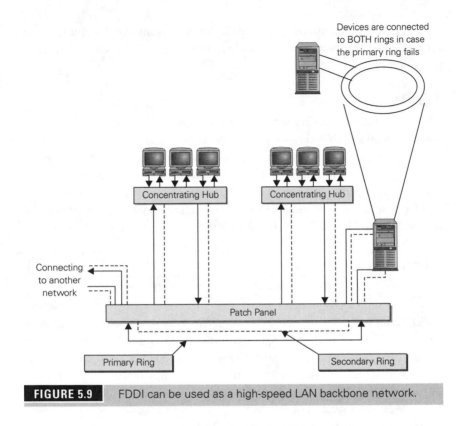

FIGURE 5.9 FDDI can be used as a high-speed LAN backbone network.

like streams flowing into a river. Figure 5-10 illustrates how different SONET rings are used to connect far-reaching LANs. This figure also shows how different types of data will be put onto different network types when it needs to be moved past the boundaries of a MAN, which would be getting into the WAN arena. Voice data would go over the telecommunications' network; Internet data-based data goes to a service provider's network; and cable TV data would be transmitted over satellite connections.

Dedicated Link

A *dedicated link* is also called a leased line or point-to-point link. It is a permanent connection between two sites. Dedicated links offer tremendous security, reliability, and QoS, but they are extremely expensive and provide no flexibility in connecting with other parties.

T-carriers are dedicated lines that can carry voice and data information over trunk lines. The most commonly used T-carriers are T1 lines that provide up to

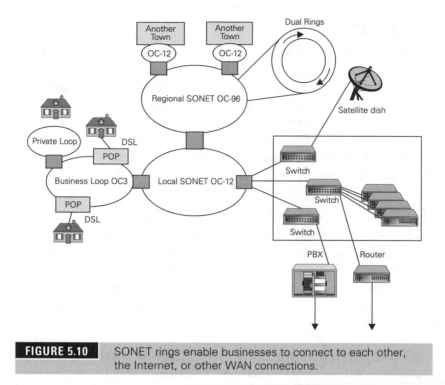

FIGURE 5.10   SONET rings enable businesses to connect to each other, the Internet, or other WAN connections.

1.544 Mbps and T3 lines that provide up to 45 Mbps in bandwidth. They are both digital circuits that multiplex several individual channels into a higher-speed channel. A *fractional* T line is a specified portion of a T1 line. These are used when the full bandwidth of a T1 is not needed.

Travel Advisory

T-carriers can offer confidentiality, but introduce a single point of failure.

Data is multiplexed onto these dedicated lines through *time-division multiplexing* (TDM). What does this multiplexing stuff really mean? Let's take a T1 line, which can multiplex up to 24 channels. If a company has a PBX connected to a T1 line, which in turn connects to the telephone company switching office, then 24 calls can be chopped up and placed on the T1 line and transferred to the switching office at once. If this company did not use a T1 line, they would have to have 24 individual twisted pairs of wire to handle this many calls at once.

CSU/DSU

Channel Service Unit/Data Service Unit (CSU/DSU) hardware is required when digital equipment will be connected to a telephone network, T1, and T3 lines. The DSU device converts digital signals from routers, bridges, and multiplexers into signals that can be transmitted over the telephone company's digital lines. The DSU device is the component that ensures that the voltage levels are correct and that information is not lost during the conversion. The CSU is the unit that connects to the telephone company's line. The CSU/DSU is not always a separate device and can be part of a networking device.

S/WAN

Secure WAN (S/WAN) was originally an initiative of RSA Security, which worked with many firewall and protocol vendors in the effort to build secure firewall-to-firewall connections through the Internet. S/WAN is based on VPNs that are created with IPSec. IPSec is the newest and most secure tunneling protocol because it provides hard-to-break encryption, gives the option of encrypting the header information (not just the payload data), and it incorporates authentication based off of cryptographic keys.

The idea was to create industry standards that all firewall vendors would follow to increase interoperability between the different products. The initiative did not catch on as planned, but there is currently an open-source version of S/WAN that provides VPN services in Linux environments. It provides secure gateways and VPN connections and is called FreeS/WAN.

ISDN

Integrated Services Digital Network (ISDN) is a set of digital communication services provided by service providers. This set of services, and necessary equipment, allows for data, voice, and other types of traffic to travel over a medium in a digital manner that was previously used only for analog voice calls. The telephone companies' networks actually went all digital many years ago, except for the local loop. The local loop is the copper wiring that connects houses and businesses to their carrier provider's central offices. These central offices contain the telephone company's switching equipment and are where the analog-to-digital transformation takes place. But the local loop was always analog, thus slower. ISDN was developed to replace the aging telephone analog systems, but has yet to catch on at a level that was expected.

ISDN provides a digital point-to-point, circuit-switched medium and establishes a circuit between the two communicating devices. An ISDN connection can be used for anything a modem can be used for, but it provides more functionality and higher bandwidth.

As stated in an earlier section, analog uses a full channel for communication, but ISDN can break this channel up into multiple channels, which allows for full-duplex communication and a higher level of control and error handling. ISDN provides two basic services, which are *Basic Rate Interface* (BRI) and *Primary Rate Interface* (PRI). BRI has two B-channels, which allow data to be transferred, and one D-channel, which provides for call setup, call management, error control, caller ID, and more. The bandwidth available with a BRI is 144 Kbps, compared to a top-performing modem at 56 Kbps. There is 1.544 Mbps of bandwidth available on a PRI, with 23 possible B-channels and one D-channel.

It is the D-channel that provides for a quicker call setup and connection process. An ISDN connection may require only 2–5 seconds to set up the connection, whereas a modem may require 45–90 seconds. This D-channel provides for out-of-band communication between the local loop equipment and the user terminal. It is out-of-band because the control data is not mixed in with the user communication data. This makes it harder for intruders to gather and manipulate control information from the line.

DSL

DSL has grown in popularity recently, but still has some significant barriers. *Digital Subscriber Line* (DSL) is another type of high-speed connection technology used to access the Internet and possibly other networks. It can provide 6 to 30 times higher bandwidth speeds than ISDN and analog technologies and uses existing phone lines. This does indeed sound better than sliced bread, but there is a catch. Only certain people can get this service because you first must find a provider that offers this service and then you have to be within a 2.5 mile radius of the phone company's central office. As the distance between the residence and the central office increase, the transmission rates for DSL decreases.

DSL is a broadband technology that can provide up to 52 Mbps transmission speed without replacing the carrier's copper wire. The end user and the carrier equipment do need to be upgraded for DSL, however.

DSL actually has several different types of services. The services can be symmetric, which means that traffic flows at the same speed upstream and downstream, or asymmetric, where the downstream speed is much higher than upstream. In most situations, an asymmetric connection is fine for residential users because they usually download items from the Internet more often than they upload data.

The primary security concern with DSL is that it is always connected. There is no dial-up connection with DSL, so the connection remains constant. It is a good idea to install a personal firewall for the DSL device and shut down the system when it is not in use.

> **Travel Advisory**
>
> Although DSL and cable modems are considered "always on" technologies, many service providers will time-out idle connections, which will require the user to reestablish the connection when needed.

Cable Modems

Cable modems provide high-speed access, up to 50 Mbps, to the Internet through existing cable coaxial and fiber lines. The bandwidth and coaxial cable is shared between users in local areas, therefore it will not always stay at a static rate. Sharing the media brings up a slew of security concerns because users with network sniffers can easily view their neighbors traffic and data as it travels to and from the Internet. Many cable companies are looking into encryption and other security mechanisms to reduce these types of threats. The growth of cable modems has also increased the use of personal firewalls.

WAN Switching

A *WAN switch* is a multiport device used in carrier networks to deliver multiservice access and switching functionality across public and private networks. There are two main types of switching: *circuit-based switching* and *packet-based switching*. Circuit switching sets up a virtual connection that acts like a dedicated link between two systems. When Barry calls Daphne, a protocol will actually set up the call through specific switches before any of his voice data is transmitted. Once this circuit is set up, all of the data that passes back and forth between Barry and Daphne will go through these switches. This is different than packet switching, which does not set up a circuit that all data will follow. In packet switching, messages can be split up and follow different routes, even though they have the same destination. They can follow different routes because one link may go down or one may be congested. This can result in the packets ending up at their destination out of order.

The characteristics of each switching type are shown here:

Circuit switching

- Connection-oriented virtual links.
- Traffic travels in a predictable and constant manner.
- Fixed delays.
- Usually carries voice-oriented data.

Packet switching

- Packets can use different dynamic paths to get to the same destination.
- Supports traffic that is bursty.
- Variable delays.
- Usually carries data-oriented data.

Frame Relay

Frame relay is a WAN protocol that operates at the data link layer. It is a MAN and WAN solution that uses packet-switching technology to allow multiple companies and networks to share the same media, devices, and services. While direct point-to-point links have a cost based on the distance between the end points, frame relay has a cost that is based on the amount of bandwidth used. Because several companies and networks use the same media and devices (routers and switches), the cost can be greatly reduced per company compared to dedicated links.

If a company knows that it will usually require *x* amount of bandwidth each day, it can pay a certain fee to make sure that this amount will always be available. This is called a *committed information rate* (CIR). Companies that do not have the high bandwidth requirement can pay lower fees but do not have the guarantee that extra bandwidth will be available if it's needed.

Frame relay forwards frames across virtual circuits. These circuits can be permanent, meaning that they are programmed in advance or the circuits are switched, which means that the circuit is quickly built when it is needed and torn down when the connection is finished. The *permanent virtual circuit* (PVC) works like a private line for a customer with an agreed-upon bandwidth availability. When a customer sets up an account with a service provider and pays the CIR, a PVC is programmed for that customer to ensure that they will always receive the specified amount of bandwidth.

Unlike PVCs, *switched virtual circuits* (SVC) require a type of dial-up connection procedure. It is similar to setting up a phone call over a telecommunication network. During the setup procedure, the required bandwidth is requested, the destination computer is contacted and must accept the call, a path is determined, and forwarding information is programmed into each switch along the SVC's path. SVCs are good for teleconferencing temporary connections to remote sites, data replication, and voice calls. Once the connection is no longer needed, the circuit is torn down and deleted from the switches.

> **Local Lingo**
>
> A logical circuit is created over a packet-switched network and provides a logical dedicated link.

X.25

X.25 is an older WAN protocol that defines how devices and networks establish and maintain connections. Like frame relay, X.25 is a switching technology that uses carrier switches to provide connectivity for many different networks. Subscribers are charged on the amount of bandwidth they use instead of a flat fee, as in dedicated links. Also like frame relay, PVCs are configured when a customer sets up an account, which programs their connection requirements into the switches that connect the different sites.

Frame relay is much more advanced and efficient than X.25. This is because the X.25 protocol was developed and released in the 1970s. During this time, many of the devices that were connected to networks were dumb terminals and mainframes, the networks did not have the built-in functionality and fault tolerance they have today, and the Internet was not as foundationally stable and resistant to errors and disruptions. These deficiencies required X.25 to compensate and provide many layers of error checking, error correcting, and fault tolerance. This made the protocol fat, which was required back then, but today it slows down connection times. Because today's Internet is more efficient, frame relay was developed without this overhead and provides quicker transmission rates.

ATM

Commonly mistaken by the nontechnical as the place where you get money, *Asynchronous Transfer Mode* (ATM) is actually another switching technology, but instead of using packet switching, it uses cell-switching methods. ATM is a high-speed networking technology used for LAN, WAN, and service provider connections.

Cell switching means that data is segmented into fixed-sized cells, 53 bytes, instead of variable-sized packets. This provides for more efficient and faster use of the communication paths. ATM sets up virtual circuits, which act like dedicated paths between the source and destination. These virtual circuits can guarantee bandwidth and quality of service (QoS), unlike IP. For these reasons, ATM is a good carrier for voice and video transmission, because it promises a bandwidth level and a dedicated path. ATM allows companies to replace individual voice and data lines and combine them into one.

Quality of Service

Quality of Service (QoS) is the ability to deliver traffic with a minimum amount of delay so that the network can deliver the expected traffic loads. The highest QoS is provided when using dedicated links that are not shared by other entities. But when dedicated links are not used, protocols that have been developed to provide QoS can be implemented to allow administrators to prioritize traffic types and ensure that certain types of traffic will be transmitted in an acceptable time frame. A QoS capability that is available is classifying traffic that has different priorities, where the higher priorities have higher bandwidth available, which is what takes place in packet-switched networks. For delay-sensitive applications, this can reduce the amount of jitter and latency that is experienced. QoS allows for real-time traffic to coexist with "best effort" traffic, which is more data-oriented.

Local Lingo

Jitter is a variation in arrival times of frames and is experienced because routers and switches have to queue traffic.

SMDS

Switched Multimegabit Data Service (SMDS) is a high-speed, packet-switching technology used to enable customers to extend their LANs across MANs and WANs. When a company has an office in one state and needs to communicate with an office in a different state, the two LANs can use this packet-switching protocol to communicate across an already-established public network. This protocol is connectionless and can provide bandwidth on demand. This technology did not take off as planned and has been replaced with frame relay and ATM.

SDLC

Synchronous Data Link Control (SDLC) protocol is used on networks that use dedicated, leased lines with permanent physical connections. SDLC is a bit-oriented, synchronous protocol that has evolved into other communication protocols such as High-Level Data Link Control (HDLC), Link Access Procedure (LAP), and Link Access Procedure—Balanced (LAPB). It is used mainly for communications to IBM mainframes within Systems Network Architectures (SNA). SDLC provides a polling media access technology, which is the mechanism that enables secondary stations to communicate on the network.

HDLC

High-Level Data Link Control (HDLC) protocol is also a bit-oriented link layer protocol used for transmission over synchronous lines. HDLC is an extension of SDLC, and provides high throughput because it supports full-duplex transmissions and is used in point-to-point and multipoint connections. Like SDLC, HDLC provides a polling functionality where primary stations contact secondary stations to establish data transmissions.

Multiservice Access Technologies

Communications are getting faster, better, and more flexible thanks to *multiservice access* technologies. These technologies combine different types of communication (data, voice, video) over one network and transmission line. They provide higher performance, reduced operational costs, and greater flexibility, integration, and control for the customers because two or more networks do not need to be built and maintained to move around these different types of data. An analogy for this is allowing all types of motor vehicles on one road. If at one time we had one road for motorcycles, another road for trucks, another road for cars, and yet another one for buses, it would cost a lot of money to build all of these similar roads and maintain them. But if we allowed all of these different vehicles to go over the same road, it would be cheaper and less complex. This is what multiservice access allows—different communications to share the same road.

The division line between service providers and telephone companies is becoming more blurred with this type of technology because they can offer each others' services. Voice services are being developed with several transport technologies, including IP, ATM, and frame relay. They are referred to as VoIP (voice over IP), VoATM, and VoFR.

The public switched telephone network (PSTN) is being replaced with data-centric, packet-oriented networks that can support voice, data, and video. The new VoIP networks use different switches, protocols, and communication links than what the PSTN currently uses. This means that VoIP, along with other new technologies, have to go through a tricky transition stage that enables the old systems and infrastructures to communicate with the new systems until the old is dead and gone.

Objective 5.06 Remote Access Methods and Technologies

Remote access covers several technologies that enable users to connect to networks external to them, which, in turn, grants them access to the necessary network resources they need to perform their tasks. Most of the time, these users must first gain access to the Internet through an ISP, which will then set up a connection to the destination network.

For many corporations, remote access is a necessity. It allows users to work from the road or home and still have access to corporate resources. From the company's perspective, remote access can also help in reducing networking costs by using the Internet as the access media instead of expensive dedicated lines.

Remotely accessing resources and information can be streamlined through Internet and intranet connections. This allows for a competitive advantage by allowing partners, suppliers, and customers to have closely controlled links. The most common types of remote connectivity methods used are VPNs, dial-up, ISDN, cable modems, DSL connections, and wireless technologies.

Remote Access

Remote access is usually gained by connecting to a *network access server* (NAS) at an ISP or the corporate network. The NAS acts as a gateway and an end point to a PPP session. If the NAS is at an ISP, it will then set up a connection that links the remote user to the corporate network using PPTP or L2TP. The NAS provides authentication and authorization functionality to ensure that only authorized individuals are allowed this type of access.

Security is a real concern for an administrator of remote access, but there are several configurations she can use when users attempt to connect to the network through a NAS. One option is requiring the user to use a preapproved phone number. Typically, when users dial in for remote access, they are asked for their usernames and passwords and are then authenticated and admitted into the network. However, a Remote Access Server (RAS) can be configured to disconnect the call in order to call the user back at the predefined phone number, referred to as *callback*. This is a security mechanism that is used to try and ensure that only authenticated users are provided access to the network, and it reverses the long-distance charges back to the company. Even if an attacker finds out the logon credentials necessary to gain remote access, it is unlikely that the attacker will also be at the predefined phone number. But this security measure can be compromised if someone implements call forwarding.

Caller ID can be configured on the NAS as well. The *caller ID* functionality can review the source telephone number and make a decision to allow access based upon a predefined list of approved phone numbers. For attackers to get around this, they must call from a preauthorized telephone number or compromise the telephone company's central office equipment.

Remote access best practices:

- All dial-up modems and servers should be in a central bank with a firewall between them and the internal network.
- Justify all remote users and their access rights yearly.
- Publish a remote access policy and enforce it through education and auditing.
- Use VPN for sensitive data transmissions.
- Configure modems to answer after a predetermined number of rings to counter war dialers.
- Use phone lines restricted to outbound access for dial-out services.
- Secure diagnostic ports and disable when not in use.

Travel Advisory

War dialers are programs that dial telephone numbers looking for hanging modems, which are usually easy entry points into a network. You should set your modems to answer after the third or fourth ring, because most war dialers will drop the connection after that many rings and move onto another phone number.

Wireless Technology

Wireless devices are no longer an alternative means of communication; they have become an integrated data transmission mechanism in networks throughout the world. It is an attractive technology because networks and users can communicate without all of those pesky cables. But it also means that data is traveling over airwaves, which can be easily sniffed or used to gain unauthorized access to corporate and personal networks.

Wireless communication can take place over long distances and work as a MAN technology, or they can work over a shorter distance and provide wireless LANs (WLAN). In a WLAN, users can take their laptops, or other wireless devices, throughout different parts of the building and never lose network connectivity. Great, but what is wireless communication?

When two people are talking, they are using wireless communication because their vocal cords are altering airwaves, which are signals that travel to another person with no cables attached. Wireless communication involves transmitting signals via radio waves through air and space, which also alters airwaves. Signals are measured in frequency and amplitudes. The frequency of a signal dictates how much data it can carry and how far. The higher the frequency, the more data that the signal can carry, but the higher the frequency, the more susceptible the signal is to atmosphere interference, thus it cannot go as far.

Spread Spectrum

In wireless technologies, the data is put onto radio carrier signals that work at specific frequencies, and the more frequencies that are available, the more carrier signals that can be used to move data from point "A" to point "Z." This is similar to comparing a one-lane highway to a six-lane highway. If you only had one lane (one frequency), you would not be able to move as many cars (data) as you would with six lanes. But how do we get the data onto these signals within these different frequencies?

Spread spectrum is a technology that places different types of data onto the signals that work at specific frequencies that have been allotted for data transmission. A spectrum is a subset of available frequencies that can be used to allow unrelated products to share the same spectrum with minimal interference. *Direct Sequence Spread Spectrum* (DSSS) and *Frequency Hopping Spread Spectrum* (FHSS) are techniques used in the spread-spectrum technology, which are ways to get the data onto a carrier wave for transmission. (Think of the horse and the cowboy again.) FHSS is part of the first IEEE-approved WLAN standard (802.11) that supports data rates as high as 2 Mbps, which we know is nothing to write home about. So, along came the next standard (802.11b), which incorporated DSSS techniques, which worked at the 2.4 GHz frequency and offered data rates up to 11 Mbps. Much better! But not so fast. In 1999, a third wireless standard (802.11a) was adopted that would give users data rates as high as 54 Mbps, which worked in the 5.5 GHz frequency. Now, we're talking!

> **Travel Advisory**
>
> The 802.11b 2.4 GHz frequency range is shared with Bluetooth, cordless phones, microwave ovens, and other products. This is referred to as a "dirty" range because so many different types of devices work here.

WAP

The 802.11 standard series uses the *Wireless Application Protocol* (WAP), which is a set of communication protocols used to standardize the way that wireless devices interface with each other, networks, and the Internet. The WAP model contains protocols that perform similar functions as the protocols within the TCP/IP stack, but because wireless devices have a smaller amount of memory and processing power, a different networking stack had to be developed for them.

Because these devices use Web-based technologies, there must be a way to present Web pages to the users. Personal computers and servers use HTML or XML to present Web-based material and possibly JavaScripts to perform the processing in the background. WAP uses *Wireless Markup Language* (WML) and *WMLScript* to perform these similar tasks. WAP also has its own session and transaction protocols and security protocol called *Wireless Transport Layer Security* (WTLS), which is similar to TLS and SSL.

If encrypted data needs to travel over the Internet, it needs to be translated from WTLS to SSL or TLS. During this translation, the data has be decrypted and re-encrypted with SSL or TLS. This means that sensitive data can be exposed for a short period of time without the control of the sender or receiver and this is referred to as the "gap in the WAP" problem. If the data is confidential, it may be unacceptable for a third party to perform this activity and potentially have access to a decrypted form of the information.

The IEEE 802.15 Working Group for Wireless Personal Area Networks is working to integrate the Bluetooth and 802.11 (WLAN) standards, which use the same 2.4 GHz frequency range. Bluetooth is a technology that allows devices within a short range to spontaneously set up wireless networks. There are mice and keyboards that have Bluetooth technology which do not require any cables to be connected to computers. And if you had a Bluetooth-enabled PDA and mobile phone, you could just set them next to each other and they could update each other's contact and calendar information by establishing a dynamic wireless network.

Access Points

In a WLAN environment, access points (AP) are the transceivers that wireless devices communicate with for network connectivity. In most implementations, the AP is connected to an Ethernet cable, which plugs directly into the wired network, as illustrated in Figure 5-11. So, the AP is the doorway for the wireless devices to be able to participate on the pre-existing wired network.

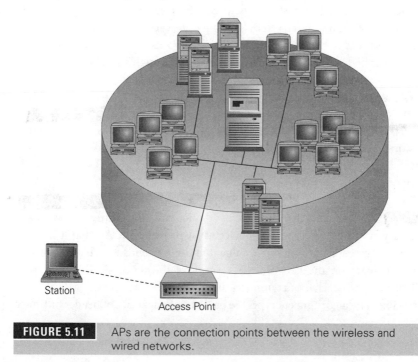

Station

Access Point

FIGURE 5.11 APs are the connection points between the wireless and wired networks.

The APs are in fixed locations throughout a network and work as communication beacons. Both the AP and the user's device must have wireless network interface cards (NICs), which enable both sides to communicate through specific frequencies.

APs exist only in something called an *infrastructured* WLAN, where the wireless network extends the current wired network. However, it is possible to construct a purely wireless network, called an *ad hoc network*, where each host has a wireless NIC and works in a peer-to-peer relationship.

SSID

Any host that wishes to participate in a particular WLAN must be configured with the proper *Service Set ID* (SSID). Hosts can be segmented into different WLANs by using different SSIDs, similar to how we use subnets today. Hosts may be segmented based on the resources they need to access, by different business functions or by levels of trust.

In most environments, the host must supply the correct SSID during its authentication phase. The host may be preconfigured with the necessary SSID value, or the AP may advertise it by sending out beacons to any listening hosts. The SSID should not be seen as a reliable security mechanism because it is usually broadcasted by the AP, thus easily accessible through sniffing.

OSA and SKA

APs have two basic methods of authentication. The first is *open system authentication* (OSA), where no encryption is required, and negotiations and data transmissions take place in clear text. In this type of authentication, the wireless station usually just needs to be configured with the correct SSID value to be authorized access to the network.

The second method is *shared key authentication* (SKA), where encryption is required, which means that the wireless device must be configured with the necessary cryptographic key. The device must prove to the AP that it has this key, usually by using it to encrypt a value that the AP sends to it, before the user can participate on the network. SKA employs the *wired equivalent privacy* (WEP) protocol, which uses a symmetrical algorithm (RC4) with key sizes of 40 bit or 104 bits. The algorithm encrypts the payload of packets, not header or trailer data and the same key is used for encryption and decryption processes. Unfortunately, the WEP encryption protocol has many weaknesses that make it easy to defeat.

War driving is a type of an attack where attackers drive around with a laptop or two, identify APs, sniff wireless traffic, and attempt to gain access to a company's network through an AP entry point.

There are several countermeasures you can take to fend off attackers of wireless technologies, however, such as the following:

- **Enable WEP**   Even though it is flawed, it does provide a level of protection.
- **Change SSID default values from vendor's configuration**   Attackers can easily get a list of all default SSID values used by all wireless technology vendors.
- **Disable broadcasting SSID values from APs**   Attackers can gather this information and use it to authenticate to the AP.
- **Implement another layer of authentication**   Require RADIUS or Kerberos authentication before a user can access network resources.
- **Physically place the AP in the center of the building**   This helps control the span of the signals leaving the building.
- **Logically place the AP in a DMZ with a firewall between the AP and internal network**   The firewall can investigate the traffic before it enters the internal network.
- **Use 104-bit WEP, not 40 bit.**
- **Implement a VPN for wireless stations to use**   This adds another layer of encryption for data transmission.
- **Configure ACLs on the AP and/or firewall to only allow known MACs**   Restrict access to only MAC addresses of the known and approved wireless devices.
- **Assign static IP addresses to stations and disable DHCP**   Otherwise, if an attacker gets through an AP, she is quickly assigned a valid company IP to allow for network activity.

Cell Phone Cloning

Cell phones are wireless devices that remote users utilize every day. Even Great Grandma Ethel is using a cell phone these days! These handy toys, however, can be vulnerable to foul play.

Each cell phone has an *electronic serial number* (ESN), which identifies the phone and a *mobile identification number* (MIN), which is the phone number assigned to it. These numbers are sent with the transmission signal and can be intercepted by attackers. The attacker, or cloner in this case, captures the numbers and gives them to a person in another city where they are not recognized as being in use. This new person programs the numbers into a new mobile phone. The cloner can then either sell the phone or use it himself without being easily traced. Another common trick that attackers use is called *tumbling*. In this scenario, an attacker tries combinations of ESN/MIN numbers until a valid set is found. The valid set is then programmed into the phone.

The telephone carrier can combat this practice if they require these numbers to be validated before calls are allowed to be made. This technology is maturing, but today it takes too long to validate these numbers through different carriers before allowing someone to use their phone.

PBX Threats

Companies use telecommunication switches called *Private Branch Exchanges* (PBXs) to interface with several types of devices that can take advantage of different telephone services. PBXs are located on the company's property, but have dedicated links to the telephone company's central office.

PBXs use switching devices that can control analog and digital signals between a company's telephones and devices and the telephone carrier's switching equipment. Older PBXs may support only analog devices, but most have been moving quickly to digital. This move to digital has reduced a number of the PBX and telephone security vulnerabilities that used to be available. That in no way means that PBX fraud does not take place today, however. Many companies have modems hanging off their PBXs to allow vendors to dial in and perform maintenance on the system. This can be an open door for intruders to enter the PBX, reconfigure it, and obtain free long-distance calls that are billed to the unsuspecting company. The modems should actually be activated only when there is a problem that requires the vendor to dial in, and then it should be immediately disabled.

Also, many PBX systems have default administrative passwords that are never changed after implementation. These passwords are set by default when the switch is shipped; thus, if 100 companies install 100 PBX systems from vendor ABC, and none of the companies reset the password, then a phreaker has access to 100 PBX systems. Once a phreaker breaks into a PBX system, she can cause mayhem by rerouting calls, reconfiguring switches, or enabling access to free long-distance calls. This type of fraud happens often without being noticed because many companies do not closely watch their phone bills.

> **Local Lingo**
>
> A phreaker is a type of hacker that specializes in telephone fraud.

PBX systems are also vulnerable to brute-force attacks, where phreakers use scripts and dictionaries to guess the necessary credentials to gain access to the system. There have also been cases where phreakers listen to an employee's voice message and then change the greeting. So when people call to leave Bob a message, they might not hear his usual boring greeting, but instead a new greeting that is filled with screaming obscenities and insults.

Another threat that a PBX is susceptible to is information disclosure. The intruder could be an outsider, or an employeee, but regardless, this person can gain access to the PBX and monitor conversations. This is a major security concern for publicly held companies trying to conceal important information about stocks, mergers, or any other confidential corporate issues.

There are a number of steps that can be taken to secure a PBX:

- Change administrative password regularly.
- Disable maintenance modems.
- Change default configurations.
- Block remote calling after business hours.
- Review telephone bills.
- Block unassigned access codes.

Objective 5.07 Fault Tolerance Mechanisms

Network and resource availability is not fully appreciated until it is gone. That is why administrators and engineers need to implement effective backup and redundant systems to make sure that when something happens (and something will happen), that the users' productivity and network functionality will not be drastically affected.

A single point of failure can bring a lot of potential risk to a network because if the device goes down, a segment or the entire network can be negatively affected. Devices that could provide single points of failure are firewalls, routers, network access servers, T1 lines, switches, bridges, hubs, and authentication servers, to name a few. The best way to cover your bases is to identify possible single points of failure, make sure you have proper maintenance, put backups and redundancy in place, and properly plan for how to deal with device failure or data corruption *before* it takes place.

RAID

Redundant Array of Inexpensive Disks (RAID) is a technology used for redundancy and performance improvement. It combines several physical disks and aggregates them into logical arrays. When data is saved, it is written across all drives, which is called *striping*. This striping activity requires dividing the data and writing it onto several different drives. Because of this, it dramatically improves the read function because more than one head is retrieving data at one time. There are different levels of RAID; the most common are 1, 3, and 5. RAID is covered more in Chapter 10.

Clustering

Clustering is a fault-tolerant server technology similar to redundant servers except each server takes part in processing requests that are made. A server cluster is a group of servers that are viewed logically as one server to users and are managed as a single system. Clustering provides availability and scalability capabilities. For example, if one of the systems within the cluster fails, processing continues because the rest of the systems just pick up the load (although there could be a degradation in performance). This approach is much more efficient than simply having a backup system waiting in the wings until the primary system goes down; the backup system remains idle, which is a wasted resource.

Backing Up

Backing up software and having hardware backup devices is a big part of network availability and fault tolerance. The first step in this enormous task is to figure out what gets backed up, how often, and how these processes should take place. Backups can occur once or twice a week, every day, or even every three hours. It is up to the company to determine this policy. The more frequent the backups, the more staff time will be dedicated to it, so there needs to be a balance between the costs and maintenance of backing up data and the actual risk of potentially losing data. You can find out much more about backup issues in Chapters 4 and 7.

CHECKPOINT

✔**Objective 5.01: TCP/IP Suite**   TCP/IP is the suite of protocols that is used to move data across many different types of networks and provides a wide range of functionality. It contains several protocols, but the two main protocols are TCP and UDP. TCP is reliable and connection-oriented, whereas UDP is unreliable and connectionless.

✔**Objective 5.02: Cabling and Data Transmission Types**   There are several types of cabling that can be used in networks today: coaxial, UTP, STP, and fiber. Cabling standards were developed to protect data from outside influences such as noise, lighting, magnetic forces, and electronic devices. Coaxial cabling offers high bandwidth, long cable runs, and is less susceptible to outside interference. Twisted-pair cabling is the most common type of cabling and is used primarily in LAN environments. It comes in a shielded form (STP) or unshielded form (UDP). Fiber is the most secure cabling type. Plenum cabling should be used in drop ceiling areas in case of fires.

✔**Objective 5.03: LAN Technologies**   The physical arrangement of computers and network devices is called a network topology. Examples of network topologies are bus, star, ring, and mesh. Ethernet and Token Ring are two examples of media access technologies that enable devices to communicate on the same network. Ethernet uses CSMA/CD, which means all computers "listen" to see when they can transmit data, with the goal of avoiding collisions. Token Ring employs a token passing system where stations are not allowed to communicate until they receive the token. Polling requires a primary system to communicate with a secondary system before the secondary can transmit data.

✔**Objective 5.04: Network Devices and Services**   Devices within LANs, MANs, and WANs allow networks and computers to communicate. The main networking devices used today are repeaters, bridges, switches, routers, and gateways. The differences in these devices lie in their functionality, capabilities, intelligence, and network placement. Firewalls serve as a choke point in the network to enforce security policies. The different types of firewalls are packet filtering, proxy-based (application and circuit), and stateful. The main types of firewall architectures are dual-homed, screened host, and screened subnet.

✔**Objective 5.05: Telecommunications Protocols and Devices**   There are several WAN technologies that companies can use to connect to the outside world. Each offers advantages, disadvantages, and security vulnerabilities. Some examples are FDDI, SONET, ISDN, dedicated links, DSL, cable modems, frame relay, and ATM.

✔**Objective 5.06: Remote Access Methods and Technologies**   Remote access can be a necessity for companies and their employees. Callback and caller ID are two access mechanisms that can be used to help authenticate valid users. Wireless is a new, up and coming technology that has several security issues. The wireless devices use WAP because of a lack of resources. WTLS is the transport security protocol that presents the "gap in the WAP" issue. Wireless devices connect with an access point station in order to connect with a wired network. WEP is used to encrypt data and can use 40- or 104-bit keys. PBX s are vulnerable to fraudulent behavior within companies; preventive steps should be taken to prevent unauthorized individuals from receiving free telephone services.

✔**Objective 5.07: Fault Tolerance Mechanisms**   The existence of single points of failure within a network can be a serious threat to production. It is important to establish redundancy and fault tolerance mechanisms to help fight these threats. RAID is a technology used to provide data backups and improve performance. Clustering is a fault-tolerant server technology that provides availability and scalability.

REVIEW QUESTIONS

1. Telephone fraud is performed by a _____.

  A. Hacker

  B. Phreaker

  C. Cracker

  D. Thief

2. Which of the following best describes attenuation?

  A. Disruptions on a line caused by things like florescent lighting, motors or computers

  B. Corruption due to the crossing of electrical signals

  C. The loss in signal strength as it travels

  D. The digital regeneration of a signal

3. Which of the following network topologies consists of a single cable run with nodes attached through drop points?

    A. Star

    B. Bus

    C. Ring

    D. Mesh

4. What is a MAC also referred to as?

    A. Single point of failure

    B. Collision domain

    C. Logical address

    D. Physical address

5. Which of the following is true of the TCP protocol?

    A. Is a reliable and connectionless protocol

    B. Uses less overhead than UDP

    C. Uses sequence numbers within packets to make sure each packet within a message is received

    D. Does not perform handshaking

6. How is a bridge different than a repeater?

    A. Bridges amplify electrical signals.

    B. Bridges work with IP addresses.

    C. Bridges work with MAC addresses.

    D. Bridges provide line conditioning and work at the physical layer.

7. Which of the following is a disadvantage of packet filtering?

    A. Scalability

    B. Does not keep track of the state of a connection

    C. Provides high performance

    D. Does not depend on other applications

8. Another name for tunnel is _____.

    A. Pipeline

    B. Packet switching

    C. VPN

    D. Firewall

9. SOCKS is an example of a _____?

    A. Circuit-level proxy

    B. Application-level proxy

    C. TCP/IP protocol

    D. Screened host

10. Which of the following is true of UDP?

    A. Acknowledges every packet it receives

    B. Connection-oriented protocol

    C. Performs handshaking

    D. Is considered a "best effort" protocol

11. Which of the following allows companies to use private addresses, which can save money and provide a level of protection?

    A. Dual-homed firewall

    B. UDP

    C. NAT

    D. PBX

12. A standard T1 has how many channels?

    A. 24

    B. 28

    C. 56

    D. 2, plus 1 for signaling

13. Which of the following technologies uses cell switching?

    A. Frame relay

    B. ATM

    C. T-carriers

    D. X.25

14. How many B-channels does a PRI have?

    A. 1

    B. 56

    C. 23

    D. 24

15. Which of the following is a disadvantage of DSL?

    A. Provides 6 to 30 times higher bandwidth rates than ISDN.

    B. Service can be symmetric or asymmetric.

    C. Uses existing copper wire infrastructure.

    D. Typically works within a 2.5-mile radius of the service provider.

16. Which of the following is a characteristic of CHAP?

    A. Used the same way PAP is used, but provides a lower level of security

    B. Authenticates using a challenge/response method

    C. Is vulnerable to man-in-the-middle attacks

    D. Sends credentials in clear text

17. Which of the following technologies combines several physical disks and aggregates them into logical arrays?

    A. Clustering

    B. UPS

    C. RAID

    D. EAP

18. In frame relay networks, what is a guaranteed level of bandwidth called?

    A. SVC

    B. Fairy tale

    C. DCE

    D. CIR

REVIEW ANSWERS

1. **B**   A phreaker is an attacker who specializing in committing telephone service fraud.

2. **C**   Attenuation is the loss of signal strength as it travels through a medium such as copper cabling, fiber, or airwaves. Repeaters can be used to regenerate a signal's strength.

3. **B**   In a bus topology, individual nodes are attached and dependent upon the single cable run. That single cable is the single point of failure, and one node going down could negatively affect other nodes on the topology.

4. **D**   A physical address is also referred to as a media access control (MAC) address. It is the hardware address that is permanently programmed into the network interface mechanism. ARP is used to translate IP addresses to their corresponding MAC addresses.

5. **C**   TCP is a reliable, connection-oriented protocol that performs handshaking, error detection, and correction. It also uses sequence numbers so that the receiving end can determine if specific packets were lost during transmission. Because of the additional functionality, TCP uses more overhead than UDP.

6. **C** Repeaters work at the physical layer and do not understand addressing. A repeater amplifies and conditions signals so that they can travel over longer distances. Bridges work at the data link layer and forward frames based on their MAC addresses.

7. **B** One of the disadvantages of packet filtering is that it does not keep track of the state of the connection. Stateful firewalls do, however. Keeping state means to understand and make access decisions based on the different stages of a communication dialog.

8. **C** Tunneling and VPN are interchangeable terms because both provide a logical channel that can be used to move data from one point to another, usually through a different network, as in the Internet. The terms are related because VPNs use tunneling protocols. Encryption can be enabled to provide a secure and private channel for data to travel through.

9. **A** SOCKS is a circuit-level proxy firewall. It looks at header information to make access decisions and clients need to have SOCKS software installed to be able to communicate with the SOCKS firewall.

10. **D** UDP is considered to be a "best effort" protocol because it does not check to see if its packets were delivered successfully. UDP is a connectionless and unreliable protocol.

11. **C** NAT enables a company to use private addresses and still be able to communicate transparently with computers on the Internet. It is a cheaper solution than purchasing and using public, Internet-routable addresses. It also hides the company's internal address scheme.

12. **A** A T1 is multiplexed into 24 individual channels.

13. **B** ATM is a LAN and WAN technology that uses cells instead of packets to achieve faster and more efficient communication paths. The cells are 53 bytes in size.

14. **C** A PRI is T1 provisioned with one signaling channel, thus 23 bearer channels are left for voice or data. The PRI has 23 B-channels and one D-channel for call setup, maintenance, and teardown.

15. **D** Distance limitation is a major disadvantage of DSL. The farther away a subscriber is from the service provider, the lower the bandwidth. In most cases, if the subscriber is not within a 2.5-mile radius of the service provider's point of presence, the service will not even be offered.

16. **B** CHAP's challenge/response mechanisms protect the communication channel from man-in-the-middle and replay attacks, and because of this, CHAP has a higher level of security than PAP. PAP sends credentials in clear text; CHAP actually encrypts a value sent over from the authentication server and never sends the user's password over the wire.

17. **C** RAID is used for redundancy and performance improvement by aggregating physical disks into logical arrays. Striping alone does not provide fault tolerance; parity would have to be used.

18. **D** Committed information rate (CIR) guarantees a level of bandwidth at all times in a frame relay network. When users sign up for frame relay, they must decide how much bandwidth they will require, which will determine the CIR they will need to pay. The different switches are then programmed to ensure this level of bandwidth for this customer connection.

Cryptography

CHAPTER 6

ETA	NEWBIE	SOME EXPERIENCE	EXPERT
	6 hours	4 hours	3 hours

Cryptography has been used by many different civilizations, all over the world, throughout time. In fact, a simplistic form of cryptography can be traced back to over 4,000 years ago. So what is cryptography, you ask? It's a science of protecting information by encoding it into an unreadable format. Its evolution is impressive. Cryptography has taken the form of disguised stone carvings, as in Egyptian hieroglyphics, writings on a type of paper to be wrapped around a stick (Scytale), and complex rotor machines that drastically affected the events of World War II. And today, cryptography is deeply integrated within almost all of our computing systems and technologies.

Unfortunately, just as technology improves, so does the ability of the bad guys. So, it's important to point out that although cryptography strives to hide sensitive information, most cryptosystems can be broken if the attacker has enough time, desire, and resources. So a more realistic goal of cryptography is to make it so difficult for attackers to break that it deters most from even trying. You want the attacker to move on to an easier victim. In this chapter, we go into what makes a strong cryptosystem, how they can be broken by attackers, and some practices that should be followed to make it much harder for the bad guys to break your encryption process.

Cryptography Definitions

T his chapter contains new terms and definitions that are important to know and understand for the CISSP exam. In future sections, we go into greater detail about the concepts that back these definitions up, technologies that provide some of the services listed, and examples of many of these items – but for now let's get the actual definitions of these terms down before we move on.

Definitions

- **Cryptography**   The science of protecting information by encoding it into an unreadable format.
- **Confidentiality**   Unauthorized parties cannot access information.
- **Authenticity**   Validate the source of a message.
- **Integrity**   Provides assurance that a message was not modified in an improper way, either accidentally or intentionally.

- **Nonrepudiation** A sender cannot deny sending a message at a later date.
- **Cipher** Something that transforms characters or bits into an unreadable form.
- **Plaintext** Readable text; once it is encrypted, it is referred to as ciphertext.
- **Cryptographic algorithm** A set of procedures or equations used for encryption and decryption purposes.
- **Cryptanalysis** The science of studying and breaking the secrecy of encryption algorithms and their necessary pieces.
- **Cryptology** The study of both cryptography and cryptanalysis.
- **Cryptosystem** A mechanism that carries out encryption and decryption processes. It usually refers to the total package of the algorithm, the keys, the software, and protocols necessary to perform encryption and decryption.
- **Encipher** The process of encrypting text.
- **Decipher** The process of decrypting encrypted text.
- **Key clustering** The instance when two different keys generate the same ciphertext from the same plaintext.

Keys and Text

So now that you know all of the terms, let's dive into how these items work together.

It all starts with an *algorithm*, which is a set of procedures or mathematical functions that are used during the encryption and decryption processes. Typically, the algorithm is not the secret piece of the encryption process, in fact, many of them are publicly known. Instead, a secret value, known as a *key*, is used with an algorithm, which dictates what parts of the algorithm will be used, in what order and with what values, as shown in Figure 6-1. The key is usually a large set of random numbers or values.

Encryption works by changing *plaintext* (readable) into *ciphertext* (unreadable). The plaintext is the message or document that a user creates; the ciphertext is the resulting encrypted message or document.

Local Lingo
A key is also called a cryptovariable.

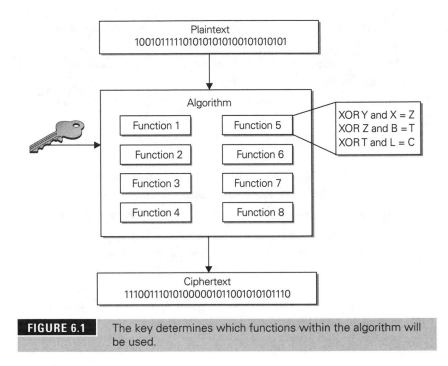

FIGURE 6.1 The key determines which functions within the algorithm will be used.

Keyspace

An algorithm creates a large number of possible key values, referred to as the *keyspace*. The keyspace is a large set of random values that the algorithm chooses from when it needs to create a key. The larger the keyspace, the more possibilities for different keys, which makes it much more difficult for an attacker to uncover the correct key value. For example, a 40-bit key can produce 2^{40} (over 1 trillion) possible key values. Algorithms should use the entire keyspace available to them, and they should not choose the same values over and over.

Algorithms that use larger key sizes, thus larger keyspaces, provide more possible values to be used when the key generation process takes place, as illustrated in Figure 6-2.

An analogy is if you had a pot of different keys. Every 30 days you changed the lock on your door and used a different key from the pot. Attackers might steal your pot of keys, but the more keys in the pot, the harder it will be for them to figure out which one to use. They will have to try each key until they identify the one that actually opens your door this month.

So if long keys are harder to break and provide more protection, why doesn't everybody just use really long keys? The main reason is that longer keys require

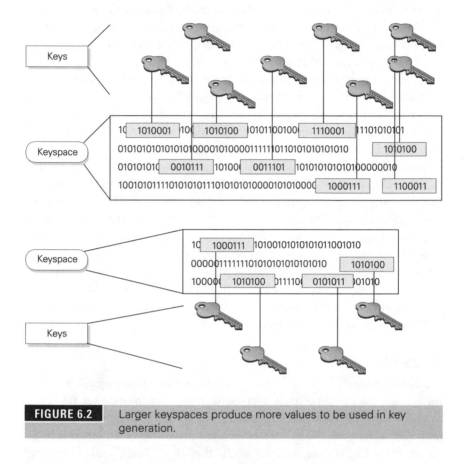

FIGURE 6.2   Larger keyspaces produce more values to be used in key generation.

more computation and processing power. When deciding upon the length of the keys to be used in an environment, two factors should be considered: the desired level of protection and the amount of resources available for this process.

Strength of Cryptosystem

The strength of cryptography is derived from secrecy, whether that is the key or the algorithm. Typically, the key is the secret ingredient, so an attacker's number one objective is trying to figure out the right combination of the random values that make up this secret key. The usual approach to uncovering the correct combination is by performing a *brute force attack*, which is a process of trying every possible key value combination. Some algorithms are so well designed that this process could take an eternity. How vulnerable an algorithm is to a brute force attack helps to determine its strength. For example, if a key can be broken with a Pentium III processor in four hours, the cipher is not considered very strong. But if the key can be uncovered only by using multiple high-end systems and it takes millions of years to accomplish, it is considered to be pretty darn strong.

As we mentioned before, the real objective of cryptography is to make it incredibly difficult for a potential attacker to figure out your secret. *Work factor* is the amount of time and processing power required to break an encryption mechanism. Stronger algorithms have larger work factors, and using longer keys usually has a direct correlation to increasing this work factor value.

When the chips do fall and a cryptosystem has been compromised, we can usually look behind the curtain and see a *person* who made a mistake, not the actual technology. Strong algorithms, random-valued keys, and long work factors don't add up to a hill of beans if keys are not properly managed and if users share their keys. The management and use of cryptography is usually the actual weakness taken advantage of by attackers because it takes less effort and resources. We go into proper key management practices later in this chapter, but realize that a cryptosystem can be broken via brute force attacks or through other methods as in tricking someone into sharing their key (social engineering) or capturing keys that are not properly protected.

Attacks

A common method of attack on cryptosystems is called *frequency analysis.* This method looks for patterns to uncover so that reverse engineering can take place to uncover the key value that was used during the encryption process. In every language, certain words and phrases are used more often than others. For instance, in the English language, the words "the," "and," "that," and "is" are very frequent patterns of letters used in messages and conversations. Messages usually start with the words "Hello" or "Dear" and end with "Sincerely" or "Thanks." Attackers can look for patterns in ciphertext that may resemble these types of phrases, which would give them insight into how the message was actually encrypted.

There is also something referred to as the "ETAONRISH" frequency, which are the letters most used in the English language. The letter "E" is the most frequently used, then "T," then "A," etc. Understanding these patterns and frequencies allows attackers to look for specific patterns in ciphertext. If they can be uncovered in the encrypted message, this basically gives the attacker the stronghold she needs to reverse engineer the process and uncover the key used during encryption, which will then allow her to decrypt other encrypted messages.

Today, the complexity of our algorithms put up a good fight against frequency analysis attacks because they, for the most part, do not allow patterns to emerge in the encrypted messages. And as we increase our key sizes, the right amount of randomness is added to the recipe. But these attacks are still taking place today, which is why we need to be aware of them and learn how to prevent them from being successful.

Another attack on cryptography is referred to as a *rubber hose* attack. This is where the person holding the actual key is threatened, blackmailed, or tortured. A *purchase key* attack is when someone is bribed for a key, and social engineering is tricking someone into providing a desired key. So how do we protect ourselves from these attacks? 1) Carry a big stick; 2) Stay honest; 3) Stay alert.

Spy-Like Ciphers

The running key cipher and the concealment cipher are the kinds of things likely to pop up in a spy novel or movie, instead of running in the software within our computers.

The *running key cipher* is not based off of complex mathematical algorithms and random bits, but instead it relates to the physical world by offering up clues. Let's walk through an example.

I get a letter in the mail that to most would not make sense, but because I'm a former secret agent I can properly decode it. At the bottom of the letter are the numbers "385." I know that this means for me to look at the third page of today's newspaper, the eighth line down, and the fifth word from the left. The word in the newspaper reads "donut." Now I know that I have to go to the Krispy Kreme to meet my partner who's on the run. Either that or I've just received a hint that I need to lose some weight. There was a reason I got out of the spy business.

Another type of spy-novel-like cipher is the *concealment cipher,* which hides messages within other messages. This is a way to place certain words in a message so that it can be discovered only by the person who knows where they are located. If my partner's letter read "furry rabbits eat in gardens more than in vegetables stores," then I could decipher it. I know from my agent-training program that I should pay attention to every third word only, thus my message is "Eat more vegetables". (My partner and I were never very close.)

Steganography

Steganography is another way of hiding data, but this approach attempts to hide the *existence* of the data instead of transforming it into an unreadable format, as in encryption. Messages can be hidden in graphics, WAV files, the slack space of hard drives, or document headers. This can be done manually or through automated means. Several programs are available that allow people to insert their messages into a graphic. (Graphics are used most often because they contain so much information that inserting extra bits will usually not distort the picture in a way that is noticeable.) This graphic can then be sent via e-mail, or another transmission method, and if it was intercepted the capturer would need to know that a message was hidden within the graphic and then have the means to properly extract it. So steganography is a science of hiding data in some type of media with the hopes of not being noticed.

 **Cipher Types**

Cryptographic mechanisms have been under the watchful eye of the U.S. government (and most governments) for quite some time. Harry Truman created the National Security Agency (NSA) in 1952 with its main objective being to listen in on communications in the interest of national security. The government has also attempted to restrict the use of public cryptography so that the enemies of the United States could not employ encryption methods that were too strong for the NSA to break. These restrictions have been relaxed over recent years, but there are still limits on what encryption mechanisms can be sold or sent to the nations that the government has labeled as "terrorist" or "hostile."

The government adopted an encryption device called the Clipper Chip that received a lot of criticism and resistance. The chip was to be placed in all American-made communication devices and would allow the government to listen in on encrypted conversations when it seemed necessary. Personal privacy debates ran rampant and spelled the end for the chip, but there were also other logistical reasons the Clipper Chip failed. It used an algorithm, called SkipJack, which was never publicly tested and used a key of only 80 bits. Most algorithms are publicly tested to ensure that there are no flaws or weaknesses, but this algorithm was developed by the NSA, which does not release its source code for public review. The fact that the SkipJack algorithm was classified hurt the public's trust and confidence in its effectiveness, but their main beef with the Clipper Chip was that it was just too "Big Brother-ish."

Exam Tip	
It is important to remember that the Clipper Chip used the SkipJack algorithm and that is used an 80-bit key.	

Governments have had other involvement in cryptography. In 1998, 33 countries signed the *Wassenaar Arrangement*, which limits the selling and exportation of encryption products to specific countries and groups. They decided to not control products that use symmetric algorithms with up to 56-bit keys and asymmetric products that uses up to 512-bit keys. Most governments have the necessary processing power and resources to break this level of encryption if they needed to, so they lifted any restrictions that were in place on this type of cryptography.

The U.S. has the following controls over importing and exporting cryptographic mechanisms:

- Retail cryptography of any length can be exported once a technical review has been completed and approved.
- Any mechanism with any key length can be exported under a license exception, after a technical review and approval, to any country not deemed a terrorist country.
- Open and publicly available source code can be exported under a license exception without technical review.

Kerckhoff's Principle

Auguste Kerckhoff published a paper in 1883 stating that the only secrecy involved with a cryptosystem should be the key. His stance was that if the strength of a cryptosystem relies on the fact that an attacker does not know how an algorithm works, it is only a matter of time before that attacker reverse-engineers the algorithm and the secret flies out the window.

As stated earlier, most algorithms are released to the public so that the people within the cryptography field can review it and identify any errors, weaknesses, or flaws. These issues are reported, and the developers go back to the drawing board and improve the algorithm. Cryptographers usually have more trust in algorithms that go through this process and are more satisfied if they can walk through the code and the logic of the beast themselves before giving their stamp of approval.

The NSA does not take this approach. They do not release their algorithms for public review, because they feel it provides more secrecy and protection. This can easily turn into a religious debate, and it has in many cases.

> ### Travel Advisory
> Although the NSA does not release most of their algorithms to the public, they have the top cryptographers working on them, so just because the public cannot test them does not mean they are not strong.

Key Escrow

We've all probably seen movies where the police put a wiretap on a suspect's phone line. Have you ever wondered how this works or if it's being done to you? Well, you'll be happy to know that it's not as simple as a flip of a switch. It does take a little work.

When the police need to listen in on phone conversations (or review e-mail and other electronic transmissions) for things like drug deals, murder investigations, or terrorist attacks, they have to cut through some red tape. This is done to protect our privacy and limit corruption.

With the idea of the Clipper Chip, the key that is necessary to decrypt communication data is escrowed. The *key escrow* provides a checks and balances system by bringing in other parties to the process. To decrypt the necessary information, the law enforcement agent needs the key to unlock the encrypted message. Each key is divided into two pieces, which are submitted and protected by two different escrow agencies. The reason the keys are split is to make sure that one agency cannot decrypt an individual's data on its own. Adding another agency makes corruption that much harder and less probable. Key escrow usually involves three groups—two key escrow agencies and one law enforcement representative.

To get this type of wiretap started, a law enforcement agent cannot just demand the key from both agencies. Instead, a court order must be obtained first. Once the court order is submitted to both agencies, the pieces of the key are released to the agent. The key pieces are put together to form one key, which is used to decrypt the communication data.

The Clipper Chip uses a hardware encryption chip, but key escrow can also be used in purely software-based cryptosystems using public key cryptography. Similar to the previous example, a private key is divided into two pieces and stored separately. When decryption is needed, the two pieces are put back together to form a functional private key. This software-based escrow process is referred to as *fair cryptosystems*.

Key escrow is used in companies today for key recovery procedures. The company needs to ensure that it can access its data that Bob encrypted with his key, even after he falls off of the side of a mountain or for some other reason becomes unavailable. So the necessary key is escrowed, or split and stored separately, and it usually requires two or more people to be involved in reconstructing the key.

Substitution Cipher

A *substitution cipher* replaces one character or bit for another character or bit. Julius Caesar developed a simplistic substitution cipher by replacing each letter with the letter three places beyond it in the alphabet, also known as a shift alphabet.

If this method was used with the English alphabet, a message of "KEY" would encrypt to "NHB." The only way a person could properly decrypt this message is to know the key, which is to move up the alphabet three spaces. This may seem too simplistic to you to be of any use, but in those days many people could not read in the first place! Today's algorithms use substitution but with much more complexity.

Exam Tip
A Caesar cipher is an example of a simple substitution cipher.

Transposition Cipher

Transposition ciphers move characters or bits to another place within the message block instead of substituting them with another value. This is also called permutation. The only way to properly unscramble the text, or decrypt it, is to know the key, as illustrated in Figure 6-3. The key indicates how the scrambling of characters will take place and how that process is to be reversed to decrypt the message.

Once again, this is the basic form of transposition and does not represent the true complexity in which it is used today.

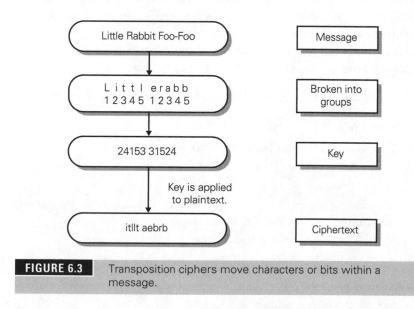

FIGURE 6.3 Transposition ciphers move characters or bits within a message.

Block Cipher

Block cipher algorithms break the plaintext message into several blocks of bits and then work on the individual blocks one at a time. The algorithm puts the bits within these blocks through several rounds of substitution and transposition. Each round is a separate process of mathematical functions and logic that take place on the block over and over again in different order. It really shakes, rattles, and rolls the bits until it is basically impossible to decrypt without the necessary key.

The framework of block ciphering creates two problems for an attacker: confusion and diffusion. The unknown key values and the complexity of the algorithm cause confusion, and sending the bits through different rounds of encryption processes creates the diffusion. An analogy is when Katie is given the task of finding 35 people. The 35 people start off as one group in her living room and have their own map that lays out paths to their destinations. Each person has a destination of a particular city in a different state. The 35 people disperse and reach their destinations, and it is up to Katie to find them. Because she does not have a copy of each and every person's map (or their keys), it brings confusion to the game. Because each person is in a different state, it brings along diffusion also. The same thing takes place within a block algorithm. Attackers do not know which rounds were performed on the plaintext because they do not have the key, and because the data goes through so many different rounds, they can not easily retrace the steps that have been taken.

The available rounds of substitution and transposition are provided in the algorithm's S-boxes, shown in Figure 6-4. Different algorithms can specify different numbers of rounds that are to be used.

This example uses two rounds and blocks of 4 bits. Typically, many more rounds of S-boxes are used with blocks of 64 bits or more.

The block cipher in this example has the following characteristics:

- 4-bit blocks.
- Two rounds of S-boxes (substitution boxes).
- Each S-box contains a lookup table that instructs how the bits should be encrypted.
- The key that is used in the encryption process dictates what S-boxes are used, in what order, and with what values.

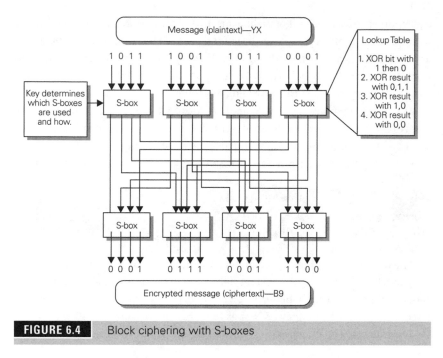

FIGURE 6.4 Block ciphering with S-boxes

An algorithm can be analogous to a large building with many rooms, and the bits can be thought of as people entering the building. In Figure 6-4, the building has eight rooms, and each room has different transposition and substitution functions that each person will need to go through when they enter the room. The key is the map that each person must follow, which tells them which room to enter and in what order. A person may enter all the rooms or only some of the rooms, and they may enter a room more than once, depending on that individual's key. Once everyone has entered their predetermined rooms, they exit out another door. The result is encrypted bits or confused people, depending on what we are working with.

Exam Tip

Data Encryption Standard (DES) is the best-known block cipher.

Stream Cipher

The *stream cipher* is different from the block cipher in that it works on the message as a continual flow of bits instead of individual blocks of bits. During the encryption process, each bit of plaintext is turned into a different bit of ciphertext through an assembly line approach. This takes place by using a *keystream generator,* which basically creates a continual flowing stream of bits that are used to turn the plaintext into ciphertext. The output of the keystream generator is exclusively ORed (XOR) with the original message, as shown in Figure 6-5

XOR is an operation in binary mathematics that is applied to two bits. The rules of this function are as follows: If both bits are the same, the result is zero (1 + 1 = 0, 0 + 0 = 0). If the bits are different, then the result is one (1 + 0 = 1, 0 + 1 = 1).

Example of how bits from a keystream generator are used to encrypt data:

Plaintext	1001010111
Keystream output	0011101010
Ciphertext	1010111101

The one-bit-at-a-time approach that stream ciphers use is very resource-intensive, which is why they are best implemented in hardware instead of software. Block ciphers are usually better implemented in software, when compared to stream ciphers, because they are not as resource-intensive.

The following characteristics are important to know and understand:

- Stream ciphers and block ciphers are two types of symmetric algorithms (covered in next section).
- Stream ciphers are usually much faster than block ciphers.

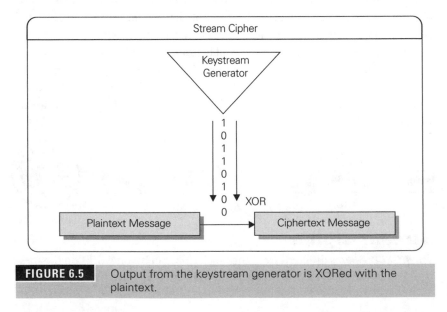

FIGURE 6.5   Output from the keystream generator is XORed with the plaintext.

- Stream ciphers operate on smaller units of plaintext (bits), whereas block ciphers work on larger units (blocks of bits).
- Stream ciphers are more suited for hardware implementation than block ciphers.

For a stream cipher to be considered strong, it should exhibit the following characteristics:

- Long periods of no repeating patterns within keystream values.
- Statistically unpredictable results.
- The keystream is not linearly related to the key.
- Statistically unbiased keystream (as many 0s as 1s).

Symmetric Cryptography

Symmetric cryptography is a technology where the sender and receiver use two instances of the same key for encryption and decryption purposes. So if Eric encrypts a message and sends it to Barry, Barry needs to have a copy of the key Eric used to properly decrypt the message.

A symmetric key has dual functionality, meaning one key can be used for encryption and decryption. So Eric does not need to have one key for encryption and one key for decryption—one key can perform both functions.

If Eric wants to communicate to someone and use encryption, he needs to figure out how to get the necessary key to that person *before* sending an encrypted message. It is important that Eric gets the key to the destination in a secure fashion. This is one of the largest obstacles when using symmetric encryption mechanisms. Simply sending the key via e-mail is not secure, so Eric must find a way to deliver the key through an *out-of-band* method, so intruders cannot intercept it. Some examples of out-of-band methods are saving the key to a floppy disk and hand delivering it (sneakernet), sending it via snail mail, or having a secure carrier deliver it. Each creates a huge hassle and would not allow us to process data at the speed we are accustomed to today.

Symmetric encryption provides confidentiality, because that is the main security service provided by any type of encryption, but this type of cipher cannot provide nonrepudiation or true user authentication. If someone encrypted a message with a symmetric key and was later questioned about it, at least two people have the same key so we cannot prove which of the two people actually sent the message.

Symmetric algorithms also have a scalability issue. If you want to communicate with one friend, you have one key to keep track of; if you want to communicate with three friends, you need to keep track of three different keys. The number of keys that need to be maintained grows as more users are involved. The equation that is used to calculated the number of keys that are needed is $N(N-1)/2$. So if 5 people are going to communicate using symmetric keys, a total of 10 keys will be needed. [5(5-1)/2 = 10 keys]

It seems like some pretty glaring weaknesses have been identified with the use of symmetric keys, and you are probably wondering why these kinds of encryption algorithms are even implemented. Quite simply, they are very fast and hard to break. Compared to asymmetric systems, symmetric algorithms scream in speed and they do their particular job (encrypting and decrypting data) quite well. It is also very difficult to uncover data that is encrypted with a symmetric algorithm if a large key size is used. Like many things, symmetric algorithms have their place in life in which they shine, and as we have evolved in our computing skills and cryptography knowledge we developed something that helped overcome their identified downfalls, which is covered in the next section.

There are several different symmetric algorithms used today. It is important that you can identify the following algorithms as symmetric:

- Data Encryption Standard (DES)
- Data Encryption Algorithm (DEA)
- Blowfish
- International Data Encryption Algorithm (IDEA)
- RC4
- Advanced Encryption Standard (AES)
- Rijndael
- SAFER

The actual algorithm used for the Data Encryption Standard (DES) is Data Encryption Algorithm (DEA), and the algorithm used for the Advanced Encryption Standard (AES) is Rijndael. We go into more detail on both standards and algorithms later in this chapter.

A summary of symmetric algorithm characteristics is shown here:

Strengths

- Much faster than asymmetric systems
- Hard to break if using a large key size

Weaknesses

- **Key distribution** It requires a secure mechanism.

- **Scalability**   Each pair of users needs a unique pair of keys, so the number of keys grows as the number of users increase.
- **Limited security**   It can provide confidentiality, but not authenticity or nonrepudiation.

Asymmetric Cryptography

Asymmetric algorithms use two different keys for encryption and decryption purposes: a *public key* and a *private key*.

Public keys can be known to everyone and are usually readily available by storing them in publicly accessible directories. The private key, on the other hand, must be known and available only to the owner.

Public and private keys work together to perform encryption and decryption processes. If data is encrypted with a user's public key, it must be decrypted with that user's private key. It is impossible to encrypt and decrypt data with the same key in asymmetric cryptography, meaning someone could not encrypt data with a public key and decrypt the data with the same public key. The two keys are mathematically related, but cannot be derived from each other. It should also be noted that each key type can perform an encryption or decryption function, so don't think that one does the encrypting and the other does the decrypting. Let's look at an example:

Russ encrypts data with his private key and sends it to Andy. In order for Andy to decrypt the information, he must have a copy of Russ' public key. So, Andy uses Russ' public key to decrypt the data and he can then read it. Now, if Andy wants to reply back to Russ with an encrypted message, he simply uses Russ' public key again to encrypt it. Russ then uses his private key to decrypt the reply.

Local Lingo

Asymmetric algorithms are also known as public key cryptography.

Asymmetric algorithms can provide user authentication and nonrepudiation. Authentication and nonrepudiation are provided because only one person should have access to a particular private key. If Russ encrypts data with his private key, Andy is assured that it really came from Russ because he is the only person that is supposed to have a copy of that key.

The mathematics involved with asymmetric algorithms is more complex and resource-intensive, thus slower than symmetric algorithms. They are approximately 100 to 1,000 times slower. Because these algorithms are slow, they are used only to encrypt small amounts of data.

We looked at two main disadvantages to using symmetric algorithms: key distribution and scalability. If we are using symmetric keys, we have to figure out how to get the key to the receiver through secure means, and it has to take place through some type of out-of-band process. Also, as more people need to communicate to each other, the number of symmetric keys grows and can become unmanageable. Asymmetric algorithms do not have these issues because each person needs only one key pair (public and private keys). Anyone that Russ needs to communicate with can use his public key, thus he does not need to keep track of different keys for each person. This allows the process to be more scalable. Also there is not a need to get a key securely to the receiver because anyone can have access and use Russ' public key.

The following are asymmetric algorithms you need to be familiar with:

- RSA
- Elliptic Curve Cryptosystem (ECC)
- Diffie-Hellman
- El Gamal
- Digital Signature Algorithm (DSA)
- Knapsack

Exam Tip

The RSA algorithm is named after the individuals who developed it; Ron Rivest, Adi Shamir, and Leonard Adleman.

A summary of asymmetric cryptography characteristics is listed here:

Strengths

- Better key distribution than symmetric systems
- Better scalability than symmetric systems
- Can provide confidentiality, authentication, and nonrepudiation

Weakness

- Much slower than symmetric systems

Travel Advisory

The Merkle-Hellman and Chor-Rivest knapsack cryptosystems have been broken, but are two examples of knapsack algorithms.

Objective 6.03 Hybrid Approach

A hybrid approach is a combination of both symmetric and asymmetric algorithms. It is the ultimate form of encryption because it uses the strengths of both algorithms to provide more overall efficiency. The actual message is encrypted with the symmetric key, and it pays to remember that the weakness of this method was finding a way to get the key to the receiver through a secure method. This is why the asymmetric algorithm is brought in. The asymmetric key is then used to encrypt the symmetric key. The encrypted symmetric key is then appended and sent along with the message. So we have the message encrypted with a symmetric key and the symmetric key encrypted with an asymmetric key. As shown in Figure 6-6, when the receiver accepts the message she uses an asymmetric key to decrypt the symmetric key and then uses the symmetric key to decrypt the message.

The hybrid method allows for secure distribution of symmetric keys. The following are the necessary points you need to understand pertaining to the algorithm types:

- Asymmetric algorithms perform encryption and decryption by using public and private keys.

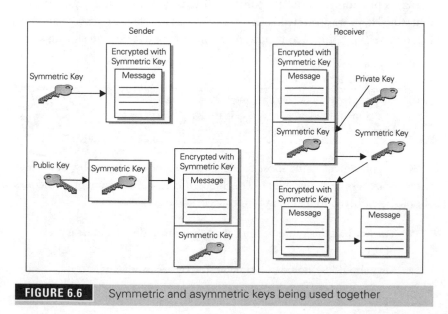

FIGURE 6.6 Symmetric and asymmetric keys being used together

- Symmetric algorithms perform encryption and decryption by using the same key.
- A symmetric key is used to encrypt the actual message.
- Public and private keys are used to encrypt and decrypt the symmetric key.
- An asymmetric key refers to a public key or private key.

Key Management

The hybrid approach introduced a secure way of transmitting symmetric keys, which is referred to as key distribution. So we have that covered, but what about ensuring that keys are generated and stored securely? If we overlook these issues of cryptography, we make it much easier for the bad guy to obtain our precious keys without much effort. If an attacker has access to our cryptography key, then he can decrypt and read messages that we need to be confidential.

Typically, protocols are used to automatically manage keys and their distribution. In Chapter 2, we looked at the Kerberos protocol, which uses a key distribution center (KDC) to handle functions such as key storage, distribution, and maintenance. The KDC receives requests for keys from various devices and users, generates them, and securely distributes them. This task is automated in order to reduce possible errors—meaning it isn't done manually by human beings. But there are things that people need to make sure take place even if technology is providing a lot of the functionality, as in not sharing keys, ensuring that stored keys are protected, selecting key sizes that provide the necessary protection level, and proper configuration of the software using and storing keys.

Exam Tip
Other key exchange protocols are RSA, Diffie-Hellman, and a variation of the Diffie-Hellman algorithm called the Key Exchange Algorithm (KEA).

Key management is the most challenging part of cryptography, because it takes awareness and discipline. The following key management principles should be enforced to maintain proper security levels:

- The key length should be long enough to provide the necessary level of protection.
- Keys should be stored and transmitted by secure means.

- Key values should be random, and the full spectrum of the keyspace should be used.
- The key's lifetime should correspond with the sensitivity of data that it is protecting (less sensitive data = longer key lifetime; more sensitive data = shorter key lifetime).
- Split knowledge and dual control should be used to protect centrally stored keys.
- Multiple copies of keys increase the chances of disclosure and compromise.
- Use one key or key pair per application. (Using the same key for multiple uses increases potential for compromise.)
- Keys should be backed up or escrowed in case of emergency.
- Keys should be properly destroyed when their lifetime ends.
- Keys should not be presented in cleartext anywhere.

> **Exam Tip**
>
> Key zeroization is properly destroying any remnants of a key, which should take place at the end of its lifetime.

Data Encryption

When two people or devices are communicating in an encrypted form, they are usually using a *session key*, which is a symmetric key that is only good for one session of communication. So, if an attacker intercepted a session key, she would only be able to use it for a small window of time. This is not true for static symmetric keys, which if compromised could be used to decrypt confidential messages for as long as the users use the same key.

Session keys can be created and exchanged before actual messages are transmitted. During a handshaking process, the two computers agree upon what algorithm and key size to use to create the session key. One of the systems can then create the session key, encrypt it with the other user's public key, and securely send the session key to the receiver. The two parties then use this session key to encrypt all the data they send back and forth to each other, which provides a secure virtual connection. When they are finished communicating and the session is finished, the session key is destroyed. The next time they want to communicate securely, the same dance must take place and a new session key must be created.

Travel Advisory

Secret and session keys are types of symmetric keys. Secret keys are static, meaning they are not dynamically created and destroyed for each communication dialog, whereas session keys are dynamically created and destroyed.

Security Goals

When employing any type of security, it is important to understand the goal(s) one is trying to accomplish with the security mechanism. This applies to the different cryptography technologies and components that can be used as well. Typically, there are three goals that encryption can provide:

- **Confidentiality**   A technique called *secure message format* can be used, which ensures that only the intended party can decrypt and read the message. To do this, the sender would encrypt the symmetric key with the receiver's public key. This way only the receiver's private key can be used to decrypt the symmetric key. The symmetric key is then used to decrypt the message.

- **Authenticity**   A technique called *open message format* can be used, which verifies who actually sent the message. To do this, the sender uses his or her private key for encryption purposes. Anyone who has access to the sender's public key can decrypt and read the encrypted data. Because anyone and everyone has access to her public key, confidentiality is not provided, but there is the guarantee that it came from one particular sender, because she is the only one who is supposed to have access to his or her private key.

- **Confidentiality and authenticity**   A technique called *secure and signed format* can be used. In this instance, the sender can encrypt the session key with his or her private key and then encrypt it again with the receiver's public key. To decrypt the session key, the receiver must first perform decryption using the sender's public key and then his or her own private key. If this takes place successfully, the receiver can be assured that the message came from the actual sender (authenticity) and that confidentially was provided, meaning no one else could have read this information during transmission.

Travel Advisory

In most cases, a digital signature is used in the secure and signed format, which we look at shortly.

Types of Symmetric Algorithms

This section details a few of the different types of symmetric algorithms available today. Although these are different algorithms, they are symmetric, meaning the sender and receiver use the same key for encryption and decryption processes.

DES

Data Encryption Standard (DES) has had a long and rich history within the computer community. In 1974, the National Institute of Standards and Technology (NIST) constructed this standard and chose an algorithm to fulfill it to be used for encrypting government data that was classified as "sensitive but unclassified." *Lucifer* was the algorithm chosen by NIST, which had been developed by IBM. Lucifer originally used a 128-bit key size, but was modified to use a 64-bit key (56 bits are true key bits and 8 bits are used for parity). After Lucifer was modified, it was then called the Data Encryption Algorithm (DEA).

DES is a block cipher that uses block sizes of 64 bits. This means that a message is chopped up into blocks of this size and each block is passed through the algorithm for encryption and decryption procedures. There are 16 rounds of substitution and transposition that take place on each and every block within a message. When all of the scrambling and substituting is done, the 64-bit block of plaintext ends up as a 64-bit block of ciphertext.

Block ciphers use different modes of operation that work better in some environments than in others. We cover four distinct modes used by DES in the next sections.

> **Exam Tip**
>
> DES uses MAC for integrity and authentication.

Electronic Code Book (ECB) Mode *Electronic Code Book* (ECB) mode operates just like its name states—a codebook. Every key is a codebook within itself, which dictates the substitution and transposition that will take place on the different blocks of data. Each block that is encrypted does not have interdependencies with the previous blocks that were encrypted, which is how the other three modes actually work. This means that one block of plaintext that is encrypted will end up to be the exact same ciphertext every time it is encrypted when using the same key, as shown in Figure 6-7. So if "X" is encrypted, and the result is "T," "X" will always encrypt to "T," which provides patterns for attackers to identify and use to reverse-engineer the process and possibly uncover the key. When using the other modes we look at, "X" may encrypt to "B" one time, "R" another time, and "z" the time after that. This is because these modes introduce much more randomness to the process.

ECB is very susceptible to Known Plaintext attacks, where the attacker has some plaintext and ciphertext of messages and works to reverse-engineer the steps within the algorithm to uncover the key that was used. Because of this, ECB is usually used in encrypting small amounts of data, such as encryption keys and challenge-response values. It can also be used in ATM machines to encrypt personal identification numbers (PINs).

Cipher Block Chaining (CBC)   *Cipher Block Chaining* (CBC) works differently than ECB, thus does not have the same weaknesses. ECB shows patterns of behavior because each time the same key is used to encrypt a block, the same ciphertext is always produced. CBC, on the other hand, takes some of the ciphertext created from encrypting a previous block of text and inserts it in the encryption process of encrypting the next block. Basically, each 64-bit block of text, the key, and ciphertext from the previous block is sent through the algorithm, as shown in Figure 6-7.

CBC introduces interdependencies between the blocks because they are chained together, hence the name Cipher Block Chaining.

Cipher Feedback (CFB) Mode and Output Feedback (OFB) Mode   *Cipher Feedback* (CFB) and *Output Feedback* (OFB) are modes used to emulate a stream

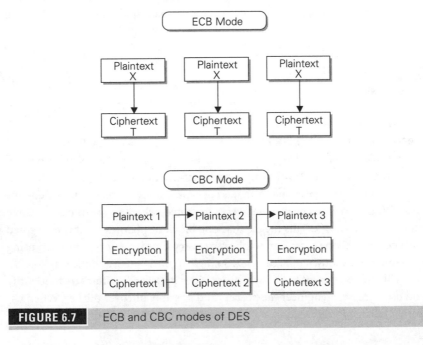

FIGURE 6.7   ECB and CBC modes of DES

cipher. Remember that we are talking about modes of DES, which is a block cipher. But if DES is used in one of these modes it is actually working as a stream cipher. The difference between block and stream ciphering is in the way they carry out encryption and decryption. Block ciphers work on blocks of messages; stream ciphers work with streams of bits. CFB and OFB make life confusing because they cross the line between block and stream, but this functionality is necessary in some implementations.

Triple-DES (3DES)

Triple-DES (3DES) is the new and improved version of DES. Hey, wait a minute. What happened to Double-DES? Fair question. Double-DES provides no more security than DES, although it does have a 112-bit key. It turned out that DES and Double-DES had the same work factor, thus Double-DES was no harder to break than single-DES.

As processing power and cryptanalysis skills increased over the years, the 56-bit DES algorithm became vulnerable to attacks and was eventually broken, which prompted for the creation of 3DES. 3DES uses 48 rounds in its computation, or three times that of single-DES, which uses 16 rounds. Increasing the activity that takes place during the encryption and decryption processes makes it highly resistant to cryptanalysis attacks and much stronger than DES. A drawback, however, is the performance hit. 3DES can take up to three times longer than DES to perform encryption and decryption procedures.

3DES can encrypt and decrypt messages differently depending upon the mode of operation. These modes are shown here:

- DES-EEE3 uses three different keys for encryption.
- DES-EDE3 uses three different keys and encrypts, decrypts, and then encrypts the data.
- DES-EEE2, DES-EDE2 are the same as the previous modes, but the first and third operation uses the same key.

The developer implementing DES or 3DES can make the decision on what mode is best for his or her specific product and environment.

Advanced Encryption Standard (AES)

After over twenty years as the standard, NIST decided to replace DES as it became more susceptible to attacks. The new standard, called *Advanced Encryption Standard* (AES), was announced in January 1997 and required a symmetric block algorithm supporting variable key sizes to fulfill the standard's requirements. A block cipher called *Rijndael* was chosen by NIST and on May 26, 2002 became the U.S. official standard for encrypting "sensitive but unclassified" data. This algorithm has key sizes of 128, 192, and 256 bits.

Other Symmetric Algorithms

The following are other symmetric algorithms used today for data encryption:

- **International Data Encryption Algorithm (IDEA)**   A 64-bit block cipher that puts the blocks through eight rounds of computation and uses a 128-bit key. At one time it was thought that IDEA would replace DES, but it is patented, so fees would have to be paid to use it.

- **RC5**   A block cipher that has a variety of parameters it can use, as in block size, key size, and the number of rounds that are used. It was created by Ron Rivest and analyzed by RSA Data Security, Inc. The possible block sizes that can be used in this algorithm are 32, 64, and 128 bits, and the key sizes go up to 2,048 bits. RC5 was patented by RSA Data Security in 1997.

- **Blowfish**   A block cipher that works on 64-bit blocks of data. The key length can be up to 448 bits, and the data blocks go through 16 rounds of cryptographic functions. Bruce Schneier designed it.

Travel Advisory

There are other symmetric algorithms out there; we covered only a few that will most likely be covered on the CISSP exam.

Asymmetrical Algorithms

The RSA algorithm has become a worldwide de facto standard when public key cryptography functionality is needed. It provides key distribution, data encryption, and digital signature capabilities. RSA's patent expired in September 2000, and as a result, it is now being incorporated as a mandatory asymmetric cryptographic algorithm in many protocols and cryptosystems.

RSA is based on a mathematical principle called a *trapdoor one-way function*, which means that it is easier to compute its mathematical functions in one direction than in the opposite direction. A common analogy used to get this concept across is when you drop a glass on the floor. Dropping a glass on the floor is the easy part, putting the pieces back together is next to impossible.

RSA bases it security on the difficulty of factoring large numbers into their original prime numbers. This is a type of one-way function because multiplying two prime numbers and coming up with a large resulting number is the easy piece of the algorithm. Factoring this large number back into its original prime numbers is basically impossible. Factoring numbers into prime numbers may not seem that difficult, but we are talking about numbers that are 10^{308} in size. Factoring these numbers is next to impossible if you do not have a secret or insight into how the number was created in the first place. This secret is known as a *trapdoor one-way function.*

Let's look at another analogy so we don't hurt our brains too much here. If Emily knows which school locker Daphne uses, she can shove a note through one of the slits on the top of the locker. This allows Emily to leave a message for Daphne without having to know the combination to Daphne's locker. Because Daphne is the only one who is supposed to know the combination to her locker, Emily can be assured that no one else will be able to open the locker and read her note. This analogy describes how the trapdoor one-way function works. The public key has the functionality of packaging data up in a way that only the private key can open, which is similar to knowing what locker to slip a note into. Only the private key knows the necessary combination to unlock the data. Without knowing this combination, or trapdoor, it is impossible to uncover the data we have safely encrypted with a public key.

Diffie-Hellman Key Exchange

As stated earlier, hybrid cryptography is based on two types of algorithms, asymmetric and symmetric. The asymmetrical functions deal with securely delivering symmetric keys to each party so that symmetrical encryption can be performed. The first algorithm developed for this type of key exchange was by Dr. W. Diffie and Dr. M.E. Hellman in 1976. Their algorithm, *Diffie-Hellman*, allowed users to handle key distribution electronically in a secure fashion without a previous relationship.

The Diffie-Hellman algorithm is used for key distribution only, not data encryption or digital signatures. This algorithm is vulnerable to man-in-the middle attacks, however, this weakness can be countered by using digital signatures. It is not based on the difficulty of factoring large numbers, but instead is based on calculating discrete logarithms in a finite field.

Local Lingo

A man-in-the-middle attack means that someone can insert themselves into a current dialog going on between two computers. This can be successful if authentication of the two parties is not required before the dialog begins.

El Gamal

El Gamal is a public key algorithm that can be used for digital signatures, data encryption, and key exchange. It is also based on calculating discrete logarithms in a finite field.

Elliptic Curve Cryptosystems (ECC)

An *Elliptic Curve Cryptosystem* (ECC) is another asymmetric algorithm that uses far less resources than other asymmetric algorithms because of the different type of mathematics that it uses. ECC cryptosystems use the properties of elliptic curves in their public key systems. The elliptic curves provide ways of constructing groups of elements and specific rules of how the elements within these groups are used together. The properties between the groups are used to build cryptographic algorithms.

Because of ECC's efficiency, it can provide the same level of protection as RSA, but with a smaller key size. ECC can perform encryption, digital signatures, and secure key exchange. Because of the low amount of processing required, ECC is a good choice for wireless devices and cellular telephones that have fewer resources than actual computers.

 **Objective 6.04**
Message Integrity and Digital Signatures

We mentioned the words confidentiality, authenticity, nonrepudiation, and integrity before when we were defining terms and security goals. Confidentiality relates to data being encrypted. Authenticity and nonrepudiation involves asymmetrical keys, which allows for the verification of the source of the message (authenticity) and not allowing that source to deny sending it at a later time (nonrepudiation). Integrity is a term that we haven't touched on yet, however. It revolves around a method called hashing, which is covered in this section.

Message Integrity

We spent all this time encrypting messages and making sure we know where they came from, but another important security measure is ensuring that the message has not been altered in any way during transmission; this is called *message integrity*.

One method of verifying message integrity has been the use of parity bits or cyclical redundancy checking (CRC) functions. Typically, these bits are used in protocols to identify any modifications. The downside is that they can only uncover unintentional modifications, such as power spikes or wire interference. This is not much help when dealing with an attacker changing a message as it travels from one computer to the next. An attacker can work around these mechanisms fairly easily by changing the message and then replacing the old parity value with a new one. To combat these kinds of threats, a function called a one-way hash is used.

One-Way Hash

A *one-way hash* takes a message of any length and creates a fixed-length value referred to as a *hash value*, or a *message digest*. It is created for the sole purpose of allowing the receiver to ensure that a message was not modified in an unauthorized manner as it was being transmitted. Let's look at an example.

Kathleen wants to send a message to Tom, and she wants to ensure the integrity of this message. To do this, she first needs to calculate a message digest for the message and append it to the message itself. When Tom receives the message, he has to use the same hashing algorithm that Kathleen used. He puts Kathleen's message through the algorithm and creates his own message digest value. So now Tom has two message digest values, one that Kathleen sent with her message and the one he calculated. He compares the two results and if they are the same, Tom knows that the message has not been modified. If the values do not match, it was either intentionally or unintentionally altered. This is illustrated in Figure 6-8.

Travel Advisory

Hashing does not encrypt the message; it only creates a message digest that is used to verify the integrity of the message.

Hashing algorithms are also used on users' passwords in many authentication products. When a user enters her password, it is then sent through a hashing algorithm. The resulting hashing value is what is actually sent to the authentication server. The server contains a database or file of hashed passwords, not the passwords themselves, and compares the hashed value sent by the user to the value held in the database for that user. If the two values match, the authentication server knows that the user typed in the correct password and authenticates her.

Hashed values of passwords are used so that the actual password is not transmitted or stored in cleartext. This means that if an attacker captured a password value as it was being transmitted or stole a password file, she would not have the

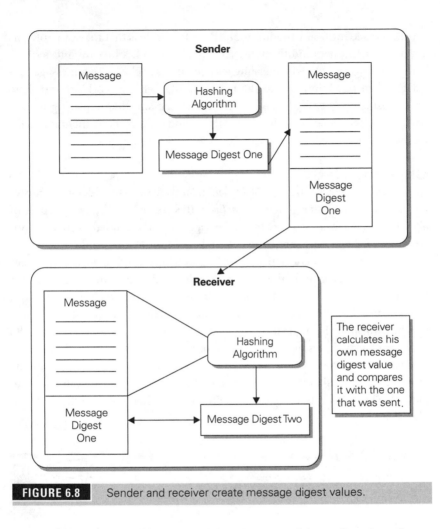

FIGURE 6.8   Sender and receiver create message digest values.

keys to the kingdom. She would have to continue working to figure out the actual passwords from the obtained hashed values.

Local Lingo

Cleartext is similar to plaintext. It is data that is not encrypted or hashed and therefore readable.

Attacks on Hashing Functions

Virtually every security mechanism has some type of weakness or potential attack areas to worry about and hashing is no different. So, it's important to understand different attacks and how certain security mechanisms can actually be vulnerable to them.

A *collision* is when a hashing algorithm produces the same message digest for two different messages. This should not happen. Collisions make it much easier for attackers to reverse engineer the process because it produces patterns, which provide insights into how the process works. It can be understood better when comparing it to a phenomenon in statistics referred to as the birthday paradox. This can be a little confusing, so take a deep breath.

How many people must be in the same room for the chance to be over 50 percent that another person has the same birthday as you? Answer: 253

How many people must be in the same room for the chance to be over 50 percent that at least two people share the same birthday? Answer: 23

In the first example, you are looking for someone in the room who shares your birthday, thus you are looking for one specific value that matches your value, or your birthday date. In the second example, you are looking for any two people who share the same birthday, or two matching values. Obviously, the second scenario produces greater odds, because it is easier to find two values that are the same than to look for one specific value in particular. This is referred to as the birthday paradox. It also has relevance to cryptography. A common method for attacking a one-way hash function is called the *birthday attack*.

The birthday attack is similar to the birthday paradox. During a brute force attack, an attacker will attempt to find a message digest value that matches one that has already been calculated. For example, if Andrea's password is "England01," an authentication system will run this through a hashing algorithm and come up with a value we are going to call "x." If an attacker wants to find out Andrea's password; he would capture the hashed version of her password, which is "x." The attacker will then try all possible characters until he finds one that hashes out to "x." If successful, he has found the necessary characters that make up Andrea's password.

This can be compared to finding someone with a specific birthday. If he finds two messages with the same hash value, it is the same as finding two people with the exact same birthday. The main point of this paradox and this section is to show how important longer message digest values truly are. A hashing algorithm that has a larger bit output will produce less collisions and is less vulnerable to brute force attacks like a birthday attack. For example, the MD5 algorithm creates a message digest of 128 bits, and the SHA-1 algorithm creates a message digest of 160 bits. SHA-1 has more possible message digest values, which means there is a smaller chance of collisions. Attackers try to identify these collisions in the birthday attack, so the less collisions, the more protection provided.

The following are characteristics of a strong hashing algorithm:

- The message digest value should be computed over the entire message.
- Data can't be disclosed by its message digest value.
- It produces no collisions.

Hashing Algorithms

In this section, we look at some of the available hashing algorithms used in cryptography today.

- **MD2**   A hash algorithm that is slower than the other MD hash functions. It was designed by Ron Rivest, as were all of the MD hashing algorithms. All MD hashing algorithms create a 128-bit message digest value.
- **MD4**   Used in software implementations for high-speed computations. The first two rounds were successfully attacked, so MD5 was created.
- **MD5**   A more complicated version of MD4 because it adds a fourth round of hashing functionality, which provides more security and is much more difficult to break.
- **HAVAL**   This is a variable-length one-way hash function and is a modification of MD5. This algorithm is not restricted to creating a specific size message digest value.
- **Secure Hash Algorithm (SHA)-1**   SHA-1 produces a 160-bit message digest. It is used in digital signatures and is a required component of the U.S. government's Digital Signature Standard (DSS).

Message Authentication Code

So far, one-way hashing has taken place without the use of any keys. A user would calculate a message digest, append it to the message and send it to the receiver. The purpose was merely to ensure integrity, not to secure the hashing function. However, it is possible for an attacker to obtain the message, alter it, calculate a new message digest, append it to the message, and send it onto the intended receiver. The receiver will calculate a message digest and compare it to the one that was appended, never knowing that the message was intercepted and altered. To provide the necessary protection to make sure any modifications are actually identified and to ensure that attackers cannot just calculate a different message digest value to fool the receiver, something else needs to be put into place.

This type of security is provided by using a hashing algorithm and a symmetric key, which is referred to as *message authentication code* (MAC). Message authentication code is the same thing as a one-way hashing function, except that the resulting hash value is the function of the message and the symmetric key. The symmetric key is concatenated with the message and the result of this is then passed through a hashing algorithm. If an attacker modifies the message while it is being sent from one person to another, she will not have the necessary symmetric key to produce the same message digest value that the receiver will generate, as shown in Figure 6-9. This means that the receiver will identify this unauthorized modification attempt and not accept the message in its received form. So one point for the good guys and no points for the bad guys.

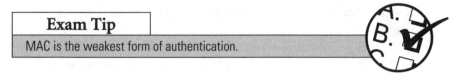

Exam Tip

MAC is the weakest form of authentication.

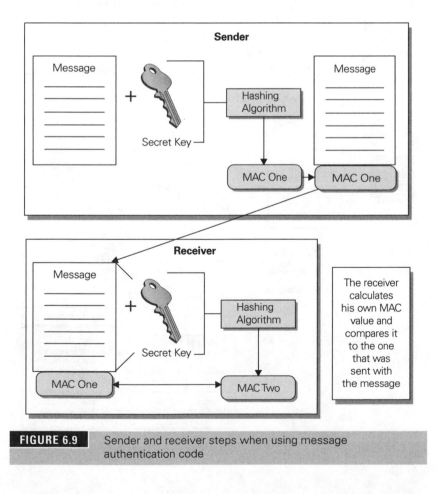

FIGURE 6.9   Sender and receiver steps when using message authentication code

Electronic Signing

A digital signature is not the process of signing your credit card receipt on the computer screen at Circuit City; that is actually referred to as a digitized signature. A digitized signature is an electronic form of an actual static signature we use when making credit card purchases. A *digital signature* is a hash value encrypted with a private key. A message that is to be digitally signed is passed through a hashing algorithm and the resulting message digest value is encrypted with that user's private key. Because the user is the only one that is supposed to be able to use his or her private key, this technology provides authenticity, nonrepudiation, and integrity. The steps of a digital signature are outlined in Figure 6-10.

When digital signatures are performed, the cryptosystem will use some type of hashing algorithm (SHA-1, MD5, HAVAL) and an algorithm that provides digital signature functionality (RSA or Digital Signature Algorithm). Once the hashing algorithm creates the message digest, the digital signature algorithm takes this value and encrypts it with the user's private key.

Digital signatures can be used in electronic contracts, to prove the identity of a software developer, and to protect software's integrity by identifying modifications

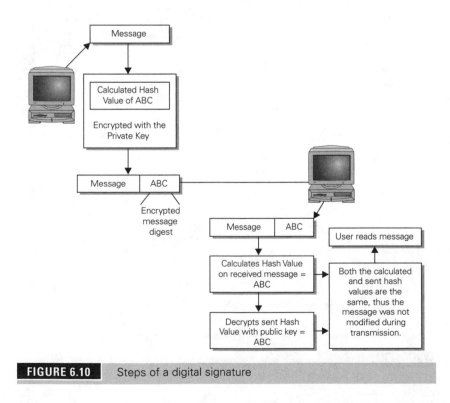

FIGURE 6.10 Steps of a digital signature

that have been introduced. Many software developing companies digitally sign their code to give the receiver a higher level of confidence in the software and to ensure that no one altered it after it left their facility. (Software signing and Authenticode is addressed in Chapter 9.)

DSS

The U.S. government and military likes everyone to be doing the same thing (wearing the same types of clothes, having the same haircut)—this is why it is a structured environment. Along with the DES and AES standards, they also developed a standard outlining how digital signatures should be carried out and validated. To make things simple, they called it the *Digital Signature Standard* (DSS). It was created by NIST so that the standard could be used by federal agencies, but over time, many vendors have incorporated DSS into their products for public use as well.

The algorithms specified in DSS to be used are Digital Signature Algorithm (DSA), RSA, and Elliptic Curve Digital Signature Algorithm (ECDSA) and the Secure Hash Algorithm (SHA-1). SHA-1 was designed to provide a more secure digital signature algorithm for federal applications. The sender computes a 160-bit hash value, and one of the digital signature algorithms encrypts it with her private key (signs it), appends it to the message, and sends it to the receiver. The receiver decrypts the value with the sender's public key, runs the message through the same hashing function, and compares the two values. If the values are the same, the receiver can be sure that the message has not been tampered with while in transit, and he knows exactly who sent the data.

RSA and DSA are the best-known and most widely used digital signature algorithms. Unlike RSA however, DSA can be used only for digital signatures. RSA can be used for digital signatures, data encryption, and key distribution. DSA has different characteristics when compared to RSA, which are listed here:

- DSA uses smaller key sizes than RSA.
- DSA is slower than RSA.
- DSA has not been put through a public analysis because it was developed by the NSA.

Exam Tip

Zero-knowledge proof means telling someone information without giving up the farm. A digital signature proves that a user has the necessary private key without actually sharing the key with the receiver. This is an example of zero-knowledge proof.

Cryptography Applications

As we learned in the previous chapter, computer systems need protocols and standards in place to allow for communication and interoperability. Cryptosystems need the same kind of framework in place so that different products and technologies can carry out intercommunication processes and understand each other to provide a seamless environment. This section discusses the various protocols, standards, and applications that make up this cryptography framework.

Public Key Infrastructure

Nearly everything discussed so far are components that can be used to construct a *Public Key Infrastructure* (PKI); this means all the programs, data formats, protocols, algorithms, standards, and procedures used in cryptography. This infrastructure is an ISO authentication framework. Just as other standards are developed to ensure interoperability, PKI was developed to provide authentication services across different networks and the Internet. However, PKI is simply a framework, not a technology; it does not specify protocols, products, and algorithms that have to be implemented, thus it provides a great degree of flexibility.

Along with authentication, PKI also ensures confidentiality, nonrepudiation, and message integrity by using both symmetric and asymmetric algorithms and hashing and digital signature algorithms. There are many components that make up PKIs, and they are covered in the following sections.

Certificate Authority (CA)

In order to participate in a PKI, you need a *digital certificate*. This is a credential containing your public key along with personal identification information. Digital certificates are created and managed by an entity called a *certificate authority* (CA). CAs are responsible for providing the following services: verifying an individual's identity, creating and digitally signing certificates, delivering certificates, and maintaining certificates over their lifetime.

A CA is a trusted third party that can be internal or external to an organization. Internal CAs provide a few advantages—the company can control the CA server, manage the authentication requirements and configurations, have in-house control over certificates, and can revoke certificates whenever necessary. External CAs can be a convenience if a company does not want the extra burden of the work required to build and maintain a PKI. Examples of external CAs are Entrust and VeriSign.

When a user requests a certificate, that individual's identity must be verified before a certificate is generated. Once the person's identification information is validated, a certificate is created, which binds that person's public key to their identity. The CA is the trusted third party that is used to vouch for other people's identity when secure communication needs to takes place, and it is the component that allows one person to trust another person and his or her public key.

An analogy for this process is the department of motor vehicles (DMV). When Emily gets her driver's license, she will then use that to prove her identity in different situations. When she writes a check at a retail store, the merchant will ask to see her identification. Emily provides her driver's license, and the merchant accepts her check. The merchant does not trust Emily directly, but he does trust the DMV, who is vouching for Emily's identification. This is basically the same role the CA plays in a PKI.

The CA is responsible for certificate generation, maintenance, and destruction when that time comes, which is referred to as a *key lifecycle*, because the public key is held within the certificate.

Registration Authority

Sometimes CAs need a little help. That is when the *registration authority* (RA) comes in. The RA is a portion of the CA that actually accepts certificate registration requests and verifies the requesting person's identification. After the identity has been verified, the RA sends the request to the CA, who actually generates the certificate and binds it to the requesting individual. The RA cannot generate and issue certificates, only the CA can.

There are different types of certificates which outline what the associated public/private keys can be for. The key pairs can be used for digital signatures or software signing, or they can allow an entity to perform CA responsibilities. The type of certificate being requested will determine the kind of information that must be submitted to prove one's identity. The more powerful certificates (software signing and CA responsibilities) usually require the requesting individual to go into the RA office for a face-to-face meeting.

Certificate Revocation List (CRL)

There are times when certificates are recalled, such as when an employee leaves the company or when a private key has been compromised. If Joe's private key has been stolen and someone else is using it to perform digital signatures, we want to provide some way that the receivers can be told not to trust Joe's private/public key pair any longer. In this situation, Joe would report to the CA that his private key was stolen, and the CA would add the serial number of his certificate to a *certificate revocation list* (CRL). Now when someone receives Joe's certificate and public key, she can go and check the CRL to see if it has been re-voked for some reason to find out if she should really trust who sent her the certificate and the corresponding public key.

The CA is responsible for maintaining the CRL and digitally signs it to ensure the integrity of the list and prove that it was actually created and maintained by the trusted third party, the CA itself.

Travel Advisory

Unfortunately, CRLs are not used properly in many PKI implementations, so one would not really know if they should trust a certificate or not. This piece of the PKI technology is being improved upon.

Components of PKI

When the CA issues a *certificate*, it is accompanied with a public key. The certificate is a critical piece in a PKI because it associates a user to a public key, and will provide authentication when messages are exchanged. Certificates contain serial numbers, version numbers, algorithm information, certificate lifetime, and the CA's signature, as shown in Figure 6-11.

How do CAs know how to create a certificate in this format and what values are supposed to be used to fulfill these fields? This is outlined in the certificate standard we use today, X.509, which is currently at version 3.

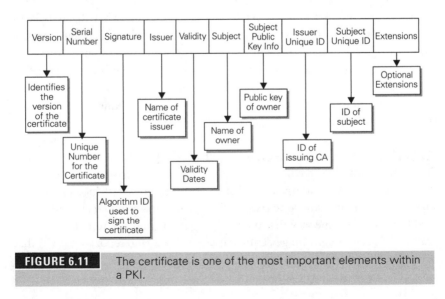

| FIGURE 6.11 | The certificate is one of the most important elements within a PKI. |

Once a certificate has been created and bound to a public key it needs to be in a place that is readily available to the public, or whoever will need to access it. Certificates are stored in certificate directories or repositories. The standard does not dictate what type of directory this needs to be, but today LDAP directories are usually implemented. In network directories (as in Active Directory) certificates can be held in repositories that hold other user information, as in their physical and logical addresses, phone number, network profiles, and network resource access permissions. When a user needs to get a copy of another user's certificate, she just needs to consult this centralized directory. (In reality the user will not be doing this herself, but her client software will carry out these activities for her.)

PKI Steps

So how do all of these components of a PKI actually work together in a real PKI environment? Let's walk through an example to see.

John needs to establish a private/public key pair. He can either create the pair himself and provide the public key during the registration process with the RA, or the CA can generate them for him. If the CA generates them, there must be a secure way to get the private key to John. In our example, John will generate his own private/public key pair, because that is usually how it takes place.

John sends a certificate registration request to the RA. The RA asks John to provide the necessary identification information required for the type of certificate John is requesting, as in a copy of his driver's license, his phone number, address, or a face-to-face meeting. Once the RA receives the required information and verifies it, it sends the request along with John's submitted public key to the CA. The CA creates a certificate and binds it to John's public key and identity information embedded within the certificate itself. Now John is registered and can participate in a PKI.

So, he decides he wants to communicate with Diane and requests her certificate and public key from a public certificate directory. The directory sends both components to John, and he validates the CAs digital signature that is embedded within the certificate. This means that John takes the CA's public key and decrypts the encrypted message digest stored within the certificate. Once the digital certificate is verified, John trusts the certificate and has confidence that the received key is really Diane's. John creates a session key and encrypts it with Diane's public key and sends it along with his own certificate and public key to Diane.

When Diane receives John's certificate, her client software looks to see if it trusts the CA that digitally signed the certificate. Diane's software is configured to trust this CA, so she validates the CA's digital signature and makes a request to review the CRL to see if the certificate is still valid or if it has been revoked. She finds that John's certificate is not on the CRL, so she trusts the validity of the certificate and John's public key.

Diane decrypts the session key with her private key. Diane and John will use this session key to encrypt the data they exchange, which provides a secure and confidential communication channel.

But why would we go through all this work? We have protocols that can actually create symmetric keys for us and exchange them securely using asymmetric algorithms without the use of a PKI. The answer is that two parties may not trust each other, especially if they have never interacted before. In our PKI example, John and Diane do not trust each other, but they both trust the CA. The CA vouches for each other's identity so John and Diane trust each other indirectly.

One-Time Pad

Throughout this entire chapter, we have discussed encryption mechanisms, their functions, their strengths and most importantly their weaknesses. The ultimate goal is to find a technique that an intruder cannot compromise. This section addresses a technique that offers the most foolproof method of encryption so far, the one-time pad.

A *one-time pad* is referred to as an unbreakable system because it uses a large random set of bits (the pad), which is used to encrypt and decrypt the message. The pad is as large as the message itself, thus can be thousands of bits long. The pad should be random and used only one time, meaning after it is used once it is destroyed, and another pad is generated for the next message. This is where the real strength of a one-time pad actually comes in.

Let's walk through how a one-time pad actually works. The plaintext data of the message is XORed with the pad, which is the same size as the message. The first bit in the pad is XORed with the first bit in the message, this continues until the whole message is converted into ciphertext. The receiver must have a copy of the exact same pad to reverse the process to uncover the original plaintext message. After this pad has been used, it is destroyed. If the same two users want to communicate again, another pad must be generated and used.

One-time pads can be integrated into applications and require a random number generator that supplies random values to the algorithm, which in turn creates the one-time pad.

The fact that one-time pads are destroyed after they are used makes it nearly impossible for an attacker to inflict much harm. Even if she were to intercept a copy of the pad, it would only be good for a small window of time, much like a session key. The steps of encryption using a one-time pad are shown in Figure 6-12.

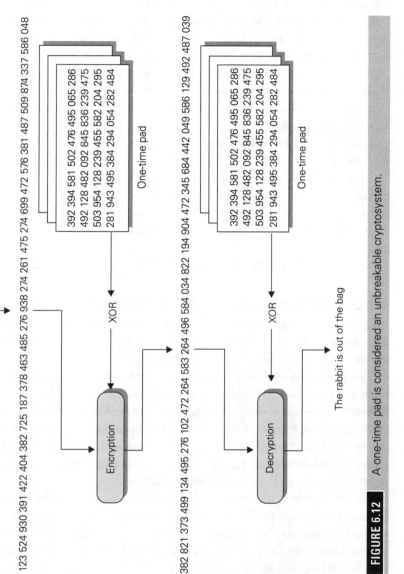

FIGURE 6.12 A one-time pad is considered an unbreakable cryptosystem.

You knew this was coming—there is a weakness in the one-time pad. Distribution of the pads is a nightmare. It is impractical in most situations because it is difficult to distribute the large pads of random values to all the necessary parties. Users must receive the pads in order for this process to work, and the pads are as long as, or longer than the actual message. The resources required for this process can be overwhelming and requires more overhead than it is worth in most situations. Government organizations that require the level of protection that one-time pad cryptosystem can provide are willing to commit the necessary resources and time needed, but in other environments this system is impractical because of all the barriers that need to be overcome to actually get the large pad to the receiver.

Another issue is creating a truly random pad. In most implementations, only pseudo-random number generators are available, which eventually repeat values and provide patterns. For a one-time pad to be truly unbreakable, a purely random number generator must be used, which again requires a lot of extra overhead.

So we created the perfect encryption scheme, but can't really use it. Great.

Encryption at Different Layers

Encryption can occur at different communication levels in our networking environments. We look at the two main types, link and end-to-end encryption, and review their characteristics and security issues.

Link encryption, which is also referred to as online encryption, provides extra security by encrypting everything over a specific communication channel. In link encryption, all the control information, such as headers, trailers, and routing information, is encrypted along with the actual message. This type of data can be beneficial if an attacker is trying to uncover where the message is going or where it came from. Some examples of where link encryption is typically used are satellite links, T3 lines, and telephone circuits.

End-to-end encryption, on the other hand, simply encrypts the message, or the data payload of a packet. The routing and control information held within the packets' headers and trailers are left unencrypted. Because end-to-end encryption does not encrypt these parts of a packet, it provides less overall protection when compared to link encryption.

Link encryption does have a downside, however. Because all of the information is encrypted, including data link and network layer headers, routers and switches must be able to decrypt this information so they know how to properly forward or route the traffic. The intermediate devices (routers, bridges, switches) must have the necessary algorithms, keys, and software to perform encryption and decryption processes. The other choice is to have link encryptors between the hops performing this activity for the intermediate devices. With end-to-end encryption, the routing information is not encrypted, so the routing equipment does not have to do this extra work in order to get the packets to their destinations properly.

Objective 6.06 Cryptographic Protocols

E-mail has become an extremely popular method of communication within businesses and for individuals everywhere. Because of its extensive use, e-mail has become more of a target for attackers, so standards and protocols have been put in place to provide interoperability and better security levels for our messages as they get passed back and forth. Before we discuss each of the standards and specific protocols, let's look at the way a typical e-mail message is secured. The following walks through the steps of a sender encrypting a message and digitally signing it and what the receiver goes through to verify it:

Sender's Steps

1. Calculate message digest on the message.
2. Encrypt message with session key.
3. Encrypt message digest with private key (digital signature).
4. Encrypt session key with receiver's public key.

Receiver's Steps

1. Decrypt session key with receiver's private key.
2. Decrypt message digest with sender's public key.
3. Decrypt message with session key.
4. Calculate new message digest and compare with the one sent.

There is nothing new here that we have not learned already in earlier sections. It is important to realize that these are the foundational steps to how almost all encryption and decryption procedures take place within technology today. Once you have these core pieces understood, you are well on your way to understanding how all products, protocols, and standards work pertaining to cryptography.

Privacy-Enhanced Mail (PEM)

Privacy-Enhanced Mail (PEM) is a standard for secure e-mail over the Internet and within corporations. It was developed to address compatibility issues with encryption products and key management functions. The protocols within PEM provide authentication, message integrity, encryption, and key management, and it works in a hierarchical trust model, which is similar to PKI. PKI and PEM use a hierarchical trust model, meaning all users and resources trust one entity. Because everyone trusts that one entity, it allows them to indirectly trust each other.

PEM was developed by several groups and uses DES-CBC for data encryption, MD2/MD5 for integrity, and RSA for sender authenticity, key management, and nonrepudiation.

PEM did not catch on as it was planned because it did not allow for enough flexibility. PKI does provide levels of flexibility and has been integrated into many e-mail products and corporate environments.

Message Security Protocol (MSP)

Message Security Protocol (MSP) is the military's version of PEM and was developed by the NSA. It is an X.400-compatible application-level protocol used to secure e-mail messages. MSP can be used to sign and encrypt messages and perform hashing functions. Applications that incorporate MSP enable different algorithms and parameters to be used to provide greater flexibility and options. When sensitive data needs to be encrypted (secret, top secret classifications), algorithms that have been developed by the NSA are employed. These algorithms have not been released to the public.

MSP provides confidentiality, authenticity, integrity, nonrepudiation, digital signatures, and return-receipts.

Local Lingo	
A return-receipt is something a receiver sends back to the sender to indicate that the message reached its destination. It also ensures that the receiver cannot deny receiving this message at a later time.	

Pretty Good Privacy (PGP)

Pretty Good Privacy (PGP) is a freeware e-mail client that allows users to choose from a variety of algorithms for data encryption and digital signatures. The key pair generation takes place by the user entering a passphrase. (Passphrases are covered in Chapter 2.)

PGP operates differently than the PKI framework we covered earlier. In a PKI environment, the CA verifies all users' identities and vouches for them. All users trust the CA, and this establishes a hierarchical trust structure. PGP takes a different approach by allowing a "web of trust" to be built by having users distribute and sign public keys themselves. This means that all users do not trust one entity (like a CA) but instead determine to what level they will trust each other.

Phil Zimmerman created PGP, which was released in 1991. It was the first widespread public key encryption program.

> **Exam Tip**
> PGP is a cryptosystem that uses session keys for message encryption.

Internet Security

Before we get into the different security protocols used on the Internet today, we need to clarify a few points. First, the Web is not the Internet. The Web runs on top of the Internet, in a sense, and is a collection of Hypertext Transfer Protocol (HTTP) servers that hold and process the Web sites that we see. The Internet is a collection of physical devices and communication protocols used to transverse these Web sites and interact with them. So the World Wide Web is the software that is used to create and maintain Web sites and the Internet is the underlining infrastructure that needs to be put into place to support connection to these sites.

Many times the activities we are performing over the Web are confidential (making purchases, performing online banking transactions, looking for a date) and we need to ensure that these actions are done securely. The next few sections look at different protocols that can be employed to secure our electronic transactions.

Secure Hypertext Transfer Protocol (S-HTTP)

Secure Hypertext Transport Protocol (S-HTTP) is basically HTTP with extra security sprinkled in. When a browser (the client) makes a request for sensitive information from a Web site, the Web server will recognize that this data needs to be encrypted before it is put onto the wire. The server and the client then agree upon an encryption method through a handshaking process. The client sends the server its public key, the server generates a session key, encrypts it with the client's public key, and sends it to the client. The client and server can then use this session key to encrypt messages.

S-HTTP is usually confused with HTTPS, but they are different technologies with different goals. S-HTTP encrypts individual *messages*; HTTPS, which is SSL working with the HTTP protocol, encrypts *a whole channel*—not individual messages. S-HTTP and SSL both use public key cryptography.

HTTPS

HTTPS protects the entire communication channel between two computers, not just individual messages. We see this protocol being used most when we are buying items from Web sites or performing online banking activities. You know that a HTTPS session has been established successfully when you see the small padlock at the bottom of your browser. HTTPS uses SSL and HTTP to provide a protected circuit between a client and server.

Secure Sockets Layer (SSL)

Secure Sockets Layer (SSL) is a protocol that was developed by Netscape for secure Web transactions and is the de facto standard in use today.

When a browser makes a request to a Web server, say a user wants to view his or her checking account information via an online banking site; the server initiates the process to establish a SSL connection. Before any confidential information is sent between the client and server, a secure SSL channel must be established. Theses necessary steps are listed here:

1. Server sends the client a certificate to authenticate itself.
2. Client checks to see if it trusts the CA that signed the server's certificate.
3. Client uses the CA's public key to verify the digital signature embedded within the certificate.
4. Client computes a message digest of the certificate and compares it with the message digest in the certificate to ensure its integrity.
5. Client checks validity dates and URL in the certificate.
6. Client extracts Web server's public key from the certificate.
7. Client creates a session key.
8. Client encrypts session key with the server's public key and sends it to the server.
9. Server decrypts session key with its private key.
10. Server and client communicate through an encrypted channel using this session key.

SSL protocol requires an SSL-enabled server and browser. SSL works within the transport layer so that it is not tied to application-related protocols and can take advantage of Internet transport standards.

The Web server can require the client to authenticate to it by requiring the Web browser to send over the user's certificate, but this configuration is rare. Usually only server side authentication is required.

S/MIME

When electronic mail was first developed, the e-mail clients allowed for only text-based messages to be sent back and forth. We came to a point where we saw the necessity of being able to attach binary attachments to these messages, so the Multipurpose Internet Mail Extensions (MIME) was developed to allow us to send spreadsheets, WAV files, small games, viruses, and pictures of our dogs to our friends and family. But we did not necessarily want just anyone to see our pictures of our dogs, so we needed to come up with a way to protect them.

Secure MIME (S/MIME) extends the MIME standard by allowing users to secure their e-mail messages and attachments by adding cryptographic security services. This standard provides confidentiality, authenticity, nonrepudiation, and integrity.

The following are components used within the S/MIME standard:

- Uses DES, 3DES, or RC4 (older) for content encryption
- Uses MD5 or SHA-1 for data integrity
- Uses DSA or RSA for digital signatures
- Uses Diffie-Hillman or RSA for symmetric key encryption
- Uses X.509 public key certificates

Because this is a standard, that means that if different e-mail client vendors follow it users could secure their e-mail and attachments in a way that could be understood by a variety of e-mail clients. This is exactly what took place. This means if I sent you an encrypted message and attachment using Outlook, as long as your e-mail client vendor followed the specifications outlined in the standard you do not need to use Outlook to properly decrypt my message and verify its source.

SSH2

Secure Shell2 (SSH) is used in remote connectivity situations by allowing a user to connect to a remote computer by creating a secure tunnel between the two systems. This type of connection provides much more security than programs such as Telnet, FTP, rlogin, rexec, and rsh. These programs allow for remote connectivity, but do not encrypt the session and usually do not provide a high level of authentication between the systems. SSH uses public key cryptography to construct the encryption tunnel, which is used to pass data back and forth.

> ### Local Lingo
> Rlogin, rexec, and rsh are referred to as UNIX r-utilities. They allow for communication to take place between two systems, but usually do not provide a high level of security.

SET

Secure Electronic Transaction (SET) was originally developed to replace SSL for secure Web transactions, but has gained little acceptance. SET, originally created by Visa and MasterCard, is a method of securing credit card transactions by using a public key infrastructure. The main perceived downfall to SET is that users and companies have viewed it as a hassle because each party involved needs specific software they do not currently have, configurations need to be put into place to allow for intercommunication, financial institutions would need to buy more hardware, collaboration of efforts needs to be made, and the overall cost is much higher than the currently used SSL. Let's walk through an example of how SET could be used.

Katie is buying a gift for her husband online. She must have an electronic wallet that contains her virtual credit card information, which she obtained from her credit card company (the issuer). Katie (who is the cardholder) must enter her credit card information when making the purchase. The payment information is transmitted to the merchant's Web server in an encrypted form so attackers cannot intercept it. The merchant does not decrypt this information, but instead digitally signs it and sends it on to a payment gateway. The payment gateway sends this information onto the acquirer (the merchant's bank). The acquirer checks with the issuer to make sure Katie has the necessary funds in her account for this purchase. Once that is confirmed, the message goes back to the merchant, who completes the transaction.

The virtual credit card information that Katie uses can be a voucher that is only payable to the merchant or an actual virtual credit card that can be used at different merchant sites. One big difference between this architecture and using SSL is that the merchant never decrypts and obtains the cardholder's credit card information. Today, merchants have to house hundreds or thousands of credit card numbers in databases, which have to be highly protected. Several merchant databases have been attacked and compromised, which hurts the merchant and its reputation. In a SET architecture, they would not have this burden because they would not be responsible for obtaining and protecting customer credit card data.

The following outlines the players that have to be involved to make a SET transaction successful:

- **Issuer**   Cardholder's bank
  - Financial institution that provides a virtual credit card to individual.
- **Cardholder**
  - Individual authorized to use virtual credit card.
- **Merchant**
  - Entity providing goods or services.
- **Acquirer**   Merchant's bank
  - Financial institution that processes payments.
- **Payment gateway**
  - Processes merchant payment.
  - Acquirer can act as the payment gateway.

Each entity has its own certificate and private /public key pair. Data being passed back and forth is encrypted, and they authenticate to each other during a transaction using digital signatures.

Travel Advisory
MONDEX is a different payment system where the currency is stored on smart cards. Security is provided by cryptography and tamper-resistant hardware.

IPSec

The *Internet Protocol Security* (IPSec) is a framework that provides the necessary functionality that allows two computers or network devices to securely transmit data. IPSec is actually a suite of protocols that was developed because the IP protocol has no security built into it. Data can be easily sniffed, modified, spoofed, and compromised if only the TCP/IP protocol suite is used during data exchange activities. Because we like to keep our secrets secret, the smart people developed exactly what we needed to provide the necessary level of confidentiality, integrity, and authenticity.

IPSec works and provides its protection at the network layer of the OSI model. Although it can be used between computers, it is most commonly provided by different router or firewall devices as a VPN solution between different networks that are connected by an untrusted network, as in the Internet.

IPSec is widely accepted because it is flexible and inexpensive. IPSec provides access control, confidentiality, integrity, and system authentication through public key cryptography, symmetric algorithms, and message authentication code (MAC).

SA   Before two devices can communicate via IPSec, they must go through a handshaking process. During this process, they will agree upon how they will communicate, if encryption is going to be used, what algorithms and key sizes to employ, what protocols will be called upon, and what modes those protocols will work in. Once all of this is agreed upon, it must be documented and stored so that each device remembers how to properly process future packets from each other. The agreed upon parameters are stored in a security association (SA). SAs are directional, meaning you need one per direction. So if I am going to allow communication to take place between my router and another router, I will need at least two SAs to be constructed, one SA for traffic going to that router and one SA for traffic coming from that router.

IPSec allows a device to have several tunneled sessions going on at one time; this is how one router can simultaneously communicate with several different networks at once. Each connection needs its own SAs so the router knows what parameters to follow to properly process traffic from each of these networks.

When a router receives an IPSec packet, how will it know which SA to call up? The packet header will contain a security parameter index (SPI) value that tells the IPSec software which SA needs to be called upon, as shown in Figure 6-13.

Another item held within the SA is if one of the following protocols needs to be called upon to process the traffic: *Authentication Header* (AH) and/or *Encapsulating Security Payload* (ESP). These are two of the main protocols within the IPSec suite and are described in the next sections.

AH   AH is a protocol that uses a key-hashed function (MAC) to ensure the integrity of a packet and provide data origin authentication. A portion of the packet is combined with a symmetric key and then passed through a hashing algorithm, which generates a message authentication code value, called the *Integrity Check Value* (ICV). This is the same technique we covered when we looked at how MACs work earlier in this chapter. Because a hashing algorithm is being used, integrity is being assured, and because we are using a symmetric key and not a private key, data origin or system authentication is provided. To supply

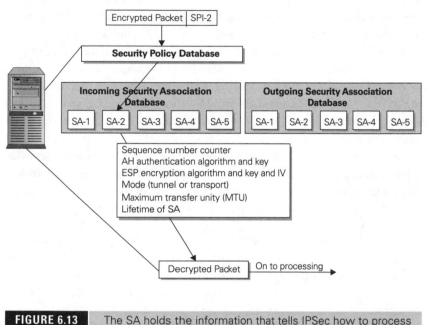

FIGURE 6.13 The SA holds the information that tells IPSec how to process received packets.

user authentication, an actual private key would need to be used because it is bound to an individual's identity. A symmetric key is not bound to an identity, but will tell the device that the packet came from the other device that has the necessary symmetric key, or system authentication.

Local Lingo

Data origin and system authentication mean the same thing.

When the receiving device accepts a packet it will compute its own ICV value and compare it with the ICV that was appended to the packet. If the values are the same, the receiving device can be assured that the packet was not modified during transmission.

ESP AH provided system authentication and integrity, but it does not provide encryption functionality. If we need to encrypt our data, we are moving back and forth between networks we will need to configure the devices to use the ESP protocol.

ESP actually provides integrity by calculating an ICV and system authentication through the use of a symmetric key, the same way that the AH protocol does, but it adds encryption functionality, which AH cannot provide.

AH and ESP can work in one of two modes, transport or tunnel. If the protocol is working in *transport mode*, that means it is only protecting the data payload. If it is working in *tunnel mode*, the payload and headers are protected. So if AH is working in transport mode it calculates an ICV value over the data payload; if it is working in tunnel mode it calculates an ICV value of the packet's payload and headers. If ESP is working in transport mode, it encrypts only the payload; if it works in tunnel mode, the payload and the headers are encrypted. If tunnel mode is being used, a new IP header is created and appended to the front of the packet. The packet could not be properly routed if all of its header information were encrypted so this new unencrypted IP header is used for routing purposes.

Key Exchange Protocols with IPSec   So we said IPSec provides system authentication through the use of symmetric keys, but how do the devices receive the actual keys in a secure manner? The keys within IPSec can be installed manually or through automated means, which would mean we would need to call upon more protocols to carry out proper key exchange. The Internet Key Exchange (IKE) is the de facto standard for exchanging symmetric keys in IPSec environments. It is used to generate, exchange, and manage cryptographic keys between the devices.

Because life just cannot seem to be simple, IKE actually contains two protocols: Internet Security Association and Key Management Protocol (ISAKMP) and OAKLEY. ISAKMP sets up the framework for the items that can be negotiated during the handshake process (algorithm type, key size) and the OAKLEY protocol is the one that actually carries out these negotiation steps.

- **Internet Key Exchange (IKE) protocol**   A subset implementation of ISAKMP and the OAKLEY protocol
- **Internet Security Association and Key Management Protocol (ISAKMP)**   Provides the framework for key negotiation although does not actually do the negotiation
- **OAKLEY Protocol**   Negotiates key information using the Diffie-Hellman algorithm

The negotiation process goes through two main phases. The first phase of IKE establishes a session key by using the Diffie-Hellman algorithm. After each end has the necessary session key, they can use it for the second phase. The second phase of IKE conducts another negotiation, but this is where the items that populate the SA are agreed upon (use of AH and/or ESP, protocol modes, encryption and hashing algorithms, key sizes).

So once the two devices agree upon how they will communicate and they have created the necessary SAs, they can now communicate through an untrusted environment securely.

Other Security Technologies

To keep one step ahead of the attackers, many protocols have been updated to include cryptographic security services. These extra measures mitigate potential vulnerabilities that exist in the earlier versions of the protocol or technology so that attackers cannot exploit them.

Some examples are listed here:

- **Secure RPC (S-RPC)** Remote Procedure Call (RPC) is a protocol that allows two devices to communicate. But if you need to protect this communication channel, S-RPC is required, which uses the Diffie-Hellman public key cryptography algorithm to generate the shared secret key for encryption. This allows for RPC traffic to be encrypted and protected.

- **Domain Name Service Security (DNSSEC)** A Domain Name Service (DNS) server responds to client requests to translate host names to IP addresses. The client does not know if the response actually came from a legitimate DNS server or if the data had actually been improperly modified, which would map the host name to an incorrect IP address. If a DNS server has DNSSEC enabled, it will digitally sign the data that is sent to the client, so that it can be assured of where it came from (the correct DNS server) and make sure that it was not modified in an unauthorized manner.

Objective 6.07 **Attacks**

A *passive attack* is when an attacker simply listens in on a conversation, as in eavesdropping and network sniffing. An *active attack* is another story however. This is when an attacker is taking deliberate actions against a system or network that can be harmful, as in a denial of service attack, IP spoofing, or packet modification. This section covers active attacks that pertain to cryptography.

Ciphertext-Only Attack

A *ciphertext-only attack* is when an attacker captures the ciphertext of one or more messages. Without the key, the ciphertext is useless, but the attacker can try and capture several messages and look for patterns that may give clues that will aid in uncovering the key that was used to turn the plaintext into ciphertext. This is the most common type of cryptographic attack because it is not hard to obtain ciphertext.

Known-Plaintext Attack

In this type of attack, the attacker has the plaintext and ciphertext of one or more messages. The goal is to discover the key that was used to encrypt the messages so that other messages can be deciphered and read. With the plaintext and ciphertext available to the attacker, she has more information to work with to try and attempt reverse-engineering the process.

> **Travel Advisory**
>
> A linear cryptanalysis is a plaintext attack because it uses linear approximation to describe the behavior of block ciphers.

Chosen-Plaintext Attack

The *chosen-plaintext attack* is when an attacker can choose the plaintext that gets encrypted. In this type of attack she has access to the plaintext and the resulting ciphertext. Having the ability to choose the plaintext that gets encypted gives the attacker more power and possibly a deeper understanding of the way that the encryption process works so that she can gather more information about the key that is being used. Once the key is discovered, other messages encrypted with that key can be decrypted.

How can an attacker choose the plaintext to be encrypted? She could type a message that she thinks you will believe, as in "We will bomb Iraq on Tuesday." She assumes that you will not only believe it, but also encrypt it and send it onto someone else. So she uses a sniffer to capture the encrypted version of her message, and she then has the plaintext and the ciphertext of that message.

This is also referred to as a *differential cryptanalysis attack* because it studies the differences between two related plaintext messages through a sampling process. Probabilities are assigned to each key until the most likely key is identified.

Adaptive Chosen-Plaintext Attack

An adaptive chosen plaintext attack is the same attack as the previous one, but the attacker can chose the plaintext samples that will be encrypted dynamically. The results of the ciphertext that she gathers can then alter the attacker's choice of the next plaintext to work with.

Chosen-Ciphertext Attack

This is similar to the chosen-plaintext, but in this attack, the attacker can choose the ciphertext to be decrypted and has access to the resulting decrypted plaintext. Again, the goal is usually to figure out the key that has been used during the encryption process so that future communications can be deciphered.

Adaptive Chosen-Ciphertext Attack

This is the same as the previous attack, but it is a situation where the attacker has free use of the actual decryption hardware, but does not have the proper procedures to extract the decryption key from it.

If the word "adaptive" is used in the attack name, this means the attacker has more control over the process and can choose what gets encrypted or decrypted in a dynamic manner.

Man-in-the-Middle Attack

A *man-in-the-middle attack* is when attackers inject themselves between two users that are participating in an active session. The attackers can simply read the messages to gain useful information or manipulate them somehow.

Digital signatures and sequence numbering can be used to circumvent these attacks.

> **Exam Tip**
>
> Man-in-the-middle attacks are also called Bucket Brigade attacks. Key exchange protocols can be very vulnerable to this attack.

Algebraic Attack

Block ciphers exhibit a high degree of mathematical structure, so techniques have been developed to understand these and more easily break them, which is an *algebraic attack*.

Analytic Attack

This attack manipulates the algorithm and algebraic functions used in specific algorithms. Two examples of this type of attack are the double DES attack and the RSA factoring attack.

CHECKPOINT

✔**Objective 6.01: Cryptography Definitions** Cryptography is the science of protecting information by encoding it into an unreadable format. The purpose of cryptography is to make the act of deciphering a message too expensive or too time consuming, to protect the confidentiality of the sensitive data, and to identify corruption or modification of data. Encryption is a method of transforming original data, called plaintext, into a form that appears to be random and unreadable, which is called ciphertext.

✔**Objective 6.02: Cipher Types** The two basic types of symmetric algorithms are substitution and transposition. Substitution ciphers change a character (or bit) out for another and transposition ciphers scramble the characters (or bits). Steganography is a method of hiding data within another data format, like a graphic, wave file, or document. The Clipper Chip was a hardware encryption chip the U.S. government wanted to implement into many American-made devices so that they could listen to suspicious communications. Block ciphers use S-boxes, or substitution boxes, to create confusion and diffusion. In symmetric key algorithms, the sender and receiver use the same key for encryption and decryption. In asymmetric key algorithms, the sender and receiver use different keys and public and private keys.

✔**Objective 6.03:** **Hybrid Approach**   Key management is one of the most challenging pieces of cryptography. It pertains to creating, maintaining, distributing, and destroying cryptographic keys. The Diffie-Hellman protocol is a key exchange protocol and does not provide encryption for data or digital signature functionality. When symmetric and asymmetric key algorithms are used together, this is called a hybrid system. The asymmetric key is used to encrypt the symmetric key and the symmetric key encrypts the data. A session key is only good for one communication session; it is destroyed when the session ends.

✔**Objective 6.04:** **Message Integrity and Digital Signatures**   Message integrity can be ensured by using hashing algorithms. When a hashing algorithm is applied to a message, it produces a message digest. If this value is signed (encrypted) with a private key, a digital signature is produced. Examples of hashing algorithms are SHA-1, MD2, MD4, MD5, and HAVAL. A birthday attack is an attack on hashing functions through brute force. The attacker tries to find two messages with the same message digest, referred to as a collision.

✔**Objective 6.05:** **Cryptography Applications**   A public key infrastructure (PKI) is a framework of programs, procedures, communication protocols, and public key cryptography that enables a diverse group of individuals to communicate securely. A certificate authority (CA) is a trusted third party that generates and maintains user certificates, which hold their public keys. A registration authority (RA) is responsible for the certificate registration process and confirming individual identities, and submitting requests to the CA on behalf of users. However, the RA cannot issue certificates to users. Certificates are held in directories, and revoked certificates are listed in CRLs.

✔**Objective 6.06:** **Cryptographic Protocols**   Pretty Good Privacy (PGP) is a freeware e-mail security program that uses public key cryptography. It uses a "web of trust" model instead of the hierarchical structure used in PKI. S-HTTP provides protection for individual messages that are sent between two computers, but not the actual link. HTTPS does protect that communication channel however. Secure Electronic Transaction (SET) is a proposed electronic commerce technology that provides a safer method for customers to perform transactions over the Internet.

✔**Objective 6.07:** **Attacks**   A passive attack is when an attacker simply listens in or eavesdrops on traffic and does nothing to alter it. An active attack, on the other hand, is when an attacker changes a message or masquerades as a legitimate user to gather information. Some examples of active attacks are cipher-text only, known-plaintext, chosen-plaintext, chosen ciphertext, and man-in-the-middle.

REVIEW QUESTIONS

1. Which of the following is a set of mathematical rules used in cryptography?

   A. Key

   B. Algorithm

   C. Keyspace

   D. Work factor

2. Which of the following is most accurate about the strength of a cryptosystem?

   A. The strength of the cryptosystem comes from the algorithm, secrecy of the key, and length of the key.

   B. The strength of the cryptosystem is determined by its message integrity.

   C. The strength of the cryptosystem relies on whether or not it's been publicly tested.

   D. Strong cryptosystems have secret algorithms.

3. Which of the following is the method for hiding data in another message or data format so that the very existence of the data is concealed?

   A. Substitution

   B. Shift alphabet

   C. Transposition

   D. Steganography

4. Which of the following is a described weakness of the Clipper Chip?

   A. It was software-based, and the public wanted hardware implementations.

   B. It was publicly tested, so it was not viewed as a secure mechanism.

   C. Its 80-bit key was considered too small.

   D. It was based on the Lucifer algorithm.

5. Which of the following is considered a strength of symmetric cryptography?

   A. Key distribution

   B. Processing speed

   C. Scalability

   D. Provides user authenticity as well as confidentiality

6. Which of the following was approved for DES?

   A. SkipJack

   B. Rijndael

   C. Twofish

   D. Lucifer

7. What does ECB stand for?

   A. Electronic Code Book

   B. Encryption Control Board

   C. Encryption Code Book

   D. Elliptic Curve Barometers

8. Which of the following is a framework of programs, data formats, procedures, protocols, and public key cryptography mechanisms working together to enable secure communications?

   A. CA

   B. DSS

   C. PKI

   D. RSA

9. Which of the following best describes a one-time pad?

   A. An encryption scheme that is impossible to break due to its randomness and pad length.

   B. An encrypted hash value of a message.

   C. A function that takes a variable-length message and turns it into a fixed-length value.

   D. A mathematical function that is easier to compute in one direction than in the opposite direction.

10. Which of the following is a standard for encrypting and digitally signing e-mails with attachments?

   A. PGP

   B. S/MIME

   C. SET

   D. SSL

11. Which of the following is use by DES for integrity and authentication purposes?

   A. SSL

   B. SA

C. ESP

D. MAC

12. Which truly describes the difference between using message authentication code and digital signatures?

   A. Digital signatures provide system authentication through the use of symmetric keys.

   B. Data origin is provided through the use of private keys in MAC.

   C. MAC can only provide system authentication and not user authentication because a private key is not used.

   D. Digital signatures uses private and symmetric keys to provide data origin and system and user authentication

REVIEW ANSWERS

1. **B**   An algorithm, usually publicly known, is a set of mathematical rules or functions that dictates how enciphering and deciphering take place.

2. **A**   The critical pieces in encryption are the algorithm, secrecy of the key, and the length of the key.

3. **D**   Steganography is used to hide messages in other media types or message formats.

4. **C**   The Clipper Chip was a hardware chip that used the SkipJack algorithm, which was developed by the NSA and not publicly released. Its 80-bit key and 16-bit checksum were both considered weak and easy to defeat, but in the end it was seen as a threat to individual privacy.

5. **B**   Symmetric encryption is much faster than asymmetric encryption, but key distribution and scalability is difficult because each set of users needs their own pair of symmetric keys. The use of symmetric keys does not provide authenticity or nonrepudiation.

6. **D**   Lucifer was developed by IBM and accepted by the NIST in 1974 as the DES standard. The Lucifer algorithm was modified, though, and that algorithm, which was the one used for DES, is called Data Encryption Algorithm (DEA).

7. **A**   Electric Code Book (ECB) is an encryption mode used by DES. It does not use any chaining, so patterns can emerge if large amounts of data is encrypted using this mode.

8. **C** PKI is an infrastructure or framework that includes all the components of public key cryptography. It provides a hierarchical trust model.

9. **A** A one-time pad is the ultimate form of encryption because the pad is random and as long, or longer, than the actual message. It is impractical in most uses because the pad is so large and hard to securely transmit to the receiver. Also creating a truly random pad is very hard to accomplish.

10. **B** S/MIME is an encryption standard designed specifically to secure e-mail that has attachments.

11. **D** Message authentication code (MAC) is used by DES and IPSec to provide integrity of data and to provide data origin or system authentication.

12. **C** MAC provides system authentication, also called data origin authentication, through the use of symmetric keys. Digital signatures provide user authentication through the use of private keys.

Disaster Recovery and Business Continuity

CHAPTER 7

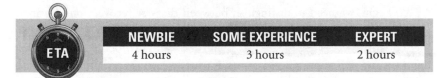

	NEWBIE	SOME EXPERIENCE	EXPERT
ETA	4 hours	3 hours	2 hours

Floods, fires, tornados, terrorist attacks, and vandalism are all examples of disasters that take place every day around the world. Any one of these threats could cripple a business for days, weeks, months, or even cause its doors to close permanently. Many companies do not have the foresight to imagine such events happening, much less create a detailed plan of how to respond to such situations. However, it is important to know that organizations that do the necessary planning and research in preparing for disasters are almost always the only ones left standing when these tragedies strike.

The existence of a disaster recovery plan (DRP) and business continuity plan (BCP) could mean the difference between a company's survival and ultimate demise. Over 65 percent of companies today would go out of business if they had to be closed down for only one week. The ability to restore operations with little or no service interruption to the customer is imperative and nearly impossible to put a price tag on. The loss of revenue, market share, reputation, and customers are likely without a thorough recovery strategy. However, most companies are reluctant to make the commitment due to the time, energy, and money needed to complete such a task. Less than five percent of companies are fully prepared for a disaster. A full-scale disaster recovery plan can take up to three years to finish. During this time, the company's resources (employees and funds) are consumed with no seemingly direct return on the investment. However, without the vision to plan for the worst, the most budget-efficient and profitable companies in the world could end up bankrupt in the event of a disaster.

Objective 7.01 Disaster Recovery versus Business Continuity

To begin, we need to distinguish between disaster recovery and business continuity. A disaster recovery plan (DRP) contains procedures to implement during and immediately following a tragic event in order to reduce further damages and maintain critical systems. It usually revolves around getting critical IT systems back online so that production is not negatively affected. A disaster recovery plan is developed to help individuals know what needs to take place in the chaos of an emergency. On the other hand, business continuity is a long-term strategy for keeping a business functional following the disaster. The continuity plan ensures the stability of critical business functions and reduces the overall impact of the interruption. For example, responding to emergencies, ensuring everyone's safety, and getting essential components back online would be encompassed in the disaster recovery plan. Defining how to continue operations effectively in a new environment or with less available resources would be part of the continuity plan.

Disaster recovery planning (DRP) includes the following:

- Showing employees how to respond to disasters or disruptions
- Developing emergency responses procedures
- Reducing the impact of immediate dangers
- Restoring critical IT systems

Business continuity planning (BCP) includes the following:

- Showing employees how to keep critical business functions operational
- Reducing overall impact of business interruption
- Restoring backups and necessary procedures to get back to original production

A common misconception in disaster recovery is the notion that backing up data and providing hardware redundancy is a sufficient solution. Although these are important, they are only two pieces in the overall planning of a full-scale recovery plan. Hardware and computers need people to configure and operate them; data is usually not useful unless it is accessible by other systems and possibly outside entities. A disaster also creates mass confusion and most likely a significant change in the way employees carry out their daily responsibilities. It is important to understand how to manually carry out automated tasks, how to reconstruct a workable environment, and how to keeping going forward even though the floor just fell out from under you.

Security issues are also a major factor when planning for disaster recovery. When a company is hit with a large disturbance or disaster, it is usually at its most vulnerable state. Confidential data needs to stay protected even during emergencies, and planning properly can guarantee that the necessary level of protection is maintained. A good way to ensure that two plans are implemented and continually updated is to integrate them into the company's security program. The importance of security does not reduce just because the company experiences a disruption or disaster; in many cases, it becomes even more important. This is why it is critical to have it tied into the company's overall security program and efforts.

Objective 7.02 **Project Initiation Phase**

To get things off on the right foot, some items should be outlined and ad dressed before actual data gathering activities are underway. These issues are addressed in the initial planning phase of BCP/DRP development.

- Obtain management support
- Establish need of plans
- Define scope of project and objectives
- Establish team—technical and functional representatives
- Identify responsibilities
- Schedule formal meetings and milestones
- Determine need for automated data collection tools
- Present initial report to management

The first step in the project's initiation to develop DRP and BCP strategies is to obtain management's support. Management must be convinced of its necessity so that they will *truly* support it. A business case should be presented that includes current vulnerabilities, regulatory and legal obligations, current status of recovery plans, cost versus benefit estimates, and recommendations. Management support will also hinge on the fact that most executives can be held liable if proper disaster recovery plans are not established. Stockholders, customers, or anyone directly affected by how the company does or does not react to a disaster can bring civil lawsuits against the company.

Without management's support, the team will not receive the necessary attention, funds, and resources, and in the end will be marginally successful, if at all. DRP and BCP need to be business decisions, rolled into meetings and budgets, and not treated as an entity that stands alone and does not directly affect the business's possible survival. A greater understanding of this process at all levels of the company will help the company endure disruptions and disasters.

Senior management should define roles and responsibilities from all levels of management down to staff echelons that have some level of accountability for these efforts. A multilevel team should be identified, with both technical and functional representatives. It is important for all levels of personnel—from executives to front-line employees—to understand their purpose in this endeavor. Roles and expectations of each level are shown next.

Senior executive management

- Consistent support and final approval of plans
- Drive all phases of the plan
- Ensure testing of the plans is carried out
- Oversee budget and funding needs

Senior functional management

- Identify and prioritize mission-critical systems
- Monitor progress of plan development and execution

Recovery and continuity committee

- Committee members should be representatives from critical departments
- Coordinate with other department representatives
- Develop analysis group
- Outline milestones, checkpoints within project, and delivery dates

Travel Advisory

The people who will be expected to carry out these plans should be involved in their development.

Objective 7.03 **Business Impact Analysis**

Disaster recovery and continuity planning deals with uncertainty and chance, but these things can become less mysterious and seem more do-able if credible data is gathered and analyzed. The first task for the committee is to perform a *business impact analysis (BIA)*, which has the goals of identifying the company's assets, uncovering all possible threats to those assets, and qualifying and quantifying the effects these threats can have on the company overall. Identifying these possible threats, calculating their potential damage, and presenting them in a clear and understandable format are the basis of the BIA.

A BIA is performed at the beginning of disaster and continuity planning to identify the areas that would suffer the greatest financial or operational loss in the event of a disaster or disruption. It identifies the company's critical systems needed for survival and estimates the outage time that can be tolerated by the company as a result of different unfortunate events. The outage time that can be endured by a company is referred to as the *maximum tolerable downtime (MTD)*.

Here are some MTD estimates:

- Non-essential = 30 days
- Normal = 7 days
- Important = 72 hours
- Urgent = 24 hours
- Critical = Minutes to hours

Each critical asset should be placed in one of the previous categories, depending upon how long the company can survive without it. These estimates will help the company determine what backup procedures are necessary to ensure the availability of these different resources. For example, if being without a T1 communication line for three hours would cost the company $130,000, they should put in a backup T1 line from a different carrier. If a server going down and being unavailable for ten hours will only cost the company $250 in revenue, they may not need to have a fully redundant server waiting to be swapped out and instead choose to count on their vendor's service level agreement (SLA), which promises to have it back online in eight hours.

The BIA should provide tangible alternatives for the company as a whole to consider, but it must also be applied to distinct and separate business functions within the organizations. This will be key in developing departmental procedures and establishing priorities. Every department has a specific role in a company, and some are more critical than others. The BIA should identify the departments that must come online first for the company's survival and the resources those departments depend upon.

Critical business functions can include the following:

- IT network support
- Data processing
- Accounting
- Software development
- Payroll
- Customer support
- Order entry
- Production scheduling

- Purchasing
- Communications

It is important to look at the company as a complex and ever-changing animal instead of a static two-dimensional entity. It is comprised of many types of equipment, people, tasks, departments, communication methods, and interfaces to the outer world. The complexity of true disaster recovery and continuity planning lies in understanding all of these intricacies and their interrelationships. Plans to back up and restore data, implement redundant data processing equipment, educate employees on how to perform tasks manually, and obtain redundant power supplies are of no use if the separate departments are unable to work together in a new environment. Interdependencies must be addressed in the planning process. The following issues should be researched and addressed:

- Define essential business functions and supporting departments.
- Identify interdependencies between these functions and departments.
- Identify all possible threats that could affect the mechanisms necessary to allow these departments to work together.
- Gather quantitative and qualitative information pertaining to these threats.
- Provide alternative methods of restoring functionality and communication.

Once the threats are identified and critical business functions acknowledged, specific loss criteria must be applied as well. The criteria can contain:

- Loss in reputation and public confidence
- Loss in profits
- Loss of competitive advantages
- Increase in operational expenses
- Violations of contract agreements
- Violations of legal and regulatory requirements
- Delayed income costs
- Loss in revenue
- Loss in productivity

Loss can be direct or indirect, potential or delayed, and must be properly accounted for. For example, if the disaster recovery planning team is identifying a terrorist bombing as a potential threat, it is important to predict which business function would be most likely targeted, how all business functions could be affected, and how each bulleted item in the loss criteria would be directly or indirectly affected. Many times, the timeliness of the disruption can cause everlasting effects. If the customer support functionality was out of commission for two days, it may be acceptable, but if it is out five days, the company could be in financial ruin. So, time-loss curves that show the total impact over specific time periods should be developed and analyzed, as shown in Figure 7-1.

Threats and potential losses must also be prioritized according to the likelihood of occurrence and severity of the damage. A DRP\BCP should provide the necessary level of security within the economic constraints. For example, if a company has a facility in a flood zone and they could lose up to $1.2 million if a large flood hit, it would not make sense for the company to spend $2 million in protection against a flood. The possibility of the more likely and damaging disasters should be addressed and planned for first, followed by the less severe and less likely threats.

The eight steps of a BIA are listed here:

1. Select interviewees for data gathering.

2. Determine data gathering techniques.

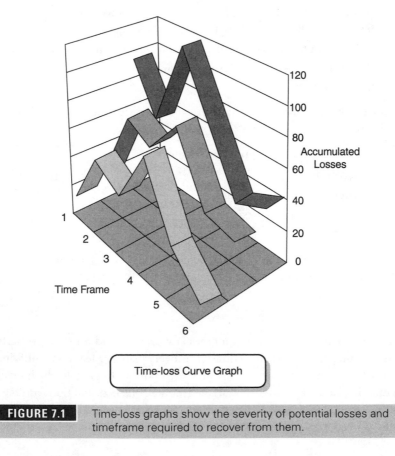

Time-loss Curve Graph

FIGURE 7.1   Time-loss graphs show the severity of potential losses and timeframe required to recover from them.

3. Develop questionnaires to obtain economic and operational impact information (qualitative and quantitative questions).

4. Analyze gathered data.

5. Determine time-critical business systems.

6. Calculate maximum tolerable downtimes (MTD) for each critical system.

7. Prioritize critical systems based on MTDs.

8. Document findings and submit to management, along with recommendations.

Objective 7.04 Possible Threats

It was stated previously that one of the earlier steps within the BIA is to identify all possible threats. But what are they? Natural disasters can be tornados, floods, or earthquakes. Man-made disasters could come in the form of arsonists, terrorists, or even simple mistakes that produce serious outcomes. And, technical disasters can be data corruption, power loss, hardware failure, or network outages. It is important to identify all possible threats and estimate the probability of each happening. The more issues that are identified, the better prepared the company will be. There are three main categories of disruptions to consider:

- **Non-disaster** A disruption in service as a result of a device or software malfunction. The solution could include hardware, software, or file restoration.
- **Disaster** An event that causes the facility to be unusable for a day or longer. This may require the use of a different facility temporarily and the recovery of backed-up data and software being housed locally or at an off-site facility. The alternate site must be available to the company until the main facility is operational.
- **Catastrophe** A major disaster that destroys the facility altogether. This requires short- and long-term solutions. The short-term remedy would be an off-site facility equipped for immediate operation; the long-term solution may require rebuilding the original facility.

Disasters and catastrophes are rare compared to the occurrence of non-disasters. Non-disasters are usually solved by replacing a device or restoring a file. Because non-disasters are so common, the existence of an on-site backup procedure is vital. A reliable backup plan can help the company restore critical information and be back to the same production level in minutes or hours.

Critical equipment should be prioritized and statistics should be calculated on each device's *mean time between failure (MTBF)* and *mean time to repair (MTTR)*. MTBF is an estimate of how long a device, or its components, will be functional, and MTTR is an estimate of how long it will take to repair a device and bring it back into production. Proper forecasting and planning of hardware performance and possible failures can eliminate a good percentage of non-disasters.

Objective 7.05 Backups and Off-Site Facilities

There are several things that need to be looked at when ensuring that a company can properly respond and bounce back after a disaster or disturbance has taken place. These have to do with making sure that the current environment can be rebuilt if needed, ensuring that data is continually backed up, choosing a site to store software backups, and choosing an alternate site for potential relocation of the company. The following sections discuss each of these items.

Employees and the Working Environment

The first issue pertaining to employees is notifying them of the disaster. A calling tree should be established within the management staff to notify all employees of the situation and explaining to them their new job function and expectations.

Because the end-users are usually the worker bees of a company, it is important that they are provided a functioning environment as soon as possible after a disaster hits. This means the current functioning environment needs to be understood and critical pieces examined so they can be replicated. This dictates more than just knowing which specific servers are critical. There are many more detailed-oriented issues that can get easily overlooked. Some of these issues are listed here:

1. Do we have backup copies of all necessary operating system and application software?
2. Do we have system configurations documented and saved off-site?
3. Do we need redundant connections to remote sites?
4. Which users need to be back online first?

5. If we need to purchase new equipment, how quickly can it be available and will it be exactly like what we have today?

6. Are there possible interoperability issues if we need to purchase different hardware and software?

7. Do we have proper configurations of all routers, bridges, switches, multiplexers, etc. documented and saved off-site?

8. Do we have access to proprietary hardware from any vendors if our current devices become unavailable?

9. Do we have copies of source code of our proprietary software backed up that will be available to us if our facility is ruined?

This list can go on and on, and it should to ensure *all* items are addressed and examined from different perspectives.

Software usually changes more often than hardware, so backup operations must happen on a continual basis. Software requiring backup can come in the form of applications, files, utilities, databases, and operating systems. The on-site backup software should always be stored in a fire-resistant safe. It is important to have a software backup process that is appropriate for the requirements of the operating environments. If data in critical files changes several times each day, backups may need to occur every day to ensure that the copies are current. Also, some or all data from user machines and different servers may be backed up and kept off-site. The planners must be aware of what data is backed up and provide procedures for retrieving the data and installing it after a disruption or disaster.

The different types of software backups need to be understood and used together in the right combination:

- **Incremental backup**   A procedure that backs up only those files that have been modified since the previous backup of any sort. It does remove the archive attribute, indicating that the item has been backed up.

- **Differential backup**   A procedure that backs up all files that have been modified since the last *full* backup. It does not remove the archive attribute.

- **Full backup**   A procedure that backs up all files, modified or not, and removes the archive attribute.

Incremental backups usually finish more quickly than differential backups, but they take longer to restore because each incremental backup since the last full backup has to be restored in sequence.

Manual backup procedures can be very time-consuming, error prone, and costly. Several technologies serve as automated backup alternatives; they can be expensive, but they do provide more speed and accuracy.

Databases require specialized backup operations that are usually integrated into the database management software as a feature. They can be configured to use *disk-shadowing*, or data-mirroring technologies. A disk-shadowing subsystem uses two physical disks (or two different media types), and the data is written to both at the same time for redundancy purposes. The subsystem performs data-mirroring functionality, and if one disk or media fails, the other is readily available.

Electronic vaulting is the transferring of data to an off-site facility via communication lines. It is mainly a batch process of moving data to an alternate site for backup procedures. *Remote journaling* is the activity of saving changed data to the local location and the alternate site in a parallel process, instead of doing it in a batch process. These technologies are used to provide fault tolerance and data backup activities.

Choosing a Software Backup Storage Facility

Backups of software and critical data should not be stored just at the local facility, but should be also kept at an off-site facility in case the primary site is destroyed. Several issues need to be addressed when a company is deciding upon a storage facility for its backup software and data. The following provides a list of just some of the issues that need to be thought through before committing to a specific company for this type of service:

- Can the backups be accessed in the necessary timeframe?
- Is the facility closed on weekends and/or holidays, and does it operate only during specific hours of the day?
- Are the access control mechanisms tied to an alarm or the police station?
- Does the facility have the correct fire safety measures in place?
- Does the facility have the capability to properly store company backup media?
- What is the availability of a bonded transport service?
- Are there any geographical environmental hazards, such as floods, earthquakes, tornados, and so on?
- Does the facility provide temperature and humidity monitoring and control?
- Is the facility guarded and protected?

A company should expect their resources to be protected at least at the same level as what is provided for them in their main facility. These items need to be clearly understood and documented, and lines of liabilities need to be drawn so that if a disaster occurs, everyone is in agreement as to what should take place and who is responsible.

Backup Facility Alternatives

Backup alternatives can come in the form of hardware, data, personnel, and off-site facilities. It is up to each company and its continuity team to decide if all of these components are necessary for its survival.

For the larger disasters that negatively affect the primary facility, an off-site backup facility may be required. Different companies offer subscription services, meaning companies pay for off-site facilities to be available to them in their time of need. The type of site best suited for a company will be determined by the results of the BIA. Companies can choose from three main types:

- **Hot site** This is a facility that is fully configured and would be ready to operate within a few hours. The equipment and system software must be compatible with the data being backed up from the main site and cause no negative interoperability issues. This is a good alternative for companies that cannot afford to be off-line for more than two days. A hot site can allow for short- and long-term outages, configuration changes, and constant testing abilities. The disadvantages of a hot site are the expense (most expensive of all subscription services) and that it can create problems for companies with proprietary or unusual hardware or software needs.

- **Warm site** This is a facility that is usually partially configured with some peripheral and telecommunications equipment, but not the actual computers. They are the most widely used backup alternatives. Warm sites are attractive to companies with proprietary or unusual hardware or software. The negative aspects are testing limitations and expected delay in bringing a site online following the disaster.

- **Cold site** Cold sites provide only the basic environment; electrical wiring, air conditioning, plumbing, and possibly raised flooring, but they provide the most inexpensive alternative to companies. The biggest downside is the delay in service turnaround. It can be weeks before a cold site is operational.

Travel Advisory

The location of a backup facility should be far away enough from the original site so that it will not be affected by the same disaster. The off-site facility should be at least 25 miles away from the primary site.

The three main costs involved with these types of facilities are initial cost (first purchasing the subscription service), recurring operation costs (maintenance), and activation costs (once the site needs to be used).

Backup tapes, or other media, should be tested periodically on the equipment kept at the hot site to make sure the media is readable by those systems. If a warm site is going to be used, the tapes should be brought to the primary site and tested on those systems. The reason for the difference is that when a company uses a hot site, it will be depending on the systems kept at that site; therefore, the media needs to be readable by those systems. If a company is depending on a warm site, they will most likely be bringing their original equipment with them, so the hardware at the primary site must be capable of reading the backup media.

Another alternative in choosing a backup facility is establishing a *reciprocal agreement* with another company. This means that company A agrees to allow company B to use its facilities if company B is hit with a disaster, and vice versa. This is cheaper than the other alternatives, but it is not necessarily a good choice. Most environments have already reached capacity levels for facility space, resources, and computing capabilities; the co-existence could prove to be detrimental to both companies.

Reciprocal agreements are also not enforceable, thus providing no guarantee to the company that the facility would actually be available if the need arises. It is best to have an actual off-site facility (hot, warm, cold, or redundant site) available and have a reciprocal agreement in place in case this alternate site is unavailable to the company for one reason or another. For example, a company can pay to have a warm site available, but if that facility was affected by the same disaster, then the company can fall back on the reciprocal agreement.

A planner should ask the following questions before deciding on a reciprocal agreement:

- How long will the facility be available to the company in need?
- How much assistance will come from the staff in terms of integrating the two environments and ongoing support?
- How quickly can the company in need move into the facility?
- What are the issues pertaining to interoperability?

- How many of the resources will be available to the company in need?
- How will differences and conflicts be addressed?
- How does change control and configuration management take place?
- How often can drills and testing take place?
- Are there hardware and software compatibility issues between the different environments?
- What is the protection level of the environment? Does it provide the necessary level of security required?

A *rolling hot site* is an additional backup option to consider. It is a processing center located in the back of a large truck or trailer. A rolling hot site can be positioned at any location (company's parking lot) and can be implemented and initiated in a very short time period. So if a company's primary site is damaged and they need certain functions up and running in hours, and do not have a hot site available, a trailer can be delivered and the company's processing can begin again in this mobile environment.

A *redundant site* is another option but more expensive because it is a site that the company builds and maintains specifically for disaster recovery and business continuity. The redundant site provides an exact duplication of networks, systems, and configurations for immediate transition if a disaster hits. The cost to build and maintain it limits most companies from using it as an alternative, however.

> **Travel Advisory**
>
> Any changes that take place at the primary site should be replicated at hot or redundant sites to ensure interoperability and that items are continually kept up-to-date.

Objective 7.06

DRP and BCP Planning Objectives

Recovery planning involves developing a plan and preparing for a disaster before it takes place with the hopes of minimizing loss and ensuring the availability of critical systems and personnel. Anyone who has been involved in large projects that must also deal with many small, complex details knows that at times it is easy to lose track of the major goals of the project. Goals are established to keep everyone on track and ensure that the efforts pay off in the end. The main goals of a disaster recovery plan are to improve responsiveness by the employees in different situations, ease confusion by providing written procedures, and help make logical decisions during a crisis. If the employees know where to go when the "all-hands-on-deck" alarm is called and are familiar with what tasks are expected of them and how to perform these tasks, the people in a position to make bigger decisions on how to properly deal with the overall event can do so in a more calm and controlled manner. This can prove to be a crucial element in disaster recovery.

> **Travel Advisory**
>
> Disaster recovery planning should not be viewed as a discretionary expense.

To be useful, a DRP goal must contain certain key information, such as the following:

- **Responsibility** Each individual involved with disaster recovery and business continuity should have his or her responsibilities spelled out in writing to ensure a clear understanding in a chaotic situation. All tasks should be divided and assigned to the appropriate individuals. However, these individuals must know what is expected of them, which is conveyed through training, drills, communication, and documentation. So, instead of just running out of the building screaming, an individual knows he or she is responsible for shutting down the servers before exiting the facility in panic-mode.

- **Authority** In times of crisis, it is important to know who is in charge. Teamwork is important in these situations, and almost every team does much better with an established and trusted leader. These people must know they will be expected to step up to the plate and understand what type of direction they should be providing to the rest of the employees. Clear-cut authority will aid in reducing confusion and increasing cooperation.

- **Priorities** It is extremely important to know what is critical versus nice to have. Different departments provide different functionality for an organization. The critical departments must be singled out versus the departments that provide functionality that the company can live without for a week or two. It is necessary to know which department must come online first, which comes second, and so on. This way, the efforts are used in the most useful, effective, and focused manner possible.

Along with the priorities of departments, the priorities of systems, information, and programs must be established. For example, it may be more necessary to ensure that the database is up and running before working to bring the file server online. The general priorities must be set by the management (with the help of the different departments and IT staff).

- **Implementation and testing**   It is great to write down very profound ideas and developed plans, but unless they are actually implemented, tested, and carried out, they may not add up to a hill of beans. Once a disaster recovery plan and continuity plan is developed, it actually has to be put into action. It needs to be documented and put in places that are easily accessible in times of crisis, the people that are assigned specific tasks need to be taught and informed, and actual dry runs need to be done to walk people through different situations. The drills should take place at least once a year, and the entire program should be continually updated and improved.

Large corporations may need each department to develop their own disaster recovery and continuity plans that detail their own specific procedures uncommon to other groups. Each department can then integrate their departmental plans into the overall recovery plan for the company, as shown in Figure 7-2.

The overall business interruption and resumption plan should cover all organizational elements, identify critical services and functions, provide alternatives for emergency operations, and integrate each departmental plan. This can

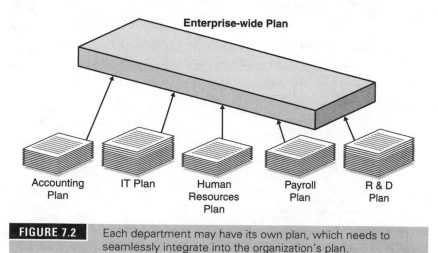

Enterprise-wide Plan

Accounting Plan   IT Plan   Human Resources Plan   Payroll Plan   R & D Plan

FIGURE 7.2   Each department may have its own plan, which needs to seamlessly integrate into the organization's plan.

be accomplished by in-house employees, outside consultants, or a combination of both. A combination can bring many benefits to the company because the consultants are experts in this field and know the necessary steps, questions to ask, issues to look out for, and general reasonable advice, whereas the in-house employees know their company intimately and have a full understanding of how certain threats can affect operations.

It is important to know when to activate the plans. The DRP should be activated after a damage assessment and evaluation has been completed; triggers should be integrated in the plan to help know when it should be initiated.

Emergency Response

Protection of life is of the utmost importance and should be dealt with first before looking to save material objects. Training and drills should teach people how to evacuate personnel, who to call for help in different situations, how to administer basic emergency procedures (CPR, wrapping wounds, etc.), and all personnel should know their designated emergency exits and destinations. If the situation is not life threatening, systems should be shut down in an orderly fashion and critical data files or resources should be removed during evacuation. The documented disaster recovery and continuity plans should be located and taken to the secure location as well.

Travel Advisory

When media needs to be removed, security policies, standards, and procedures should be enforced to ensure that data is not compromised during evacuation.

It is common to overlook the moments immediately following the disaster when order has been restored. The following items are considered secondary issues, but should be addressed and the plan should incorporate how to deal with each of them:

- Looting and vandalism
- Fraud opportunities
- Media and press responses
- Responsibilities to families
- Legal responsibilities
- Further expenses

At least one person should be prepared to talk to the press so that a clear, direct, and informative message can be given to the company's customers, stockholders, and partners. The substance and direction of this information and who should deliver it should be agreed upon beforehand so that the company provides a uniform response to the disaster.

Recovery and Restoration

A restoration team should be divided into two groups. One group has the responsibility of getting the alternate site into a working and functioning environment; the second team, or salvage team, has the chore of returning the primary site back to its original condition. The teams must know how to do many tasks, such as how to install operating systems, configure workstations and servers, string wire and cabling, configure the network, install equipment and applications, restore data from backup facilities, and possibly work with outside vendors to complete other configurations.

A company is not out of an emergency state until it is back in operation at the original primary site. Operations should not be moved back to the original site until the salvage team has approved it. There are many logistic issues to consider when a company returns from the alternate site to the original site. Mission critical issues such as operational procedures should be prioritized so that production is not negatively impacted.

The least critical business components should be the first moved back to the primary site so that if it was not reconstructed correctly, the company will not be severely impacted. When business returns to normal operating conditions, it is referred to as a reconstitution or resumption phase.

Documentation

Documentation seems to be a dreaded task to most people, and many will find any other task to take on to ensure that they are not the ones stuck with documenting processes and procedures. However, a company can do a great and responsible job of backing up hardware and software to an off-site facility, maintaining it, keeping everything up-to-date and current, and when a disaster hits, no one knows how to put it back to together again.

Disaster recovery documentation is vital because when it is needed, it will most likely be during a chaotic and frantic time with a demanding time schedule. The recovery plan should include the following categories of information:

- Facility issues (main facility and backup sites)
- People (operations, technical, end-users, business requirements)
- Hardware (servers, workstations, devices, replacement timeline)
- Software (operating systems, applications, data)
- Supplies (HVAC, UPS, office supplies)

- Recovery procedures
- Emergency procedures
- External contact information

Testing and Drills

It should be assumed that the disaster recovery and continuity plans are not complete until testing has taken place. Each test or drill should have a goal or objective that helps confirm that the company can indeed recover from a disaster or disruption. Tests should take place at least once a year and whenever there are significant changes within the company or within the disaster and continuity plans. Although it is difficult for many companies to accomplish full-scale testing at once, the combination of tests and drills should cover all areas, including hardware, software, personnel, procedures, and communication lines. If the test will include moving some equipment to an alternate site, then transportation, extra equipment, and alternate site readiness must be addressed. Compatibility with the backup facility is a key element in testing to ensure that the plan is effective.

Testing results should identify all weaknesses so they can be addressed properly. Team members should expect mistakes to take place, which will help them identify what needs to be improved upon. All of the results should be reported to management so they are aware of the overall status of the project.

Predetermined scenarios should be developed for each test, which will walk employees through different disaster possibilities and see how they react to various situations.

The following are the different types of drills that can take place:

- **Checklist test** In this type of test, copies of the disaster recovery and business continuity plans are distributed to different departments and functional areas for review. This is done so that each functional manager can evaluate the plan and ensure that nothing pertaining to her department has been left out. This is a method that ensures that some things have not been taken for granted or omitted. Once the departments have reviewed their copy and made suggestions, the planning team then integrates those changes into the master plan.

- **Structured walk-through test** In this test, representatives from each department or functional area come together to go over the plan and ensure its accuracy. The group will go over the objectives of the plan, discuss the scope and assumptions of the plan, review the organization and reporting structure, and evaluate the testing, maintenance, and training requirements. This allows for brainstorming, storyboarding, exchanging of ideas and gives the people responsible for disaster recovery execution the ability to sign off on the plan or suggest changes.

- **Simulation test**   This type of test takes a lot more planning and resources. In this situation, all employees who participate in operational and support functions come together to practice executing the disaster recovery plan based on a specific scenario. The drill continues until the moment the actual relocation to the new facility would take place. This is done to ensure that specific steps were not left out or certain glitches were not identified. This test will act as a catalyst to raise the awareness of the individuals involved.

- **Parallel test**   A parallel test is done to ensure that specific systems can actually perform adequately at the alternate off-site facility. Some systems are moved to the alternate site where duplicate processing occurs. The results are compared with the processing at the primary site to identify mistakes or areas that need more attention.

- **Full-interruption test**   This type of test is the most intrusive to regular operations and business productivity. The original site is actually shut down, and processing is moved to the alternate site. The recovery team must ensure that the new facility is operation-ready and all processing will be done on devices at the alternate facility. This is a full-blown drill that takes a lot of planning and coordination, but can identify many holes in the plan that need to be fixed before an actual disaster hits.

Travel Advisory

The first four tests are usually carried out before a full-interruption test takes place.

Maintenance

Like any other type of documentation or policy, disaster recovery and continuity plans can quickly fall out of date. The following are common reasons why:

- Reorganization of company
- Personnel turnover
- Environmental changes
- Hardware and software changes
- Plans simply forgotten about

However, there are several methods of ensuring that the plan stays current:

- Integrate it into job descriptions
- Include the ongoing maintenance of the plan as part of personnel evaluations

- Conduct regular audits
- Centralize responsibility for continual updates
- Require regular reports
- Make disaster recovery and continuity planning a part of every business decision

The disaster recovery and continuity plans are only as good as they are relevant to the company and the current times, so it is important that the plans are not shoved in a desk drawer as everyone pats each other the back claiming, "Job well done on that planning project!" Developing the plans falls under due care, but discipline needs to be continually practiced to keep the plans current and useful. Thus, it needs to be integrated into other business activities and clear responsibilities need to be drawn.

Phase Breakdown

Disaster recovery and business continuity planning is a systematic way of providing a checklist of actions that should take place right after a disaster. The complete program is divided into different phases, as shown in Figure 7-3.

Prevention

Although having these plans is a good idea in preparing for the worst, it makes good business sense to research ways to prevent a disaster from ever happening in the first place. We can't control the natural disasters and the unknown, but there are several preventive steps that can be taken to mitigate the extent of the damages and prevent smaller disruptions to production:

- Understand all risks and alternative countermeasures.
- Institute strict physical and information security.
- Establish emergency response procedures to help mitigate further damages.
- Acquire adequate insurance coverage.
- Have a backup communications link (ISDN, T1, dial-up).
- Continually back up critical business data.
- Ensure that backup hardware and software is available.
- Have redundant power supplies.
- Secure all devices and ensure access to them.
- Train employees and communicate requirements to them.

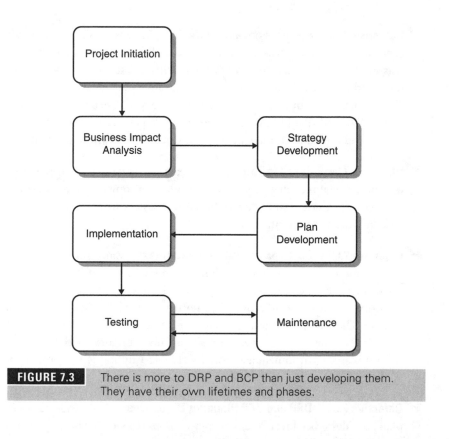

FIGURE 7.3 There is more to DRP and BCP than just developing them. They have their own lifetimes and phases.

CHECKPOINT

✔ **Objective 7.01: Disaster Recovery versus Business Continuity**   DRP outlines activities that should take place during and right after a disaster. It usually focuses on emergency procedures and recovering critical IT systems. BCP pertains to keeping a company in business in an alternate environment and under different circumstances.

✔ **Objective 7.02:   Project Initiation Phase**   Executive commitment and support are the most critical elements in developing the disaster recovery and business continuity plans. A business need must be made to gain executive support by explaining regulatory and legal requirements and vulnerabilities, and it should be accompanied with recommendations.

✔**Objective 7.03:   Business Impact Analysis**   The business impact analysis is one of the most important first steps in the planning development phase. It is used to identify the company's most critical departments and equipment and estimates the outage time the company can endure without them. The team carrying out the BIA also ascertains alternative backup methods. Qualitative and quantitative data needs to be gathered, analyzed, interpreted, and presented to management for direction on how to proceed.

✔**Objective 7.04:   Possible Threats**   Threats can be natural, man-made, or technical. The three categories of disruptions for a company to consider are disaster, non-disaster, and catastrophe. Non-disasters are the most common and the easiest to prevent.

✔**Objective 7.05:   Backups and Off-Site Facilities**   Many things need to be understood pertaining to the working environment so that it can be replicated at an alternate site after a disaster. A reciprocal agreement is when one company promises another company they can "move in" if they experience a disaster. These agreements are hard to enforce and rarely work out, but do provide for a cheap alternative. A hot site is fully configured with hardware, software, and environmental needs. Electronic vaulting is the process of backing up bulk data immediately to an off-site facility.

✔**Objective 7.06:   DRP and BCP Planning Objectives**   A disaster recovery plan provides procedures for emergency responses, extended backup operations, and post-disaster recovery. There should be an enterprise-wide plan, and each individual organizational unit should have its own disaster recovery plan. A business continuity plan ensures continuity of critical business functions and provides rapid recovery to reduce the overall impact of a disaster or disruption. Testing and drills demonstrate the actual ability to recover and can verify compatibility of backup facilities.

REVIEW QUESTIONS

1. What is the first step that needs to take place before developing a disaster recovery plan?

   A. Choose an off-site facility or implement a reciprocal agreement with another company.

   B. Perform a risk analysis and identify assets.

    C. Perform software and hardware backups and implement electronic vaulting.

    D. Perform a business impact analysis.

2. If a company is paying for a warm site facility, what is the best way to assure the reliability of the information on backup tapes and the ability to properly restore data from them?

    A. Test restoration of data on the devices at the primary site.

    B. Have the off-site staff verify that the tapes are properly labeled.

    C. Inventory the tapes at the site each month.

    D. Have the off-site staff verify that the tapes are readable on their equipment.

3. Emergency actions are taken at the first stage of a disaster with the goals of preventing injuries or loss of life and …

    A. Protecting evidence

    B. Preventing looting and fraud

    C. Mitigating further damage

    D. Determining the extent of the property damage

4. How often should a business continuity plan be tested?

    A. At least once a year

    B. Every two years

    C. Only after a merger takes place

    D. Every three years

5. Which of the following describes remote journaling?

    A. Sending data to two different disks, one being a shadow disk

    B. Sending tapes of transaction data to an off-site facility in a batch process

    C. A batch process that captures transaction data and sends it to multiple storage facilities

    D. Electronic forwarding of transactions to an off-site facility

6. What areas of a company require a business continuity plan?

    A. Financial and information areas

    B. Management, marketing, and critical areas

    C. All areas of the enterprise

    D. Areas the directly support the company and integrate with outside entities

7. Which of the following is not one of the items identified during a business impact analysis?

   A. The critical departments and equipment that the company depends upon

   B. The areas that would suffer the greatest financial loss in the event of a disaster

   C. The outage time that can be tolerated by the company

   D. Names of people to contact during a disaster

8. Which of the following describes a parallel test?

   A. It is performed to ensure that specific systems will run at the alternate site.

   B. All departments receive a copy of the disaster recovery plan and walk through it.

   C. Representatives from each department come together and go through the test collectively.

   D. Normal operations are shut down.

9. Which of the following describes a structured walkthrough test?

   A. It is performed to ensure that critical systems will run at the alternate site.

   B. All departments receive a copy of the disaster recovery plan and walk through it.

   C. Representatives from each department come together and go through the test collectively.

   D. Normal operations are shut down.

10. When is the emergency actually over for a company?

    A. When all people are safe and accounted for

    B. When all operations and people are moved back into the primary site

    C. When operations are safely moved to the off-site facility

    D. When a civil official declares that all is safe

11. Which of the following does not describe a reciprocal agreement?

    A. Agreement is enforceable.

    B. It is a cheap solution.

    C. It may be able to be implemented right after a disaster.

    D. It could overwhelm a current data processing site.

12. Which of the following describes a cold site?
    A. Fully equipped and operational in a few hours
    B. Partially equipped with data processing equipment
    C. Expensive and fully configured
    D. Providing environmental measures and no equipment

13. What is the first thing to accomplish in the project initiation phase of a business continuity planning effort?
    A. Establish scope of project and necessary funding
    B. Obtain management support
    C. Draw up disaster scenarios
    D. Develop documents to be used for the business impact analysis

14. Which of the following best describes what a disaster recovery plan should contain?
    A. Hardware, software, people, emergency procedures, recovery procedures
    B. People, hardware, off-site facility
    C. Software, media interaction, people, hardware, management issues
    D. Hardware, emergency procedures, software, identified risk

REVIEW ANSWERS

1. **D** The first step before developing a disaster recovery plan is to perform a business impact analysis, which will look at the threats that could affect the company and alternative ways of dealing with it.

2. **A** Because this is a warm site facility, the company will be bringing their own equipment after a disaster hits, so it is important that the tapes can be read on their equipment at the primary site, not the site maintainer's equipment.

3. **C** All steps taken in disaster recovery have to do with preventing or mitigating further risks and damages.

4. **A** Both plans should be reviewed and tested at least once a year so that they do not go out of date and that they can continue to be improved upon.

5. **D** Remote journaling is used to send data to an off-site facility electronically so that valid data is saved and available in case of a disaster or disruption. Remote journaling is a parallel process of saving data locally

and remotely and electronic vaulting does the same thing, but performs the activities in a batch process.

6. **C**　Every department should have a DRP and BCP and there should be DRP and BCP enterprise-wide plans also. Every department is important to some degree and should be prepared for threats that may directly affect them.

7. **D**　The first three items are the main functionalities of a business impact analysis. The plan will not identify what individuals should be contacted. That information should be on a document that the BIA references.

8. **A**　In a parallel test, certain systems are run at the alternate site and results are compared with how processing takes place at the primary site. This is to ensure that the systems work in that location and productivity is not affected.

9. **C**　During a structured walkthrough test, functional representatives meet and review the plan to ensure its accuracy and that it correctly and accurately reflects the company's recovery strategy.

10. **B**　The emergency is not actually over until the company moves back into their primary site (or into a new primary site) because the company may still be functioning in a "crippled" state at the alternate site and can still be vulnerable to other threats that affect productivity and production.

11. **A**　A reciprocal agreement is not enforceable, meaning this new facility may or may not be available to the company in need during an emergency.

12. **D**　A cold site provides only environmental measures; wiring, air conditioning, and raised floors. It is basically a shell of a building and no more.

13. **B**　The first crucial step in the initiation of the project is to obtain management support; without it, all other efforts could be fruitless.

14. **A**　The recovery plan should provide encompassing information about how to deal with people, hardware, software, emergency procedures, recovery procedures, facility issues, and supplies.

Law, Investigation, and Ethics

	NEWBIE	SOME EXPERIENCE	EXPERT
ETA	5 hours	3 hours	2 hours

Since the earliest of times, crime has taken place, with or without a computer. Computers simply add more complexity to the game. Crooks now have more opportunities to trespass, eavesdrop, scavenge, and steal without much risk of being caught. And in today's computer world, they don't even have to leave the comfort of their own homes. The introduction of the computer has not thwarted the trend of criminal activity; in fact, it has created entirely new forms of crime.

Remote and internal attacks are a big part of computer crime and have now become a serious concern to companies. They have to deal with these new criminal activities—the effect they have on the company, liabilities involved with protecting themselves, question of prosecuting an identified criminal or not, loss in revenue and reputation, and the consequences that come along with each.

This chapter deals with the ethical and legal responsibilities of security professionals, executives and employees, as well as the investigation process that takes place after a crime has been committed. We look at some popular attacks that take place, laws that are being used to protect companies from these types of attacks, and profiles and motivations of many of the attackers today.

Objective 8.01 Ethics

Information security professionals are the good guys. Now, although we know that ethical practice comes naturally to the good guys, it is still important to understand the rules and guidelines that have been laid out. It's also a good thing to know come exam time.

(ISC)²

The International Information Systems Security Certification Consortium, (ISC)², requires all certified information system security professionals to commit to fully supporting its Code of Ethics. If a CISSP intentionally or knowingly violates this Code of Ethics, she can be subject to a peer review panel, which will decide if the certification should be relinquished.

The full set of (ISC)² Code of Ethics is listed on their Web site at www.isc2.org; an overview is included here. Please read the full version before taking the exam.

Code of Ethics Summary

- Act honestly, justly, responsibly, legally, and protect society.
- Work diligently and provide competent services and advance the security profession.

- Encourage the growth of research—teach, mentor, and value the certification.
- Discourage unnecessary fear or doubt, and do not consent to bad practices.
- Discourage unsafe practices; preserve and strengthen the integrity of public infrastructures.
- Observe and abide by all contracts, expressed or implied, and give prudent advice.
- Avoid any conflict of interest, respect the trust that others put in you, and take on only those jobs you are fully qualified to perform.
- Stay current on skills and do not become involved with activities that could injure the reputation of other security professionals.

Computer Ethics Institute

One group that concentrates specifically on ethics in the technological industry is the Computer Ethics Institute. This group works to help advance technology by ethical means. It is a nonprofit organization concerned with the impact computer technology has on society. Their Web site is www.cpsr.org. You can visit this site and read through their Ten Commandments of Computer Ethics.

Internet Activities Board

The Internet is a big focus when discussing computer ethics and crime. Because it has grown so much and so quickly, there is a lot of potential for unethical behavior. The *Internet Activities Board* (IAB) is the coordinating committee for Internet design, engineering, and management. It is an independent committee of researchers and professionals with a technical interest in the health and evolution of the Internet. The IAB sees the use of the Internet as a privilege and works to protect it against unethical behavior.

The following are acts considered unethical by the IAB:

- Purposely seeking to gain unauthorized access to Internet resources
- Disrupting the intended use of the Internet
- Wasting resources (people, capacity, and computers) through purposeful actions
- Destroying the integrity of computer-based information
- Compromising the privacy of others
- Involving negligence in the conduct of Internet-wide experiments

Objective 8.02   Hacking Methods

Now that we have the ethics down, let's look at what can lead to unethical behavior.

When a detective is presented with a crime case, oftentimes he first tries to figure out a motive. Learning why a crime was committed can often lead to the criminal. Computer crime can be treated the same way.

Motivations are the "who" and "why" of crimes and they can be influenced by different factors. One factor is referred to as an internal condition. This can be human emotion such as committing a crime for the thrill of it, the excitement, or the challenge that it imposes. Internal conditions are difficult to identify. However, external conditions are usually much easier to uncover. This could be a case where a person is having financial trouble and feels he has no other option but to commit a crime. Figuring out the motivation of a crime is an important first step in solving it.

The next step is to look at how the crime happened, meaning where were the holes that allowed this attacker to commit the crime in the first place. These are called opportunities.

Opportunities are the "where" and "when" of a crime. Some examples of opportunities are when no firewalls are present in a network, lax employee auditing, or users with excessive permissions that would allow them to cause grave damage.

Finally, how did the criminal carry out this act? This is called the *means* or capability of the criminal. For example, computer crime is almost always committed by someone with extensive knowledge of computers. Looking at each suspect's technical ability will help in discovering the actual person guilty of the crime.

Characteristics of an Attacker

You must always be on the look out for a potential attacker. They come in all forms and there is no full-proof way of spotting them, but it is a good idea to know their general characteristics. Historically, hackers have been curious young males who want to test their technical abilities or see what kind of destruction they can cause. The more serious crimes, however, are usually carried out by a small group of attackers or a dedicated individual. They are usually seeking financial gain by stealing money electronically, obtaining credit card numbers, or embarrassing companies, disrupting services, or acquiring confidential information and/or military secrets.

It is also a good idea to know what kinds of things attract a hacker to you. These characteristics are included here:

- Lack of awareness
- Inadequate safeguards
- Insufficient security staff, skills, and resources
- Lack of incident-response capability
- Companies that do not press charges

> **Local Lingo**
>
> The word "hackers" has taken on the meaning of the word "crackers." Hackers used to be viewed as computer gurus and not people with malicious intent, whereas crackers aimed to bypass security controls for one purpose or another. Today, they are used interchangeably.

Problems with Prosecuting Attackers

Another reason hackers continue to flourish is because it can be difficult to prosecute them for their crimes. The reasons are varied.

- Cross-jurisdiction problems.
- Lack of understanding and skill on the law enforcement side.
- No laws that cover some of the newer crimes.
- Lack of crimes reported in the private sector.
- Difficulty of setting appropriate punishments.
- Traditional crimes usually have tangible evidence; computer crimes have intangible evidence.
- Not always viewed as serious crimes.

If a hacker in the Netherlands attacked a bank in the United States, where did the actual crime take place (in the Netherlands or the U.S.)? Whose jurisdiction would that fall within? If an attacker is captured, how hard is it to find a lawyer who understands these types of cases and is willing to take them on? How are complex technical issues explained to a jury and judge? How are bits and commands that were used to carry out the crime captured and properly presented in court as evidence?

These are just some of the issues law enforcement and the legal system are working hard to define and develop the necessary processes and procedures to deal with today's current computer crimes.

Types of Attacks

There are many types of computer crimes. Each type has different methods that an attacker can use to accomplish specific goals. The following section goes over some of the more popular types of computer crime.

Salami

A *salami* attack is when small crimes are committed with the hopes that the ultimate larger crime is not identified. For example, small amounts of money can be purposefully transferred from different banking accounts to an attacker's account. Because the amount is so small, it often goes unnoticed. But, if this act is done over and over again for a long period of time, the result can add up to some pretty big sums. This kind of criminal activity was shown in the movie *Office Space*, where a computer program was written to subtract fractions of a penny for every transaction that is processed. In fact, there have been reports that these types of activities have taken place in many different industries all over the world.

Data Diddling

Data diddling is when data is modified before being inputted into an application or computer system or as soon as it comes out. If a company wants a better credit rating or wants to show that the company is actually producing profits instead of losses, bogus figures may be entered into some type of accounting application.

Another place this can happen is if a cashier enters into a system that a customer purchased an item that costs $20, but charges the customer $30 and pockets the difference. In this case, the cashier is entering incorrect information into the system to try and cover up the actual transaction that took place.

This kind of crime is very hard to control, especially in environments that are constantly changing. Retail industries can suffer greatly because of the heavy volume of cash transactions that occur every day. These environments also usually have heavy turnover with limited employee supervision.

Excessive Privileges

Granting a user access to resources that he does not absolutely need can open up huge holes in security. This is referred to as *excessive privileges*. A good example is when an employee changes positions within the company. An accounting employee may have access to payroll information, financial records, accounts receivables, etc. If this employee were to transfer to the customer service department, his privileges should be changed appropriately. Oftentimes, this is overlooked and the employee's permissions grow over time, which means that he could have a window of opportunity to commit fraud or cause more extensive damages through mistakes.

Password Sniffing

Password sniffing is when a hacker monitors, or sniffs, network traffic with the hopes of capturing useful data being sent between computers. Many times the useful data that the attackers are out to obtain are passwords so that they can authenticate as legitimate users and gain more privileged access to a company's resources. The Internet can supply attackers with many tools to accomplish this kind of attack.

IP Spoofing

IP spoofing is one of the best disguises an attacker can use. This means that an attacker manually changes her IP address so she cannot be traced. Spoofing is necessary because computers have IP addresses assigned to them, and when a crime is committed, the investigation will lead back to this address. Attackers will often use hacking tools that will automatically change their IP address for them. The majority of computer crimes that are committed use spoofed IP addresses.

Dumpster Diving

Dumpster diving is when someone goes through another person's trash looking for useful information. This is common in the corporate world as spies are looking for insider trading information, confidential documents, network schematics, or customer information.

To carry out this act, an intruder needs to gain access to the dumpster area of a company. Typically, this is not difficult because these areas are usually not guarded by security personnel or with surveillance equipment.

Exam Tip	
Although dumpster diving is considered legal, it is highly unethical.	

Wiretapping

Wiretapping is the act of eavesdropping on an electrical signal. It is referred to as a *passive* attack because it usually goes undetected and the attacker is not actually doing anything actively. Attackers can use wiretapping tools such as cellular scanners, radio receivers, microphone receivers, tape recorders, network sniffers, and telephone-tapping devices. Wiretapping is illegal under the U.S. Federal Wiretap Law without a court order.

> **Exam Tip**
>
> A danger of sniffers is that their presence is usually undetectable and cannot be audited.

Social Engineering

Social engineering is the art of tricking people into giving up sensitive information. It can be as simple as calling a customer service representative and pretending to be an employee of the company in order to obtain confidential information.

Masquerading is another attack type that attempts to fool others about the origin of a message or attack. E-mail viruses use masquerading methods all the time by tricking users into thinking they have just received an e-mail from a friend or acquaintance. In actuality, a computer program sent out the message, which contains a harmful computer virus. As soon as the user opens the e-mail or an e-mail attachment, the virus is activated. In addition to crippling the user's computer system, it usually automatically forwards the virus to every address contained in the user's address directory, which causes the virus to spread exponentially.

More Attack Types

- **Superzapper**   An attack that uses a tool, called a superzapper, to modify files or configurations without being detected or audited.
- **Scanning**   A process of presenting data sequentially in an automated method in the hopes of receiving a positive response. This is basically a brute force attack, made by trying all possible combinations.
- **Information Warfare**   An attack against the information infrastructure of a nation or its critical systems.
- **Pseudo Flaw**   A loophole planted in an operating system or application as a trap for intruders.

> **Travel Advisory**
>
> A superzapper tool used to be a mainframe utility used by administrators. Today, it is a general term for a tool that can make changes that are undetectable.

Attack Categories

There are three categories of attacks that take place in relation to information security: physical security, personnel security, and operations security. Each of the attack types listed previously can be placed in one of the categories outlined in Table 8-1.

Phone Fraud

Phreakers are hackers who specialize in telephone service. They are known for tricking phone systems into giving them free long-distance service or reconfiguring telecommunication devices.

A method called *blue boxing* was a scheme where phreakers used devices that simulated frequency tones that took advantage of a weakness in the public telephone system. This simulated tone tricked the system into believing long-distance access should be granted.

Another type of fraud involved pay telephones. Phreakers used a device that simulated coins being deposited into the pay phones in order to receive free calls. This scheme was referred to as *red boxing*. A line voltage scheme called *black boxes* was used to trick older toll switches into providing free long distance calls.

One other interesting case took place in 1972 with a phreaker called Cap'n Crunch. This phreaker's blind friend discovered that a toy whistle found in boxes of Cap'n Crunch cereal could generate the 2,600-Hz tone, which in turn could be used to get free long-distance phone service.

As the telephone companies advanced their systems and went digital, most of the phreaker phone tricks became ineffective. However, a lot of fraud still takes place in PBX systems. Today, phreakers steal phone services by reconfiguring PBXs and other systems and by charging the long-distance tolls to the owners of those systems. This crime is very hard to trace, but it is mainly successful because many companies do not audit their phone bills.

TABLE 8.1	Physical security, personnel security, and operations security are the three categories of attacks.	
Physical	**Personnel**	**Operations**
Dumpster diving	Social engineering	Data diddling
Wiretapping	Masquerading	IP Spoofing
	Pseudo flaw	Password sniffing
		Salami
		Superzapping

Organization Liabilities and Ramifications

Objective 8.03

The extent to which companies are held liable for activities and crimes has changed dramatically with the evolution of computers and information technology. In the old days, a company would need to do things like install burglar alarms and smoke detectors, and maybe even shred some important documents to ensure that they did not get into the wrong hands. Today, companies are required to do things like install firewalls, encrypt their data, and establish virtual private networks (VPNs). More extreme measures need to be taken to protect assets, and these measures are required to protect companies from a variety of liabilities.

Companies that are taking these necessary steps are said to be practicing *due care*. This means that a company did everything reasonably possible to try to prevent security breaches. Along with preventative steps, due care also means that if a breach were to occur, damages would most likely be far less when compared to not practicing due care. To look at it more simply—due care means that a company practiced common sense and prudent management practices with responsible actions.

One type of liability that can be imposed upon companies is referred to as a *downstream liability*. This means that one company that does not implement the necessary due care practices could negatively affect the security of another company that is somehow connected. Downstream liabilities are often related to a company's extranet or other shared network platforms. If two or more companies are going to connect their networks in some way, there should be a contract in place indicating the security level expected of each party and what should happen if a compromise takes place. If one company does not follow and honor these practices, the other company can sue them because of their negligence.

Security Principles

Best practices have been developed to help companies deal with liability. The *Generally Accepted System Security Principles* (GASSP) is a set of guidelines intended to help guide organizations when establishing new policies, practices, or infrastructures. These guidelines were originally modeled after the Organization for Economic Cooperation and Development (OECD). The GASSP committee has created these guidelines hoping to promote good security practices worldwide and to provide a point of reference for IT and security professionals.

Legal Liability

Companies that do not practice due care are vulnerable to negligence suits. In order for this to hold up in court, the company must be said to have a *legally recognized obligation*. This means that there is a standard of conduct expected of the company that protects others from unreasonable risks. In addition, a *proximate causation* must be demonstrated, which means that someone can prove that the damage that was caused was the company's fault. So there needs to be a rule and someone must be able to prove a company broke that rule.

Other liabilities that companies can be exposed to are

- Violation of law   Regulatory, criminal, or civil suits
- Violation of due care   Stockholders, employee, or customer suits
- Violation of privacy   Employees or customer suits

Privacy Issues

Corporations have responsibilities to their employees just as they do their stockholders and customers. An employee's right to privacy is an issue that organizations must understand and protect. This concept relates to the computer world because confidential information is usually held by one type of computer or another. If an agency's computer is holding an individual's private information, it must provide the necessary security mechanisms to ensure that it cannot be compromised or obtained in an unauthorized way.

The next few sections detail the various privacy regulations in place that companies may need to abide by or face legal consequences.

Privacy Act of 1974

The *Privacy Act of 1974* deals with what information U.S. government agencies can collect and keep on its citizens and what they can do with this information. It applies to records and documents developed and maintained by specific branches of the federal government, such as executive departments, government corporations, independent regulatory agencies, and government-controlled corporations. An actual *record* is information about an individual's education, medical history, financial history, criminal record, employment history, and other types of information. Agencies can only maintain this type of information if it is necessary and relevant to accomplishing the agency's purpose. The Privacy Act dictates that an agency cannot disclose this information without written permission from the individual. However, like most government acts, legislation, and creeds, there is a list of exceptions.

The information collected needs to be used for the reason it was collected and citizens should have access to this data and be able to submit corrections if it is incorrect.

Electronic Communications Privacy Act of 1986

The *Electronic Communications Privacy Act of 1986* extended the wiretapping and privacy laws to cover electronic communications. As new technologies were developed in the 1980s, giving hackers additional communication mechanisms, this regulation was put into place to ensure that all boundaries of wiretapping and eavesdropping would be covered by the law. Court approval is required to intercept messages in this manner.

Health Insurance Portability and Accountability Act (HIPAA)

The *Health Insurance Portability and Accountability Act* (HIPAA) is a new federal regulation that helps protect the medical records of individuals. This law addresses the advancements in information technology by requiring agencies to meet certain standards and procedures when storing medical records electronically, as well as transmitting them.

HIPAA dictates facility security procedures for any agency that deals with medical records and provides guidelines to ensure integrity and privacy when handling this type of information. This and the act described in the following section is basically forcing these different types of businesses to implement a security program and follow through with it or be faced with monetary fines and possible jail time for those responsible.

Gramm Leach Bliley Act of 1999

This regulation protects the privacy of an individual's financial records. The *Gramm Leach Bliley Act of 1999* specifies that financial institutions cannot share nonpublic information with a nonaffiliated third party unless the customer has given consent. Before this type of data is shared with a third-party entity, the financial institution is supposed to give the individual the opportunity to forbid this action.

Another provision of the act states that the board of directors for a financial organization is responsible for security issues, risk management, and ensuring that all employees are trained on information security issues. Security measures must be implemented and tested and a written policy was to be put into place by July 1, 2001.

Employee Monitoring

How many times have you heard this message when calling a customer service line, "Your call may be monitored for quality assurance?" This is common practice for employers to evaluate the performance of their employees and track their service levels. However a company must follow certain guidelines to be able to carry out such activities.

An employer must inform its employees that certain types of monitoring could be taking place and that the data gathered must be relevant to work activities. When you log in to your company's network and are presented with that long paragraph no one reads, it is stating that monitoring may take place, and that if you perform actions deemed unethical or illegal, the ramifications could be termination or prosecution. I'll bet you are going to read that paragraph next time. Monitoring can take place through screening phone calls, e-mail messages, or keystroke monitoring.

> **Local Lingo**
>
> Keystroke monitoring is recording each and every key punched at a specific computer.

Legally, the employer must inform an employee about possible monitoring activities *before* it actually takes place, or it can be seen as invading that person's privacy. Informing employees of these types of issues should take place through security awareness, posted bulletins, new employee training, and the dialog box presented to users before they can log in to a system.

> **Exam Tip**
>
> If a company wants to monitor an employee but has not informed her that it could take place, the company should not do any monitoring until all employees have been given notice of its possibility.

Here are some general guidelines to employee monitoring:

- Establish a policy outlining the expected use of company resources and ramifications if not followed.
- Notify users that monitoring may take place.
- Ensure that monitoring takes place in a lawful manner.
- Individuals cannot be singled out, monitoring must happen uniformly.
- Only work-related events can be monitored.

Transborder Information Flow

Many companies communicate internationally everyday through e-mail, telephone lines, satellites, fiber cables, and long-distance wireless transmission. It is important for a company to research the laws of different countries pertaining to information flow and privacy.

Many times, data can route through many different countries before arriving at its destination. Network routing should be analyzed regularly to understand how data moves from one place to another. Some countries restrict the flow of personal information and financial data, or deem it illegal. It all depends on the laws of the countries you are passing data through, so you should be aware of them.

Other issues to consider pertaining to the privacy of confidential information include:

- **Data retrieval advances**   Ways of collecting vast amounts of personal data and storing it in central repositories
- **Convergent technologies**   Technical methods of gathering, analyzing, and distributing information
- **Globalization**   Distributing information beyond national borders

If these technologies and methods are used to collect and store private data, the data must be properly secured and access drastically restricted.

International Issues

A hacker in another country can be difficult to prosecute because of differing laws, evidence ruling, and punishment guidelines. Many times, governments will not work together in these types of cases, thus many computer criminals have been caught but not prosecuted because of the perspective and attitude of the country the attack originated from. Jurisdiction issues and differing law systems have made it very hard for the secret service and FBI to successfully fight computer crime and bring identified suspects to trial.

Exam Tip

The secret service and FBI are responsible for dealing with many computer crimes.

Objective 8.04 Types of Law

There are different types of laws because there are different types of crimes. Segmenting them into these different categories increases the understanding and efficiency of the proper activities that should take place to conduct investigations, trial procedures, and the types of punishments that map to specific crime types. The three main types of common law are civil, criminal, and administrative (or regulatory). Each is covered in the following sections.

Civil Law

A *civil law* is a wrong against an individual or company that causes damage or loss. A person filing a civil law suit may be seeking financial restitution for the harm that was caused. This type of law does not impose jail sentences to the guilty party. Civil law, also called *tort*, is typically easier to convict than criminal law because it requires a reduced burden of proof. Criminal law, on the other hand, makes it possible to find someone liable for damages.

Criminal Law

Criminal law is a violation of rules established by the government to protect the public. Unlike civil law, criminal law can impose jail sentences to guilty parties depending upon the severity of the crime. Because penalties can be more severe, and guilt has to be proven instead of just liability, it does take a much stronger burden of proof to convict than in civil law. In fact, it is not uncommon for an individual to be found not guilty in a criminal case and then found liable in a corresponding civil case. This is exactly what happened to O.J. Simpson.

For criminal law to be effective in the computer world, the punishment has to work as a real deterrent. Today, most hackers are not caught, prosecuted, or punished appropriately. Punishment should take into account the money and time that is required for the investigation of the crime.

Travel Advisory

In a civil suit, an individual or company is attempting to sue another individual or company. In a criminal case, the government is attempting to prosecute an individual or company.

Administrative Law

Administrative laws are government-imposed standards for companies and agencies in specific industries to follow. They are the standards of performance that government agencies expect from companies and organizations.

Officials and executive management of organizations are held accountable for administrative laws and can be prosecuted if they are not adhered to properly. Some examples of administrative laws are: companies transferring financial information must ensure its confidentiality and integrity; restaurants must set personal hygiene requirements for employees; and organizations maintaining medical information must keep certain types of data confidential and protected.

Federal Policies

Even though computer crime legislation still has a long way to go, there are some laws in place today that help protect companies and U.S. citizens. Many of the laws deal with computer-related crimes and abuses (e.g., denial of service), software piracy, illegal content (e.g., child pornography), malicious code, wire and mail fraud, Internet jurisdiction issues, and economic and financial criminal activities. This section touches on only a few of the current laws in use for these purposes today.

Exam Tip

The definition of property has been expanded to include intangible materials, which allows existing laws to protect companies' electronic information.

Computer Fraud and Abuse Act of 1986

The *Computer Fraud and Abuse Act of 1986*, which was amended in 1996, is the primary federal anti-hacking statute. It categorizes seven forms of activity as federal crimes, mainly dealing with computers used by the federal government. This act includes felonies and misdemeanors with a range of large to small fines and jail sentences.

Economic Espionage Act of 1996

The *Economic Espionage Act of 1996* was developed to strengthen guidelines on espionage activity and enforce harsher penalties for the individuals convicted of these acts. This was done primarily because incidents of corporate espionage were rising because no real guidelines were in place to stop it. The Economic Espionage Act of 1996 defines trade secrets as technical, business, engineering, scientific, or financial in nature and imposes strict penalties that could reach up to $10 million in fines or 15 years in prison.

Federal Sentencing Guidelines of 1991

The *Federal Sentencing Guidelines of 1991* provided guidelines for judges so that they could dole out sentences and punishments in a more uniform manner when it comes to computer and white-collar crimes. It also deems senior executive management responsible for their company's security issues and allows for up to $290 million in fines that can be applied to these individuals.

Intellectual Property Laws

Companies put a lot of time, money, and resources into developing proprietary products and methods, collecting information, and coming up with catchy logos, jingles, and names for their products. It would not be fair for a company to go through all of this work and spend this kind of money and then let another company use the same information for their purposes. We should have some types of laws to deal with this! Oh yeah, we do.

The laws outlined in this section are put into place to protect a company's ideas and marketing efforts and what is considered to be rightfully theirs.

The first step a company must take when proving that an intellectual property law has been broken is to show what they did to protect this resource in the first place. This is an example of when due care comes into play. If the company feels that it has been violated, it must then prove that it took every reasonable step to protect itself against this kind of behavior and followed up on these steps to ensure it was working. Let's look at an example.

Joe makes a copy of a proprietary document and gives it to his friend David, who does not work for the same company. The company discovers what has happened and decides to charge Joe with illegally sharing intellectual property. For the company to be successful in this case, they must show the court why this document is so important, that the employee had been informed that this type of activity was unacceptable previous to the act, the damage that has been caused, and most importantly, what the company did to protect that document in the first place. No one else is going to help you protect your stuff if you don't even protect it yourself.

Some examples of intellectual property laws are shown in the following sections.

Trade Secret

A *trade secret* is a resource that gives a company a competitive advantage. This resource must not be generally known, must require a special skill, or must have required a significant amount of money to develop it. The trade secret must also be vital to a company's survival or profitability. Examples of trade secrets can be development methods for a piece of software and its internal components, or the recipe for the secret in a "secret sauce."

If this resource is stolen or used without consent, the violators can be charged under the trade secret law. For protection, most companies with intellectual property requires their employees to sign a *nondisclosure agreement (NDA)*. This contract prohibits employees from sharing company information and provides a full understanding that if an employee shares a trade secret, he can be fired and/or prosecuted.

Copyright

Copyright law protects expression of an idea, such as writings, lyrics, drawings, paintings, or even programming code. Though this book is protected by a copyright law, it does not protect the idea itself.

The law protects the creator and owner of the idea and his right to control the public distribution, reproduction, display, or adaptation of the work. For example, a print of an artist's painting requires the artist's consent. If the painting was simply copied without consent and sold, the violator could be charged under copyright law.

Copyright law is a big part of information technology as well. Computer programs are protected, which can include both the source and object code. Sometimes, even the structure of a program can be protected. However, the law does not cover things like concepts or procedures because they are considered subject matter rather than ideas.

> **Local Lingo**
> Source code is the programming code a developer writes; object code is after that source code has been compiled.

The copyright symbol, ©, is a warning or signal to others stating that the item is protected by law. However, owners of copyrighted items are not required to display the symbol even though it is strongly encouraged.

> **Travel Advisory**
> The copyright law outlines what the owner can do with the work and what others cannot do with it. It does not deal with the actual profits of the work.

Trademark

A *trademark* is a word, name, symbol, sound, shape, color, device or any combination of these. Companies trademark items like these because they help to uniquely identify the company, such as the golden arches of McDonalds, the red and gold circles of the MasterCard logo, and the ram head of Dodge trucks. A trademark can be said to be the "look and feel" of a company.

Most things that help distinguish a company from its competitors or are easily recognizable are worth trademarking. This ensures that you will be protected if others attempt to copy it.

Patent

Patents are for inventors, creators, and developers of new concepts, applications, or mechanisms. A patent is given to the owner of the invention, which grants him the right to exclude others from using or copying it. The requirements for obtaining a patent are that the invention is original, novel, useful, and nonobvious. Thus, you cannot patent stupidity, because it's everywhere.

An interesting rule in patent law is that once it is granted, it is good only for a certain amount of time. After this time period, the owner's rights are relinquished. Pharmaceutical companies experience this often with their patented drugs. During the window of time that the patent is valid, the company holding the patent is the sole manufacturer of the drug, but once the patent expires, all of its competitors are allowed to manufacture it also. This is why the medication you have been on for years suddenly dropped from $12 a pill to 50 cents. While that patent is good, the original company is the only one who can sell it, thus you have to pay *their* price.

In the computer world, algorithms are often patented allowing the creators to maintain complete control of their use during this time frame. But, once the time is up, other vendors can use and implement the algorithm without having to pay a fee.

Software Piracy

Software piracy occurs often today. It is the act of copying software without permission or compensation to the developer.

This happens a lot within companies when one person has a license for a software program and then copies it and shares it with other people. If caught, the person and the company can be held liable. In the past, there has been no real effective way to monitor or control this kind of activity, but software companies are making progress and hope to have more reliable mechanisms in place in the near future.

Licensing is a major issue to software companies. It is how they generate revenue and control piracy. Because software companies have lost a good amount of money in potential profits to software piracy, the Software Protection Association (SPA) has been formed by major software companies to enforce proprietary rights on software and licensing agreements. Licensing is a survival issue for many software companies because it represents how they generate the majority of their revenue.

Other international groups that protect against software piracy are the Federation Against Software Theft (FAST) and the Business Software Alliance (BSA).

Objective 8.05 Computer Crime Investigation

As mentioned earlier in the chapter, fighting cybercrime is far from easy. Law enforcement is usually not properly trained and the laws are hard to understand, if they're even in place. In addition, investigating a computer crime can open up a new can of worms due to the complexities that are involved. Collecting evidence from a computer is much different than dusting for fingerprints at a crime scene. This section goes over some of these barriers and the guidelines that have already been put into place.

Who Should Investigate?

One of the first and sometimes hardest decisions a company is faced with is deciding who should do the actual investigation of a computer crime. There are three groups to choose from: employees, consultants, and law enforcement. Many companies do not have a staff skilled in computer crime investigation and must bring in experts. Many companies are hesitant or unwilling to contact law enforcement because they do not want security compromises to be publicized, which could quickly hurt their reputation.

> **Travel Advisory**
>
> Before reporting a crime to law enforcement, permission should be obtained from management.

Incident Response Plan

A company should plan for dealing with computer crimes, security breaches, and incidents before they actually take place. This allows for better planning, proper procedures, and better chances of actually catching the bad guy.

Immediately following a computer crime, the area should be cleared of employees, vendors, customers, or other individuals that may compromise the scene. A crime scene is a fragile environment that must be secured quickly so that proper investigation can take place.

Most companies have security procedures already established for emergency situations. The same kind of preparation and detail should be put into an *incident response plan*.

> ### Local Lingo
> An incident is an adverse event that impacts the security or ability of a company to conduct normal business activities.

The incident response plan will help key personnel decide how to handle attacks, computer crimes, and production disturbances. There are some tough decisions that must be made and very little time to make them. For example, the decision of whether or not to shut down computer systems must be made. This is often a tough call because shutting down certain systems can affect customers and productivity, but leaving them on can impose danger also, especially if the attacker planted a logic bomb or virus. There is also the possibility that evidence can be destroyed if the system is not immediately turned off. The incident response plan should detail different possible scenarios and prioritize key systems so that individuals are not left with these dilemmas during a chaotic time.

> ### Local Lingo
> A *logic bomb* is a small program that is configured to carry out some kind of destructive activity at a specific time or when a certain event takes place.

Incident Response Team

Assuming that the company decides to handle future computer crimes and incidences with its own employees, then an *incident response team* should be formed. It is important that the team members bring a diverse skill set to the team. Generally speaking, the team should have someone from management, a network administrator, a security officer, possibly a network engineer and/or programmer, and a liaison for public affairs. The team should have the following resources at its disposal:

- A list of outside resources or agencies to contact
- A list of computer and forensic experts to contact
- A list of procedures that indicates how systems should be treated and prioritized
- Steps on how to search for evidence
- Steps on how to secure and preserve evidence
- A list of items to include on the crime report

Travel Advisory

If a suspect is an internal employee, a representative from human resources should be involved.

Incident Handling

The primary objectives for the response team immediately following a computer crime are to contain the damage that was caused and prevent further damage. If the team is going to perform the investigation and attempt to collect evidence, they should have these skills, be trained in these activities, have written procedures outlining the steps they should follow, and understand the demands and complexity of *properly* collecting evidence.

Collecting Evidence

Evidence is material presented in a court that is used to prove the truth or falsity of a fact. Collecting evidence can be a very complicated and detailed process, and it is critical that proper steps are taken and established procedures are followed. If they are not, it is highly likely that the evidence will not be admissible, thus it cannot be used during the trial. Extracting information, copying files, or even simply analyzing data on a computer can be very complicated; one mistake could mean the difference between a crook being convicted or acquitted.

Depending on how critical the affected system is to the company's current productivity and what the company decides should be done to this system will play into the decision as to whether the computer should be taken off the network and powered down. In most cases, the system will be taken offline, but a few things should take place first. The system and surrounding area should be photographed and configurations logged. The system's memory should also be dumped to a file before the system is powered down, because there could be crucial information being held within the memory of the computer.

The incident response team will need special tools, such as an evidence collection notebook, containers, a camera, and evidence identification tags. Evidence can be volatile, fragile and easily dismissed from a courtroom, so it must be handled carefully. As the team collects the evidence, it must ensure that a proper *chain of custody* of the evidence is maintained.

Chain of custody refers to the following:

- Who obtained the evidence?
- When and where was it obtained?
- Who secured it?
- Who had control or possession of the evidence?

The following checklist details some of the common steps that need to take place when gathering evidence:

- Photograph area; record what is on the screen.
- Dump memory.
- Power down system.
- Photograph inside of system.
- Label each piece of evidence.
- Record who collected what and how.
- Involve legal department and possibly human resources.
- Give items to forensics.

Travel Advisory

Among the most common reasons that evidence is deemed inadmissable are the following: no established incident response team, no established incident response procedures, poorly written policy, and a broken chain of custody.

The three main steps in incident response are triage, action/reaction, and follow-up. *Triage* is the process of identifying that an event has become an incident, meaning it is negatively affecting business activities. Triage deals with receiving, sorting, and prioritizing information pertaining to this incident. *Action/reaction*

pertains to dealing with the incident in a legally appropriate manner to mitigate and reduce its negative impact.

If law enforcement is involved in an investigation, they may need to confiscate systems, peripherals, and data. This can have a direct impact on a company's productivity; thus, critical business systems and data should be identified. This should be explained to the law enforcement agents so that possible copies can be made and implemented to ensure that production is not negatively affected.

Once the emergency is over and items are either shipped off to forensics or the environment is restored back to normal, a *follow-up* should be performed. This means a debriefing should take place to determine what went wrong and what was done correctly. These findings should be fed back into the incident response process for continual improvement.

> **Exam Tip**
>
> The goal of incidence response is to contain and mitigate damage and to prevent similar incidents from reoccurring.

Search and Seizure

Before the investigation begins, the response team needs to be sure of a few things. First, if law enforcement is involved, there needs to be probable cause before search and seizure activities can be initiated. American citizens are protected by the Fourth Amendment against unlawful search and seizures. Many times, a warrant, subpoena, or voluntary consent will need to be granted before an investigation can begin. However, if law enforcement is not involved, these controls aren't needed. Employees who are acting as part of the response team can begin investigations immediately because they are not police officers and are not bound by the Fourth Amendment restrictions. This could mean copying and obtaining employee files and resources for investigative purposes. Companies can have this ability if the employees are using company systems, if these issues are stated in a company policy, and if employees have been informed that this type of activity could take place. The company still needs to understand any and all privacy laws that may be in affect protecting the employees from this type of activity. Education of all rights and laws within a particular region is necessary to ensure that the investigation can be carried out legally and successfully.

One exception to the Fourth Amendment rule when law enforcement is involved is called *exigent circumstances*, which means that the suspect is about to destroy critical evidence. In order for the police to seize the evidence in this situation, it must be related to criminal activity and there must be probable cause.

Exam Tip
Private citizens are not required to follow the procedures outlined in the Fourth Amendment when searching for evidence, unless they are acting as police agents.

Forensics

Forensics is the study of computer technology as it relates to law. Forensics uses specialized tools, procedures, and individuals to extract evidence from computer systems and devices. When collecting evidence, it is a best to send computer systems to a forensics lab to be analyzed, although it can be done onsite.

When collecting evidence from a computer, it is a good idea to make a sound image of the attacked system first. It is never a good idea to begin work on the original system. Working on a copied version allows for mistakes to be made that do not torpedo the entire investigation.

Imaging the disk ensures that deleted files, slack spaces, and unallocated clusters are all preserved. A message digest should also be created for files and directories before any work begins to make sure the team can identify if something changes the original data during testing and investigation procedures.

The following should take place to uncover possible evidence:

- Look for hidden files.
- Review slack space.
- Search for Trojan Horses, logic bombs, and viruses.
- Examine deleted files.
- Extract data from the swap file.
- Review temporary files.

Local Lingo
Message digests are created by a hashing program that is used to ensure the integrity of files and to detect whether changes were made.

Admissibility of Evidence

You have probably heard the term *inadmissible evidence* in detective or court-room movies. It means that the evidence cannot be used during the trial for one reason or another. This is the reason that so much preparation is put into evidence collection and investigation. For evidence to be considered admissible in court, it must be competent, meaning that a proper process of collecting and producing evidence was followed; it must be relevant, meaning that there must be sensible relationships to the case and prove or disprove a fact; and it must be material, meaning that it must be pertinent to the case.

Other requirements of evidence are listed here:

- **Foundation of admissibility**   The collection process of evidence must be proved trustworthy.
- **Legal**   No illegal acts took place, such as unlawful search and seizure.
- **Evidence identification**   Evidence must be marked, tagged, and sealed appropriately, and the process must be fully documented.
- **Preservation of evidence**   Evidence must have been controlled and secure at all times.

> **Exam Tip**
>
> The life cycle of evidence includes identification and collection of evidence, analysis, storage, preservation, transportation, presentation in court, and eventual return to the owner.

Evidence Types

Evidence can be written, oral, computer-generated, visual, or audible. Oral evidence is a testimony of a witness. Computer-generated evidence can be files or data logs; visual or audio evidence is usually recorded during an event or immediately following it. Some of these types of evidence are considered more reliable than others and can be categorized in different ways. This section goes over a few categories evidence is put into depending upon its type and trustworthiness.

Best Evidence

Best evidence, like its name implies, is considered to be the best or most reliable form of evidence. Original documents, such as signed contracts, are examples of best evidence. Oral evidence can be used in correlation with original documents, but it is not considered to be a form of best evidence. Oral evidence can be used to help interpret a document but not to dispute it.

Secondary Evidence

Secondary evidence is not viewed as reliable or strong in proving innocence or guilt when compared to best evidence. Examples of secondary evidence are witness testimony and copies of original documents.

Hearsay Evidence

Hearsay evidence is secondhand information. It can be in oral or written form but is not considered reliable because there is no firsthand proof. If Lance told Tanya that Erica said something, then Tanya's knowledge of what Erica actually said is considered hearsay, because she did not hear it directly herself. Also, computer files and electronic evidence are generally considered as hearsay evidence because it is hard to detect whether files have been modified before being presented in court. There is no firsthand proof that they are unaltered.

Computer-generated evidence is also considered to be copies of the original evidence, but the original evidence is usually voltage levels within the computers interpreted as bits, thus the true originals cannot be presented.

Exam Tip

The discovery phase is when the prosecution provides investigation reports, information on evidence that will be presented, a list of potential witnesses, and criminal history of witnesses.

An exception to the hearsay rule is when documents are created during regular business activities, meaning that they were not created specifically to be presented in court. Thus, documents, audit trails, and log files may be admitted if it can be proven that they were generated during regular business procedures and were not developed to prove a point one way or another for a court case.

Enticement and Entrapment

Again with the movies—the term "entrapment" is commonly used in scenes where a corrupt police officer sets up a criminal to be caught in the act of committing a crime. Entrapment is illegal and unethical. "Enticement" is a term that is not used as much and is considered legal and ethical.

Let's start with *enticement*. In the computer world, a *honeypot* is used to entice attackers. If a company suspects that an attacker is infiltrating its network, it can use decoy systems to fool the attacker and record his actions in the attempt to later press charges. The honeypot is a computer that could have many open ports, exploitable vulnerabilities, and limited security features installed on it, so that the attacker would be drawn to it. In actuality, the computer would have no useful information on it and no direct connections to important services, but when the attacker attempts to connect to the device, the company would be watching and recording. Enticement is an effective method of learning about attack techniques and possibly prosecuting computer criminals.

Entrapment, on the other hand, is deliberately tricking a suspect into committing a crime. Here is an example. An employee is suspected of accessing restricted servers to gain confidential information. The company wants to catch the employee in the act, so they place a link to the confidential information on her desktop labeled as her legitimate share on a different server. When the employee clicks on the link and reads the information, the company records the behavior and attempts to prosecute. This kind of trickery is considered entrapment because the employee was fooled into committing this crime.

Trial

There are several complications that can occur when a computer-related crime goes to trial. This section does not cover all the steps needed to prepare properly for trial, but here are some simple guidelines to follow:

- Find a prosecutor with experience in computer crime.
- Concentrate on making the jury understand the case. Computer crime can be complicated, and if there is any doubt, a not-guilty verdict may be rendered.
- Ensure that the judge also understands the technical aspects of the case.
- Line up several computer expert witnesses to interpret the crime and evidence for the jury and judge.
- Expect less stringent punishments. Computer crimes are considered "white-collar" crimes.

Exam Tip

The only time an investigator's notebook, which contains notes from the case and crime scene, can be used in court is to refresh his memory. It cannot be submitted and used as evidence.

CHECKPOINT

✔**Objective 8.01: Ethics** A CISSP must know and adhere to the $(ISC)^2$ Code of Ethics. The Internet Activities Board (IAB) sees the use of the Internet as a privilege and works hard to protect against unethical behavior. Laws are derived from ethics. And just because something is not illegal does not mean that it is ethical.

✔**Objective 8.02: Hacking Methods** There are three categories of attacks: physical, personnel, and operational. Dumpster diving is going through someone's trash to find confidential or useful information. It is legal, but unethical. Excessive privileges means that an employee has more rights and permissions than necessary to complete his tasks. Social engineering is the act of tricking a person into giving up confidential or sensitive information that could then be used against her company.

✔**Objective 8.03: Organization Liabilities and Ramifications** Due care means practicing common sense and prudent management practices. In order for a company to be held liable, proximate causation must be proven, meaning someone can prove that the damage that was caused was indeed the company's fault. Companies must notify employees that they may be monitored, and monitoring must be related to work activities. Many laws have dictated that the board of trustees and senior management can be held liable for security breaches and security faults within a company.

✔**Objective 8.04: Types of Law** There are three main categories of common law: civil, criminal, and administrative. Civil law deals with wrongs committed against individuals or companies that result in injury or damages, with no jail time. Criminal law pertains to rules developed by the government to protect the public. Administrative, or regulatory laws, are standards of performance or conduct expected by government agencies of companies, and are usually industry-specific. Trademarks protect words, names, product shape, symbol, color, or a combination of these used to identify company products. Copyright protects the expression of ideas rather than the ideas themselves.

✔**Objective 8.05: Computer Crime Investigation** The primary reason for the chain of custody for evidence is to ensure that it will be admissible in court. The life cycle of evidence includes identification and collection of evidence, analysis, storage, preservation, transportation, and presentation in court—the evidence is then returned to the owner. Evidence must be legally permissible, meaning that it was seized lawfully and the chain of custody was not broken. Enticement is luring an intruder and is legal. Entrapment induces a crime by tricking a person and is illegal.

REVIEW QUESTIONS

1. Which of the following is a set of security guidelines that was developed to provide security best practices worldwide?

   A. $(ISC)^2$

   B. IAB

   C. GASSP

   D. Computer Ethics Institute

2. Which of the following indicates that a specific person had a chance to commit a crime?

   A. Opportunities

   B. Motivations

   C. Means

   D. DMZ

3. What is data diddling?

   A. Subtracting small amounts of funds from an account with the hope that such a small amount will go unnoticed.

   B. Disguising an IP address to avoid being linked to a computer crime.

   C. Altering data before it is entered into an application or as soon as it comes out.

   D. Monitoring network traffic in order to intercept passwords.

4. Which of the following is an example of a passive attack?

   A. Salami

   B. Wiretapping

   C. Masquerading

   D. Dumpster diving

5. What type of attack is referred to as blue boxing?

   A. Social engineering to obtain insider trading information

   B. Cloning ATM cards

   C. Stealing funds from bank accounts

   D. Telephone toll fraud

6. Which of the following is an example of a downstream liability?

   A. Two companies sharing an extranet and one does not implement proper security measurements

   B. Employees suspected of stealing trade secrets

   C. Attackers accessing a company's network

   D. An employee with excessive privileges

7. Which of the following types of law deal with regulatory standards for a company's performance and conduct?

   A. Tort

   B. Administrative

   C. Civil

   D. Criminal

8. Copyright law protects _____.

   A. A resource that provides a company with a competitive advantage

   B. A word, name, object, color, or combination of these

   C. The expression of an idea

   D. A novel invention

9. Which of the following is the study of computer technology as it relates to law?

   A. Forensics

   B. Cybercrime

   C. Chain of custody

   D. Due diligence

10. Electronic information and computer-generated documentation is usually considered which type of evidence?

    A. Best evidence

    B. Direct evidence

    C. Hearsay evidence

    D. Corroborative evidence

11. Which of the following is a method of tricking an attacker into committing a crime and is illegal?

    A. Honeypot

    B. Enticement

    C. Entrapment

    D. Interrogating

12. If law enforcement is involved with an investigation, what should take place so that production is as least affected as possible?

    A. Refuse to give over systems, data, and evidence.

    B. Offer to provide backups from an offsite facility to law enforcement agents instead of them taking the originals.

    C. Ask for copies of important data to be made.

    D. Make copies of important data yourself and implement them into the environment.

13. If you find data on a system that indicates that an employee has been sniffing traffic and obtaining data to give over to a competitor, what should you do?

    A. Call the police and outline findings for them to make a decision on legal approaches.

    B. Approach individual with evidence and then go to that employee's supervisor.

    C. Do not alter any data, and report findings to management.

    D. Format the drive to ensure that this information is not obtainable by the competitors.

14. When would computer-generated documents be admissible in court and not seen as hearsay evidence?

    A. Computer-generated documents are always seen as hearsay evidence, thus never admissible.

    B. If the documents were digitally signed.

    C. If a third party can identify and verify the documents and their legitimacy.

    D. If the documents were created during regular business operations.

15. During incident response and evidence gathering activities, what should be done first?

    A. Make an image of the hard drive.

    B. Label all pieces of evidence.

    C. Take pictures of area and systems.

    D. Call the police and power down the systems.

REVIEW ANSWERS

1. **C**   The Generally Accepted System Security Principles were created to bring agreement upon security practices and security awareness internationally. They are a set of guidelines that can be used by a company to construct a security program and are linked to the Common Criteria.

2. **A**   Opportunities are the "where" and "when" of a crime, which usually arise when weaknesses are present that can be taken advantage of   A company should try and reduce the amount of opportunities its employees and external entities have to commit fraudulent activities.

3. **C**   Data diddling is the act of improperly altering data before it is processed or as soon as processing has been performed upon it. It can be committed by people who want reports to provide a different perspective than reality; for example, if someone is trying to receive a loan, he might "doctor" the form that indicates his cash flow.

4. **B**   Wiretapping is passive because the attacker is simply listening to conversations or data passing over a communication link and does not actually perform any active activity.

5. **D**   Phreakers used to be able to commit toll fraud by simulating frequency tones, which tricked the phone system into giving free long-distance phone service; it was referred to as blue boxing.

6. **A**   If a company does not follow due care by ensuring that its activities do not negatively affect others, they could be faced with downstream liabilities.

7. **B**   Administrative laws regulate companies based on certain standards that are created by government agencies.

8. **C**   Copyright law protects an expression of an idea rather than a particular resource or the idea itself.

9. **A**   Forensics experts can help recover evidence from a computer following a computer crime.

10. **C**   Electronic data can be easily modified without being detected, thus it is not seen as reliable. It is also considered to be copies of the original data.

11. **C**   Entrapment is considered illegal and unethical because it uses trickery to capture a suspect.

12. **C** To try and ensure that production is not negatively affected by losing critical systems and information, these items should be identified and their importance should be explained to the agents. There may be a way for them to make copies and return them to the company. The company should not make copies themselves because they may alter critical evidence.

13. **C** You should not approach the individual yourself or alter the data in any way. These findings should be reported to management, and they will decide how to approach and handle the situation.

14. **D** Documents that are submitted as evidence must have been generated during normal business functions and not created specifically to prove a point in court.

15. **C** The area and the computers themselves should be photographed to prove the state of the environment before investigators started working. This helps prove that evidence was not modified in an improper manner.

Applications and Systems Development

	NEWBIE	SOME EXPERIENCE	EXPERT
ETA	6 hours	4 hours	2 hours

Software and application development go through many different phases, from planning and testing to implementation and maintenance. However, one common mistake that companies make is forgetting that security should be integrated into the development efforts, and not be treated as an afterthought. It is all too common for a software program to be put into place only to discover later that huge holes exist. Implementing security mechanisms while in panic mode is never a good idea. It limits the number of security components that can be added, hurts the overall level of protection that can be provided, and usually ends up breaking something else.

This chapter covers different issues in software development, which include development models, proper security controls and coding practices, applications communicating in distributed environments, databases, and object-oriented programming. And as always, potential threats will be identified and explained. Where would security be without some risks, threats, and vulnerabilities?

Objective 9.01 Project Development

Software development, just like every other facet of the computing world, is changing and evolving to keep pace with new technologies and market demands, and it is perpetuating the continual game of trying to stay ahead of the competitors. Security should be an integral part of development efforts if companies wish to provide a secure product instead of a Swiss cheese product full of vulnerabilities that requires the customer to frantically attempt to plug the holes after purchase. So, why has security been left out of development for so long?

There are a few reasons. Software vendors are constantly rushing their products out the door in order to keep up or stay in front of their competition. Adding extra time to ensure proper and secure programming techniques and putting the product through more testing cycles costs the vendor money and causes delays in delivery. Software developers, and even their customers, have developed a bad habit of accepting certain flaws and vulnerabilities because a new and improved patch is just around the corner.

Also, when today's programmers went through school for programming, security was not as important as it is seen today, thus those techniques and disciplines were not totally understood, indoctrinated, and forced upon the students. This is changing; security is being integrated into computer science classes, but at a slow pace.

As we move forward with the new age of computers and software development, companies have a lot to worry about. Changes in environments can add complexity to an already diverse environment. Today's networks are distributed in nature with client/server models, having MAN and WAN connection, wireless attachments, and mobile users. They have a slew of different vendor products integrated into a heterogeneous network trying to accomplish different or overlapping functionality. The complexity, interoperability issues, diversity in software and devices, and different configurations provide an uphill battle in the pursuit of providing the necessary level of functionality, not to mention to properly secure it and ensure that there are no open doorways lurking at different layers.

The most prevalent approach to security is to install devices and software to provide a perimeter defense around company assets and the vulnerabilities that lie within the software that hold and maintain these assets. In this methodology, the focus is on keeping the bad guys out of the network, which has been described as having a tough outer shell and a chewy middle. If the middle were not so chewy, many companies would not have to be so dependent upon these fortress-like devices. This means that if many of the vulnerabilities within the software did not exist in the first place, the company's level of risk would be reduced, and firewalls, intrusion detection systems, and anti-virus software would not necessarily be the booming business it is today. It is not that these items would not be needed, but they would not be so heavily depended upon if our software did not contain so many flaws and vulnerabilities.

So we take a quick stroll through the phases that should take place in a development project, with an eye on where security should be inserted and integrated in the different phases of the project.

Software Lifecycle

Security that is added as an afterthought can cause many problems. One of these problems, and something that will get the attention of executives, is the cost. In most situations, it is much more expensive to add on security after software has been put into place than during the planning and development stages. This is because security will affect different components, features, and functionality of the software and possibly connecting devices. Adjustments mean time and money, because securing one thing usually negatively affects the functionality of another thing. Also, when a product is released with many security vulnerabilities, hackers will have a heyday, customers will be irate, and the press will be happy to tell everyone about it. Use cost and reputation as your arguments when trying to add security as part of the software development effort.

Security should be planned and managed throughout the lifecycle of a system. This will make a more secure and healthy product and not require the developers to scramble for a fix at the eleventh hour.

Software Development Models

There are several types of software development methods and approaches, which we look at in a later section, but they all contain the following items in one form or another. These are the different phases of a project and the evolution of the product:

- Project initiation and planning
- Functional design analysis and planning
- System design specifications
- Software development
- Acceptance testing/implementation
- Operations/maintenance
- Disposal

Although each phase has many components and activities, we focus on the security issues within each phase.

Project Initiation

Project initiation involves many things, but the first item is getting everyone on the same page so that everyone on the team understands the goals of the product. The project is usually driven by a need in the market or a specific demand of a customer. Typically, a project kick-off meeting is held so all the participating parties can understand what is being developed and why.

An initial risk analysis should be performed that will review the level of protection required of the product, the type and sensitivity of the data that this product will be processing, the type of environment it will be implemented into, the possible liabilities of the consumer of this product, and the necessary mechanisms that should be implemented that support the identified issues.

If these items are addressed in the beginning through a risk analysis exercise, security mechanisms can be identified and integrated in later phases. As with everything else in life, it is better to start off on a good foot.

The components of this phase entail the following:

- Decide upon the conceptual definition of the project.
- Identify security requirements.
- Perform an initial risk analysis.
- Analyze threats and countermeasures.

Functional Design Analysis and Planning

This is the step that many companies skip over because they are anxious to begin development of the product. However, proper analysis and planning needs to take place in order to see the broad picture of a project. In this phase, the team looks at the customer's requirements and determines how they will be met before the actual details and specifications are derived. This is still at a high level of abstraction and each future phase gets more granular in progression.

The *functional design analysis phase* provides a formal functional baseline, which is an official method of identifying how the product will perform. This baseline should include security tasks, test plans, and checkpoints along the way to ensure that everyone is on track and that everyone is on the *same* track.

Exam Tip
Security requirements are defined in the functional design analysis and planning phase.

So the initiation phase is, "Great, there is a demand for a widget!" The design analysis plan is, "Okay, this is what we need our widget to do," and the next phase is, "These are the detailed specifications of how we will actually build our widget."

Travel Advisory
This phase is also referred to as the function requirements definition phase.

System Design Specifications

The last phase outlined what the product was going to do. This phase describes what kind of mechanisms will be put into place to make that happen. This is also the time when security components and procedures will be officially laid out. A security checklist is created and the test plan is updated. The test plans should be continually updated as the project evolves and changes because the people involved have a better understanding of *what* should be tested.

If the company is developing this product for a specific customer, they will go over these specifications with the customer to help ensure that this is what the customer wants, that it will integrate within their current infrastructure, and that it will provide the necessary level of security. At this point, the customer usually has to sign a document agreeing to all of these conditions, and if they change their mind down the road, they have to pay for the extra work that will be involved. Once the specifications are hammered out, they are the holy grail of the project. Any confusion, questions, changes, or needed direction will come from these agreed-upon specifications, and when the project is finished, the customer will (should) grade the product in how it upholds and fulfills these specs.

Software Development

Software development is when the fingers touch the keyboard. This is the point where programmers are put to work developing code based on the specifications handed to them. Security is a focus here also because the code will incorporate all the security specifications laid out in the previous phase. Auditing mechanisms, access controls, encryption, intrusion alerts, file protection, and more will be built as well as unit tests being performed.

Local Lingo

A unit test is what is performed by the developer to test his or her work, which is different than the battery of tests performed by a quality assurance team.

Acceptance Testing/Implementation

When all the code is written and unit testing is complete, the resulting code is turned over to a quality assurance (QA) department, which will test the product and look for anomalies, errors in functionality, and security loopholes. If issues are uncovered, it goes back to the developers, who fix the problems, and resubmit the code to QA. This dance continues until the product meets the previously agreed upon level of functionality and security.

The customer may also put the product through user acceptance testing to make sure it performs to their expectations. And the product may need to go through a certification and accreditation process. *Certification* is a technical review of the product to ensure that it provides the functionality and security it claims. The results of this review are submitted to management, which goes through a formal process of accreditation. *Accreditation* is the act of management formally accepting this product and accepting responsibility for it.

Now it is time to install the product. This may be performed by the customer or by the vendor, depending upon the relationship and service level agreement. Implementation is the process of integrating a new device or software component into an existing environment, which may have negative affects. The security of the "new" environment needs to be evaluated also to ensure that the product has not introduced any new flaws or vulnerabilities to the network as a whole. They say that the effects of a butterfly's wings in the Amazon can affect a tsunami that hits Japan because of the interdependencies of each organism in the world. This is also true for a network. A newly added application could directly affect the security of your back-end database, which was previously extremely secure, so the security of the environment may need to be revisited.

Travel Advisory

Documentation is distributed in this phase, which includes user manuals, installation guides, and reference materials.

Operations/Maintenance

At this phase, the product is actually used within its intended environment. If the vendor has a service level agreement with the customer, their involvement and responsibilities have not stopped. If the customer requests changes or uncovers problems, the vendor may be the one called into action.

It is important to be very disciplined about security within this phase. Any patches that need to be applied should be tested before implementation, vulnerability scanning procedures should be performed periodically, and any changes to the product or environment may require another round of certification and accreditations.

Disposal

All good things come to an end, and a crucial piece of ending something is how to properly integrate the new. It can sound easy and straightforward when a company wants to perform an upgrade of something, but actually going through this process can become more hairy than it appeared on paper or in Thursday's morning meeting.

The phase of sending out the old and bringing in the new can be a vulnerable time for a company. The security that the original items provided can be diminished during the process, which could provide attackers a path directly into the kingdom. If sensitive data is being held on the system, its integrity, confidentiality, and availability needs to be protected during the disposal of the older system.

Software Development Methods

There are several different life cycle models that outline the significant phases of software development. The following provides a quick glimpse at some of these different models:

- **Waterfall** A classical method that uses discrete phases of development that requires formal reviews and documentation before moving into the next phase of the project. The project flows from one point down to the next.

- **Spiral model** A method that builds upon the waterfall method with an emphasis on risk analysis, prototypes, and simulations at different phases of the development cycle. This is used for rapid production and prototyping. This is useful for environments that are constantly changing and you can't clearly identify milestones because the project as a whole is continually moving.

- **Joint Analysis Development (JAD)**   Uses a team approach in application development in a workshop-oriented environment.
- **Rapid Application Development (RAD)**   A method of determining user requirements and developing systems quickly to satisfy immediate needs.
- **Cleanroom**   An approach that attempts to prevent errors or mistakes by following structured and formal methods of developing and testing. This approach is used for high-quality and critical applications that will be put through a strict certification process.
- **Computer Aided Software Engineering (CASE)**   Allows development to be performed quickly with automated tools to reduce redundant manual tasks (debugging, code analyzing, version control). Virtual environments and simulation engines can mimic the environment the code will eventually live in to aid developers in verifying that the development process is matching expectations.
- **Prototyping**   Produces an example or "proof of concept" of the product for quicker analysis and testing.

Change Control

Changes are inevitable in software development, but if they are not controlled, a project can become a never-ending ball of twine. If the vendor has a specific customer, the customer usually changes its mind during development, programmers come up with issues not previously addressed, and the direction of the project can actually change for one reason or another. If the vendor does not prepare a method for how to deal with these inevitable changes, the project will not meet its milestones or deadlines, the project can easily get off track and out of control, and the expense of continually working on the changes can drive the resulting price up so that no customer will be willing to pay the asking price.

The following are the steps that should be included in a change control process:

1. Change request is made formally.
2. Analyze request.
3. Develop the implementation strategy.
4. Calculate the costs of the implementation.
5. Review any security implications.
6. Record change request.
7. Submit change request for approval.

8. Recode segments of the product; add or subtract functionality.
9. Link changes in the code to the formal change control request.
10. Submit software for testing and quality approval.
11. Repeat until quality is adequate.
12. Make version changes.
13. Report changes to management.

Travel Advisory

It is also important to ensure that changes do not negate the established security policy and protection requirements.

If this process is in place, it is used as a tool to make sure that changes are thought through and approved before integrated, and that they are cost-effective, documented, tested, and approved.

Administrative Controls

Within software development environments, it is important to have clear definitions of different roles and to ensure that those lines do not become gray. For example, a group other than the programmers should test the code and product. When software has been completely tested and approved, it is to be submitted to a centralized library. The library ensures that version control is implemented, it documents who tested, approved, and submitted the code, and it also keeps track of who checks the code out of the library. The code should go from this library to the customer's production environment. Code should never go from the programmer or testing environment to the production environment, and the programmer should not be modifying code in production.

In the same vein, people working in operations should not have access to any source code. They have no need, and they could compromise the integrity of production code if it is implemented. These are examples of the separation of duties, which can be administrative controls:

Split knowledge procedures ensure that more than one person has the necessary knowledge to perform critical tasks. It is a security risk when only certain people have knowledge of a procedure or have isolated access to a product. It provides for a higher possibility of fraud and puts the company at risk if the one individual who held the keys to the kingdom were to leave the company, were abducted by aliens, or both.

Software source code and documentation about a specific product should be put into *software escrow*. This is a third party that holds a copy of code, enforces vendor license agreements, and allows the customer access to the source code and documentation as it is laid out in the vendor/customer legal agreement. The software escrow protects the customer in the event that the vendor goes out of business or burns down to the ground; the source code that they paid to be developed is being safely protected at another site by a different company.

Program Language Evolution

A program language is a set of rules used to develop instruction sets to tell the computer system what to do. Program languages are used to write applications, operating systems, and malicious programs. As with everything else in life, programming languages have undergone an evolution, which resulted in different generations:

- **Generation One**   Machine language
- **Generation Two**   Assembly language
- **Generation Three**   High-level language
- **Generation Four**   Very high-level language
- **Generation Five**   Artificial intelligence and natural language

Each generation provides more powerful functionality to be added into applications and operating systems. One of the more popular approaches to developing software uses object-oriented programming languages, which are third-level generation languages.

Objective 9.02
Object-Oriented Programming

Just as technology has improved over the years, so have software programming languages and techniques. Previous methods used a classic input-output processing style that passed data to the beginning of a program and was operated upon by sequential lines of code, as shown in Figure 9-1.

Object-oriented programming (OOP) has improved this classic approach in a number of ways, but mainly by allowing objects to be reused by other applications and in different projects. This makes for more efficient programming and a reduction of cost since objects can be reused and do not have to be re-created each time that specific functionality is required. This method is highly modular and self-contained, which reduces complexity, allows for fewer mistakes, and improves resource efficiency, which saves time and money.

But what is an object? It is a piece of code that provides some type of service or functionality to the program and other objects that make up that program. One object may send data to a printer, another object may deposit money into a

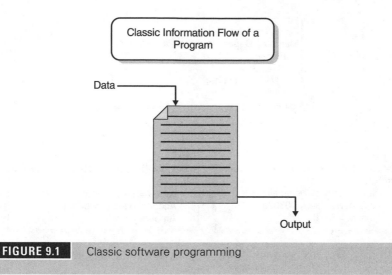

Data

Output

FIGURE 9.1   Classic software programming

checking account, another object could withdraw money from a savings account, and yet another transfers money from one account to another. Just like people in life, each object has its own job and responsibilities. And because they are self-contained and modular, they can be easily extracted and replaced with new and improved objects without negatively affecting the objects around them.

Classes and Objects

OOP uses classes to define the attributes, functionality, and interfaces of the objects that will be instantiated from them, as shown in Figure 9-2. The developer will create a class that will dictate what functions an object can perform, referred to as *methods*. It will also determine the object's interfaces and the types of messages the object will accept. When an object is created from a class, it *inherits* the attributes, methods, and specified interfaces outlined in that class.

When data is passed to an object, it is called a *message*, which is how objects communicate with each other, and an object can only accept the messages indicated by its class. An analogy is how we interact with an automated teller machine (ATM). The machine can perform deposits, transfers, and withdrawals, which are the methods that it can perform. The interface is the buttons you push to initiate one of these methods. And when you insert data into the system, it is accepting messages and processing the information passed to it. The ATM provides only the buttons (interface) of the methods it will perform for you and no more. Objects will have a specially formed interfaces that will only accept specific messages requesting the methods it can carry out.

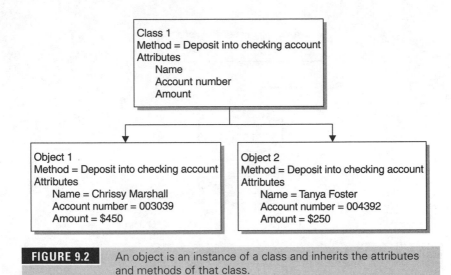

Class 1
Method = Deposit into checking account
Attributes
    Name
    Account number
    Amount

Object 1
Method = Deposit into checking account
Attributes
    Name = Chrissy Marshall
    Account number = 003039
    Amount = $450

Object 2
Method = Deposit into checking account
Attributes
    Name = Tanya Foster
    Account number = 004392
    Amount = $250

FIGURE 9.2   An object is an instance of a class and inherits the attributes and methods of that class.

Abstraction

Abstraction is a term that means the details of something are hidden. Objects provide abstraction by working like "black boxes," meaning that their actual internal code and mechanisms are hidden from other objects and surrounding code. When one object sends data to another object for processing, it needs to know only how to communicate to that object's interface and not be concerned with how the object actually works. This means that the developer of a new object does not need to know how another object actually works to be able to interact with it, but only needs to know how to format a request to that object's interface. This is similar to you not needing to know how the ATM machine works to get your money; you just need to know how to communicate with it by pressing its buttons.

Polymorphism

Two different objects can respond to the exact same message in different ways, which is referred to as *polymorphism*. The objects react differently because they are from different classes or subclasses and have inherited different attributes and methods, as shown in Figure 9-3. An example of polymorphism is the shortcuts we use on our desktops. Shortcuts belong to a certain class of objects, and when stimulated with the same input "double-click," they launch different applications.

Polyinstantiation

Sometimes "truth" is looked at as a relative term, especially when interacting with government agencies or politicians. When a government representative is talking to the press, she works very hard at getting one specific message out and not indirectly

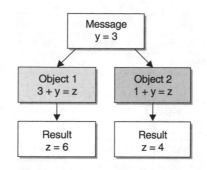

FIGURE 9.3   Two different objects reacting differently to the same message.

giving up any further information. This tactic can also be used in object-oriented programming. *Polyinstantiation* is an access control mechanism that takes a copy of one object and repopulates with different data. As shown in Figure 9-4, when a user with a security clearance lower than "top secret" accesses a database, she will see that the ship Oklahoma is on its way to Africa containing food. This way the user would know that the ship is being used and will look to another ship to move her cargo. If a user with a "top secret" clearance accesses the same database, she would see that the ship Oklahoma is actually headed towards the Ukraine containing weapons. If the first user was just told that the Oklahoma ship was unavailable, and its cargo and destination were classified, this would indirectly tell that user more information than the military would want that user to know. So, just like when they are communicating with the press, a more "sanitized" story is supplied so that the real military operations are not known to a large subset of individuals.

In this example, the act of polyinstantiation creates two versions of the same object so the lower level subjects will not know the true information. This is a technique used to keep sensitive information confidential by controlling who can access and view it.

Application Threats

There are several items that can threaten the overall security of a program, and the environment it will be implemented within, that need to be avoided during development and addressed during testing phases:

- **Object reuse**   All sensitive data should be erased from storage or memory areas before another subject accesses it.
- **Garbage collection**   A process should deallocate committed storage, memory segments, and resources when they are no longer needed by the application.

Level	Ship	Cargo	Origin	Destination
Top Secret	Oklahoma	Weapons	Delaware	Ukraine
Unclassified	Oklahoma	Food	Delaware	Africa

Copy and repopulate

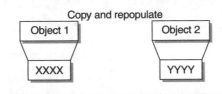

Object 1	Object 2
XXXX	YYYY

FIGURE 9.4   Polyinstantiation allows an object to be copied and populated with different data.

- **Trap doors/back doors** Mechanisms that allow an entity into the application and system by bypassing access controls.
- **Buffer overflow** When bounds checking is not implemented, long strings of data can be accepted. If the data is larger than the allocated memory buffer, the data flows over into another memory segment.
- **Time of check/time of use (TOC/TOU)** Control information is modified between the time the system checks the contents of a variable and when the variable is actually used.
- **Covert channel** When two or more objects use resources as a communication channel in a way that they were not intended.

There are two types of covert channels: storage and timing. In a *storage covert channel*, a process at a higher security level writes information to storage that should not be available to another process that resides at a lower security level. If Debbie has a "top secret" clearance, she should not be passing any data to Sam, who has a "secret" clearance. But if Debbie writes data to a pagefile on the hard drive, and Sam reads this information, they just used a resource (the pagefile) for an unintended purpose (as a communication channel), which circumvents the system's access controls.

A *timing covert channel* is when a process modulates its resource in a way that it is actually used as communication to another process. If Debbie accessed her hard drive 20 times within 30 seconds, this could communicate to Sam some predetermined message. It can be compared to Morse code, which is a way to relay messages through mechanisms not usually used for communication, as in taps on a wall or flashes of a light.

> **Exam Tip**
>
> If data is not properly erased from memory or a storage device, it is called *residual data* and can threaten the confidentiality of that data.

Objective 9.03 Distributed Computing

Today, most of our computing takes place in a distributed manner, which means that not all necessary resources are installed and implemented on one individual computer. In the client/server model, the client is closer to the user and provides a communication channel to the back-end server software, which contains much more processing power and information. When you request to print something to a centralized print server, your computer has the necessary client software that sends the request to the server software residing on a distant computer providing print server capabilities. The server software piece processes this request and sends it to the actual printer. But your system needs to know where the print server is to send this request, which is where DCOM, ORB, or Enterprise Java Bean implementations can come into play.

ORB and CORBA

An *object request broker* (ORB) is a piece of code that your client software would query to find out where the necessary server objects are located. The ORB works as a middleman in a client/server environment and points the client to the correct computer.

Many environments have applications written in different programming languages (C, Java, C#), but just because they are written in different languages should not mean that they cannot work together and share information. If these different applications are written to the specifications outlined in the *Common Object Request Broker Architecture* (CORBA), each application would have the necessary interfaces to allow other applications to send it requests and information, as illustrated in Figure 9-5. CORBA provides interoperability between different vendor products and allows for a more seamless distributed working environment.

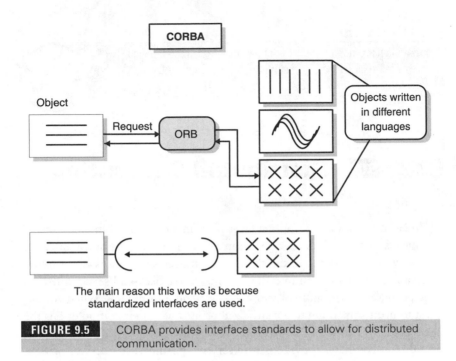

The main reason this works is because
standardized interfaces are used.

FIGURE 9.5   CORBA provides interface standards to allow for distributed
communication.

When a client sends a message that needs to be processed by an object on another system, its message is sent to the ORB, which will track down the needed object and will process the request through its security system, which enforces a security policy to ensure that the request is safe and acceptable.

Travel Advisory

ORBs and DCOM are also used to provide middleware functionality,
which usually means front-end software (possibly Web browsers)
can communicate with back-end servers (possibly databases).

COM and DCOM

We have different flavors of ice cream because people have different tastes, and not all vehicles are trucks because we are not all interested in hauling around firewood and tools. In the same sense, developers have different options when needing to provide communication between distributed applications. *Distributed component object model* (DCOM) was developed by Microsoft and is based on and is an extension of their component object model (COM). COM is a model for objects on one computer to locate each other and communicate. DCOM allows objects to communicate with objects on different computers.

DCOM uses a COM-based interface but provides additional services, such as ORB services, data connectivity, distributed messaging, security, and distributed transaction services, which are layered over its remote procedure call (RPC) mechanism.

> ### Exam Tip
> DCOM uses global unique identifiers (GUID) to keep track of different objects.

Enterprise Java Bean

Enterprise Java Bean (EJB) is a structural design for the development and implementation of distributed applications written in Java. The EJB provides interfaces and methods to allow different applications to be able to communicate across a networked environment. By using the Internet Inter-ORB Protocol (IIOP), the client portion does not have to be a program written in Java, but can be any valid CORBA client.

> ### Local Lingo
> A Java Bean is a Java component.

OLE

We are never totally satisfied with the capabilities of our tools and continue to improve upon them and change their possibilities in ways that the original developers never dreamed of. There came a point where we demanded a way of inserting a spreadsheet or funny graphic into our Word document and wouldn't take "no" for an answer. This demand introduced the birth of *object linking and embedding* (OLE). OLE uses COM as its foundation to locate objects and allows them to communicate with each other. Embedding is the capability of inserting an object inside another object. For example, when you insert a graphic into your document, you have embedded it. Linking means that the inserted object is still associated with its original program. So if you create a graphic in the Microsoft Paint program, insert it into your document, and double-click on the graphic, the Paint program will open with your graphic inside to allow you to modify the object by using its original application.

Linking is the capability of one program to call another program. Another common example of linking is adding a uniform resource locator (URL) to a document or e-mail. When readers of the document click on the URL, their Web browser is called upon to open and take users to that destination.

ActiveX

OLE seemed to work so well on individual computers, we decided we needed it everywhere. So OLE was expanded upon to provide linking and embedding within Web pages on the World Wide Web (WWW), and it was crowned with the name *ActiveX*.

Small programs are written in many different languages to provide functionality for individual applications, operating systems, and Web pages and are referred to as *ActiveX controls*. When these controls are posted and downloaded from a Web site, browsers will look to see if they trust the entity that digitally signed the control. If it is signed by an entity that the browser is configured to trust, the control is downloaded and installed. If the control is signed by an entity that is not trusted or not signed at all, the user will be presented with a dialog box indicating the situation and asks the user if she wants to download it anyway or cancel the action.

The security model for ActiveX is based on digital signatures and does not scan the code for malicious strings or program code. Once the control is deemed "trustworthy," it has a good degree of access to the computer and its resources. The control is not put into a container, where its access is restricted, which is more along the lines of the Java security model.

> **Travel Advisory**
>
> Authenticode is Microsoft's standard for digitally signing software.

ActiveX controls, Java applets, and active scripts or executables transmitted as e-mail attachments are known as *mobile code*. Although they provide a good amount of flexibility and functionality for the user, they can contain malicious code that performs activities the user is not aware of, until it is too late.

Java Applets

Java is an object-oriented, platform-independent programming language that was developed by Sun Microsystems. Its claim to fame is that it can run on many different platforms, where other languages have to be compiled for a specific platform.

Java applets are small programs written with a subset of the Java language. The applets can be developed to enrich a user's experience by providing more bells and whistles at a Web site, as in listening to sound and viewing animation. When a user visits a site and requests to perform some action that requires a specific applet, the system will check to see if it is already installed. If not, the applet's bytecode is downloaded. The browser's Java Virtual Machine (JVM) will then interpret this bytecode for the specific platform that is running. This is how

Java applets are platform-independent; the bytecode is created and is available to the different platforms. The operating system browser must have a JVM to then change this bytecode into machine code that can be understood by that system and its processor.

The JVM also sets up a *sandbox* for the applet to run in, which is a simulated virtual environment that provides a controlled working domain. The sandbox drastically reduces the amount of resources the applet can interact with and acts as a logical container for this mobile code. The sandbox ensures that the applet cannot access system files, make network connections, or interact with system resources. Of course, the smart malware writers have figured out how to climb over the sandbox walls and cause damage, but to date the amount of compromises through Java applets have been few.

CGI

Common Gateway Interface (CGI) is a method of manipulating and processing data that is entered at a Web site. When a site requests a user to enter information, that data may need to be formatted by the CGI script and sent to a back-end server for processing or the CGI script may do the processing itself. CGI uses scripts and programs that reside on a Web server to provide a more interactive experience for the user. The tasks that the CGI components perform can be very powerful, thus if an attacker could access and use them, the security of the system would be at risk.

Cookies

Cookies are small files dropped onto a user's system for one of two purposes: to help the Web site keep state information about the connection or to capture browsing and spending habits of the user. The HTTP protocol was designed to not keep state on a connection. This means that when a user requests to see a Web page, the Web server sends that page to the user and forgets that the user or connection ever existed. The Web server does not keep an active session with that user. This provides more efficiency overall, but some developers would like their site to keep state on a user's connection, so they had to get creative with the use of cookies.

When a user authenticates to a site, the Web site can create a cookie and send it over to the user's browser. The site can then periodically check for this cookie to ensure that it is still communicating to the same authorized user and makes sure that the time window allotted for authentication has not run out. If sensitive information is kept in the cookie, it should be encrypted so that an ill-intentioned individual cannot get a hold of it.

The other reason to use cookies is to build profiles on a user's browsing and buying habits and store it in cookies on the user's system. When the user returns to that specific site, the cookie can be scanned, and the Web site displays items that it thinks the user will be interested in purchasing. This is a common marketing and advertising technique, which quickly presents consumers with the products that he is most likely to buy.

Attackers can access cookies from hard drives to gain information about the user, such as personal information, passwords, and account information. And, there is a sense that personal privacy seems to be encroached upon when habits are written down and stored for vendors to later exploit.

Objective 9.04   Databases

Databases have played an important role for companies for a long time and continue to do so. They are incorporated into computing networks in companies all over the world. But, although the existence of databases remains unchanged over time, the way in which they are used has changed significantly over the years. Much of this change can be attributed to the Internet explosion and multiple technologies that allow users so many different ways to interact with databases. Today, customers, vendors, and employees access company databases through Web sites, different applications, extranets, and VPNs. Security professionals must be intimately involved with different databases' functionality, execution, design, and most importantly, their security.

Let's start with a definition. A *database* is a collection of interrelated data stored in a meaningful way to allow multiple users and applications to access, view, and modify the data as needed. If an actual database is not implemented, a company usually has important information stored on different computers throughout the company instead of having it stored in one location. Storing data in a centralized database preserves storage space and prevents inconsistencies by making changes to one central collection of information and allows for easier backups to be made.

A database administrator creates and maintains the database through *database management system* (DBMS) software. The DBMS allows the administrator to develop the database, add and subtract functionality, enforce integrity rules, implement access controls, and incorporate security mechanisms.

Databases can be built with different approaches, meaning there are different models available to create a database. A model is a formal method of defining the relationships between the data elements and how they will be presented to the users. The following sections go over a few of these models.

Relational Data Model

The most popular type of database model is a *relational database*. The database is made up of tables with columns and rows for data to be stored, viewed, and modified. Columns are referred to as *attributes* and rows are called *tuples*. Each row has a unique value, a *primary key*, that represents that row. All the data within that row are attributes of the primary key, as depicted in Figure 9-6. The tables are related to each other and linked in a way that represents these relationships. In Figure 9-6, we see that the second table is related to the first table because one of the product bundles contains an actual product listed in the first table. The attribute in the second table contains the same value as a primary key in the first table, which is referred to as a *foreign key*.

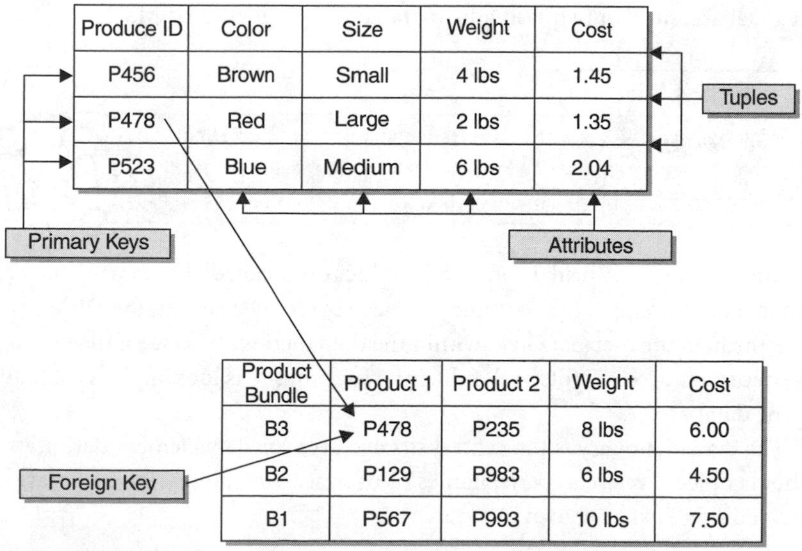

Produce ID	Color	Size	Weight	Cost
P456	Brown	Small	4 lbs	1.45
P478	Red	Large	2 lbs	1.35
P523	Blue	Medium	6 lbs	2.04

Tuples

Primary Keys

Attributes

Product Bundle	Product 1	Product 2	Weight	Cost
B3	P478	P235	8 lbs	6.00
B2	P129	P983	6 lbs	4.50
B1	P567	P993	10 lbs	7.50

Foreign Key

FIGURE 9.6 Components of a relational database table

> **Exam Tip**
>
> A foreign key is an attribute in one table that contains the same value and is linked to a primary key in another table.

Data and database integrity is very important to ensure that neither gets corrupted. The *entity integrity rule* dictates that a tuple cannot have a null value for its primary key and that each tuple contains a unique primary key value. The *referential integrity rule* deals with the integrity of table relationships. It dictates that a foreign key must be mapped to a primary key value, the foreign key value and primary key value must be the same, and that neither should contain a null value.

Data Dictionary

When a database administrator builds, manipulates, and maintains a database throughout its lifetime, she is actually modifying the database's metadata. *Metadata* is data about data, meaning that she does not actually touch the data users store in the database, but the information that is used to describe the structure and framework of the database. For example, the metadata may indicate that the database has 200 tables, and each table contains five attributes and seven rows. It could also dictate which users can access specific information within the database, database views, relationships between the tables, and how data will be accepted as input and presented as output. So, if the administrator needs to add another column to each of the tables and allow a new user access to the database, she would modify the metadata, by using the DBMS.

> **Exam Tip**
>
> A database view is an access control technique that filters what is shown to different users. Views allow a database to be logically divided based on the sensitivity of its data and who is accessing it.

This metadata is held in one logical location, called the *data dictionary*. When a user attempts to access the database by doing a search, the DBMS will look through the metadata held within the data dictionary to see if the user has the necessary access rights and if the information she is looking for is actually in the database.

The data dictionary is the central storage area for data element definitions, schema objects, reference keys, names of user accounts, integrity information, and auditing data, as shown in Figure 9-7.

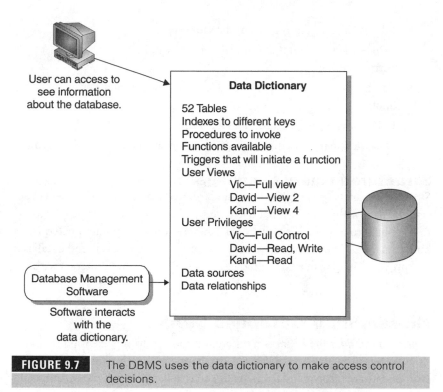

Data Dictionary

User can access to
see information
about the database.

52 Tables
Indexes to different keys
Procedures to invoke
Functions available
Triggers that will initiate a function
User Views
    Vic—Full view
    David—View 2
    Kandi—View 4
User Privileges
    Vic—Full Control
    David—Read, Write
    Kandi—Read
Data sources
Data relationships

Database Management
Software

Software interacts
with the
data dictionary.

FIGURE 9.7 The DBMS uses the data dictionary to make access control decisions.

Database Jargon

There are a lot of terms used in this section, some of which may be unfamiliar to you. The following is a list of terms used when working with relational databases to describe how data is stored:

- **Database** Cross-referenced collection of files.

- **Database Management System (DBMS)** Software that manages and controls the database.

- **Relation** Data is represented by a collection of tables.

- **Attribute** A column in a relational data model.

- **Tuple** A row in a relational data model representing a relationship among a set of values.

- **Element** Each data value in a row under a column.

- **Schema** Describes the structure of the database.

- **View** Virtual relations or partitions—controls what data is accessible to specific users.

- **File**   Collection of records of the same type.
- **Primary key**   Field that links all the data within a row to a corresponding value.
- **Foreign key**   Attribute of one table that is the primary key of another table.
- **Cell**   Intersection of a row and a column.
- **Data dictionary**   Central repository of metadata and data relationships.

Structured Query Language

Structured query language (SQL) is a standardized language to allow users to access the data within a relational database by issuing commands. Applications that are built to interact with relational databases can have predesigned queries built into them. The applications work as front ends to the back-end databases and provides users with a GUI interface, which allows them to interact with the database.

Hierarchical Database Model

A *hierarchical data model* takes a different approach to representing relationships between data than a relational database model. This model has a tree structure where records and fields are linked together through parent and child relationships. Parent records can have no children, many children, or a single child. The highest node is called the root.

Hierarchical data models have predetermined relationships, so they are not as flexible as relational database models.

Network Database Management System

A database that is built with a *network model* represents its data as records and sets of records that are related and linked, forming a network. Instead of using a single parent tree hierarchy, the network model uses set theory to provide a tree-like hierarchy that allows a child table to have more than one parent. This model supports a many-to-many relationship between data elements.

Distributed Data Model

A *distributed data model* means that a database is partitioned and that each partition is located closest to the people who will need to access it, which may be at different remote sites. It is a series of databases connected together logically. Users access a database through an interface and depending upon their requests and needs, they are directed towards the appropriate database partition. This type of design is used for environments that require distinct and separate functionality within its databases. This model offers flexible functionality, but can also be difficult to manage because of the complexity involved.

Object-Oriented Database

An *object-oriented database* is designed to handle a variety of different types of data (images, audio, documents, video). The objects within the database contain information that is used to access the objects actually containing these different data types and defines their properties. An object-oriented database is more dynamic in nature when compared to a relational database because objects can be created when needed and the data *and* procedure go with the object when it is requested. In a relational database, an application uses its procedures to obtain data from the database, the database does not actually provide procedures as object-oriented databases do. The object-oriented database has classes to define the attributes and procedures of its objects.

Object-oriented databases can be used to dynamically build different Web pages for different users depending upon their requests and input to a particular Web site. The objects are used to build the page, and the procedures within the objects dictate how the data within the objects will actually be used to perform their tasks.

Database Interface Languages

Data is of no use if you can't get to it and do something with it. Applications need to be able to obtain and interact with the information stored in databases, thus they need some type of interface and communication mechanism. The following sections address several interface languages.

- **Open Database Connectivity (ODBC)**   An application programming interface (API) that allows a program to communicate with a database either locally or remotely. The application sends requests to the ODBC, which in turn translates them into database commands. ODBC tracks down the necessary database driver for the application.

- **Object Linking and Embedding Database (OLE DB)**   Separates data into components that run as middleware on a client or server. It provides a low-level interface to link information across different databases and provides access to data no matter where it is located or how it is formatted.

- **ActiveX Data Objects (ADO)**   An API that allows applications to access back-end database systems. It is a set of ODBC interfaces that expose the functionality of a database through accessible objects. The ADO uses the OLE DB interface to connect with the database and can be developed with many different scripting languages.

- **Java Database Connectivity (JDBC)**   An API that allows a Java application to communicate with a database. The application can connect through ODBC or directly to the database.
- **Extensible Markup Language (XML)**   A standard for structuring data so that it can be easily shared by applications using Web technologies. It is a markup language that is self-defining and provides a lot of flexibility in how information within the database is presented. The Web browser interprets the XML tags.

Travel Advisory

XML is a "push" technology, meaning the formatting tags used to present the information come with the data.

Concurrency Issues

Databases are busy beasts because they can be accessed and modified by different users and applications within a short period of time. When these actions happen concurrently, the database should have some type of controls to ensure that two users cannot simultaneously modify the same information.

A good example would be when booking a hotel room. Robbie and Heather are reservationists for a large hotel chain and both receive calls one day at the same time for a hotel in San Diego. They both have callers who want a room on the upcoming Friday night for a one-night stay. When looking at the database, Robbie and Heather can both see that there is only one room left that night, so they both tell their callers that a room is available and proceed to secure the reservation. However, if they are both allowed to access the record at the same time, they could effectively double-book the room. Databases have controls in place so users cannot view or change records if it being used by another party. In this case, if Robbie initiated the reservation on the final room first, then when Heather attempted to do so moments later, she would be denied access and be forced to tell the caller that the hotel had just sold out for the night.

If the necessary controls are not in place, processes can be in a deadlock situation (two processes waiting for each other to release resources), data can be corrupted, or there can be a denial of service. Databases use software locks so when one user is making a change to information no other users can access it until she is finished.

Databases have a few other tools up their sleeves to ensure the integrity of the transactions and modifications to the system:

- **Rollback**   Allows a database to cancel changes that are being made and returns to the previous state. This is a defense mechanism if the system senses a problem or a disturbance. Rather than saving portions of data that may be corrupted due to the problem, the database simply reverts to its previous state when it knows that everything was stable.

- **Commit** This mechanism is the way that changes are saved to a database. The transaction is ended and all changes to the data take effect.

- **Checkpoint and savepoints** Mechanisms that periodically save database information as it is being modified by users and applications. This is done to protect against failures, hiccups, or any other kind of disruption that causes data to be lost.

Online transaction processing (OLTP) records transactions as they occur (in real-time), which usually updates more than one database in a distributed environment. This type of complexity can introduce many integrity threats, so the database software should implement the characteristics of the ACID test:

- **Atomicity** Divides transactions into units of work and ensures that all modifications take effect or none take effect. The changes are either committed or the database is rolled back.

- **Consistency** A transaction must follow the integrity policy developed for that particular database and ensure that all data is consistent in the different databases.

- **Isolation** Transactions execute in isolation until completed, without interacting with other transactions. The results of the modification are not available until the transaction is completed.

- **Durability** Once the transaction is verified as accurate on all systems, it is committed and the databases cannot be rolled back.

> **Local Lingo**
>
> Atomicity is used so that if one step in the transaction fails, subsequent steps are not processed.

Aggregation and Inference

Aggregation occurs when a user combines individual pieces of data that she has access to in order to figure out a larger story, which she does not have access to. This can happen when a user only has access privileges to some records but draws enough information from these records to understand information that has been deemed "off limits" to her.

For example, Madison learns of a rumor that her boss, Lisa, has been fired. She asks around but cannot get a straight answer from anyone, because this information has not been officially released, and she cannot find Lisa to ask her directly. Because Madison is not a member of management, she is not included in the e-mails that have been distributed that explain her boss' firing. But, Madison knows her way around these kinds of obstacles and is anxious to find out if her boss is still employed with the company. So, she accesses the employee information database, which is accessible to everyone, and discovers that Lisa's name and profile have been removed, thus confirming her suspicions. Lisa used aggregation (piecing together clues) and inference (actually figuring out the story) to get the information she needed.

To prevent aggregation and inference, databases can enforce one of the following:

- **Containers** Placing data in logical containers and assigning access rights to those containers.
- **Cell suppression** Hiding certain cells in the database that contain sensitive information.
- **Partitioning** Dividing the database into logical parts and implementing views.
- **Noise and perturbation** Inserting bogus information into a database in order to relay a different story or set of data.
- **Context-dependent access control** Looks at the previous access attempts to try and detect an inference attack before allowing access to the requested data.
- **Zero-knowledge proof** Providing information that does not directly or indirectly give up any other information.
- **Polyinstantiation** A record at a higher security level contains different information than the same record at a lower security level.

Local Lingo

Context-dependent access control reviews the previous access attempts to try and detect an inference attack. Content-dependent access control is more static in nature and pertains to the sensitivity of the data itself and does not look at previous access attempts.

Exam Tip

Content and context-dependent access controls can provide a high level of protection but requires a lot of resources and overhead.

Data Warehousing

Data warehousing is the process of combining information from different data sources so that trend analysis can be performed and better decisions can be made by viewing the information in one system instead of being spread across different databases. It is not simply copying or mirroring different databases and placing them into one spot. Instead, the data is put into a high-integrity database, redundancies are stripped out through normalization procedures, the data is mined to find relationships between the different data elements, which produces metadata, and it is all stored in the new data warehouse.

Datamarts are components of the data warehouse and are created and placed closest to the people who would need them most. For example, a data warehouse can contain *all* of the company's information, and from it a payroll datamart can be created and stored at the New York site, if that is where that department is located; another datamart containing supplies and shipments can be stored at the Atlanta site; and a datamart containing sales, expenses, and profits can be located at the headquarters site.

Data Mining

There are different *data mining* tools that identify trends, relationships, or patterns between the data elements within the data warehouse that would be basically impossible for a person to detect. A data mining tool processes the information held within a data warehouse and creates metadata. It is this metadata that users can review to understand previously unseen patterns and relationships. Data mining can be used to forecast stock trends in the market, identify computer attack signatures in network traffic, identify customer buying habits, and uncover fraudulent activities.

For example, a call center for long-distance phone billing could use metadata to identify customers who may be fraudulently disputing their bills. Say Darren calls to complain about his bill once every three months, and has received refunds regularly for the past three years by doing this. By looking into his records, it is discovered that he makes a phone call to Tokyo once every three months and then calls to complain about other disruptions in his phone service hoping that he would receive credit on his bill to compensate for the international toll charges. Data mining can quickly uncover this kind of behavior.

Data mining is also known as *knowledge discovery in database* (KDD), which are techniques of identifying valid and useful patterns. Different types of data can have various interrelationships, and the methods used depend on the type of data and patterns that are being sought. The following are three different approaches used in KDD systems to uncover these patterns:

- **Classification** Data is grouped together according to shared similarities.
- **Probabilistic** Data interdependencies are identified and probabilities are applied to their relationships.
- **Statistical** Identifies relationships between data elements and uses rule discovery.

Objective 9.05 Artificial Intelligence

You didn't know the CISSP included a review of a Stephen Spielberg movie, did you? Well, it doesn't. Artificial intelligence, in relation to the CISSP, deals with expert computer systems that try to act more like humans than computers.

Many times, the information that is gathered through data mining needs to be processed in ways that a person would process it, not a computer. The trick is to keep things analytical but try and add a bit of intuition and reasoning into the mix.

Expert Systems

Expert systems are computer programs designed to mimic human logic. The programs use nonnumerical algorithms to solve complex problems, identify patterns, perform data mining, and apply human reasoning and ways of thinking. These types of activities cannot be performed by typical computer algorithms, methodical programming languages, or mathematical formulas.

Subject matter experts are gathered and asked a long list of questions about different scenarios, and their answers are stored in a knowledge base. The system is developed using program languages based on "if-then" statements and uses an inference engine to identify patterns.

When the expert system is in production, the user of the system actually has access to a sea of expert advice, which is cross-referenced with a large database of facts, as shown in Figure 9-8. The system may have to "fill in the gray areas," which is something regular computer systems cannot perform, but it can be carried out by systems that imitate human interpretation, rationalization, and deduction.

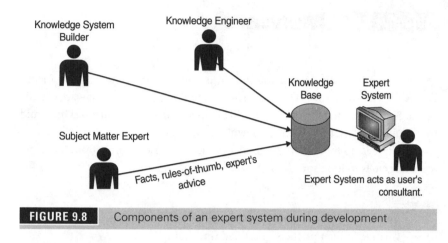

Knowledge System Builder

Knowledge Engineer

Knowledge Base

Expert System

Subject Matter Expert

Facts, rules-of-thumb, expert's advice

Expert System acts as user's consultant.

FIGURE 9.8 Components of an expert system during development

Artificial Neural Network

The *artificial neural network* (ANN) is a network model that is based on the neural structure of the brain. The goal of the model is to provide computers with the capability to identify patterns and learn from different situations and inputted values. Although computers may be superior to the human brain in crunching numbers and performing complex tasks, they have not actually been able to learn and respond differently to specific situations.

The ANN model has many small units that mimic neurons, and these different units are connected in a similar fashion as the brain. Where neurons communicate with neurotransmitters, ANN units communicate strictly through electrical voltage. The network is presented with different situations and scenarios so that it can learn from them and provide better results the more that it learns.

Travel Advisory

Just like a person, an ANN network is only as good as the experiences that it has been put through. The better the experiences, the better processing power it can provide.

When you go through something in life that has a lot of emotion tied to it, you will remember that item because it has more weight applied to it. With humans, the more emotionally charged an activity is, the more weight it has. Thus, it has a high probability of being stored and remembered. The developers and maintainers of artificial neural networks can apply more weight to one scenario than another so that it has more importance and influence on the units.

Objective 9.06   Malware

Malware is another name for malicious code. It can come in many forms, such as viruses, worms, Trojan horses, and logic bombs. Malware usually requires an action to occur before it will begin its harmful execution. This could be opening an e-mail attachment, downloading a file, or simply opening a document. There is no foolproof way to identify malicious code in action, but there are a few clues to look for:

- File size increase
- Many unexpected disk accesses
- Change in file update or modified timestamp
- Sudden decrease in hard drive space
- Unexpected and strange activity by applications

Travel Advisory

Checksums and hashing algorithms are used to detect if data has been modified, which could be the work of some type of malware.

Virus

Viruses seem to pop up all too often. Nearly everyone has heard of or experienced the effects of an e-mail virus. Even if the virus steers clear of your computer, you have probably been affected by network outages, network congestion, and disabled e-mail servers. So what is this epidemic that disrupts our work environment so often anyway?

A *virus* is a program that searches out other programs and infects them by embedding a copy of itself. When the infected program executes, the embedded virus launches itself and spreads the malicious code. A virus depends upon some type of host application for reproduction; it cannot reproduce itself on its own.

The following are several types of viruses that have been identified "in the wild":

- **Macro virus** Easy to create because of the simplicity of macro languages; used within Microsoft Office templates and documents.
- **Boot sector virus** Malicious code inserted into a hard drive or floppy disk boot sector.
- **Compression virus** Initializes when decompressed. Tries to outsmart anti-virus software by compressing itself, thus not matching a specific virus signature.

- **Stealth virus** Hides its footprints and any changes that it makes. Attempts to try and avoid detection by anti-virus software or host-based intrusion detection systems.

- **Polymorphic virus** Makes copies of itself and makes each copy slightly different by using a mutation engine (again to avoid detection).

- **Multiparty virus** Infects both boot sector and file system.

- **Self-garbling virus** Modifies own code so that it will not match anti-virus signatures to elude detection.

- **System virus** Reconfiguring BIOS configurations and other system files.

Local Lingo

"In the wild" means that the particular malware has been found in production networks and not just created in academic laboratory environments.

Worms

Worms and viruses are often confused because they are alike in many ways. The big difference is that a *worm* is a self-contained program that can reproduce on its own without the need of another piece of software. The reason they have been confused with viruses is because some malware in the past has acted like a virus *and* a worm. The ILOVEYOU virus is the most heralded. It could be spread to different computers through e-mail clients (acts as a virus), but can also reproduce itself on the infected system (acts as a worm).

Logic Bomb

A *logic bomb* executes its payload when an event occurs or at a certain date and time. This could be a disgruntled employee who places a logic bomb that is configured to execute two weeks after she is terminated. The malware may then delete all the data within the database, which will not make her former employer very happy. After a computer system has been compromised, for example, the attacker could configure a batch file so that when a regular user types in the command "dir" at the command line, instead of presenting her with a directory listing, it begins to format the hard drive.

Trojan Horse

A *Trojan horse* is a harmful program disguised as a program providing some type of beneficial service. It often looks and acts like the real thing, but in the background it is spreading malicious code, deleting files, capturing sensitive data, etc.

An example is if an attacker creates an application called notepad.exe. When a regular user runs it, she is presented with a Notepad program and is unaware that in the background the same program is e-mailing his password file to the attacker.

Denial of Service

A *denial of service* (DoS) attack is when a system is bombarded with so many requests that it can no longer accept other requests or fulfill them. This can happen maliciously where an attacker continually requests to set up connections with a specific system until that system no longer has available resources to accept other connection requests. This phenomenon can also happen accidentally, as when a large world event takes place and users all around the world connect to a Web site that provides up-to-date news. The overwhelming amount of access attempts can be too much for the Web servers to handle and in response they may freeze, reboot, or go offline.

There are several types of DoS attacks that can be launched, but the common theme between them is negatively affecting a victim system to the point where it can no longer fulfill its tasks.

DDoS

Distributed denial of service (DDoS) attacks negatively affect computers by sending hundreds and thousands of requests to it at the same time. Basically, it is the same thing as a DoS attack, but has tens or hundreds of computers overwhelm the same victim with the same attack. This is how some of the larger Web sites (Yahoo!, EBay, Excite) have been brought down and taken offline.

DDoS attacks usually use a master/zombie setup to flood a system with requests. The attacker compromises several systems through worms or Trojan horses. The master computer is controlled by the attacker, and it in turn controls the zombie computers. The zombie computers are infected systems that are used in this type of amplified attack without the users being aware of it. The zombie code lies dormant until the attacker gives the indication to attack. So the more systems an attacker can infect, the more amplified the DDoS can be.

Smurf Attacks

A *smurf attack* is a type of DoS attack that uses the Internet Control Message Protocol (ICMP). The attacker changes the source address on an ICMP ECHO REQUEST packet to that of the victim's address. When an ECHO REQUEST packet is sent to a system that is up and running, it replies with an ECHO REPLY. The attacker also makes sure that the destination address is a broadcast address. So when all the systems within the victim's subnet receive an ECHO REQUEST packet, they dutifully reply with an ECHO REPLY packet, as shown in Figure 9-9.

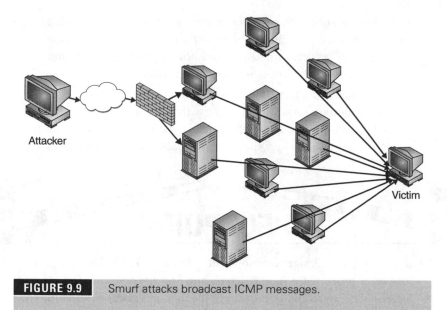

FIGURE 9.9   Smurf attacks broadcast ICMP messages.

The victim system gets hit with a large number of ECHO REPLY packets, which could negatively affect its performance or actually cause it to freeze.

An analogy could be if you went to each person in your office and told her that Bob just won the lottery and at 1:00 P.M. wanted everyone to come over to his cube because he was handing out $50 bills. At 1:01 P.M., Bob would not be able to carry out his regular tasks because of being bombarded with requests for money. Bob may perform another type of DoS attack upon you when he gets a hold of you.

Exam Tip

The Fraggle attack is the same attack as the Smurf attack, but instead of using the ICMP protocol, the Fraggle attack uses the UDP protocol.

Timing Attacks

Attacks work because computers act in a predictable manner. They have to follow a sequence of steps, and when an attacker understands these steps and figures out how to take advantage of them, she can perform a type of timing attack. The following are three types of timing attacks you should be familiar with:

- **Between the lines entry attack**   The attacker taps into and uses an active communication line. The user may not be using the connection at that time, but it is still active so the attacker jumps in and uses it.

- **NAK/ACK attack** A NAK is a negative acknowledgment to tell a system that a certain piece of information was not received. Some systems do not deal with negative acknowledgments properly and attackers used this symptom to their advantage.
- **Line disconnect attack** An attacker may access and keep a communication session open after the user attempts to terminate it. In this case, the user drops off thinking the connection is closed, but actually the attacker kept the connection active and is now using it.

CHECKPOINT

✔**Objective 9.01: Project Development** Security should be incorporated into every phase of software development. Security add-ons after software has been developed and/or implemented is a more expensive and time consuming approach. A risk analysis should be performed to identify security objectives, threats, and countermeasures. A software development effort should follow through with thought-out phases instead of just hitting the pavement running. Change control is a critical requirement of software development to ensure that changes are approved, tested, and documented. It should be verified that any approved and implemented changes do not negatively affect the application or system's security policy.

✔**Objective 9.02: Object-Oriented Programming** Object-oriented programming offers many more advantages than classic input/output programming, such as modularity, reusability, and more granular control within the programs themselves. Object-oriented programming allows for developers to create classes that dictate the attributes of the objects that will be instantiated and the methods they will perform. Objects can communicate with one another through messaging. Messaging is carried out through standardized interfaces on each object.

✔**Objective 9.03: Distributed Computing** ORBs and DCOM allow computer components to communicate within distributed environments. CORBA provides standardized interfaces that allow applications written in different languages to communicate and work together in a distributed fashion. COM deals with components on a local system; DCOM deals with components in a distributed environment. OLE provides linking and embedding services for objects.

✔**Objective 9.04: Databases** Databases are developed and maintained by software called database management system (DBMS). A relational database uses two-dimensional tables with rows and columns. A distributed database is a series of databases connected together logically. A hierarchical database uses a tree structure to provide relationships between data elements. Databases have safeguards in place, such as rollback, commit, and checkpoints, to protect data integrity. Real-time transactions should meet the ACID test to ensure consistency and integrity of information. A data warehouse is a central location where data from different data sources is stored, manipulated, and presented to the user in a useful way, usually by data mining.

✔**Objective 9.05: Artificial Intelligence** Expert systems use rule-based programming languages, a knowledge base, and on inference engine to provide nontraditional computing solutions. They attempt to provide the same service as having a room full of subject matter experts by mimicking human-logic. ANNs are based on the neurons of the human brain. They can learn and identify patterns based upon the numerous connections and data processing that occur over and over again.

✔**Objective 9.06: Malware** A virus is an application that requires a host for reproduction, whereas a worm can reproduce itself. There are several different types of viruses, which are written to evade detection by anti-virus software or host-based intrusion detection systems. Another type of malware is a Trojan horse, which seems to perform one type of activity while in the background it is also doing something malicious. A logic bomb initiates at a specific time or event. DoS attacks overwhelm a victim with requests; a DDoS is an amplified DoS. Smurf and Fraggle are examples of DDoS attacks.

REVIEW QUESTIONS

1. In which phase of a project development plan should security requirements be identified and defined?
   A. Acceptance testing/Implementation
   B. Project initiation
   C. Functional design analysis and planning
   D. Disposal

2. In which phase of software development should a risk analysis be conducted?

   A. Functional design analysis and planning

   B. Project initiation

   C. Software development

   D. System design specifications

3. Ensuring that programmers are not the only ones who test their own code is an example of what?

   A. Job rotation

   B. Change control

   C. Distributed environment

   D. Separation of duties

4. Which of the following is not a characteristic of object-oriented programming?

   A. Highly-modular

   B. Expensive and time-consuming

   C. Self-contained

   D. Uses objects and classes

5. Why are macro viruses prevalent and popular?

   A. They hide their activities when in stealth mode.

   B. They hide in the boot sector and within the file system.

   C. They are easily written.

   D. They garble their code to evade detection.

6. Which of the following can be used as middleware in client/server relationships?

   A. CASE

   B. ADO

   C. ICMP

   D. ORB

7. Which of the following is an example of OLE?

   A. Tokens used by HTTP to keep track of user profile information

   B. Embedding a graphic into a document

   C. Small mobile-code programs that run on a user's browser

   D. Scripts used to manipulate data that is inputted into a Web site

8. Which of the following database terms is the intersection of a row and column?

   A. Cell
   B. Tuple
   C. Attribute
   D. Foreign key

9. Which of the following is the result of data mining?

   A. DBMS
   B. Schema
   C. Metadata
   D. Data warehouse

10. Which of the following automatically identifies patterns within an expert system?

    A. If-then rules
    B. Inference engine
    C. Knowledge base
    D. Numerical algorithms

11. Which of the following is not a part of a Smurf attack?

    A. Amplified network
    B. ICMP
    C. UDP
    D. Victim

12. Which of the following is used to control and maintain the database centrally?

    A. Data dictionary
    B. Primary key
    C. Tuple and attributes
    D. Foreign key

REVIEW ANSWERS

1. **C** The security requirements of the product need to be identified and actually defined in the functional design analysis and planning phase.

2. **B** A risk analysis is one of the first steps in software development. It can help to set security objectives, identify threats, and determine proper countermeasures that should be integrated.

3. **D** Separation of duties protects against fraud and improves the accuracy by allowing individuals with a fresh perspective to work on the project.

4. **B** OOP saves time and money because the developed objects can be reused by other applications and reused in other projects.

5. **C** Macros viruses are easy to create because of the simplistic nature of the macro language itself.

6. **D** ORBs manage communication between components in distributed environments and act as a middleman. They tell the client piece of the application where the server components are located in the environment.

7. **B** OLE involves embedding and linking services. Linking is allowing one program to access another program, and embedding is placing an object within another object.

8. **A** The point where a row and column meet is called a cell. A row within a relational database is called a tuple, and a column is referred to as an attribute.

9. **C** Data mining analyzes data to look for patterns that could not be uncovered with typical reporting mechanisms. The data output in the process is called metadata.

10. **B** Inference engines automatically match patterns and determine which rules are applicable. The knowledge base is the database of captured information, mainly from subject matter experts.

11. **C** The Smurf attack is made up of an attacker, using an ICMP packet with a spoofed source address, and a network to amplify the attack. The Fraggle attack uses UDP; the Smurf attack uses ICMP.

12. **A** The data dictionary contains metadata about the database, which is modified by the DBMS. When the database administrator needs to make a change to the structure of the database, she makes that change to the data dictionary, which is then applied to the database itself.

Operations Security

CHAPTER
10

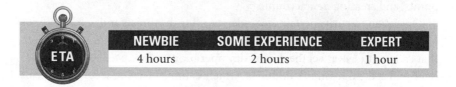

	NEWBIE	SOME EXPERIENCE	EXPERT
ETA	4 hours	2 hours	1 hour

Everything we've discussed so far points toward making sure a company and its assets are protected and ensuring its operations can run smoothly without interruption. However, all of this behind-the-scenes planning, testing, and implementing won't do a lick of good if the operations unit itself is not secure. This chapter covers the necessary procedures and security practices necessary for a company's operations department, as well as the potential threats to these efforts.

Objective 10.01 Operations Controls

You may ask yourself, "Haven't we done enough already?" I mean, we've planned for disasters, developed a security policy, performed a risk analysis, secured the facility, encrypted our data, enabled single sign-on access, trained our people on security matters, and backed up servers and files—what's left to do?

There are actually some critical pieces within the operations unit that we haven't touched upon yet; pieces that, if left unprotected, could be damaging to a company and its ability to operate.

Operations deals with the day-to-day activities that need to take place to keep everything running and functioning correctly. This usually means to fix or replace hardware when it gives out, restore data backups when information gets corrupted, investigate and correct network connectivity issues, implement new devices and applications, control changes to the current systems and software, and respond to user requests as in changing passwords, setting up new share points, and creating new accounts.

Operations security pertains to understanding the threats and vulnerabilities of the computer systems, devices, and applications within a given environment that can negatively affect the day-to-day operations. So we need to add another item under the operation's umbrella, which is implementing security controls that have been approved to protect the infrastructure's availability, integrity, and confidentiality.

Many of the key resources pertaining to operations that need to be protected are shown here:

- Sensitive data
- Source code
- Hardware
- Password files

- System utilities
- Audit logs
- Backed up files
- Main and auxiliary storage media

The actual operational controls that can be put into place to protect these resources are the following:

- Physical and logical access controls
- Configuration management
- Resource protection
- Input/output controls
- Media access controls
- Separation of duties, rotation of jobs, least privilege
- Backup and recovery procedures

The rest of this chapter explains these controls and their relationships to the resources they are to protect and the environment they reside within.

Due Care

Any company, regardless of its industry, is expected to exercise *due care*, meaning that they are to implement and maintain security mechanisms and practices that protect the company, its employees, customers, and partners. Due care can be compared to the "prudent man" concept. A prudent man is seen as responsible, careful, cautious, and practical, and a company practicing due care is seen in the same light. Although being responsible in some cases may not seem to be fun and the life of the party, when it comes to keeping things operational and legally within compliance, it wins hands down.

The right steps need to be taken to achieve the necessary level of security, but it takes continued effort and discipline to retain this level of security. This is what operational security is all about.

Administrative Control

Administrative controls cover many areas and are very important pieces of operational security. The objectives that fall into this category are usually the responsibility of a company's management team, and for good reason. As we've mentioned other times in this book, executives and senior management personnel are legally responsible for protecting company resources and assets and for maintaining proper security levels. A critical function of doing this is through employee management, which is an administrative control.

Companies could not run without people, and for the most part people are wonderful, but trying to get them to do things they don't want to do can be easily compared to herding cats. Instead of just telling people "Do not do bad things and do not defraud the company," the items discussed in the following sections should be put into place so the opportunity for fraud is not possible or at least harder to achieve.

Separation of Duties

Two of these concepts (separation of duties and job rotation) were touched upon in Chapter 1, but their importance in the workplace and on the CISSP exam allows for us to revisit them here.

Separation of duties is a control that ensures that one person acting alone cannot compromise the company's security or commit fraudulent activities. High-risk activities should be broken up into separate parts and distributed to different individuals. This way, the company does not need to put a dangerously high level of trust in one person, and fraudulent activity would require an agreement of more than one person instead of one individual acting alone.

Separation of duties also helps to prevent dangerous mistakes. For instance, a programmer should not be the only one to test her own code. A different person, or department, should perform functionality and integrity testing on the code because the programmer may have a predetermined view of how the testing results should appear.

So if someone wants to do bad things to the company, he will need to find a friend with the necessary access rights and permissions and convince her to perform these actions. By implementing separations of duties you are banking that friendship does not go that deep, and just in case it does, you should have critical activities audited and monitored.

Job Rotation

Job rotation means that more than one individual is trained for a specific position within the company. This allows the company to have more than one person who understands the tasks and responsibilities of a specific position, which provides backup and redundancy if a person leaves the company or has an unfortunate meeting with a bus. Job rotation also helps in identifying fraudulent activities as well. For example, if Dave is siphoning money from different customer accounts and you rotate Keith through his position, there is a good chance that this will be uncovered.

(ISC)²'s definition of rotation of duties is, "Interrupt opportunity to create collusion to subvert operation for fraudulent purposes." This is confusing to say the least. It means that if employees are rotated through positions, it will be harder for one employee to commit fraudulent activities without other employees finding out.

Least Privilege and Need-to-Know

Least privilege means that an individual should have just enough permissions and rights to fulfill his role in the company and no more. If an individual has excessive permissions and rights, it could possibly open the door to abuse and fraud and can put the company in greater risk than necessary.

If Kandi is the company's accountant, she should only have access rights to accounting files and only enough permissions to fulfill her tasks. This can help ensure that she is not overstepping her bounds and fraudulently creating her own nest egg with company funds. It also helps reduce the amount of critical mistakes that could take place.

Least privilege and *need-to-know* have a symbiotic relationship. Each user should have a need-to-know of the resources that she is allowed to access. If Kandi does not have a need-to-know about the company's foreign affairs, she should not have access to those documents and that information.

Authorization creep is a direct violation of least privilege and need-to-know. This takes place when an employee moves from one position to another within the organization and accrues more and more permissions and privileges. Companies should evaluate users' rights and take away the ones they no longer need to complete their tasks.

Mandatory Vacations

Mandatory vacations are another type of administrative control that may sound a bit odd at first, but they do help in providing operational security. Forcing employees to take vacations reinforces the rotation of jobs principle that we discussed earlier.

If an accounting employee has been performing a salami attack by shaving off pennies from multiple accounts into his own account, a company would have a better chance of figuring this out if that employee was required to take vacation for a week or longer. The person filling in for this employee might then uncover the activities or, at the very least, raise questions about abnormal procedures.

Many people who perform fraudulent activities at their jobs do not take the vacation they earn because they do not want to be caught. These people must be forced to take their earned time off; this is why it is called mandatory vacations.

Clipping Levels

Employees make mistakes every day, which is generally an accepted behavior. However, companies should set certain thresholds for specific errors and the number of times these errors can occur before it is considered suspicious. The threshold is a baseline for violations that may be normal for a user to commit before alarms are raised. This baseline is referred to as a *clipping level.*

Once this clipping level has been exceeded, further violations are recorded for review. Typically, IDS software is used to track these activities and behavior patterns because it would be overwhelming for an individual to continually monitor stacks of audit logs and properly identify certain activity patterns. So the clipping level indicates how many mistakes are acceptable for employees to make.

Control Categories

There are different categories that operational controls can fall within. It is important for you to understand each type, especially preventive and detective controls. *Preventive controls* are used to discourage undesirable events from taking place. They help companies avoid potential problems. Preventive controls are a company's first line of defense and include things such as access controls, security policies and standards, prenumbered forms that prevent errors, and physical security measures (guards, locks, fences).

Detective controls identify breakdowns in access controls and can help determine the effectiveness of the preventive controls currently in place. Output from detective controls are usually consulted after an event takes place to help understand the cause of the disturbance. Some examples are audit logs, access control logs, and intrusion detection systems.

The following is a list of the other control categories and how they are used in combination:

- Corrective
  - Controls used to amend a situation after undesirable events have occurred
- Deterrent
  - Controls used to discourage security violations and malicious behaviors
- Recovery
  - Controls used to restore resources and capabilities
- Compensation
  - Controls used to provide alternatives to other controls, usually when the first choice is too expensive

- Preventive–Administrative
  - Policies and procedures
  - Effective hiring practices
  - Pre-employment background checks
  - Controlled termination processes
  - Data classification and labeling
  - Security awareness
  - Separation of duties
- Preventive–Physical
  - Badges and swipe cards
  - Guards and dogs
  - Fences, locks, man-traps, and alarms
- Preventive–Technical
  - Passwords, biometrics, and smart cards
  - Encryption, call-back systems, database views, and constrained user interface
  - Antivirus software, ACLs, firewalls, routers, and clipping levels
- Detective–Administrative
  - Job rotation
  - Sharing responsibilities
  - Inspections
  - Incident response
- Detective–Technical
  - IDS
  - Reviewing audit logs
  - Reviewing violations of clipping levels
- Detective–Physical
  - Human evaluation of output from sensors or cameras
  - Motion detectors, intrusion detection, and video cameras

Travel Advisory

The three main types of controls are administrative, technical, and physical. These different controls can provide detective, preventative, corrective, recovery, deterrent, or compensation services.

Configuration Management and Media Control

Objective 10.02

How many times have you heard someone say, "This business is all about change"? Yes, change is pretty common in just about every business. A lot of companies talk about it like experts, but not all of them are preparing for it like experts. One area of change that is a serious concern to operational units is configuration management. Configuration management is a control put into place to manage how changes take place in the production environment. It is a process of approving, testing, documenting, and auditing all changes made to devices, computers, and application configurations. The following is a list of changes that a company needs to control with configuration management procedures:

- New computers or devices installed
- New applications installed
- Different configurations implemented
- Patches and updates applied
- New technologies integrated
- Updated policies, procedures, and standards
- New regulations and requirements
- Different network configuration

These types of changes need to take place in a thought-out, controlled, disciplined, and logical manner. Do you think the operations of a company would be negatively affected if people could reconfigure servers any way they see fit, install patches without testing them first, make up new policies, or throw in new networking devices without permission or approval? These things do take place and usually account for the ulcers and hair loss that network administrators and managers experience. Let's look at how changes *should* take place.

The ultimate goal of configuration management is the stability of individual systems and the environment and the integrity, confidentiality, and availability of the data they hold. This does not just take place once, but should be a discipline that is incorporated and followed throughout the operational life cycle of each system.

The following steps are examples of the types of procedures that should be part of any change control process:

1. **Formal request for a change**   Requests should be presented to an individual or group that is responsible for approving changes and overseeing how these changes are implemented and how they affect the overall environment.

2. **Approval of change**   The individual requesting the change must justify the reasons and clearly show the benefits and possible pitfalls of the change. Sometimes the requestor is asked to conduct more research and provide more information before the change is approved.

3. **Documentation of the change**   Once the change is approved, it should be fully documented and entered into a change log.

4. **Testing and presentation**   The change must be fully tested to uncover any unforeseen effects. Depending upon the severity of the change and the company's organization, the change and implementation steps may need to be presented to a change control committee. This helps show different groups the purpose and outcome of the change, as well as possible ramifications.

5. **Implementation**   Once the change is fully tested and approved, a schedule should be developed that outlines the projected phases of the change being implemented and the necessary milestones. These steps should be fully documented and progress should be monitored.

6. **Report changes to management**   A full report should be submitted to management summarizing the change. This report can be submitted on a periodic basis to keep management up-to-date and ensure continual support.

The effort of controlling changes is carried out to protect the environment and the items within it. It is important to understand that change control is a strict procedure to be used for *all* changes that take place and not something that is modified for individual changes that are requested.

Media Controls

Many times, companies will have a media library with a librarian in charge of protecting company resources (hard drives, laptops, backed up data). Users may be required to check out resources instead of having them readily available for everyone. This type of control is put into place to reduce the possibility of damages to resources, to ensure that sensitive data is not disclosed in an unauthorized manger, and to limit the opportunities of resource misuse.

The media librarian is responsible for making sure that resources are handled properly and stored safely. This can encompass keeping backups in a fireproof safe, transporting backups to an off-site facility, and ensuring proper environmental controls (temperature, humidity, cleanliness) of storage areas. The librarian is also responsible for proper logging of activities that pertain to these resources.

Detailed logs should be kept of who checked out media, the date and time, who approved it, and when it was returned and in what type of condition. If the library controls backed up data, the media it is on should be labeled with the following information:

- The date of creation
- The individual who created it
- The retention period (how long the data should be maintained)
- The classification
- The volume name and version

Other than centrally controlling access to media within a company, the following media controls should also be put into place:

- Encrypt sensitive data.
- Label media internally and externally (logically via software and physically on the media itself).
- Train users and staff on media handling, storage, and transportation procedures.
- Establish an access control policy and use privileges.
- Protect resource according to classification.

Media should be clearly marked, logged, and its integrity verified. Data on the media should be erased when no longer in use or needed. When media is cleared of its contents, it is said to be *sanitized*. This should take place if the media is going to be reused by someone else, thus any sensitive information is unavailable to those it is not intended for. There are different methods of sanitation: overwriting, degaussing, and destruction. As stated in earlier chapters, deleting files on a piece of media does not actually make the data disappear; it only deletes the pointers to where those files still live on the disk.

Exam Tip

Residual data on media after erasure is referred to as *data remanence.*

Degaussing is generating a coercive magnetic force that reduces the magnetic flux density of the storage media to zero. This is a fancy way of describing how a machine with large magnets erases data on different media types. It is the magnetic force created by the magnets that properly erases data from the media.

Zeroization is erasing electronic data by overwriting the contents with null values so that data recovery is not possible. This is carried out by software developed especially for this purpose.

If a piece of media that is holding sensitive data cannot be properly sanitized, it must be physically destroyed.

Travel Advisory

If a CD-ROM is holding confidential information and that information needs to be erased, in most cases that CD-ROM needs to be physically destroyed.

Input/Output Data Controls

Before entering data into a system or application, controls should be put in place to ensure its integrity, and the output should be compared to the corresponding input. In mainframe environments, operators are responsible for ensuring the integrity of the data being inputted into the system and the resulting output from the applications running on the mainframe.

Output procedures pertaining to operations security could also restrict access to sensitive printed materials, require signed receipts before releasing sensitive output, and create header and trailer banners with recipient's name and location on the printed materials. It is all about making sure that only the authorized individuals can view the secrets you are trying to hide.

Objective 10.03 # Reacting to Failures and Recovering

Understanding how to properly react to system and device failures is a large part of operations security, because they are inevitable. Within an operating system itself, certain controls must be in place to ensure that instructions are being executed in the correct security context. The system must be able to react to expected and unexpected situations for self-preservation and ensure that the necessary level of security is *always* in place. When it determines that something unsafe has taken place within the system, it must revert to a more secure state, which is what trusted recovery is all about.

Trusted Recovery

When a system crashes or freezes, it should not put the operating system in any type of insecure state. Typically, a system crashes because it encounters something that it perceives as dangerous and decides that it is safer to freeze, shut down, or reboot rather than perform the current activity.

A *system reboot* takes place after shutting down the system in a controlled manner in response to a trusted computing base (TCB) failure. Also, if the system finds inconsistent object data structures or if there is not enough space in some critical tables, a system reboot may also be performed. This releases resources and returns the system to a more stable and safe state.

An *emergency system restart* takes place after a system failure happens in an uncontrolled manner. This can be a TCB or media failure, which could be caused by a lower privileged process attempting to access memory segments that are restricted. The system may interpret this as an insecure activity that it cannot properly recover from without rebooting. So, the system goes into a maintenance mode and recovers from the actions that have taken place by restarting. The system is brought back up in a consistent and stable state.

A *system cold start* takes place when an unexpected TCB or media failure happens and the regular recovery procedures cannot restore the system to a more consistent state. The system, TCB, and user objects may remain in an inconsistent state while the system attempts to recover itself, and intervention may be required by the computer operator or administrator to properly restore the system.

When reacting to a failure, a system can take on one of four possible states, each of which handles the situation differently:

- **Fail-safe** Automatic termination and protection of programs and processes when a failure is identified. This is done to make sure the operating system environment does not become unstable, which could threaten the security of its components.
- **Fail-soft** Termination of affected non-essential processes when a failure is identified. This activity keeps as many of the processes up and running as possible and terminates the processes that it cannot restart or the ones causing the disturbance.

- **Fail-secure**   System preserves a secure state during and after failure. No matter what processes needs to be terminated or if the system needs to become unusable with the requirement of user intervention—the system must still be able to protect itself and the assets it has been put into place to defend.
- **Fail-over**   The backup system is activated which takes over processing. This is a recovery control.

After a system crash or failure, the following steps should be followed before allowing the user access to the system:

1. Boot into single-user mode or maintenance mode.
2. Uninstall program or process that is disrupting the system.
3. Recover file systems to before time of failure.
4. Restore missing or corrupted files from most recent backup.
5. Check security and integrity of critical files.
6. Boot into regular mode and test usability.

Facsimile Security

Just about every office has a fax machine, and that being said, just about every office that works with sensitive data has a security issue to be aware of.

Fax machines can present some security issues if they are being used to transmit sensitive or confidential information. The information has to be scanned into the device, which is then transmitted over a phone or network line, and printed out at the destination fax machine. The received fax often just sits in a bin until the recipient walks over to retrieve it. This is not a secure environment for confidential information.

Some companies use fax servers, as shown in Figure 10-1, which are systems that manage incoming and outgoing faxed documents. When a fax is received by the fax server, it properly routes it to the individual it is addressed to so that it is not actually printed, but instead it is held in electronic form. Many times, the received fax is routed to the recipient's electronic mailbox.

A fax server usually has the capability of allowing someone to print the received faxes, but this can present the same security breaches of a stand-alone fax device. In these cases, the print feature should be disabled so that sensitive documents can be stored and viewed only by authorized individuals.

Extensive logging and auditing is available for fax servers as well and should be enabled and monitored in companies that require this level of security.

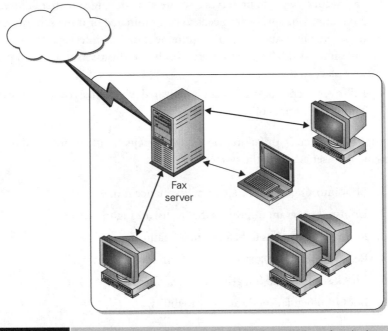

FIGURE 10.1 A fax server can be used instead of stand-alone fax devices.

Because data will be traveling to and from the fax server in a clear text form, some companies may wish to implement encryption for faxed materials. A *fax encryptor* (bulk data link encryption mechanism) may be put into place. The encryptor will encrypt any and all data that hits the network cable or telephone wire. This would be used when a company needs to ensure that all data leaving the fax server will be properly encrypted and protected.

Operational Responsibilities

The operation's department has responsibilities and tasks that are critical and far reaching within the environment. The next few sections review some of the issues not yet covered that fall within the scope of the operation's department.

Unusual or Unexplained Occurrences

Networks can be complex and dynamic creatures. At times, conditions take place that are at first confusing and possibly unexplainable. It is up to the operations department to investigate these issues, understand the problem, and come up with a logical solution.

For example, there could be ARP storms, which may indicate that the default gateway is not accessible or continual elections are taking place between domain controllers in a Windows environment. The elections could be caused because the master browser is continually taken offline for some reason. Individuals from the operation's department would arrive wearing their capes, figure out the problem, and make everything better again.

Local Lingo

ARP (address resolution protocol) resolves IP addresses to corresponding MAC addresses.

Deviations from Standards

Each system should have specific expectations of it and a certain level of performance, which is referred to as that system's standard. The standard can represent that computer's baseline, which means the level of security and performance that the system supplies to the environment. If this changes for some reason, investigations into the cause may need to take place.

For example, if three specific systems periodically experience a drastic reduction in performance and resource capabilities, it would be operations to the rescue to try and figure out what is going on. Proper troubleshooting procedures may uncover that the three systems are victims of a denial of service attack, thus the team needs to take the proper steps for correcting this issue.

Sometimes, the standard needs to be recalibrated so that it portrays a realistic view of the actual service level the system can provide. If a server was upgraded from a Pentium II to Pentium IV, the memory was quadrupled, the swap file increased, and three extra hard drives added, then the service level of this system should be re-evaluated.

Local Lingo

The word "standard" here pertains to a baseline of performance. In Chapter 1, we looked at a different standard, which is a compulsory rule derived from the company's security policy.

Unscheduled Initial Program Loads

Initial program load (IPL) is a mainframe term for loading the operating system's kernel into the computer's main memory. On a personal computer, booting into the operating system is the equivalent to IPLing. This activity takes place to prepare the computer for user operation. The operations team needs to investigate computers that reboot for no reason, which could indicate that the operating system is experiencing major problems or an attack.

> **Exam Tip**
>
> Security Administrator Tool for Analyzing Networks (SATAN) is a tool used to detect system vulnerabilities, show weaknesses, and provide corrective recommendations.

Personnel Operators

The three main categories of personnel pertaining to operations are the operators, network administrator, and security administrator. The following gives an outline of each role's responsibility pertaining to operations security:

Operators (pertains mainly to mainframe environments)

- Monitoring execution of the system
- Controlling flow of jobs
- Mounting input/output volumes
- Initial program load
- Renaming/relabeling resources
- Reassigning ports/lines

Network Administrator

- Maintenance and control of network operations
- All device and system administration tasks

Security Administrator (in some environments, the network administrator also has this role)

- Implementing dictated user clearance levels
- Setting initial password and security profiles for users
- Configuring sensitivity levels
- Implementing device security mechanisms and secure communication channels
- Reviewing audit logs

Objective 10.04 **Software Backups**

Backing up software and ensuring that a network has proper redundancy in place are critical tasks within operational units. This topic is covered in Chapter 7, but we touch on a few areas that are vital to operations.

Network Availability

Availability is one of the three fundamental components of security (the other two being confidentiality and integrity). There are a number of factors that can affect a network's availability, such as device failure, software failure, misconfigurations, user mistakes, or attacks. Operations personnel need to have a solid understanding of the overall network, how devices interconnect with one another, potential failures, redundancy options, and recovery solutions.

A term we mentioned earlier in the book, but that has specific relevance to operational units, is a single point of failure. A single point of failure in a network can cause serious limitations to both employees trying to perform tasks and customers trying to make product requests or perform transactions. It is critical that these potential problem areas be identified and redundant alternatives are implemented.

RAID

Redundant Array of Inexpensive Disks (RAID) is a technology that is an extremely practical and important tool to help the operations department. It provides redundancy and performance improvement by combining several physical disks and aggregating them into logical arrays. Redundancy and performance improvements are key objectives for operations because they usually directly affect the production and productivity of a company and its employees.

RAID performs a function called *striping*, where data is written across all aggregated drives. This technique dramatically improves the data retrieval speed because more than one of the device's heads is being used to perform read activities.

There are different levels of RAID, which dictate the type of activity that will take place within the RAID system. Some levels deal only with performance issues; other levels deal with performance and redundancy. If redundancy is one of the services that a RAID level is providing, parity is involved. Parity data holds the necessary instructions to re-create a drive if it fails. *Parity* data can be written to one or more disks, which works as a backup. If a drive fails, the parity data is used to rebuild a new drive, and all the information the failed drive held. Table 10-1 shows the different RAID levels and activities for each.

TABLE 10.1 Different RAID Levels and the Functionality They Provide

RAID Level	Activity	Name
0	Data striped over several drives. No redundancy or parity is involved. If one volume fails, the entire volume is unusable. It is used for performance only.	Striping
1	Mirroring of drives. Data is written to two drives at once. If one drive fails, the other drive has the exact same data available.	Mirroring
2	Data striping over all drives at the bit level. Parity data is created with a hamming code, which identifies any errors. This level specifies the use of up to 39 disks: 32 for storage and 7 for error recovery data. This is not used in production today.	Hamming code parity
3	Data striping over all drives and parity data held on one drive. If a drive fails, it can be reconstructed from parity drive.	Byte-level parity
4	Same as level 3, except data is striped at the block level instead of the byte level.	Block-level parity
5	Data is written in disk sector units to all drives. Parity is written to all drives also, which ensures that there is not a single point of failure.	Interleave parity
6	Similar to level 5 but with added fault tolerance, which is a second set of parity data written to all drives.	Second parity data (or double parity)
10	Data is simultaneously mirrored and striped across several drives and can support multiple drive failures.	Striping and mirroring

Most RAID systems allow for hot swapping disks (replacing drives while the system is running). When a drive is swapped out, or added, the parity data rebuilds the data on the new disk. This is important in operational environments because the ability to keep a system running while performing maintenance could mean the difference between servicing a customer or turning them away.

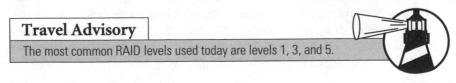

Travel Advisory

The most common RAID levels used today are levels 1, 3, and 5.

The RAID Advisory Board (RAB) has developed new classifications for RAID systems:

- **Failure Resistant Disk Systems**   Protects against loss of data or access due to a disk failure
- **Failure Tolerant Disk Systems**   Protects against loss of data access due to failure of any single component and offers continuous data availability
- **Disaster Tolerant Disk Systems**   Two or more zones are used to provide and protect the access to stored data

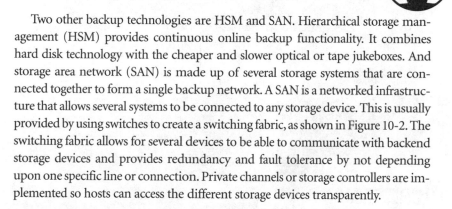

Local Lingo

Disaster Tolerant Disk Systems are server systems that are divisible into two or more zones. The mechanisms within the zones cooperate to protect against the loss of access, possibly caused by a power outage, cooling system, or component failure.

Two other backup technologies are HSM and SAN. Hierarchical storage management (HSM) provides continuous online backup functionality. It combines hard disk technology with the cheaper and slower optical or tape jukeboxes. And storage area network (SAN) is made up of several storage systems that are connected together to form a single backup network. A SAN is a networked infrastructure that allows several systems to be connected to any storage device. This is usually provided by using switches to create a switching fabric, as shown in Figure 10-2. The switching fabric allows for several devices to be able to communicate with backend storage devices and provides redundancy and fault tolerance by not depending upon one specific line or connection. Private channels or storage controllers are implemented so hosts can access the different storage devices transparently.

Backups

If you've ever lost an important file and had no backup, you know how frustrating and helpless you can feel. For operational groups, that feeling of frustration and helplessness might just be the tip of the iceberg. Not having proper backups could mean lost revenue, loss of customers, and loss of a job.

There are four questions to ask when developing a backup plan:

- What needs to be backed up?
- Where should backups be stored (safe, off-site facility)?
- How often should backups take place?

A backup plan should be developed with key personnel to decide what needs backing up and when. Another important piece is how long data should be kept.

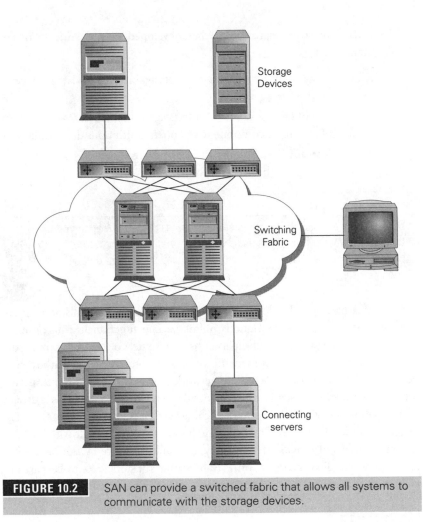

Storage Devices

Switching Fabric

Connecting servers

| FIGURE 10.2 | SAN can provide a switched fabric that allows all systems to communicate with the storage devices. |

Backing up data can require a lot of hard drive and media space, thus it cannot be kept forever. Many companies have regulations pertaining to how long records and information must be stored, so the operations department needs to ensure that these requirements are met. When deciding on how long to keep other types of data that does not fall under these rules, a balanced approach needs to be applied that looks at the possibility of the data needing to be restored and the space that is required and available to hold the data.

Exam Tip

On-demand backups are done outside of the regular backup schedule and are usually carried out due to unexpected events.

The operations department could be diligent and outline and follow an effective backup schedule that protects the company's critical data, store one copy in a fire-proof safe and another copy at an off-site facility, ensure environmental and safety controls are put into place where this data is stored, and then pat themselves on the back for doing such a fine job. But what is missing? Ensuring that this data can actually be restored properly. There have been many horror stories of companies backing up data for years and not realizing that the tapes were stored next to a device that has large magnets or that the backup and recovery software was faulty. In these cases, the operation's department (and company) had a false sense of security and when important data got corrupted and needed to be restored, yelling and finger pointing usually commenced as tempers rose and the company's production was threatened.

Travel Advisory

Backups should take place immediately following a company reorganization or a system upgrade to ensure that the most up-to-date version is being stored.

Contingency Management

Contingency management pertains to developing plans and procedures that should take place before, during, and after an incident that can directly affect operations. It is done to ensure the availability of critical systems and to provide a predictable and productive environment.

These issues are more fully covered in Chapter 7, but they are mentioned here so that the understanding of contingency management and its direct relationship to operations is apparent. Operations is all about keeping things up and running, but things *will* go wrong, and a company has to be prepared for it or be drastically affected by the ramifications.

CHECKPOINT

✔**Objective 10.01:   Operations Controls**   The goal of operational security is to ensure that hardware and software stay operational and available. Administrative controls include separation of job duties, mandatory vacations, job rotation, enforcement of need-to-know, least privilege, and due care responsibilities. Preventive controls are an organization's first line of defense. Detective controls can be used to determine the effectiveness of preventive controls.

✔**Objective 10.02:   Configuration Management and Media Control**   The major objective of configuration management is to achieve environment stability by controlling the changes that take place to individual systems and devices. Access to hardware and software should be centrally controlled via media library. When media is cleared of its contents, it is said to be sanitized, which can happen by overwriting, degaussing, or destruction activities.

✔**Objective 10.03:   Reacting to Failures and Recovering**   When a system crashes, it does so because it encounters something that it perceives as insecure. A system should always revert to a secure state after it has encountered an insecure activity. It may do this by performing fail-safe, fail-soft, fail-secure, or fail-over procedures.

✔**Objective 10.04:   Software Backups**   Single points of failure should be identified within a network to allow for proper redundancy to be added. RAID is a technology that is very useful to operational departments because it provides redundancy and improves performance levels. Data backups should occur on a regular basis and data recovery procedures should be tested.

REVIEW QUESTIONS

1. Why is job rotation an important part of operations security?

    A. Improves customer satisfaction

    B. Increases overhead

    C. Can uncover fraud

    D. Boosts employee morale

2. A user with access to the bare minimum of resources necessary to fulfill his job responsibilities is called what?

    A. Need-to-know

    B. Least privilege

    C. Due diligence

    D. Job rotation

3. What is a threshold for normal errors a user may commit before investigation begins?

    A. Due care

    B. Separation of duties

    C. Dual control

    D. Clipping level

4. Why are mandatory vacations important to companies?

   A. It is a way that fraud can be uncovered.

   B. It is part of due diligence.

   C. They have a legal obligation.

   D. To ensure that employees do not get burned out.

5. What is it called when data is magnetically erased from a media device?

   A. Fluxing

   B. Deleting

   C. Degaussing

   D. Overwriting

6. RAID level 1 performs what function?

   A. Data striping

   B. Mirroring

   C. Block-level parity

   D. Byte-level parity

7. Which of the following fault tolerance mechanisms selectively terminates non-essential processing when a failure is detected?

   A. Fail-over

   B. Fail-soft

   C. Fail-secure

   D. RAID

8. If a company wants to ensure the confidentiality of all data that is faxed, what should be put into place?

   A. Fax encryptor

   B. End-to-end encryption

   C. Print banners before and after data

   D. Enable print function

9. Which of the following is not considered an administrative—preventative control?

   A. Pre-employment background checks

   B. Controlled termination processes

   C. Data classification and labeling

   D. Intrusion detection system

REVIEW ANSWERS

1. **C** Rotating jobs may allow others to uncover fraudulent activities by teaching them the necessary tasks of that position. Once they understand what *should* be taking place in that job, they may be able to detect the activities that should not be taking place.

2. **B** Giving an employee the least amount of access to the resources to fulfill the tasks of his job is a security control called least privilege.

3. **D** A clipping level is a way of signaling potential fraud if normal errors rise above this threshold. If fraudulent activities are not taking place, most likely employee retraining is needed to reduce the number of errors occurring.

4. **A** Most people who commit fraud on the job do not take vacations because they fear getting caught, so employees should be forced to take their vacations. This will allow others to be rotated into their positions, which may uncover misdeeds.

5. **C** Degaussing generates a coercive magnetic force that reduces the magnetic flux density of the storage media to zero. This magnetic force is what properly erases data from the media.

6. **B** Mirroring is a function that writes the same data to two drives, usually using one disk controller.

7. **B** Fail-soft selectively terminates certain processing functions, which keeps parts of the system operational after a failure.

8. **A** A fax encryptor will encrypt all data traveling over a specific communication channel used by a fax server.

9. **D** Administrative controls that provide preventative services include the first three items. An intrusion detection system is a technical— detective control.

About the Free
Online Practice Exam

Mike Meyers' Certification Passport
FREE Online Practice Exam Instructions

To access your free online Practice Exam, browse to www.osborne.com/passport, where you'll be given instructions for accessing your exam. You can access the exam area as much as you'd like for 120 days from your initial registration.

Note from the Publisher: The exam is hosted by ExamWeb, a leading provider of online exams, and the question and answer content was written by Shon Harris (so you know the content is great!). It's well worth taking the time to use the online exam. It's free, and it will definitely help you prepare for the real CISSP exam. Good luck with your studying.

Exam features:

- Find explanations that teach what you need to know for all questions.
- Take a full exam, exam by subject, or exam by previously missed questions.
- Create an exam based on a keyword found in questions.
- Save and resume an exam at a later time.
- Get detailed strength and weakness reports by subject area.

System Requirements

- Browsers supported: Internet Explorer 4.0 and up; Netscape 4.0 and up
- Internet connection required

Technical Support

For questions concerning the *content* of the book or the online practice exam, contact McGraw-Hill Customer Service:

- Phone: 800-722-4726
- E-mail: customer.service@mcgraw-hill.com

For technical support for the online practice exam application or your ExamWeb online account, contact ExamWeb:

- Phone: 949-566-9375
- E-mail: support@examweb.com

Additional technology certification practice exams available for purchase at ExamWeb.com!

Career Flight Path

Career Paths in Security

Today, any career that pertains to technology has been affected by the growing demands of security, whether it is a network administrator or engineer, programmer, implementer, or consultant. An increase in knowledge and skill pertaining to security can help any one of these career fields because new security methods, processes, technologies, and threats are encroaching upon each one. This requires that current employees know more and more about complex security threats and the technologies used to fight against them. Many of today's careers now require applicants to have some type of security training and knowledge because of the demands put upon companies to protect themselves, their assets, and confidential information. Within the technology industry, one of most sought-after credentials is the CISSP. Currently, there are approximately 8,000 worldwide, but the number is growing because of the demand and the continual rise in job opportunities.

The following are just some of the available careers within the security field:

Product and technology implementer

- Implements and integrates new security products and technologies into a current infrastructure. These technologies may be public key infrastructure (PKI), IPSec (IP security), Kerberos, RADIUS, TACACS+, or Diameter; the products could be VPNs, firewalls, intrusion detection systems, remote access devices, data encryption, wireless products, and many more.
- Requires a solid network foundation and integration skills along with an understanding of how security mechanisms work together to provide the required level of protection.

Forensics

- Investigates computer crimes and properly looks for and collects evidence that may be used in court for prosecution. This profession usually requires performing expert witness services by explaining specific computer crimes and techniques to a judge and jury.
- Requires a knowledge of intrusion operations and detection, understanding hacker methodology and techniques, intimate knowledge of different operating systems, and the use of different forensics tools and software packages.

Consulting

- Assesses different companies' current environments, gauges the current protection level, and provides several different countermeasures and methods the companies can implement to increase their overall security and reduce their risk.
- Requires knowledge of how to perform vulnerability and penetration tests, understanding of current security technologies, knowledge of current weaknesses and vulnerabilities within operating systems and networking products, and an understanding of the current agreed-upon best practices within the security field. This could also require security solutions design, development, and deployment.

Security officer

- Many companies have specific regulations, laws, and industry-specific standards they must adhere to so that they will not be found liable or negligent in their activities. This has caused many companies to create new positions—security officers—which are filled by individuals who are responsible for understanding the expectations the company faces and how to properly meet them.
- Requires an understanding of business needs, goals, and requirements and how they can be affected by several different security issues. This type of position also requires a person to understand specific industry regulations and how they can be properly met and companies can stay in compliance.

Auditor

- Many companies are audited for different things: accounting, business practices, adherence to industry-specific standards, and security requirements. Different companies specialize in performing these types of audits and working with companies to ensure that they know how to meet the expectations put upon them. As more and more government-directed regulations are coming down to govern and oversee different industries (government agencies, medical facilities, financial institutions, utility companies, etc.), the need for auditing skills will only increase.
- Require intimate understanding of required methods that need to be implemented for companies to stay in compliance with different laws and regulations, and how to test for these methods.

Physical security

- After September 11, 2001, the need for physical security has increased exponentially in many different industries. There are escalating needs for people who specialize in physical security to work as consultants, technology implementers (especially biometrics), and trainers. Companies need to know how to protect themselves from physical threats and ensure that they are doing the necessary things to ensure that they are meeting their legal responsibilities.
- Require an understanding of many different types of physical threats and how they can be detected and protected against. It would also require an understanding of the old and new regulations different companies have to meet and the necessary methods to ensure compliancy.

Law enforcement

- Different fields of law enforcement (FBI, Secret Service, police, CIA) are having to deal with more and more computer crimes, which has put quite a strain on their staffing levels. All facets of law enforcement need more employees that have many different computer skills so that computer crimes can be properly investigated and prosecuted.

- Depending upon the agency, a security clearance will most likely be required. These types of positions would also require intimate knowledge of different operating systems, hacker methodology and techniques, ability to carry out investigation and forensics techniques, and a good understanding of the different laws that correlate with computer crime.

Software engineer

- Up to now, most software developers have been totally focused on implementing functionality into their programs, without much concern for implementing security and following safe programming techniques. This is slowly beginning to change as more and more software vendors are being expected to create secure products.
- Requires programming skills, but also an understanding of how different programming methods introduce various vulnerabilities and open the door to potential security breaches. Proper programming and software development skills would be necessary.

These are just some of the possible careers that are just now taking off in the security field. As the demand for different types of security (physical, system, network, information, and personnel) increases, so does the demand for skilled employees. Obtaining the CISSP certification is one of the best steps you can take to open these doors and opportunities for yourself.

Index

disasters
  definition of, 279
  preventing, 292
disk-shadowing, use of, 282
disposal phase of software, purpose of, 339
disruptions to business, categories of, 279
distributed computing
  ActiveX, 350
  CGI (Common Gateway Interface), 351
  COM (component object model) and
    DCOM (distributed COM), 348–349
  EJB (Enterprise Java Beans), 349
  Java applets, 350–351
  OLE (object linking and embedding), 349
  ORB (object request broker) and CORBA
    (Common Object Request Broker
    Architecture), 347
  overview of, 347
  role of cookies in, 351–352
distributed data model, explanation of, 356–357
DMZ (demilitarized zone),
  role in firewall architecture, 171–172
DNS (Domain Name Service),
  dynamics of, 178–179
DNSSEC (Domain Name Service Security),
  explanation of, 260
documentation
  distribution of, 339
  providing for disaster recovery, 289–292
dogs, using for perimeter security, 130–131
DoS (denial of service) attacks
  example of, 61
  explanation of, 366
downstream liability, role in extranets, 145, 308
drills and testing, implementing in DRPs,
  290–291
DRPs (disaster recovery plans)
  components of, 273, 286–287
  conducting BIA (business impact analysis)
    for, 275–279
  importance of, 272
  objectives of, 285–293
  phase breakdown of, 292–293
  project initiation phase of, 274–275
dry pipe water sprinklers, explanation of, 124
DSA (Digital Signature Algorithm)
  versus RSA, 243
DSL (Digital Subscriber Lines), use of, 185–186
DSLC (Synchronous Data Link Control),
  explanation of, 190
DSS (Digital Signature Standard),
  explanation of, 243
DSSS (Direct Sequence Spread Spectrum),
  purpose of, 193–194

dual control, role in authorization, 41
dual-home firewalls, use of, 170–173
due care, explanation of, 2–3, 375
dumpster diving attacks, explanation of, 305
durability, meaning in ACID test, 359

E

E0-E6 ratings in ITSEC, meanings of, 95
EALs (evaluation assurance levels),
  role in Common Criteria, 97
EAP (Extensible Authentication Protocol),
  explanation of, 175
EBC (Electronic Code Block) mode of DES,
  explanation of, 231–232
ECC (Elliptic Curve Cryptosystem)
  asymmetrical algorithm, explanation of, 236
ECHO packets, role in ICMP, 159
ECHO REPLY packets,
  role in Smurf attacks, 366–367
Economic Espionage Act of 1996,
  explanation of, 314–315
EDI (Electronic Data Exchange),
  purpose of, 144
EF (exposure factor),
  role in quantitative risk analysis, 11
EJB (Enterprise Java Beans),
  explanation of, 349
El Gamal asymmetrical algorithm,
  explanation of, 236
electrical power
  overview of, 114–115
  safeguards for use of, 117
  UPS (uninterruptable power supply),
    114–115
Electronic Communications Privacy Act of 1986,
  purpose of, 310
electronic signing, use of, 242–243, 251
electronic vaulting, explanation of, 282
emanation security, dynamics of, 60
emergency response, planning for, 125,
  288–289
emergency system restart, occurrence in
  system failure, 384
EMI (electromagnetic interference),
  explanation of, 115–116
employee management
  after disasters, 280–282
  dynamics of, 21–22
employee monitoring, guidelines for, 311
encipher, definition of, 211
encryption
  dynamics of, 211–212
  end-to-end encryption, 250
  link encryption, 250

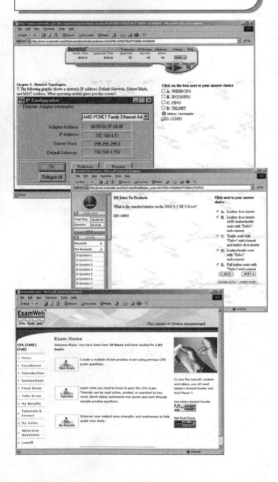